The
Great Wall
at Sea

*China's Navy in the
Twenty-First Century*

Second Edition

Bernard D. Cole

NAVAL INSTITUTE PRESS
Annapolis, Maryland

Naval Institute Press
291 Wood Road
Annapolis, MD 21402

Cole, Bernard D., 1943-
  The Great Wall at sea : China's Navy in the twenty-first century / Bernard D. Cole.—2nd ed.
    p. cm.
  Includes bibliographical references and index.
  ISBN 978-1-59114-142-6 (acid-free paper)   1. China. Zhongguo ren min jie fang jun. Hai jun.
  2. China—Military policy.   I. Title.
  VA633.C65 2010
  359.00951—dc22

                                                                      2010020184

Printed in the United States of America on acid-free paper ∞

14 13 12 11 10   9 8 7 6 5 4 3 2
First printing

This manuscript represents the views of the author alone; it may not represent those of the National War College or any other organization of the U.S. government.

Contents

Illustrations

Photos

Varyag, an aircraft carrier acquired from Russia and since renamed
Shi Lang, en route to China
Shang-class nuclear-powered submarine
Jin-class nuclear-powered ballistic missile submarine
Song-class submarine (Chinese built) moored in Hong Kong
Kilo-class submarine, acquired from Russia
Sovremenny-class guided missile destroyer, acquired from Russia
Luhu-class guided missile destroyer
Luhai-class guided missile destroyer
Luyang I–class guided missile destroyer
Luyang II–class guided missile destroyer
Luzhou-class guided missile destroyer
Jiangkai-class guided missile frigate
Jiangwei-class guided missile frigate
Houbei-class missile boat
Yuzhao-class amphibious assault ship
Fuqing-class oiler
Fuchi-class oiler/stores ship
Peace Ark hospital ship

Maps

Tables

Acronyms and Abbreviations

AAW	antiair warfare
AIP	air-independent propulsion
AMW	amphibious warfare
AOR	area of responsibility
ARF	Asia Regional Forum
ASCM	antiship cruise missile
ASEAN	Association of Southeast Asian Nations
ASUW	antisurface warfare
ASW	antisubmarine warfare
BCD	Border Control Department
BP	British Petroleum
C3	command, control, and communications
C4ISR	command, control, communications, computers, intelligence, surveillance, and reconnaissance
CCG	Chinese Coast Guard
CCP	Chinese Communist Party
CIC	combat information center
CIWS	close-in weapons systems
CLCS	Commission on the Limits of the Continental Shelf
CMC	Central Military Commission
CMS	China Marine Surveillance service
CNOOC	China National Offshore Oil Corporation
CNPC	China National Petroleum Company
CODOG	combined-diesel-or-gas-turbine

CRSB	China Rescue and Salvage Bureau
CS	continental shelf
CSC	China Shipbuilding Corporation
CSG	aircraft carrier strike group
CV	aircraft carrier
CVBG	aircraft carrier battle group
CZ	contiguous zone
DDG	guided-missile destroyer
EEZ	exclusive economic zone
EW	electronic warfare
FBM	fleet ballistic missile submarine
FFG	guided-missile frigate
FLEC	Fisheries Law Enforcement Command
GAD	General Arms Department
GDP	gross domestic product
GLD	General Logistics Department
GPCR	Great Proletarian Cultural Revolution
GPD	General Political Department
GSD	General Staff Department
ICBM	intercontinental ballistic missile
IORARC	Indian Ocean Rim Association for Regional Cooperation
IRBM	intermediate-range ballistic missile
IW	information warfare
JMSDF	Japan Maritime Self-Defense Force
km	kilometer
KMT	Kuomintang
LCU	landing craft, utility
LNG	liquefied natural gas
LPD	landing platform, dock
LSM	landing ship, mechanized
LST	landing ship, tank
MIW	mine warfare
MOFA	Ministry of Foreign Affairs
MOOTW	military operations other than war
MR	military region
MSA	Maritime Safety Administration
NCO	noncommissioned officer
NDU	National Defense University

NERA	Naval Equipment Research Academy
nm	nautical miles
NRI	Naval Research Institute
OMTE	outline of military training and evaluation
OTHT	over-the-horizon targeting
PAFD	People's Armed Forces departments
PAP	People's Armed Police
PLA	People's Liberation Army
PLAAF	People's Liberation Army Air Force
PLAN	People's Liberation Army Navy
PLANAF	People's Liberation Army Navy Air Force
R&D	research and development
RAS	replenishment at sea
RMA	revolution in military affairs
ROKN	Republic of Korea Navy
ROTC	Reserve Officers Training Corps
SAM	surface-to-air missile
SAR	search and rescue
SAREX	search and rescue exercise
SEATO	Southeast Asia Treaty Organization
SINOPEC	China National Petroleum Corporation
SLOC	sea line of communication
SOA	State Oceanographic Administration
SOE	state-owned enterprise
SRBOC	super-rapid-blooming off-board chaff
SS	diesel/electric-powered attack submarine
SSB	diesel/electric-powered ballistic missile submarine
SSBN	nuclear-powered ballistic missile submarine
SSM	surface-to-surface missile
SSN	nuclear-powered attack submarine
Tcf	trillion cubic feet
TMD	theater missile defense
UAV	unmanned air vehicles
UN	United Nations
UNCLOS	United Nations Convention on the Law of the Sea
VCP	Vietnamese Communist Party
VLS	vertical launching system
WTO	World Trade Organization

Preface to the Second Edition

On 14 December 2001, shortly after publication of my book on the Chinese Navy, *The Great Wall at Sea: China's Navy Enters the Twenty-First Century*, the two most senior officials in China, President Jiang Zemin and Minister of Defense General Chi Haotian, called for the building of a modern Navy with powerful, comprehensive combat capabilities to defend the country's maritime security. Subsequent military and civilian Chinese leaders have continued this campaign to strengthen the Navy. China's 2008 Defense White Paper emphasizes the importance of the Navy as a strategic instrument and represents a significant step from just ten years ago, when the People's Liberation Army Navy (PLAN) was first preparing to enter the twenty-first century; that decade has witnessed remarkable naval progress by China.

The twenty-first century has also witnessed China's maintenance of unprecedented economic growth, which has continued to yield double-digit increases in the annual budget of the People's Liberation Army (PLA). The PLAN has especially benefited from these increased allocations, acquiring new ships, submarines, and aircraft. These material additions have been accompanied by important changes in the administration and organization of the force, from individual ship maintenance procedures to major fleet operating practices.

The tragic events of 11 September 2001 changed the course of U.S. national security thinking, strategic policy, and perhaps even the very foundations of the American polity. The relationship with China increasingly affects the U.S. economy and security interests in a dynamic and perhaps synergistic fashion. The American military is so absorbed in the Iraqi and Afghan campaigns of the war on terror and the dire possibilities concerning North

Korea and Iran, that nascent Chinese challenges to U.S. interests may exceed available American capabilities. The other Asian nations recognize that China continues to modernize its military and expand its economy to a degree never before seen even in this region.

Ten years ago Beijing had not formulated a coherent national maritime strategy. China's dependence on coastal, regional, and global sea lines of communication (SLOCs) was recognized, but the United States was regarded as the guardian of those arteries. Now, however, Beijing has made the decision to maintain a Navy capable of safeguarding China's vital maritime interests.

Chinese maritime power is expanding from a coastal Navy with little capability against a modern opponent at sea or in the air to a twenty-first-century maritime force able to compete for important objectives in the western Pacific Ocean areas, including especially the East and South China seas and their attendant straits. Additionally, Beijing's naval planning seems aimed at projecting naval force into the Philippine Sea and perhaps the eastern (if not the entire) Indian Ocean.

Success in reaching these new goals is currently within the PLAN's sights. Whether and when it occurs will depend largely on political and economic conditions in China. Whether it results in a Sino-centric shift in the strategic situation in maritime Asia will depend also on the reactions on the part of the other major naval powers in the region, especially Japan and the United States.

We still face many unanswered questions about China's Navy, but printed materials pertaining to PLAN growth and modernization are available and plentiful in the public domain, especially if one reads Mandarin. I do not agree with accusations that the Chinese "lack transparency," despite their penchant for secrecy. Sufficient information has been and continues to be published to augment discussions with Chinese officers, and visits to ships and bases in China allowed for a meaningful rewrite of the first edition of *The Great Wall at Sea*. This second edition follows the first's scheme: an introduction, chapters on the PLAN's historic background; China's oceanic territorial claims and maritime economic interests; PLAN organization, vessels and aircraft, manning, and training; Beijing's maritime strategy; and my concluding thoughts.

· · ·

I wish to acknowledge again the debt I owe to Professor Frank L. Owsley Jr., of the Auburn University history department. I must also offer my thanks to many colleagues. At the risk of omitting some, I am particularly grateful to my fellow "PLA watchers," from whom I continue to learn: Kenneth Allen, Dennis Blasko, Andrew Erickson, Eric McVadon, and William Murray read the entire manuscript and offered a stream of corrective and enlightening suggestions. I am also indebted to Richard Bush, David Finkelstein, Taylor Fravel, Chas. Freeman, Daniel Hartnett, Evan Madeiros, Michael McDevitt, Ellis Melvin, Bernard Moreland, James Mulvenon, Alan Romberg, Robert Ross, Michael Swaine, Fred Vellucci, Alan Wachman, and Christopher Yung, who patiently assisted me in pursuing answers to many questions; Rick Fisher and Charles Au were most generous in providing pictures; U.S. Navy Chief of Information Rear Admiral Denny Moynihan also assisted in this effort. The National Defense University library, particularly Carolyn Turner and Michael McNulty, offered superb support. Many serving officers in various services were very helpful but must remain nameless. Of course, all errors of omission and commission are solely my responsibility.

Three individuals deserve special mention: the late and much lamented Ellis Joffe continues to inspire all who labor to understand China and its military; Paul H. B. Godwin continues to offer constant friendship, encouragement, and assistance; as does Cynthia Watson, to whom this book is dedicated.

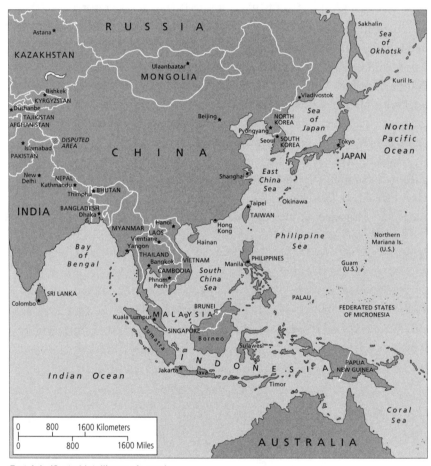

East Asia (Central Intelligence Agency)

Introduction
Strategic Context

On 23 April 2009 China conducted a fleet review to celebrate the sixtieth anniversary of the People's Liberation Army Navy (PLAN). In an interview the next day, General Guo Boxiong, vice chairman of China's Central Military Commission, "urged the Navy to beef up its combat capacity to better protect the country's maritime security." Speaking at the celebration, China's president, Hu Jintao, urged the Navy to "comprehensively push forward its modernization to constantly enhance its capability to carry out its missions in the new century." Two months later Hu argued that China "should raise our strategic capability of safeguarding our maritime security, defend our country's territorial sea and maritime rights and interests, [and] protect the security of our country's increasingly developing maritime industry, maritime transportation, and energy resources strategic channels."[1]

The naval review was larger than previous similar demonstrations and marked the PLAN's "coming out" as a modern navy. A celebratory theme reigned as many foreign military attachés and senior naval officers attended the parade, but the event also was clearly intended to demonstrate China's newfound status as a major naval power in Asian waters.[2]

Hu had previously addressed maritime missions at a December 2004 meeting of the Central Military Commission (CMC), when he delineated the "Historic Missions of the Armed Forces in the New Period of the New Century."[3] At this same meeting the PLAN commander was made a member of the CMC. China's Defense White Paper for 2004 stated that "the PLA Navy is responsible for safeguarding China's maritime security and maintaining the sovereignty of its territorial seas along with its maritime rights and interests." The white paper emphasized the importance of conducting operations well offshore, timely "preparation [of the] maritime battlefield," enhanced "integrated combat capabilities," and the ability to conduct "nuclear counterattacks," as well as "building maritime combat forces, especially amphibious combat forces . . . [and] updating its weaponry and equipment," to include "long-range precision strike capability . . . joint exercises . . . and integrated maritime support capabilities."[4]

This ambitious menu represents a huge step from 1927, when the only mission really applicable to China's Navy on the founding of the People's Liberation Army (PLA) was to "carry out the political tasks of the revolution"—not a particularly maritime assignment. It also represents Beijing's increased emphasis on deploying a modern PLAN; the decade since the first edition of this book has seen remarkable naval progress.

The historic missions in 1982 to "resist invasions and defend the homeland" attested to the PLAN's role as a coastal defense force charged to support the ground forces as they resisted a supposed Soviet invasion of China. An "offshore defense" strategy was delineated by Deng Xiaoping in 1985, while in 1993 the PLAN was directed to "safeguard the sovereignty of China's national territorial land, air, and seas" and to "uphold China's unity and security." This marked the PLA's transition to a post–Cold War world; by 2008 the PLAN was being described as "a strategic service."[5]

The four historic missions Hu listed in 2004 were (1) the traditional responsibility of ensuring the military's loyalty to the Chinese Communist Party (CCP); (2) ensuring sovereignty, territorial integrity, and domestic security, to include preventing Taiwanese separatism; and the new responsibilities of (3) safeguarding expanding national interests, including maritime security and "non-traditional security problems"; and (4) helping to ensure world peace. Of these missions, the PLAN has direct responsibilities for sovereignty and territorial integrity, maritime security, and promoting world peace. PLAN modernization today is aimed primarily at the first of these, while the 2008–9 deployments to the Gulf of Aden to combat piracy are the most prominent of the latter two.

The Navy's commander, Admiral Wu Shengli, addressed his force's missions and intentions at its sixtieth anniversary review. Wu stated that his service "will develop weaponry such as large combat warships, submarines with longer range and stealth capability, supersonic cruise aircraft, more accurate long-range missiles, deep-sea torpedoes and upgraded information technology, among others." Wu also listed strengthened logistics and support facilities "to improve far-sea repair, delivery, rescue and replenishment capacities" while establishing "a maritime defense system . . . to protect China's maritime security and economic development." Finally, he announced that the Navy's primary 2009 missions included "anti-piracy missions off the coast of Somalia, port visits, [and] the National Day parade and a sea parade to mark [the PLAN's] 60th anniversary." These remarks reinforced Wu's 2007 remarks justifying the creation of a "powerful armed force on the sea" as a "long cherished dream for the Chinese nation."[6]

Historically, national naval power has been linked directly with national economic strength. China's remarkable economic growth during the past three decades, with its concentration in coastal regions and reliance on seaborne trade, highlights the maritime arena as a national security interest of the highest priority for Beijing.

With these words of the leaders of China and its Navy as touchstones, this book analyzes and evaluates how China defines its maritime challenges, how these affect the way it identifies the capabilities the PLAN must possess, and how successfully Beijing is building and deploying the Navy. The opinions of civilian analysts in China and other countries will be surveyed, as will those of government and military officials.[7] This work describes and analyzes China's Navy: its background, organization, force composition, capabilities, doctrine, strategy, readiness, and utility as an instrument of national power.

Chapter 1 examines the efforts by the People's Republic of China (PRC) to become a maritime power. The nation's record is characterized by inconsistent development and development of naval power as an instrument of national security strategy, but that has changed in the twenty-first century.

Chapters 2 and 3 examine China's maritime territorial and economic interests. In the first edition these focused on the Yellow Sea and the South and East China seas, but the nation's dramatically increased energy demands have expanded Beijing's maritime view to include the long SLOCs to the Middle East and Africa over which most of its imported oil travels.

Chapter 4 examines the current organization of the PLAN, which reflects the service's history and also connotes its intentions and capabilities. This facet of naval modernization was highlighted in the loss of the crew of China's Ming 361 submarine in 2003, a tragic event that demonstrated literally fatal weaknesses in the PLAN's maintenance and training practices. The accident may also have demonstrated a lack of operational procedures similar to that associated with the 2000 loss of the Russian submarine *Kursk* or the 1945 loss of the U.S. cruiser *Indianapolis*.[8] The PLAN's corrective organizational measures are relatively easy to discern; much more difficult to evaluate are the corrective operational steps in the half-decade since the submarine disaster.

Chapter 5 addresses the PLAN's ships, submarines, aircraft, and weapons systems. The Navy's effectiveness is tied directly to the capabilities of its component parts, and reviewing the open literature on its ships and aircraft provides a measure for estimating how well the Navy might perform in different situations, especially as it gains experience with state-of-the-art platforms and systems.

Chapter 6 investigates how the PLAN is manned and trained, with particular attention to the interplay between concerns for professional expertise and political reliability. No area of inquiry into China's Navy is less clear than how that force manages and trains its personnel. The normal demands of recruiting, educating, training, and managing the personnel force of a modern Navy are complicated by Beijing's insistence on political reliability as well as professional expertise—the need for its personnel to be both "red" and "expert." Understanding these complex issues is made more difficult by the Chinese obsession with secrecy.

Chapter 7 looks at the way doctrine is developed and applied in the PLAN, with a focus on operations as the result of planning and implementation. A discussion of the other navies confronting China is included.

Chapter 8 traces the development of maritime strategy in China. Beijing draws on both classic Chinese concepts of strategy and the role of the military as well as on Western concepts of "sea power" and reliance on military technology.

The Conclusion sums up the elements, motivation, and capabilities of the modern Chinese Navy.

A strong Chinese Navy is being developed and deployed. How is that being accomplished, and is it an indicator of Beijing's national security posture and international ambitions in the twenty-first century? A conservative attitude is appropriate when evaluating Chinese policy and military developments; it is not helpful to "confuse aspiration with accomplishment," a caution echoed in another analyst's view that a "Chinese penchant for metaphorical writing . . . makes literal interpretation of interesting rumors problematic."[9]

China historically has been a continental rather than a maritime power, despite its more than eleven thousand miles of coastline and six thousand islands. It has more often viewed the sea as a potential invasion route for foreign aggressors than as a medium for achieving national goals, which has contributed to a weak Chinese maritime tradition. This attitude has changed during the first decade of the twenty-first century. The remarkable growth of China's economy, the broadening of Beijing's global political and economic interests, and the resolution of almost all border disputes with China's many contiguous neighbors have contributed to a newly confident international outlook. These factors in turn have contributed to increased attention to threats to the vital sea lines of communication (SLOCs) on which China increasingly depends.

Beijing continues to believe that China confronts "long-term, complicated, and diverse security threats" and "is faced with the superiority of the developed countries in economy, science and technology, as well as military affairs." China's maritime threats were discussed at length in a 2004 paper whose author averred that "China's heartland faces the sea, the benefits of economic development are increasingly dependent on the sea, [and] security threats come from the sea." He then named the United States as the threat to these interests, noting "strong [U.S.] forces in the Western Pacific" and "a system of military bases on the first and second island chains."[10]

One perceptive American scholar has identified five reasons for China's drive to modernize its military: to ensure the CCP's continuance in power; guarantee China's territorial integrity; ensure national unification, to include Tibet and Xinjiang provinces as well as Taiwan; and secure maritime interests; all without threatening regional stability.[11] The Navy features prominently in these activities.

Furthermore, a Chinese analyst has cautioned that "for a power like China, possession of strong sea power is an inevitable choice [but it] must be and can only become a component part of China's land power."[12] While the People's Liberation Army—the name given to all of China's armed services—remains dominated in numbers and command structure by the Army, the Navy and Air Force have benefited significantly from the double-digit increases in defense spending that have occurred over most of the past two decades. Additionally, non-Army commanders—the heads of the Navy, Air Force, and Second Artillery Corps—are serving as members of the CMC, China's equivalent to the U.S. Joint Chiefs of Staff, but with one important difference: the chairman of the CMC is Hu Jintao, who also serves as president of China and general secretary of the CCP.

China's increased regard for its Navy has not significantly reduced the percentage of PLA manpower assigned to the Army, but the Navy is responsible for the PLA's guiding mission—described by Hu as "three provides and one contribute": provide "an important strength safeguard for the [CCP's] effort to consolidate its ruling position, strong security . . . for the country's development, powerful strategic support for defending national interests, and contribute importantly to world peace and common development."[13] This in turn lies at the heart of the CCP's view that "all service personnel in the country's military forces [must] show absolute obedience to the Party." The PLA owes its loyalty not to "China" but to the CCP, a point often made by the most senior central government officials, both civilian and military.[14]

Beijing's strategic view of post–Cold War Asia has increasingly come to focus on offshore sovereignty and economic and resource issues. The key question to evaluating today's PLAN—whether China's leadership understands the maritime element of national strategy—has been answered in the affirmative during the first decade of the twenty-first century.

China has always depended primarily on ground forces to guard its national security interests—for the simple reason that threats to those interests have consistently arisen in northern and western Asia. China's historic focus on continental security concerns, however, has been moderated by the nation's heavy and increasing dependence on maritime trade and a view that the United States and other Asian powers are determined to "contain" China. This heightens concern about the nation's long coastline, many islands, and the constraining presence (in the eyes of some Chinese) of the "first island chain."

At the turn of the twenty-first century China has shown apparent confidence in its ability to employ its maritime strength effectively. In 1995, for instance, China fortified Mischief Reef, a bit of contested coral in the South China Sea, as a step in solidifying its sovereignty claims over that sea. Likewise, the Taiwan Strait crisis of 1996 resulted from Beijing's employment of naval and military power to threaten Taiwan.

Since 2001, Chinese maritime forces have five times interfered with U.S. airborne or seaborne intelligence-gathering efforts, once causing loss of life. These events are part of a larger effort to restrict foreign military operations in China's exclusive economic zone (EEZ) and the airspace above it. A Chinese submarine broached near a U.S. aircraft carrier in 2007, and during the past decade Chinese ships have frequently operated in waters claimed by Japan.[15] A successful antisatellite destruction shot was conducted in 2007. After many decades of isolation from navies it once considered superior, the PLAN now conducts joint exercises with them, apparently no longer concerned about being embarrassed by its backwardness or revealing its shortcomings.

PLA annual budget increases have averaged 15 percent since 1993, with the 2009 budget 14.9 percent greater than that for 2008. One analyst has estimated that China's defense budget quintupled between 1997 and 2009. Beijing continues to describe these increases as "modest" and as devoted primarily to "salaries and benefits," but that claim is not convincing given the obvious modernization of the PLA.[16]

In addition to its duties to defend the homeland and China's economic interests, the modernizing Chinese Navy plans to field a sea-based nuclear deterrent resident in the new class of ballistic missile submarines (FBM) currently joining the fleet. National status is an important factor in the modernization as well. Its leaders believe that China must deploy a world-class Navy if it is to achieve recognition as a world power. National pride is most noticeably manifested in calls for the PLAN to acquire aircraft carriers. Another factor may be interservice rivalry, as the Navy struggles with its sister services for an increasing share of annual defense allocations.

While Taiwan has furnished the primary scenario for PLAN planners for the past three decades, that is changing. China is modernizing its Navy to deal with national security situations that may occur after Taiwan is reunified with the mainland. These include conflict with Japan over disputed East China Sea territory and resources, conflict with the other claimants—Vietnam, Malaysia, Indonesia, Brunei, and the Philippines—to South China Sea land features and resources, and concern about the security of the very long SLOCs linking China with the energy resources of Southwest Asia and Africa. Finally, there is the idea that a great country should have a great Navy.[17]

CHINA'S MARITIME GEOGRAPHY

Beijing's pursuit of regional power encompasses Eurasia, the largest "island" on a globe that is more than 70 percent covered by water. This super-continent today remains dominated by Russia and China, with India a rapidly rising force. From Beijing's perspective, Japan is China's leading Asian maritime competitor; the "rim" of Eurasia is also bordered by the insular countries or enti-ties of northeastern, southeastern, and southern Asia: Taiwan, the Philippines, Indonesia, Brunei, Singapore, Australia, New Zealand, Bangladesh, and Sri Lanka. The Pacific-Indian Ocean region is arguably the most important area in global trade. One-half of the world's twenty largest container lines are owned and based in Asia, and eighteen of the world's largest container ports are located in the region; approximately one-third of the world's shipping is owned by Asian nations.

Asia is delineated by a series of geographic features beginning in the north-east with Russia's Kamchatka Peninsula and the Kurile Islands extending southward. South beyond the Soya Strait lie Japan's four large main islands and the Ryukyu Islands, extending southward beyond the Osumi Strait. The Ryukyun kingdom was a Chinese tributary state from 1372 to 1609, when it was seized by Japan and then, in 1869, annexed.[18] China does not formally challenge Japan's sovereignty over the Ryukyus, despite this history.

The Ryukyus point south-southwest to the Senkaku (Diaoyu, to China) Islands and then to Taiwan. The sovereignty of these islands is disputed between Japan and China; Taiwan agrees that they are "Chinese." Taipei also agrees with China's sovereignty claims to all of the land features in the South China Sea. South of Taiwan, the Republic of the Philippines lies across the Luzon Strait. Indonesia lies to the south and west of the Philippines and, like it, is an archipelagic nation.

Asia is bordered by the Seas of Okhotsk and Japan; the Yellow, East, and South China seas; the Philippine Sea; and the Indian Ocean. These seas in turn are linked by many of the world's most important straits. The Soya (or La Perouse) Strait between the Russian island of Sakhalin and the northern-most Japanese island, Hokkaido, divides the Sea of Okhotsk from the Sea of Japan. This 22-nm-long strait is an important ship channel—wide (24 nm at its narrowest point) and deep (almost 28 fathoms at its shallowest)—but it freezes over in the winter and is characterized by extremely strong currents.[19]

The Tsugaru Strait lies between the Japanese islands of Hokkaido and Honshu, connecting the Sea of Japan with the Pacific Ocean. This 87-nm-long strait is 15 nm wide at its narrowest point and more than 70 fathoms deep at its shallowest. Although a common path for both naval and merchant traffic, it is characterized by complicated currents, strong winds, and earthquakes.

The Tsushima (or Korea) Strait marks the southern end of the Sea of Japan and divides the Japanese island of Honshu from the Korean peninsula. This 62-nm-long strait is bisected by the island of Tsushima. It is just under 50 fathoms deep overall and 36 nm wide at its narrowest point. Even the name of this strait is disputed between Japan and the two Koreas, which insist on calling it the Korea Strait. Some charts further muddy the waters by referring to the passage south of Tsushima Island as the Tsushima Strait and calling the passage north of that island the Korea Strait or Western Channel.[20]

Just south of the Tsushima Strait, the Osumi Passage is the major route between the East China Sea and the Pacific Ocean, passing between the southern Japanese main island of Kyushu and smaller islands to the south. The passage is easily navigable and received unwelcome attention in November 2003 when a Chinese Ming-class submarine transited the strait, apparently to observe a U.S.-Japanese naval exercise in the area.[21]

The Taiwan Strait, which separates that island from the Chinese mainland by approximately 100 nm, is potentially one of the most dangerous bodies of water in the world. This 200-nm-long passage has an average depth of just 38 fathoms and is marked by even shallower areas, wide-ranging tides, unpredictable currents, and the potential for sudden bad weather. Its waters are also extremely "noisy" due to the extensive ship traffic, fishing boats, shipwrecks, and biological activity, making the use of both passive and active acoustic sensors (sonar and sonobuoys) difficult for submarine and antisubmarine warfare operations.[22]

The Taiwan Strait leads into the South China Sea, which is also marked in the north by the Luzon Strait between Taiwan and Luzon, the northernmost Philippine island. Almost all seaborne traffic between the Indian Ocean and East Asia and the Americas passes through one of these straits. The 174-nm-long Luzon Strait is relatively deep and wide (135 nm) but is divided by the Babuyan and Batanes islands into the Bashi (north), Balitang (central), and Babuyan (south) channels.

Two important straits penetrate the Philippine archipelago: from north to south these are the San Bernardino Strait between the islands of Luzon and Samar, and the Surigao Strait between the islands of Leyte and Mindanao. Both are deep enough (more than 270 fathoms) to accommodate the largest surface vessels but are challenging to navigate because of their sinuousness, the heavy small boat traffic, and the many small islands that dot their course.

The South China Sea is relatively deep (mean depth 663 fathoms) and contains the most heavily used SLOCs between the Indian and Pacific oceans. It opens to several strategically vital seaways, none more important than the Singapore and Malacca straits between the Malay Peninsula and Indonesia. These straits, commonly called simply "Malacca," form the primary corridor between the Indian and Pacific oceans and are approximately 600 nm long. Malacca's shallowest point, just under 11 fathoms (62.6 feet), limits the passage of supertankers; the channel is just 1.5 nm wide at its eastern end abeam Singapore. More than 60,000 vessels use these straits annually, carrying more than 30 percent of global trade and more than 50 percent of global energy shipments.[23]

Malacca is one of the most important navigational choke points in the world, and certainly the most important for China and the other nations of

East Asia. Through it pass 20 percent of global seaborne trade, 33 percent of global seaborne crude oil, 37 percent of global semiconductor trade, and 57 percent of total global shipping capacity. This traffic dwarfs that passing through the Panama and Suez canals.[24]

Malacca has drawn a good deal of attention from naval planners and energy analysts because of its importance to seaborne trade. Consequently, the states that border the strait—Indonesia, Singapore, and Malaysia—have been improving its safety and security. Australia, China, Japan, the United States, and other user states have been supporting these efforts, which have met with considerable success since 2005. China has not played a direct role in the counterpiracy center established in Malaysia or any of the other international actions that have dramatically lowered piracy in these waters.

To the east of Malacca, the Sunda and Lombok straits traverse the Indonesian archipelago and link the Indian Ocean to the Pacific. The Sunda Strait between the islands of Sumatra and Java is approximately 50 nm long and, at 10.5 fathoms, relatively shallow. It leads from the Indian Ocean into the Java Sea and then to the South China Sea.

The 33-nm-long Lombok Strait lies farther east, between the islands of Bali and Lombok. The strait leads from the Indian Ocean into the Java Sea and then through the Makassar Strait into the Celebes Sea. Ships may then sail into the South China Sea or directly into the Pacific Ocean. The Lombok Strait is the deepest of the Southeast Asian straits, ranging from 137 to 765 fathoms, and is thus used by deep-draught vessels not able to transit the Malacca and Sunda straits. Ships that choose it add three and a half days to their transit from the Indian Ocean to the Pacific. If all the Indonesian straits were closed, a transit around Australia would add approximately sixteen days for tankers traveling from the Indian Ocean to East Asia. The cost of a blockage is not only in the cost of petroleum directly, but also in terms of lengthier schedules and the additional tanker tonnage required.[25]

The Malacca Strait is guarded on its western end in the Andaman Sea by the Indian-owned Andaman and Nicobar island groups. The channels through these archipelagoes lead to the Bay of Bengal to the north and the main Indian Ocean to the west. The main shipping route then follows the Six Degree Channel bounded on the north by Sri Lanka and India, and on the south by the Maldive Islands.

The Arabian Sea forms the western Indian Ocean, bounded by the African continent. The North Arabian Sea is the southern terminus of two important bodies of water: the Persian Gulf and the Red Sea. The former is guarded by the

Strait of Hormuz; the latter by the Bab el-Mandeb Strait. Hormuz, bounded by Iran and Oman; is just 29 nm wide and is divided into UN-authorized traffic lanes for inbound and outbound ships. The strait is deep and very heavily used by tankers and local craft. The Bab el-Mandeb is 17 nm wide and divided by the island of Perim into two channels: 14-nm-wide Dact-el-Mayun to the west and 1.7-nm-wide Bab Iskender to the east.

The Asian maritime realm is thus marked by seas, straits, and gulfs with many narrow navigational points and areas of conflicting sovereignty claims. These waters are characterized by great distances, which mean long transit times for seaborne traffic. The distance from Shanghai to Abadan, Iran, for instance, is more than 5,000 nm, a fourteen-day trip for a ship traveling at 16 knots.[26]

The United States is the most important naval power in Asian waters. American dominance is neither limitless nor everlasting, however, a fact heightened by America's post-9/11 preoccupation with Southwest Asia and the shrinkage of its naval and merchant fleets: the nearly six hundred–ship Navy of 1990 is less than half that size in 2009, and the downward trend continues.

Other navies of note are Japan's Maritime Self-Defense Force (JMSDF), which shows few signs of significant growth, and India's powerful navy, which continues to modernize its fleet. Russia retains only the potential to redeploy a major Asian maritime force, despite August 2008 statements by Prime Minister Vladimir Putin and the commander of the Russian Navy, Admiral Vladimir Vysotsky. The former stated the intention to rebuild Russia's military, and the latter announced a plan to deploy at least six new aircraft carriers as the core of a revitalized Russian Navy.[27]

• • •

Monumental changes took place during the twentieth century. The United States debuted as a world power with the vanquishing of Spain and ended the century as a superpower stronger than any in the history of the world. At the dawn of the twenty-first century, China seems to be following much the same course. Only Japan and possibly India among Asian nations have the potential to match China in economic and military terms. All three are crucial participants in the Asian strategic calculus.

One author has described China's strategic view of the maritime Asia-Pacific region as the "territorialization of the seas," with Beijing's objective being the control of adjacent ocean areas as never before defined in international law or usage.[28] Beijing advocates a definition of sovereignty extending out at least 200 nm from its coastal baseline. China's leaders believe that the Navy's most important mission—defense of the homeland—includes defending this maritime area.

Chinese maritime strategists first justify building a strong Navy in terms of defending national sovereignty—hardly an idea unique to China—and then often cite geopolitical reasons, including the demand for increased *Lebensraum* for a nation that supports almost a quarter of the world's population on approximately 7 percent of its arable land. A PLA strategist summed up Beijing's view of the dangerous potential of the ocean in a 1996 statement: "In the last 109 years, imperialists have repeatedly invaded China from the sea . . . 470 times, . . . 84 of these being serious invasions. The ocean has become an avenue for the aggressors to bring in their troops and haul away our wealth. . . . [T]he ocean is not only the basic space for human survival, but also an important theater for international political struggle. . . . The better people can control the sea, the greater they have the sea territorial rights [which have] become inseparable from a country's sovereignty." China was urged to draw three lessons from this experience: (1) a strong naval force is a protection of the land; (2) a nation that does not understand the importance of the ocean is a nation without a future; and (3) a major sea power incapable of defending its sea territorial rights will not be a major sea power for very long.[29]

Regional maritime dominance would require the capability to project power to a distance of at least 1,500 nm from China's coast and beyond, including the areas of the Yellow, East China, South China, and Philippine seas. Beijing's naval building programs during the first decade of the twenty-first century are seeking to fulfill that ambition, supplemented by the ability to project naval power into extra-regional areas on a limited basis, as demonstrated in its 2008–10 of deployments to the Gulf of Aden.

China sees both opportunity and danger in extending its maritime power. Its offshore national security concerns include Taiwan, the East and South China seas, the SLOCs vital for commerce, insular sovereignty disputes, economic resources, and issues of national pride. Beijing believes that resolution of these concerns in China's favor requires a Navy able to prevail as a deterrent combat force.

CHAPTER 1

China's Naval Heritage

The PLAN has a long and illustrious lineage. China's naval forces have evolved through several distinct stages.

IMPERIAL CHINA

The PLAN can trace its lineage to the earliest recorded naval battle in Chin, in 549 bc, during the Spring and Autumn Period, when rival rulers used ships to attack each other.[1] Large-scale naval operations continued to play a role in Chinese warfare through the Han Dynasty (206 bc–ad 220). The sea also probably provided China's earliest trading routes with southern and western Asia.[2] Chinese mariners were the first to control their ships with sails and rudders. They also greatly increased their vessels' seaworthiness through compartmentalization, painted vessel bottoms to inhibit wood rot, and built dry docks. They developed the art of navigation to a high degree, including use of the portable compass as early as 1044.[3] Regular commercial sea routes as far as southwestern Asia and western Africa were established by the end of the Tang Dynasty (ad 907).[4]

The high point of naval development in imperial China probably occurred during the Song Dynasty (ad 960–1279) as part of a five-hundred-year period when China deployed "the world's most powerful and technologically sophisticated Navy."[5] The army organized fleets composed of several hundred warships and supply vessels in times of emergency; indeed, a fleet deployed in ad 1274 reportedly totaled 13,500 ships.[6] Chinese maritime technology also matured during this age, and the maritime sector was an important part of the national economy. Perhaps most significant, the Song regime was the first in China to establish a permanent national navy functioning as an independent service administered by a central government agency. The Imperial Commissioner's Office for the Control and Organization of the Coastal Areas was established in 1132 to supervise a navy of 52,000 men.[7]

The Song maritime experience was based on a rapidly expanding national economy with a particularly strong maritime sector encompassing commerce, fisheries, and transportation. As the navy expanded, so did port facilities, supply centers, and dockyards; soldiers were trained specifically as marines, and coast guard squadrons were established. Song navies used both sail and paddlewheel-driven craft, the latter powered by laborers on treadmills. Doctrine including the development of formation maneuvering, long-range projectile launchers, and complex tactics was formalized.[8]

China remained a sea power during some periods in the two succeeding dynasties. In fact, the overthrow of the Song regime by the Yuan (Mongol) Dynasty was largely due to the latter's mastery of naval warfare. The Yuan later used large fleets to undertake invasions of Vietnam, Java, and Japan: the 1274 expedition against Japan numbered 900 ships and 250,000 soldiers; that of 1281 included 4,400 ships.[9] Maritime commerce continued to expand during the Yuan Dynasty, and cannon made their appearance aboard ships.[10]

During the Ming Dynasty (1368–1644) China saw both the pinnacle of its overseas naval deployments and the collapse of its naval power. The crux of the successful Ming struggle to succeed the Yuan was a series of battles on the lakes of the Yangtze River valley. The waterborne forces employed by the Ming and their opponents were not independent navies, but army units assigned to ships on local lakes and rivers. Their original mission had been to transport men and supplies, but the armies quickly recognized the advantages of using these craft as warships against both land forces and each other. The Ming ships were manned by approximately twelve thousand troops and were armed with archers, cannon, and "flame weapons." The "lake campaign" was an effective use of ships and men to take advantage of the battlefield topography, but it did not result in the establishment of a regular Ming navy.

Also during the Ming Dynasty, the early-fifteenth-century voyages of Zheng He to the Middle East and Africa represented a standard of Chinese shipbuilding, voyage management, and navigation ability well beyond European capabilities. Zheng He led large fleets of ships, some displacing more than 400 tons, on seven voyages halfway around the world at a time when Portuguese explorers were still feeling their way down the west coast of

Africa in 50-ton caravels. This period of Chinese naval power lasted a mere thirty years, however; the Ming rulers ended these voyages for domestic, financial, political, and ideological reasons just as European nations were beginning to use the high seas to achieve economic wealth and to proselytize. Why end such epochal maritime expeditions? First, the voyages were expensive and the Ming pursued a rigidly conservative economic policy. Second, the court was concerned about the growing power of the eunuchs, who were the chief sponsors of the voyages. Third, "Confucian-trained scholar-officials opposed trade and foreign contact on principle."[11] Perhaps most important, the threat from Mongols and other Asian aggressors grew stronger, which increasingly focused government concerns inland and absorbed a growing portion of the national budget. By 1500, "anti-commercialism and xenophobia" had triumphed and the government was attempting to deal with maritime problems by ignoring them. The navy was allowed to deteriorate. By the end of the sixteenth century, the Ming government was unable even to defend Chinese maritime traders against pirates.

Even during the long period of brilliant maritime scientific progress and dominating power, however, the focus of China's national security concerns still lay to the north and west, where the threat to the regime lay. Imperial naval missions were for coastal defense, control of maritime trade, defending the regime against domestic threats, and ensuring economic benefit to the state. No dynasty fell as a direct result of foreign maritime invasion or pressure: usurpers emerged from the Asian interior, and the crucial battles were land battles. The navy was at various times capable and even powerful, but never was it vital to a dynasty's survival, even in the face of the centuries-long threat from Japanese "pirates," as the Chinese habitually referred to their neighbors.

Typical of the process of dynastic progression, the Qing (Manchu) Dynasty replaced the Ming Dynasty after a long period of land warfare in which naval power played a very small role. The Qing made no concerted effort to rebuild the navy or expand the maritime sector of China's economy after assuming power in 1644. This was not the result of neglect; rather, the Qing faced no significant threat from the sea during the dynasty's first century and a half in power, and there seemed little justification for a large naval investment. This was especially true after the most notable Qing maritime campaign, when the new dynasty conquered Taiwan in 1683. A historian described that island as "flat, malarial plains along the west, backed by inhospitable mountain ranges"; an "unfriendly aboriginal population further discouraged exploration or settlement."[12]

Overseas trade grew despite Qing indifference, due in part to the Chinese diaspora throughout Southeast and South Asia that had begun during earlier dynasties. The Qing navy remained powerful enough to prevent coastal piracy from getting out of hand, to maintain order on the canals and rivers, and to perform other coast guard–type functions. China had fallen so far behind the global norm in naval power, however, that it was unable to defeat the late-eighteenth- and early-nineteenth-century imperialists—who came by sea.

As the Qing reeled from the imperialist onslaught, major "restoration" movements occurred following the end of the Taiping Rebellion in 1864. These "self-strengthening" efforts, bearing the slogan "Chinese learning as the fundamental structure, Western learning for practical use," included building and training a modern navy. This slogan probably resulted from admiration of the technology in modern warships and because China's humiliating defeat by the imperialist powers had been made possible by their navies.

An arsenal was established in Shanghai to build steam-powered gunboats, but efforts to modernize China's navy too often fell victim to Confucian traditionalists, who were the rigid ideologues of the day. It was in part a case of ideology defeating professionalism, a problem that continued into the twenty-first century. Nonetheless, by 1884 China had deployed a modern navy, led by the efforts of Li Hongzhang, one of the most prominent of the scholar-bureaucrats who appreciated how far behind the foreign powers China lagged. Li used three approaches to build a navy, which he thought should be oriented toward coastal defense: indigenous production, purchases abroad, and the reverse engineering of foreign systems.

Unfortunately, the new navy suffered from corruption at high levels and weak administration.[13] It was organized into four fleets that were essentially independent navies. The Beiyang Fleet, organized by Li Hongzhang and homeported in Weihaiwei, was the most modern and powerful; by 1884 it included two 7,500-ton-displacement German-built battleships. The Fujian Fleet was homeported in Fuzhou; the other two fleets were the Nanyang, homeported in Shanghai, and the Guangdong, homeported in Guangzhou.

The new Chinese force soon became embroiled in war with two foreign navies. Disputes with France over its colonization of Vietnam led to the outbreak of hostilities in August 1884, and the local French fleet attacked the outgunned Chinese Fujian Fleet in Fuzhou Harbor, sinking every ship.[14] The other fleets were not sent to fight the French because Li wanted to conserve China's remaining naval strength. His efforts were successful—at least on paper. He established a national navy office, organized a training regimen and shore establishment, and in 1888 issued standardized naval regulations.[15]

Despite these achievements, China failed to form a coherent national navy. The Beiyang fleet came to grief in the effort to halt Japanese incursions into Korea in the 1890s. The fleet, which consisted of two battleships, ten cruisers, and two torpedo boats, lost a sea battle to the Japanese in September 1894 because its members were not trained to fight together and suffered from poor leadership. Afterward the fleet withdrew to Weihaiwei, a strongly fortified harbor on the northern Shandong coast. In January 1895, however, the Japanese landed troops who seized the forts guarding the harbor and turned their guns on the Chinese ships.[16] Chinese ship losses in conjunction with the suicides of the fleet commander and other senior officers eviscerated the Beiyang Fleet.[17] Again, the other Chinese fleets failed to join the fight.

These naval conflicts with the French and the Japanese demonstrated that while Beijing had successfully acquired the ships and weapons of a modern navy, it had failed to institute effective central administration, training, logistical and maintenance support, and command and control. Furthermore, operational doctrine was almost completely lacking; naval leaders failed to establish interfleet coordination, exercises, or mutual support. Finally, China failed to provide its new navy with a coherent strategy tied to national security objectives. As a result of these factors, China's attempt to deploy a modern navy in the late nineteenth century failed miserably.[18]

REPUBLICAN CHINA

Chinese naval forces during the republican period consisted almost entirely of ships left over from the Qing Dynasty or obtained from foreign nations. No significant efforts were made to build up the navy; in any case they probably could not have been justified amid China's political and economic disarray. Individual warlords occasionally made effective use of naval forces, but always to augment ground forces. The low point probably occurred during the height of the warlord period in the mid-to-late 1920s. A Western observer remarked: "There has been a steady deterioration in the discipline of the Chinese Navy since the establishment of the Republic, and it has now ceased to exist as a national force, the different units being under the control of various militarists, who treat the vessels as their own private property.... It is impossible today to obtain a complete list of Chinese warships, showing to which party or militarist faction they belong. Vessels have been changing their allegiance ... with bewildering frequency.[19]

The government did not develop a maritime strategy because the primary threats to the new regime were ground forces of the Chinese Communist Party (CCP), Russia, and warlords. Naval actions took place chiefly on the rivers—especially the Yangtze and the waterways of the Pearl River delta. Many of the warlords who struggled to gain control of various provinces and districts during the revolutionary period, from 1916 to 1928, used China's inland waterways for transportation, as military barriers, or as sources of revenue by taxing the dense river and canal traffic. These efforts led to frequent skirmishes between provincial forces and the imperialist gunboats that patrolled China's rivers and lakes but were not a coherent maritime presence.

There were two notable exceptions. First was a battle at the upper Yangtze River port city of Wanhsien in September 1926. The local warlord, General Yang Sen, had commandeered British-owned steamers to transport his troops. When the British gunboat HMS *Cockchafer* attempted to free the steamers, it ran into an ambush very capably managed by Yang and suffered severe casualties.[20] There was also an October 1929 naval and land engagement on the Heilong (Amur) River between Chinese and Soviet forces that foreshadowed the 1969 incident over disputed boundaries.[21]

Foreign sea power was an effective "force multiplier"; that is, foreign powers were able to use sea and river transport to move troops rapidly from crisis area to crisis area.[22] Great Britain, the United States, and Japan were thus able to influence the course of events in revolutionary China with relatively small military forces. Japan introduced a new element of maritime warfare in 1932 when bombers from an aircraft carrier stationed off Shanghai bombarded Chinese forces threatening Japanese interests in the city. Republican China was unable to contest such maritime strength.

China's record as a naval power during the long period of empire and republic shows an understandable focus on the continental rather than the maritime arena. Navies were built and employed almost entirely for defensive purposes. Maritime strength was regarded as only a secondary element of national power.

THE PEOPLE'S REPUBLIC OF CHINA

China's navy began to come into its own with the establishment of the PRC.

The Early Years: 1949–1954

The Communists' victory in 1949 was an Army victory, not a Navy one; the People's Liberation Army was unable to project power across even the narrow Taiwan Strait. The Kuomintang (KMT) Navy continued raiding coastal installations, landing agents, attacking merchant craft and fishing vessels, and threatening invasion of the mainland on a larger scale. The new government in Beijing sought to defend its coastline and island territories against both the United States and the KMT regime on Taiwan.

Coastal defense was emphasized in January 1950 with the creation of a new East China Military Command headquartered in Shanghai and deploying more than 450,000 personnel. Beijing ordered these troops to defend China's coast against "imperialist aggression from the sea," to continue the fight against Chiang's forces, and to help with economic reconstruction.[23] The East China People's Navy was established on 1 May 1949 as part of this command. This first PRC Navy was formed mostly by defectors from the former KMT Second Coastal Defense Fleet.[24] The new Navy's commander defined its mission as "to safeguard China's independence, territorial integrity and sovereignty against imperialist aggression[,] . . . to destroy the sea blockade of liberated China, to support the land and air forces of the People's Liberation Army in defense of Chinese soil and to wipe out all remnants of the reactionary forces."[25]

The CCP Politburo charged the new Navy with "defending both [eastern and southeastern] China coasts and the Yangtze River."[26] It was also to establish law and order on coastal and riverine waters, help the Army capture offshore islands still occupied by the KMT, and prepare for the capture of Taiwan. The first commander (and political commissar) of the East China Navy was General Zhang Aiping. Zhang's first acts included the establishment of a naval staff college at Nanjing in August 1949, organization of a rudimentary maintenance and logistical infrastructure, and in September 1949 a visit to Moscow to discuss Soviet naval assistance. The PLAN was officially established in May 1950 under the command of General Xiao Jingguang. The Chinese wanted a defensive force that would be inexpensive to build and quickly manned and trained.[27]

Zhang and Xiao were typical of early PLAN leaders: revolutionary officers who had spent their entire careers as ground commanders and were transferred to the Navy for reasons of political reliability and proven combat record rather than for any particular naval experience. This trend, in fact, continued until 1988; Liu Huaqing was an Army officer before he was appointed to head the PLAN in 1982. After six distinguished years in that position, Liu again became a general when he was appointed to the CMC vice chairmanship. Some recent personnel moves have continued this practice.[28]

The new PLAN was established with Soviet assistance obtained by Mao Zedong during his 1949–50 visit to Moscow. Mao planned to use half of the initial Soviet loan of $300 million to purchase naval equipment. The new PLAN also ordered two new cruisers from Great Britain and attempted to obtain surplus foreign warships through Hong Kong, but those efforts were nullified by the outbreak of the Korean War.[29] China acquired mostly small vessels suitable to combat the coastal threat from Taiwan.

China initially obtained four old Soviet submarines, two destroyers, and a large number of patrol boats. The new force also included about ten corvettes; forty U.S. landing craft; and several dozen miscellaneous river gunboats, mine-sweepers, and yard craft seized from the Nationalists. The Soviets helped the Chinese establish a large shore-based infrastructure, including shipyards, naval colleges, and extensive coastal fortifications.[30]

Beijing's goal was to seize the offshore islands still occupied by the KMT, with the invasion of Taiwan scheduled initially for the spring of 1950 but soon postponed to the summer of 1951. Mao Zedong considered the capture of Taiwan "an inseparable part of his great cause of unifying China."[31] He lacked experience in naval warfare but quickly learned that a successful campaign against Taiwan would require amphibious training, naval transportation, "guaranteed air coverage," and the cooperation of a "fifth column" on the island—requirements that still apply.[32]

China achieved a major victory in April 1950 when the PLA occupied Hainan, after Taiwan the second-largest island held by the Nationalists. The campaign cost Beijing heavy personnel losses but included the capture of more than 90,000 Nationalist troops. This victory resulted from the PLA's careful planning, its ability to neutralize superior Nationalist naval and air forces by use of shore-based artillery to gain effective control of the sea and airspace between Hainan and the mainland, and a typically poor performance by Taiwan's senior commanders.

China's fear of American aggression was heightened in June 1950 when President Harry Truman ordered the U.S. Seventh Fleet into the Taiwan Strait at the outset of the Korean War. Although Truman explained America's

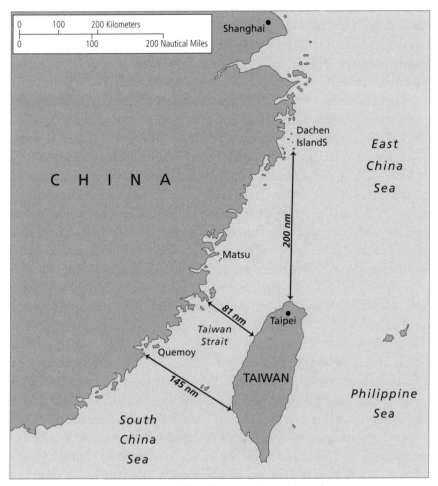

Distances between Taiwan and mainland China (Central Intelligence Agency)

reentry into the Chinese civil war as a means of preventing either side from attacking the other, Beijing understood that he was committing the United States to defend Taiwan—after having refused for many months to do so.[33] Premier Zhou Enlai called Truman's move "violent predatory action by the U.S. Government [that] constituted armed aggression against the territory of China and total violation of the UN charter."[34] Beijing also understood, as it does today, that the United States had complete air and sea superiority in Asian waters.

Beijing's concern was reinforced in February 1953 when President Dwight Eisenhower withdrew the U.S. fleet from the Taiwan Strait, thus in theory "unleashing" Nationalist forces to attack China.[35] In December 1953 Mao Zedong assigned the PLAN three priority missions: eliminate KMT naval interference and ensure safe navigation for China's maritime commerce, prepare to recover Taiwan, and oppose aggression from the sea.[36]

The PRC's young Navy faced many problems, including the lack of trained personnel and amphibious ships, as demonstrated in its spotty record of assaults on KMT-held coastal islands. Furthermore, in February 1952 Mao diverted the Navy's ship-acquisition funds to the purchase of aircraft needed to fight in Korea.[37] Budgetary limitations and Western reluctance further constrained acquisition of equipment from foreign sources. In addition, despite several visits to Moscow by senior PLA leaders to plead China's case, the Soviets continued to insist on payment for their ships, even though most of them were obsolete and of little use to the USSR.[38] The PLAN also lacked air power and was just beginning to establish a modern maintenance and logistical infrastructure. None of these problems should have been unexpected, but they remained characteristic of the PLAN during its first half-century of existence.

1955–1959

The Korean War presented mixed naval lessons to China. The allies' amphibious landing at Inchon in September 1950 was a major turning point of the war, and their command of the sea allowed free employment of aircraft carriers and battleships to bombard Chinese and North Korean forces. The UN forces suffered at least one significant maritime defeat when a planned amphibious assault on the east coast port of Hungnam in October 1950 had to be canceled because North Korea mined the harbor. Overall, however, Korea was not a maritime conflict, and the PLA's success in land and air battles contributed to a continued reliance on a defensive, coastal Navy.

This conclusion was not unanimous among the PLA's leaders; after witnessing the effects of modern weaponry firsthand in Korea, including the threat of nuclear warfare, some wanted to modify Mao's theory of "people's war" to become "people's war under modern conditions." The most prominent proponent of the latter was Peng Dehuai, who had commanded the Chinese forces in Korea. Peng reportedly stated that "people's war and such stuff are outdated [at sea because] in battle the Navy relied upon the tonnage of its vessels, the caliber of its guns and the slide rule." Peng's attempts to regularize and modernize the military brought the accusation that he was trying to "negate the principle of people's war" by placing "military technique" ahead of ideology. His effort to modify Mao's military theories was one of the reasons he was dismissed from office in disgrace in 1959.[39] Conforming to Maoist ideology meant continued concentration on large ground formations, with the Navy remaining in a subsidiary role.

Beijing initially relied on Soviet nuclear forces to counter the American nuclear threat during the 1950s. The stresses in the alliance with Moscow became more divisive as the decade progressed, however, in part because Mao was determined that China develop its own nuclear forces. "Even if it takes 10,000 years," he proclaimed, "we must make a nuclear submarine."[40] The budgetary emphasis on nuclear weapons, the economic disruptions resulting from the disastrous Great Leap Forward, and the continuing belief in Maoist orthodoxy all contributed to the lack of resources for developing a strong Chinese Navy during the late 1950s and 1960s.

PLAN operations in the mid-1950s continued to focus on turning back KMT attacks against the mainland and on capturing islands still held by Taiwan. During the 1954–55 Taiwan Strait crisis the PLA used its superior air power and a well-coordinated amphibious assault against an outlying island to capture the Dachen Islands.[41]

In neither of the decade's crises did Beijing expect to capture Quemoy (Jinmen) or Matsu (Mazu), but the incidents drew the United States more firmly into the conflict between China and Taiwan and emphasized the PLAN's weakness. Furthermore, Chiang Kai-shek used the 1954–55 shelling to pressure Secretary of State John Foster Dulles into signing the mutual security treaty with the Republic of China. The incident did not redound to Beijing's benefit.[42] The 1950s ended with China possessing all the disputed islands except Jinmen and Mazu, and of course Taiwan. The PLA also stopped most of the KMT raids on the mainland, as well as attacks on merchant and fishing vessels.[43]

The Navy's First Aviation School was founded at Qingdao in October 1950; the Navy's air force—the People's Liberation Army Navy Air Force (PLANAF), or Naval Aviation—was formally established in 1952. Its mission was support of anti–surface ship and antisubmarine defensive operations. Initial inventory was 80 aircraft, including MiG-15 jet fighters, Il-28 jet bombers, and propeller-driven Tu-2 strike aircraft. The PLANAF had grown to about 470 aircraft by 1958.[44]

PLAN operating forces were organized into three fleets. The North Sea Fleet included the majority of the submarine force, perhaps because it was the fleet nearest the U.S. naval forces based in Japan.[45] The East Sea Fleet was the busiest and most important because it faced the American-supported KMT forces across the Taiwan Strait. The South Sea Fleet, once the Vietnamese-French war ended in 1954, faced a hostile Southeast Asia Treaty Organization (SEATO) but a relatively quiet maritime situation. The PLAN had been organized, sent to sea, and proven effective as a coastal defense force within ten years of its founding.

A New Situation: 1960–1976
The 1960s were marked by major foreign and domestic events that further constrained the PRC's development of a seagoing navy. Most important was the split with the Soviet Union, signaled during Nikita Khrushchev's October 1959 meeting with Mao Zedong in Beijing, and dramatically executed in mid-1960 when Soviet advisers (and their plans) were withdrawn from China. The Navy suffered with the rest of the PLA as military development projects were left in turmoil.[46]

Other significant events in the early 1960s included war with India, the reemerging Vietnam conflict, turmoil in the new African states, and revolutionary movements throughout Southeast Asia. None of these major international events directly involved the Navy. They did not provide justification for improving the PLAN, and in fact served to limit naval modernization. Maoist orthodoxy continued to dominate strategic thinking.

Minister of Defense Lin Biao apparently wanted to change the situation by instituting a policy of technological development with "politics in command." He did not succeed, and at the end of the decade changed direction and came down solidly on the side of "politics," writing "long live the victory of people's war."[47] This may have simply resulted from Lin's belief that the CCP had to remain firmly in control of the PLA for China to survive; hence, ideological reliability was more important than modern hardware.

Taiwan was too weak to act on its invasion rhetoric; America's involvement in Vietnam and determination not to repeat its 1950 provocation of Beijing meant that China faced no overseas threat during the 1960s. By the end of the decade, however, relations with the Soviet Union had deteriorated to the point of armed conflict along the Amur River. The former ally was now the enemy; soon the United States would be China's ally.

Mao remained determined that China would join the nuclear club. Despite the ideological turmoil of the late 1950s and the 1960s, Beijing invested heavily in developing nuclear-armed missiles and the nuclear-powered submarines to launch them. These were national rather than PLAN projects, however, and did not significantly increase the Navy's ability to obtain the military resources necessary for modernization.

Beijing viewed the Soviet Navy at this time as capable of a major amphibious invasion. This estimate owed more to the history of threats and invasions from the north—and to the Soviet Union's proximity to Beijing and the economic resources of northeastern China—than it did to the weak Soviet amphibious forces actually present in the Pacific.[48] The Great Proletarian Cultural Revolution (GPCR), lasting from approximately 1966 to 1976, precluded significant naval developments. The PLAN continued to serve as an extension of the Army, and modernization was limited because people's war ideology portrayed technology and weaponry as insignificant compared to revolutionary soldiers imbued with Mao's ideology.

The GPCR seriously hampered technological development in general; even the relatively sacrosanct missile, submarine, and nuclear weapons programs were affected.[49] A review of global naval developments indicates that PLAN modernization was retarded by perhaps two decades as a result of the program's restrictions and the personnel losses that resulted from this political maelstrom.[50] Except for the evolution of nuclear power, the PLAN missed or was very late joining common developments in most warfare areas, including guided missiles in antiair (AAW), antisurface (ASUW), and antisubmarine warfare (ASW); automation and computerization of command, control, and communications (C3); the use of shipborne helicopters; automation of gunnery and sensor systems; and even the advent of automation and gas turbine technology in ship propulsion.

PLAN modernization was still hamstrung at the end of the GPCR by the "Gang of Four." Mao's widow, Jiang Qing, led the attack on naval missile development. Another member of the clique, Zhang Chunqiao, expressed the Gang's anti-Navy position and support for the "continentalist view."[51] Despite this attitude and a lack of resources for major conventional force development, the PLAN had moved into the missile age by 1970, deploying a Soviet-designed ballistic missile submarine and ten Soviet-built patrol boats armed with cruise missiles.[52]

After the Cultural Revolution

When Mao Zedong reportedly directed the development of a modern Navy at a May 1975 meeting of the CMC,[53] he was probably reacting both to the Soviet threat and to the development of a powerful navy by China's ancient enemy, Japan. The PLAN's first priority in the 1970s was defending against possible Soviet amphibious assault from the northeast. Other missions included combating criminal activities such as smuggling, piracy, and illegal immigration; sea and air rescue (SAR); and safety of navigation.

China perceived the Soviet naval revolution of the 1970s as a direct threat, even though that event was defensive in motivation and aimed primarily at the United States. Moscow viewed China as a significant national security concern as well, however, a fact that Beijing understood. China's concern about Soviet maritime power was strengthened when Moscow demonstrated its new global navy in the 1975 Okean exercises.

Chinese interests threatened by the Soviet Navy in the late 1970s and 1980s included sea lines of communication (SLOCs) vital to Beijing's rapidly increasing merchant marine as Moscow's maritime forces maintained a continual naval presence in the Indian Ocean and North Arabian Sea. The Soviet Pacific Fleet almost doubled in size during the 1970s and was upgraded by the assignment of Moscow's latest combatants, including nuclear-powered and nuclear-armed surface ships and submarines. Soviet merchant and fisheries ships were also omnipresent in Pacific waters historically vital to China's economic interests.

Several factors continued to impede the development of a large, modern Chinese Navy. The political aftershocks of the GPCR, as Hua Guofeng and Deng Xiaoping contested for leadership of post-Mao China, limited the resources devoted to military modernization,. This struggle was not resolved until 1980, with Deng emerging on top. After the Gang of Four were arrested in October 1976, Premier Hua Guofeng had seemed to move away from a strictly continentalist position, at least so far as to emphasize the PLAN's nuclear deterrent mission. In 1980, however, Deng Xiaoping reemphasized the Navy's role as a coastal defense force, and that view was retained throughout the first half of the decade. "Our navy," Deng asserted, "should conduct coastal operations. It is a defensive force. Everything in the construction of the navy must accord with this guiding principle."[54]

Naval growth was also limited by the disorder in China's economic and social structures that lasted beyond the end of the GPCR. In particular, this turmoil affected China's military-industrial complex, hindering modernization efforts in the PLA. Furthermore, the lessons of the 1979 "punishment" of Vietnam must have been sobering to the PLA. This conflict did not involve significant naval efforts, however, and the PLAN probably benefited only marginally from corrective budgetary measures.

The allegiance shifts among China, the Soviet Union, and the United States meant that by 1980 Beijing could rely on the world's largest and most modern navy to counter the Soviet maritime threat. With the U.S. Navy in the region, China had no need to develop a similar force. Furthermore, given the U.S.-Japan security treaty, Beijing could subsume any concern about future Japanese aggression within its strategic relationship with Washington.[55]

Major changes in China's domestic and international situation in the 1980s altered Beijing's view of the PLAN, and maritime power was a more important element of national security strategy by the end of the decade. Beijing's second maritime priority, after the Soviet threat, was securing offshore territorial claims. Taiwan was the most important of these, but the South China Sea was also significant. Although successful action against South Vietnamese naval forces in 1974 had given China possession of the disputed Paracel Islands, this fight was an indication that other claimants to the islands and reefs of the South China Sea would not accede meekly to Beijing's territorial claims. Furthermore, the Soviet naval base at Cam Ranh Bay was flourishing as the 1980s began.

These factors contributed to a significant change in the South Sea Fleet's organization: the Marine Corps, first formed in 1953 but disbanded in 1957, was reestablished in December 1979 as an amphibious assault force and assigned to the southern fleet. The PLAN's slender amphibious assets were concentrated in the south because that fleet's training regimen included "island-seizing" exercises. In 1980, for instance, a major fleet exercise in the South China Sea focused on the seizure and defense of islands in the Paracels.[56]

The South Sea Fleet's organization benefited from the PLAN force structure changes, which for the first time centered on Chinese-built warships. Although China still relied heavily on Soviet designs, the Luda-class guided-missile destroyers, Jianghu-class frigates, and Houjian fast-attack missile boats marked a significant increase in China's maritime capability. The submarine force included the first Chinese-built nuclear-powered attack submarines as well as about sixty conventionally powered boats. A seaborne nuclear deterrent force continued under development, following Mao's earlier insistence that the Navy had to be built up "to make it dreadful to the enemy."[57]

Deng Xiaoping's Navy

Naval expansion and modernization were spurred during the 1980s by the coastal concentration of China's burgeoning economy and military facilities. China's dramatic economic development and increasing wealth supplied the necessary resources. Recovery from the GPCR, well under way by 1985, included a reinvigorated if more decentralized military-industrial complex.

Three events contributed prominently to the development of China's Navy in this decade. The first was Deng's evaluation of the military at an expanded CMC meeting in 1975 as "overstaffed, lazy, arrogant, ill-equipped, and ill-prepared to conduct modern warfare"—an opinion strengthened by the PLA's poor performance during the 1979 conflict with Vietnam.[58] The Soviet naval presence in the South China Sea probably inhibited the employment of Chinese naval forces in that conflict, and the Navy could contribute little to the overland invasion of Vietnam.[59]

Second was Beijing's 1985 strategic decision that the Soviet Union no longer posed a major threat to China in terms of global nuclear war, and that in the future the PLA would have to be prepared instead for "small wars on the periphery" of the nation.[60] The emphasis on a "peripheral" (to a significant extent maritime) rather than a continental strategic view improved the PLAN's ability to obtain resources within the PLA.

Third was the rise to prominence of General Liu Huaqing. Liu had been schooled in the Soviet Union, served most of his career in the science and technology arms of the PLA, and was close to Deng Xiaoping.[61] His appointment to head the Navy was unusual because Liu held substantive (general/admiral) rank senior to that (lieutenant general/vice admiral) normally held by the PLAN commander, and represented Beijing's determination to improve its maritime power.

Liu exerted a strong force on naval developments both as Navy commander from 1982 to 1987, and then as vice chairman of the CMC until 1997. He is best known for promulgating a three-stage maritime strategy for China that provided justification on which PLAN officers and other navalists could base their plans for a larger, more modern Navy. More important were his accomplishments in reorganizing the Navy, redeveloping the Marine Corps, upgrading bases and research and development facilities, and restructuring the school system.[62]

China's widening maritime concerns and increased budget resources in the 1980s raised interest in a strong, modern Navy. PLAN modernization proceeded along three paths—indigenous construction, foreign purchase, and reverse engineering—much as Li Hongzheng's "self-strengthening" navy had a hundred years earlier. The 1980s program proceeded at a measured pace, however; Beijing did not embark on a major naval building program.

Construction included guided-missile destroyers and frigates, replenishment-at-sea ships, conventionally and nuclear-powered attack submarines, and support craft including missile-tracking ships and officer-training vessels. Foreign purchases were concentrated in the West, with the United States selling China five modern ship engines, ASW torpedoes, and electronic warfare systems; and Western European nations selling weapons and sensor systems including Italian torpedoes, French cruise missiles, and British radars.

Protecting offshore petroleum assets, other seabed minerals, and fisheries also received increased attention.[63] The PLAN acquired its only Xia-class fleet ballistic missile submarine. The successful submerged launch in 1988 of the Ju Lang-1 (JL-1) intermediate-range ballistic missile (IRBM) from this submarine meant that China for the first time could deploy nuclear strategic weapons at sea.[64]

During the 1980s the PLAN also demonstrated its increasing capability in other maritime missions. China invested in four large space-surveillance ships to support its growing military and commercial space programs, with these ships conducting the first long-range PLAN deployments, in support of space launches, in 1980. Task forces supported scientific expeditions to the Arctic and Antarctica. The PLAN's first foreign port visit was conducted in 1985, when two East Sea Fleet ships visited Bangladesh, Sri Lanka, and Pakistan. The officer-training ship *Zheng He* became the first PLAN vessel to visit the United States when it made a 1989 port call to Hawaii.

During the 1990s Beijing continued to expand and modernize the Navy at a measured pace. The PLAN engaged in a series of long-range deployments throughout East and South Asia as well as deploying a three-ship task group to the Western Hemisphere, visiting the United States, Mexico, Peru, and Chile in 1998. Foreign purchases of improved ships, submarines, and aircraft earned the PLAN headlines as China acquired *Sovremenny*-class DDGs, Kilo-class submarines, and Su-27 and Su-30 fighters from Russia.

Naval modernization has intensified throughout the first decade of the twenty-first century, characterized by three important factors: (1) concentration on modernizing the PLAN's submarine force; (2) focus on the "softer" aspects of maritime power: dramatic increases in merchant ship numbers, shipyard capability, and port cargo-handling capacity; and (3) determination to improve personnel education and training, fleet maintenance, and resupply procedures, with increasing at-sea operational capability a priority. Fleet air and missile defenses have improved significantly, and China's ongoing nuclear and conventional submarine acquisition program is unprecedented.

CONCLUSION

The communist regime was quick to recognize the need to deal with maritime issues, but only after forty years and a dramatically altered international situation did Beijing begin preparing to deploy a modern Navy capable of operating on the high seas. Beijing currently views the sea "as its chief strategic defensive direction" because "China's political and economic focus lies on the coastal areas[, and] for the present and a fairly long period to come, [its] strategic focus will be in the direction of the sea."[65]

The Chinese Navy steamed into the twenty-first century with a history marked by notable consistencies. First is recognition of the maritime element of China's national security. Second, Chinese naval efforts have been closely linked to the nation's economic development.[66] Hence, China's naval modernization during the past thirty years has been unexceptional and is going to continue in view of China's continuing economic growth and reliance on maritime trade.

Third, Chinese naval development since the nineteenth century has been marked by significant interaction with foreign navies. Qing Dynasty modernization efforts drew on Japanese, German, British, and American naval professionals as advisers, administrators, and engineers. This trend has continued under the PRC, with a sporadic but pervasive reliance on Soviet/Russian advisers, strategy, equipment, technology, and engineers. Russia also has been an important influence on the development of naval thought in the PRC.[67]

Fourth, the Chinese government has not hesitated to employ naval force in pursuit of national security goals. These efforts have often achieved some success, as in 1950, 1954–55, and 1958 in the Taiwan Strait; and in 1974, 1988, 1995, and 1998 in the South China Sea. Beijing's willingness to resort to naval force even when significantly outgunned bears a cautionary message for foreign strategists evaluating China's possible actions during a crisis. Finally, China typically has employed naval force over issues of sovereignty concerning specific islands and provinces, including Taiwan, the Diaoyu Islands, and South China Sea claims.[68]

China today deploys a modern navy capable of becoming "a Great Wall at Sea" operating on, above, and below the ocean surface. Beijing has developed the coherent fleet structure and nation maritime strategy previously lacking from Chinese naval efforts. What are the capabilities and strategy of China's twenty-first-century Navy? What are Beijing's parameters for employing that Navy? Answering those questions requires a closer look at China's maritime interests and priorities.

CHAPTER 2

China's Maritime Territorial Interests

Territorial sovereignty is a vital interest of any nation, but it holds a special place in Beijing's national security calculus. This is in part the result of the "hundred years of humiliation"—the period from approximately 1840 to 1949 during which China was torn by foreign aggression and was, in Mao Zedong's words, "a semi-colonial country."[1] Chinese civilian and military officials remain extremely sensitive to sovereignty claims, no matter how contested or tenuous under international law.

Beijing is party to six of East Asia's more than two dozen maritime territorial disputes: the Diaoyu/Senkaku Islands with Japan; Taiwan; the Paracel Islands with Vietnam; the Spratly Islands in the South China Sea with Taiwan, Vietnam, the Philippines, Brunei, and Malaysia; water areas of the South China Sea with the foregoing nations and Indonesia; and the maritime border with Vietnam.[2] All of these disputes include significant economic issues.

UNITED NATIONS CONVENTION ON THE LAW OF THE SEA

Maritime claims in East Asia must be considered within the context of UNCLOS, which Beijing signed and ratified in 1996. This convention, promulgated in 1982 after almost a decade of international negotiations, embodies important changes from previous maritime and international laws. UNCLOS changes the concept and limit of "territorial seas," now defined as the offshore area subject to a state's sovereignty, including the airspace above the sea as well as the seabed and subsoil.[3] The convention retains the previous delineation of territorial seas as 12 nm from a state's coastline, but also defines three additional areas of sovereignty.

A state's territorial waters continue to be sovereign. The state may, for instance, require submarines to transit those waters on the surface, and may require ships of any sort to obtain approval before transiting the area. It may also impose sea-lanes and traffic separation schemes requiring transiting ships to follow specific, limited routes through the area.

As the first new area, UNCLOS establishes a contiguous zone (CZ) extending an additional 12 nm, or 24 nm from a state's coastline. A state does not possess full sovereignty within the CZ but may exercise the control necessary to "(a) prevent infringement of customs, fiscal, immigration or sanitary laws within its territory or territorial seas; and (b) punish infringement of the above laws and regulations committed within its territory or territorial sea."[4]

The second new area delineated by UNCLOS is a state's exclusive economic zone (EEZ), "an area beyond and adjacent to the territorial sea" in which the state has "sovereign rights for the purpose of exploring and exploiting, conserving and managing the natural resources, whether living or non-living." The nation's EEZ also includes jurisdiction over artificial islands, installations, and structures; marine research; and protection and preservation of the environment. The EEZ may not extend beyond 200 nm from the state's coastline.[5]

Finally, UNCLOS defines a state's rights on its continental shelf (CS), comprising "the sea-bed and subsoil of the submarine areas that extend beyond its territorial sea" to a maximum distance of 350 nm. The state has sovereign rights over the CS "for the purpose of exploring it and exploiting its natural resources," both living and nonliving. The state does not, however, have any legal rights on the water surface or the airspace above the CS area.[6]

Two other UNCLOS provisions are particularly important to China's maritime claims. UNCLOS defines an "island" as "a naturally formed area of land, surrounded by water, which is above water at high tide." This affects Beijing's insular claims in the East and South China seas. An island possesses the territorial sea, CZ, EEZ, and CS characteristics of a continental state.[7] The UNCLOS provision for delimiting the EEZs between states less than 400 nm apart—and the CS between states less than 700 nm apart—particularly affects China's maritime territorial claims with North Korea, South Korea, Japan, and several Southeast Asian nations. States with conflicting EEZ or CS claims are urged to "achieve an equitable solution." If they cannot agree, they are supposed to submit the dispute to UNCLOS-created adjudication bodies for resolution.[8]

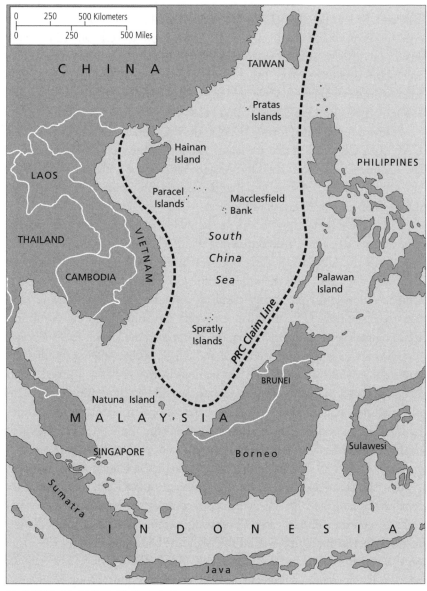

South China Sea (U.S. Pacific Command)

In its effort to resolve old questions of maritime law, UNCLOS has raised some new problems, two of which particularly apply to China's claims in Southeast Asian waters. First is the creation of the 200-nm EEZ in a region where multiple claims often overlap. One extreme example is the Gulf of

Thailand, where the EEZ claims of Cambodia, Malaysia, and Vietnam theo-retically leave Thailand with no EEZ.[9] Second, the UNCLOS-related right of states to impose navigation restrictions within their territorial waters allows archipelagic states to make troublesome claims. Indonesia, for instance, has tried to limit the freedom of navigation of ships transiting the vital Sunda and Lombok straits into the South China Sea.[10]

Many states included formal "Declarations and Statements" when ratifying UNCLOS. China listed five, for reasons including the view that international law historically has been used by Western nations for imperialistic purposes against developing countries and that the sea has often served as an avenue for the invasion and exploitation of China.

China's first qualifying statement claimed "sovereign rights and jurisdic-tion" over its EEZ and "the continental shelf," a claim that appears to contra-vene both the UNCLOS description of limited sovereign rights over the EEZ and the UNCLOS definition of the CS. This statement is the basis of China's rationale for protesting—and on several occasions employing mili-tary force against—U.S. surveillance aircraft and ships operating within the EEZ. China's second qualifying statement opposed the UNCLOS-suggested method of delineating contested EEZ and CS claims by applying equidistance criteria, instead favoring bilateral negotiations by the parties concerned. Third, China declared that all boundary disputes would be settled through bilateral consultations, not by reference to the international tribunals recommended by UNCLOS. Fourth, China attempted to qualify the UNCLOS provision for foreign warships having the right of innocent passage through its territo-rial (i.e., sovereign) waters, stating that "foreign ships for military purposes shall be subject to approval by the Government of the PRC for entering the territorial sea of the PRC." This includes, contrary to Washington's view, the right to control military vessels operating within its EEZ. Finally, Beijing reaffirmed its sovereignty over all the islands it had claimed in its 1992 Law on the Territorial Sea and the Contiguous Zone. These include "Taiwan and all islands appertaining thereto," as well as the Penghus, Dongsha, Diaoyu (Senkaku), Xisha (Paracel), Nansha (Spratly), and other South China Sea land features. This would remove from discussion exactly the sort of issues UNCLOS was created to address.[11]

In 1996 the UN Commission on the Limits of the Continental Shelf (CLCS) established a period, ending 13 May 2009, during which states could submit survey findings on the limits of their continental shelves. China submitted its survey on 11 May. In it, Beijing claimed a continental shelf

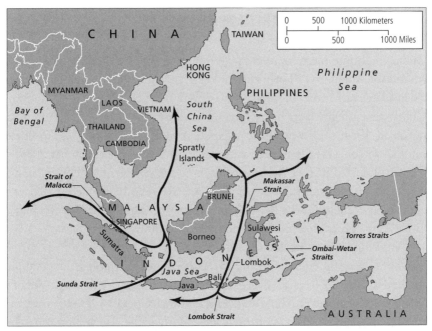

Strategic chokepoints: the Straits of Malacca, Sunda, and Lombok and SLOCs passing the Spratly Islands. (Institute for National Strategic Studies, Washington, D.C.)

beyond 200 nm in the East China Sea—in fact, all the way to the western slope of the Okinawa Trough. China based this claim on data collected over ten years of marine scientific research undertaken by China's Academy of Sciences, the Hydrographic Department, and the PLAN.[12]

China's claim will further exacerbate the dispute between Beijing and Tokyo over these waters. The CLCS is not authorized to decide the issue: it can only evaluate the scientific merits of a state's claim to a continental shelf beyond 200 nm, as permitted under UNCLOS article 76. Even if the continental shelf commission were to rule that Beijing had demonstrated the scientific basis for a continental shelf claim beyond 200 nm, it would not be the same as granting China exclusive jurisdiction over the area. Japan is still entitled to claim an EEZ as far as 200 nm as well, although to date it has only claimed an EEZ as far the median line between the waters it claims and those claimed by China. Only the two parties can resolve the dispute. Furthermore, a CLCS ruling would not resolve China's and Japan's dispute over the Senkaku/ Diaoyu Islands, because this issue lies outside its authority. Additionally, China's continental shelf claim to the UN commission may overlap with the extended continental shelf claimed by South Korea.

MARITIME INTERESTS

China's maritime interests now range from the Arctic to the Antarctic and around the world. The PLAN's initial long-range mission took place in 1980 when a large task group of ships was deployed to the South Pacific to monitor China's first satellite launches. China sent its first expedition to the Antarctic region in 1984; the twenty-fifth expedition took place during the 2008–9 summer season, and the twenty-sixth departed Shanghai in October 2009.[13] China conducted its first Arctic expedition in the summer of 1999, engaging in oceanographic studies and sea-bottom research—both of which have operational implications for the PLAN's antisubmarine warfare (ASW) capability. Three Arctic expeditions had been completed by 2009.[14]

China underlined its interest in Indian Ocean economic and political issues by joining the Indian Ocean Rim Association for Regional Cooperation (IORARC) in 2000 as a "dialogue partner." Ministry of Foreign Affairs (MOFA) spokesperson Zhu Bangzao stated that China "will take an active part in cooperation projects of the association [and] is also willing to make joint efforts . . . in establishing a new international political and economic order."[15] Organized to promote regional economic construction, IORARC has accomplished little of note, but Beijing maintains its interest in using multinational forums to extend China's economic and political influence.

Taiwan is China's most important maritime issue, but next in importance are its territorial claims in the South China Sea. Larger than the Mediterranean and just as much a maritime crossroads, the South China Sea stretches from the Taiwan Strait in the north to the Malacca Strait in the south and comprises one of the world's busiest international sea-lanes. It is rich in oil, natural gas, and fish, and lies at the center of Southeast Asia, scene of dramatic economic activity during the past fifty years. Sovereignty claims in the area are also driven by national pride.

The South China Sea contains several hundred small islands, rocks, cays, and reefs categorized as "land features." The Spratly Islands include more than one hundred islets, reefs, and sea mounts scattered over 158,300 square miles, many submerged even at low tide; the Paracels number about two dozen land features within 5,800 square miles. The total land area of the Spratlys is less than 3 square miles; that of the Paracels even less. The highest point of land in the Spratlys is 13 feet, on Southwest Cay; the highest point of the Paracels is 46 feet above sea level, on Rocky Island. Claimants have built artificial structures on some of the subsurface reefs and other spots in attempts to qualify them as "islands," although UNCLOS specifies that an "island" must be naturally formed. All are susceptible to being wiped clean by typhoons, which are most likely to occur from June to November.[16]

There are few real islands of size in any of these groupings. The largest in the Spratlys, Itu Aba (called Taiping Dao by China), is about half a square mile in area and is the only island in the South China Sea with a natural water supply. About fifty of the Spratlys are occupied by one or another of the claimants. Taiwan occupies Itu Aba, on which in 2007 it completed a paved, 3,773-foot-long runway—far too short for safe use by any of Taiwan's tactical fighters. Malaysia has occupied five islands, the Philippines eight, China seven, and Vietnam twenty-seven. Taiwan also occupies the Pratas Reef group, which lies northeast of the Paracels and is also claimed by China. China occupies all of the Paracels.

The South China Sea can be divided into five areas that are in dispute:

1. Eastern Gulf of Thailand, where Thailand, Malaysia, and Cambodia claim overlapping maritime boundaries.
2. Northern part of the Natuna Islands, where Indonesia and Vietnam disagree over ownership of three small islands. China may also claim part of this area based on Beijing's 1992 map, discussed below.
3. Gulf of Tonkin (called the Beibu Gulf by Beijing), where China and Vietnam make conflicting maritime territorial claims.
4. Paracel Islands, claimed by China, Taiwan, and Vietnam.
5. Spratly Islands, claimed by China, Taiwan, Vietnam, Malaysia, the Philippines, and Brunei.[17]

ECONOMIC INTERESTS

Petroleum is China's preeminent offshore economic interest. The northern and extreme southern parts of the South China Sea have long been a source of oil and natural gas reserves from which China, Vietnam, Brunei, Indonesia, the Philippines, and Malaysia all benefit. The presence of petroleum reserves around the Spratly Islands is problematic, although it inspires numerous territorial claims to those islands.

China's most inclusive counterclaimant to South China Sea energy resources, Vietnam, argues that Beijing's claims violate both UNCLOS and Vietnam's CS.[18] Fortunately for Beijing, Hanoi has had neither the naval nor the economic strength to contest successfully for those territories, although in 2009 Hanoi was poised to purchase six very capable Kilo-class submarines and additional Su-30 fighter aircraft from Moscow. These acquisitions clearly are intended to counter China's increasing naval and air strength, a point Beijing appreciates. In May 2009 a Beijing source accused Vietnam of planning to establish a "submarine ambush zone" in the South China Sea with the intention of interfering with China's access to the Malacca Strait.[19]

None of the Southeast Asian nations with counterclaims in the South China Sea wants to provoke Beijing, however, precisely because of China's overwhelming naval and economic superiority. In fact, Vietnam, Malaysia, and the Philippines have signed various agreements with China to resolve differences peacefully. Jakarta is simply trying to wish away its conflicting claims with Beijing over the Natuna Islands and their attendant gas fields in the southern South China Sea.[20] The region's nations cannot muster enough commonality of purpose to present a united front to China, a strategic reality supporting China's view that it will get its way. At present, China, the Philippines, Brunei, Indonesia, Malaysia, and Vietnam are all harvesting energy resources from the South China Sea. Disagreements about maritime boundaries are being negotiated or ignored except for the most contentious area—the Spratly Islands.

The potentially dangerous situation in the Spratlys is kept in check by the fact that meaningful oil or gas reserves have not been found. Several energy companies, including such giants as Phillips, ExxonMobil, China National Offshore Oil Corporation (CNOOC), British Petroleum (BP), Amoco, and Shell, have been exploring for oil in the South China Sea since the early 1970s, but with no success in the Spratlys.[21] If commercially valuable petroleum deposits are found, Beijing will undoubtedly adopt an even less flexible position on its sovereign rights to the area, and will have a modernized PLAN to enforce its claims.

Ships carry more than 85 percent of China's trade, and the South China Sea's SLOCs are vital to the Chinese economy. More than half of the world's total merchant shipping passes through the Malacca, Sunda, and Lombok straits into the South China Sea. More than three times as many ships pass through the Malacca Strait as pass through the Suez Canal, and more than five times as many as pass through the Panama Canal. Half this traffic— dominated by cargoes of raw materials, particularly petroleum products— passes near the Spratly Islands. Nearly two-thirds of the tonnage transiting the Malacca Strait and half of that passing near the Spratlys is crude oil from the Middle East—15.2 million barrels per day in 2006; liquefied natural gas

(LNG) shipments through the South China Sea constitute approximately two-thirds of the world's total LNG trade.[22]

TERRITORIAL CLAIMS

China, Taiwan, and Vietnam claim all of the Paracels and the Spratlys; Malaysia and the Philippines claim several islands in the latter group. Brunei in 1984 established an "exclusive fishing zone" that includes Louisa Reef in the southern Spratlys, the sovereignty of which it disputes with Malaysia. Indonesia does not claim any of the Spratlys, but the rich oil and natural gas fields surrounding its Natuna Islands extend into the area of the South China Sea claimed by China; hence, Jakarta is a very concerned participant in the region's territorial disputes.[23]

Japan occupied the Paracel and Spratly islands from 1938 to 1945, using them as a naval resupply base during World War II. In 1945 the islands were surrendered to Chinese forces, although the 1951 U.S.-Japanese peace treaty did not specify to whom Japan was formally ceding the islands.

The South China Sea's fishing and shipping routes have been crucial for seafarers from China and many other nations since ancient times. Hence, the sovereignty claims of China/Taiwan and Vietnam have some historical validity. Hanoi cites fifteenth-century historical evidence in support of its claims but relies on a more modern series of nineteenth- and twentieth-century factors, particularly the 1933 claim by France, when its colonial regime in Vietnam established administrative control over the islands. This claim is undercut, however, by China's 1887 treaty with France, which included a map showing the Spratly Islands within Beijing's jurisdiction. Furthermore, Hanoi twice in the 1950s acknowledged China's sovereignty over these islands. In 1958 North Vietnam agreed with China's claims "on China's territorial sea" in a note to Beijing which it has since dismissed as resulting from the pressure "when Vietnam had to fight against U.S. intervention and aggression."[24] In addition to occupying more than two dozen Spratly land features, only nine of which naturally remain above water at high tide, Vietnam claims a continental shelf in excess of 200 nm.

China has been steadfast in claiming all of the land features in the South China Sea. In December 1947 the CCP formally announced the incorporation of the Paracels and the Spratlys into Guangdong Province. In 1951 Beijing criticized the U.S.-Japanese peace treaty for not specifying Chinese sovereignty over the islands. Beijing formalized its claim in China's 1992 Law on the Territorial Sea and Contiguous Zone; in 2007 created a new municipality that includes the Spratlys and Paracels; and in May 2009 reiterated its claim. Beijing describes the twenty-five islands and more than "230 reef shoals and sand banks" in the South China Sea as accounting for "more than one quarter of China's three million square kilometer marine territory" and explains its policy as "maintaining sovereignty, shelving disputes and seeking common development."[25]

China's historical claims include evidence of voyages through the area in the Han Dynasty (206 BC–AD 220), nominal administration of the islands during the Tang Dynasty (AD 618–906), and Chinese artifacts from that dynasty found on the islands. These claims by themselves do not establish sovereignty under the conventions of modern usage. Furthermore, China uses "straight baselines" to demarcate its territorial claims along all of its coastline and the Paracels, a method contrary to the 1982 UNCLOS agreement.[26] Taiwan's Territorial Sea and Contiguous Zone Law, passed in 1993, claimed sovereignty over the same U-shaped line in the South China Sea that Beijing claimed in its 1992 legislation.[27]

PLAN forces defeated a Vietnamese naval group near the Spratly Islands in March 1988, sinking three ships and killing seventy-two Vietnamese. Afterward China occupied Fiery Cross Reef and continued to militarize the Spratlys. Best known are its activities on Mischief Reef, but Beijing has also built significant military outposts on Fiery Cross, Gaven, and Johnson reefs in the Spratlys, in addition to the large air base on Woody Island (Yongxing Tai to China; Phu Lam to Vietnam) and other military facilities on Lincoln and Duncan reefs in the Paracels.[28]

Vietnam maintains military garrisons on perhaps twenty Spratly landforms, only nine of which naturally remain above water at high tide. Hanoi also claims a continental shelf in excess of 200 nm.

The dispute over the Paracel and Spratly islands is the most serious in the South China Sea, made so because of the petroleum reserves present there. China and Vietnam have twice fought sea battles over these islands and have come close to blows over oil rigs just west of the Spratlys. Vietnam claims that "China attacked and seized Vietnam's Paracel Islands" in January 1974, and "in March 1988, after a military attack on Vietnamese freighters, . . . occupied Chu Thap, Chau Vien, Ga Ven, and Tu Nghia reefs." Vietnam derides Beijing's May 1992 contract with Crestone, an American oil company, as based on an "absurd claim" because the area covered by the contract is part of

Vietnam's continental shelf; and further accuses China of deliberately ignoring UNCLOS in occupying the Paracels and various Spratly islands as part of a plan to "monopolize the Eastern Sea by [the] early twenty-first century."[29]

Vietnam is widely engaged with foreign oil companies to exploit petroleum fields in its claimed territorial waters and on its continental shelf. The first such effort was a 1972 agreement with the Italian company Agenzia Generale Italina Petroli to explore parts of the continental shelf. Vietnam hired Compagnie Generale de Geophysique of France in 1976 to survey offshore areas off the southern Vietnamese coast, and a 1984 joint venture with the Soviet Union to explore Vietnam's southern continental shelf found oil.

Hanoi signed an exploration agreement with the U.S. company Conoco in 1992 to explore blocks 133, 134, and 135, an area that overlaps China's Wan Bei-21 field being explored by Crestone. China's April 1994 announcement that it had commenced drilling was followed within hours by Vietnam's announcement that it had signed exploration contracts with American, Japanese, and Russian companies for an adjoining field within China's claimed area. This situation resulted in minor incidents between the two nations' ships, but none involved loss of life or property.[30]

Beijing and Hanoi agreed on a maritime boundary in 2000 that roughly bisects their respective claims for both fisheries and energy reserves; it came into force in June 2004 but has proven only marginally effective. The Vietnam Petroleum Corporation (PetroVietnam) and the CNOOC signed a joint exploration agreement in November of that year. The two nations conducted the first of five joint naval patrols in April 2006.[31]

China and Vietnam agreed to settle their contested land border in a treaty signed on 30 December 1999, and their maritime boundary in the northern Beibu Gulf (Tonkin Gulf) between Vietnam and Hainan Island in 2004, but neither had been fully implemented by mid-2009. Hanoi bases its claim on the line established by the French in the 1887 treaty with China; Beijing has responded that the boundary should be equidistant between the two nations.[32] Neither of the agreements addresses the more serious disputes in the central South China Sea over territorial sovereignty and seabed resources. By the end of 2000 China and Vietnam had signed the Agreement on the Demarcation of Waters, Exclusive Economic Zones and Continental Shelves in the Gulf of Tonkin, under which both sides agreed to "refrain from taking any action that might complicate and escalate disputes, resorting to force or making threats with force,"[33] and the Agreement on Fishing Cooperation in the Gulf of Tonkin.

Problems nevertheless continue in the area. In January 2005 eight Vietnamese fishermen were killed by Chinese law enforcement officials. In March 2005 a clash occurred between Chinese and Vietnamese fishermen that may have been a dispute over fishing grounds or simple robbery. This was followed in May by a strange incident: a Vietnamese cargo ship sank off the coast of Shanghai, reportedly during a PLAN exercise that may have included gunnery. It would not have been the first time civilian merchant vessels were accidentally fired on during naval exercises, but naturally it raised press speculation about China's intentions.[34]

Despite these and similar incidents, Beijing and Hanoi continue the periodic discussions that began in November 1995. The talks have not resolved any territorial sovereignty issues because China insists that only the Spratlys are open to discussion while Vietnam insists that the Paracels' sovereignty should also be discussed. The sovereignty issue for both groups of islands includes not just the land features—almost all of which lack intrinsic value—but the maritime sovereignty domains that ownership might warrant under UNCLOS.

In April 2006 the Tenth National Congress of the Vietnamese Communist Party (VCP) adopted a resolution that the nation should "develop a strong maritime economy, [and] maintain national defence and security in a spirit of international cooperation." In January 2007 the VCP's fourth plenum noted economists' estimates that by 2020 the marine economy could be capable of contributing up to 55 percent of GDP and between 55 and 60 percent of exports, but that no comprehensive plan existed to integrate the development of maritime resources with Vietnam's overall economy. This concern gave rise to two decisions. First, the government was directed to design and articulate a national "maritime strategy toward the year 2020" that would integrate economic development, environmental concerns, and national security. Second, the Vietnam People's Army was given the mission of "defending territorial waters and safeguarding national sovereignty." The strategy was reportedly completed by the end of 2007 but had not been promulgated by 2010.[35]

Beijing was undoubtedly displeased by these directives—since they formalize Hanoi's intention to take action in waters claimed by China—and that displeasure may have led directly to a series of Chinese-sparked incidents. These have included apparent pressure against foreign firms involved in developing Vietnam's offshore resources. In March 2007 BP announced an extensive project for a $2 billion investment in Vietnam's energy sector. The proposal included exploiting offshore natural gas fields and constructing a power station. Beijing immediately attacked BP's proposal. On 10 April 2007

Chinese MOFA spokesperson Qin Gang responded to a question about the proposal: "China has indisputable sovereignty over the Nansha Islands and their adjacent waters and neighbouring marine areas.... Vietnam's new actions, which infringe on China's sovereignty, sovereign rights and administrative rights on the Nansha Islands [are] illegal and invalid."[36] Hanoi's response cited the validity of its own claims in the South China Sea. While this exchange was occurring in April 2007 PLAN ships stopped four Vietnamese fishing boats near the Spratly Islands and fined their crews.

China continued to provoke incidents in the disputed maritime areas, and in June 2007 BP announced that it was halting seismic work off southern Vietnam. A particularly nasty incident nevertheless occurred on 9 July 2007, when a Chinese warship reportedly fired on and sank a Vietnamese fishing boat, killing a fisherman. PLAN exercises in the area of the Paracel Islands in November 2007 evoked protests from Vietnam accusing the Chinese of violating Vietnam's sovereignty. China's Foreign Ministry dismissed Vietnam's statement and issued its usual claim of "irrefutable sovereignty" over the South China Sea island groups.[37]

Perhaps Beijing's most provocative action in this dispute to date was legal rather than naval; in late 2007 the Chinese central government assigned administrative authority over the South China Sea land features to the government of Hainan Province. Hanoi protested, and anti-China student demonstrations in Vietnam evoked protests from Beijing. Incidents at sea continued, and in May–June 2008 senior officials from the two nations' Communist parties met in Beijing in an attempt at least to paper over the sovereignty disputes in the South China Sea.[38]

The two sides have now reached a de facto agreement in the Tonkin Gulf. In May 2008 Secretary General Nong Duc Manh of Vietnam met with President Hu Jintao in Beijing, where they issued a joint statement declaring that "the two sides will continue to implement the [Gulf of Tonkin] Demarcation Agreement and the Agreement on Fishery Cooperation in the [Gulf of Tonkin] and carry out joint inspection in the fishing zone, joint survey of fishery resources, and joint naval patrols. The two sides will accelerate the implementation of the Framework Agreement on Oil and Natural Gas Cooperation in Agreed Zones in the [Gulf of Tonkin]."[39]

Resolution of the South China Sea disputes remains to be accomplished, although China and Vietnam have conducted discussions. The fourth meeting on this issue was held in Beijing in January 2008. Afterward, Chinese and Vietnamese leaders "pledged to continue joint naval patrols . . . to conduct a joint survey of waters" in the Gulf of Tonkin."[40] The fragility of this "pledge" was demonstrated in July 2008 when an ExxonMobil executive reported that China was exerting pressure to prevent that company from forming a business partnership with PetroVietnam. In October, a Chinese official insisted that China will "further maintain" its sovereignty in the South China Sea with the establishment of a "regular marine patrol and rights protection system."[41] At the end of 2008 the two nations' military chiefs of staff met and issued a statement pledging to "cooperate" and to "step up bilateral military relations."[42] Despite these pronouncements, the disputes over South China Sea sovereignty claims remained unresolved and subject to continuing Chinese naval pressure in mid-2009.

The atmosphere of "cooperation" was adversely affected by the near-simultaneous revelation in June that China was constructing a major new naval base on Hainan Island near Sanya. Publicly available satellite imagery depicts facilities capable of supporting both surface combatants and nuclear-powered submarines, supplementing the facilities in southern China already used by the PLAN's South Sea Fleet.[43] Construction of this base probably indicates Beijing's intent to improve its ability to exert military pressure against Vietnam and other disputants in Southeast Asia and the PLAN's desire to better disperse vital naval assets, especially the Type-094 (Jin-class) fleet ballistic-missile-carrying submarines currently under construction.

Like Vietnam, the Philippines has unresolved South China Sea sovereignty issues, in its case based on the 1947 "discovery" and "occupation" of the Spratlys by a Filipino businessman. These claims were not announced until 1956 and were "deeded to the Philippine government" in 1974. An indeterminate number of Philippine troops are stationed on some of the eight Spratlys claimed by Manila, including Thitu Island (Pagasa), which also features a short airstrip. The Philippines' territorial disputes in the South China Sea include disagreements over island sovereignty with Indonesia, Malaysia, and Vietnam as well as with China.[44]

There are two categories of disputes between Manila and Beijing. First, the Philippines' most important offshore energy sources, the Malampaya and Camago natural gas fields, are located in eastern South China Sea waters also claimed by China. Philippine oil exploration in the Spratlys actually preceded Chinese efforts, as Manila granted concessions to AMOCO, Salen, and the Philippine Oil Development Company in the early 1970s and 1980s, and drilled wells on Reed Bank (Liyu Tan and Lile Tan). As of 2009, energy exploration and recovery contracts for Philippine waters were held by Australian, Dutch, Japanese, Malaysian, Singaporean, and U.S. companies.[45]

Second, the Philippines and China have been engaged in a contentious dispute about ownership of land features in the Spratly Islands. Beijing claims all of the Spratlys; Manila claims eight of the land features. China's actions on Mischief Reef (Meiji Jiao to China, Panganiban to the Philippines), located just 140 nm from the Philippine island of Palawan—well within the Philippine-claimed EEZ—have received the most attention. China first built this reef, normally barely above the sea's surface, into a sizable artificial island and then constructed buildings; installed communications equipment, sensors, and antiaircraft emplacements; and built helicopter landing platforms and mooring facilities.[46]

A similar pattern seemed to be emerging in the late 1990s on Scarborough Shoals (Hung Yen Tao), 122 nm off Luzon, but has not resulted in the construction of permanent facilities. Chinese fishing boats continue to visit this reef and have been confronted on several occasions by Philippine patrol craft. China has been unbending about its ownership of both Mischief Reef and Scarborough Shoals.

The Philippines lacks an effective navy or air force and cannot stop China's actions, although Philippine leaders have been trying to modernize the nation's military. President Corazon Aquino urged the Philippine Congress in 1990 to fund a $1 billion modernization program, with emphasis on the navy and air force. Her successor, Fidel Ramos, was especially concerned about Philippine claims in the South China Sea and convinced Congress to pass a five-year, $12.6 billion armed forces modernization program, but the military saw very little of that money.[47] Succeeding presidents—Joseph Estrada and now Gloria Macapagal-Arroyo—have made little progress. In fact, in June 2008 the commander of the Philippine military, General Alexander Yano, stated that "the Philippine military cannot fully defend the country." While the army and marine corps have been periodically effective fighting insurgents in the southern islands, Yano stated that "modernization of the ill-equipped Navy and Air Force would have to wait."[48]

The Chinese activities on Mischief Reef undoubtedly were a prime reason Manila ratified the Visiting Forces Agreement with the United States in 1999, which facilitated renewal of exercises between the two nations. The first joint exercise following the VFA signing took place in January–February 2000. Balikatan 2000 involved U.S. and Philippine Air Force and Army units on Luzon and Palawan. After this successful exercise, one prominent Philippine legislator, Senate President Blas Ople, boasted, "I have no doubt in my mind that our American friends in accordance with the treaty obligation, will not

hesitate to join us in repulsing any forcible aggression against our territory."
President Joseph Estrada emphasized, however, that the U.S.-Philippine exercises were not aimed at "any country, including China." These exercises have
continued on an annual basis, with the 2008 Balikatan hailed by President
Macapagal-Arroyo "as a means to wipe out the Abu Sayyaf and end their
atrocities and exploitation of Filipinos." The most recent Balikatan exercise
took place in March 2010.[49]

U.S. military support notwithstanding, the Philippines' relationship with
China has changed significantly since the 1995 clash over China's fortifica-
tion of Mischief Reef. Simply put, President Macapagal-Arroyo, whose term
ends in 2010, has apparently decided that the economic benefits gained
from a cooperative relationship with Beijing outweigh her nation's territorial
claims. The Sino-Philippine disputes have been in a diplomatic hiatus with
the signing of a series of economic and diplomatic agreements between 2002
and 2009—agreements that gained little for Manila and strengthened China's
presence in Southeast Asia. The 2009 Philippine Baseline Law has drawn the
disapprobation of China and other South China Sea claimants but actually
amounts to further withdrawal by Manila of its claims.[50]

This dispute has illustrated both Beijing's "two-track" strategy in the South
China Sea and Manila's helplessness in the face of that strategy. Although
the Philippines successfully engaged the support of its ASEAN neighbors
following China's February 1995 actions on Mischief Reef, Manila's appeals
in 1999 to ASEAN and the UN following further Chinese actions in 1998
were rebuffed.[51] Secretary for Policy Lauro Baja of the Department of Foreign
Affairs described Manila's position as "a lose-lose situation."[52]

Estrada struck the most positive note possible during his May 2000 visit
to Beijing, agreeing with President Jiang Zemin that the South China Sea
disputes should be "resolved through peaceful means." The two presidents
signed five agreements, including the Joint Statement on the Framework
for Cooperation between the Governments of China and the Philippines in
the Twenty-first Century. The joint statement issued following the January
2007 visit to Manila by Chinese premier Wen Jiabao underlined that attitude as Wen and President Macapagal-Arroyo declared that "Sino-Philippine
relations are experiencing a 'golden age of partnership' as the two countries
upgrade bilateral cooperation and launch more dialogues on political, defense,
and socio-cultural affairs."[53]

Other nations in the region have South China Sea interests as well. Malaysia bases its claims on two legal principles: continental shelf extension and discovery/occupation. Kuala Lumpur's claims include five land features in the Spratlys, three of which—Swallow Reef (Terembu Layang Layang), Ardasier Bank (Terumbu Ubi), and Mariveles Reef (Terumbu Mantanani)—are occupied on the basis that they are part of the nation's continental shelf. Similarly, Brunei's implied claim to Louisa Reef is based on location because that feature falls within its 200-nm EEZ.

Malaysia has been a leader among Southeast Asian nations professing to see no "China threat." Although China's 1995 occupation of Mischief Reef came as a "shock" to Malaysian leaders, they have since reverted to a studiously noncontentious policy with Beijing. Ironically, Kuala Lumpur has pursued an aggressive policy of occupying and building up the Spratly Islands that it claims. Malaysia's foreign minister signed a Joint Statement on Framework for the Future Bilateral Cooperation between China and Malaysia in Beijing in May 1999, and the two nations issued a joint communiqué in June 2004 in which they "agreed to maintain peace and stability in the South China Sea and to promote the settlement of disputes through friendly bilateral consultations and negotiations."[54]

Indonesia has played the leading role in striving to establish international processes to resolve territorial disputes in the region, beginning with a 1990 "workshop" on the Spratlys. At the tenth meeting of the South China Sea Informal Working Group in Bogor in December 1999, Minister of Foreign Affairs Alwi Shihab "guaranteed" that "Indonesia will stay with its commitment to endorse peace, stability and cooperation" in the dispute over the Spratly Islands.

Foreign Minister Ali Alatas of Indonesia had warned in 1991 that the Spratly Islands dispute might become a "conflict area" for the ASEAN states. Beijing emphasized its claims at a 1993 Indonesian-sponsored workshop on the Spratlys, displaying a map that depicted its claim line extending well into Jakarta's claimed EEZ. Jakarta queried Beijing about the claim in 1994. China did not then and has not since commented on the issue other than to maintain that China's sovereignty over the claimed South China Sea area (presumably including part of the Natuna fields) is based on "inheritance from past dynasties." Indonesia refuses to accept this rationale, but Jakarta and Beijing have continued to keep the dispute quiet.

Jakarta has, however, established four maritime region commands under the control of its navy, nominally to "focus on development of the country's marine resources." Despite this move, Jakarta is following the lead of Manila and Kuala Lumpur in seeking accommodation rather than confrontation with Beijing; the two nations' presidents, Hu Jintao and Susilo Bambang Yudhoyono, issued a joint statement in April 2005 announcing a "joint strategic partnership" between China and Indonesia.[55]

THE PLAN IN THE SOUTH CHINA SEA

China has built an air base with a paved 8,200-foot runway on Woody Island in the Paracels, 200 nm southeast of Hainan Island. With an area of 1.1 square miles, Woody is the largest island in the group, although it lacks a natural source of fresh water. Ship-handling facilities and a ship channel through the surrounding reef have been constructed there as well. The PLAN has designated Woody Island as headquarters for its South China Sea forces. The island is capable of handling China's tactical jets (up to and including the Su-30), with covered revetments for an estimated eight and paved apron space for approximately two dozen aircraft. It possesses extensive radar and electronic monitoring facilities but limited maintenance capability. China has also built supporting facilities on nearby Lincoln and Duncan reefs.[56]

The greater the value placed on maritime interests such as the Spratly Islands, the greater the Navy's advantage in PLA budget competition and the greater the willingness of the Beijing leadership to authorize naval modernization and growth. Some observers even argue that China's aggressive stance in the South China Sea is being driven by the PLAN over the objections of the Foreign Ministry.[57]

One revealing case involved Beijing officials telling the Crestone chairman in 1992 that the PLAN would be deployed to protect his activities, if necessary. That same year, PLAN deputy commander Vice Admiral Zhang Xusan stated that "it was high time for China to readjust naval strategy and make greater efforts to recover South China Sea oil and gas resources."[58] The conjunction of these three events—territorial claim, oil exploration contract, and naval strategic pronouncement— indicate Beijing's national security policy of improving China's maritime strength.

The PLAN commander argued in that same year that the seas were the "new high ground of strategic competition."[59] PLAN strategists have written much about China's lack of access to the open Pacific due to the presence of the "first island chain." This is cited as one reason why China must control

Taiwan to "break" this restriction. As a practical matter, and considering the geography, it is difficult to accept an assertion that Taiwan or any other entity significantly limits China's access to the Philippine Sea or other parts of the Pacific Ocean, any more than Cuba could be seen as blocking U.S. access to open ocean. If there is a threat to China's access to the open Pacific, it comes from Japan and U.S. bases in that country.

RESOLVING THE DISPUTES

There are legal problems with both the Chinese and the Vietnamese sovereignty claims in the Spratlys. One authority describes the claims as "incomplete, intermittent, and unconvincing," because none demonstrates "effective control, administration and governance of sovereign territory." The claims of the Philippines, Malaysia, and Brunei, based on the EEZ, continental shelf, proximity, or some combination of these, have a much stronger case under UNCLOS than do those of China, Taiwan, and Vietnam, which are based on history. In fact, the validity of all these claims is weakened by both the lack of continuity in historic occupancy of the various islands and by the lack of clearly defined national continental shelves in the restricted South China Sea.[60]

At the July 1995 meeting of ASEAN, Foreign Minister Qian Qichen expressed China's willingness to participate in multinational discussions to "resolve the dispute over ownership of the Spratly Islands according to international law and UN conventions."[61] China's apparently cooperative attitude in 1995 was probably due to at least two factors. First, following the PLAN's initial incursions onto Mischief Reef early that year, the Philippines successfully enlisted ASEAN's verbal support against Beijing's actions. This multinational opposition probably surprised the Chinese and caused them to restrict their South China Sea actions. Second, when President Lee Teng-hui of Taiwan visited the United States in the summer of 1995, Beijing expressed its displeasure through extensive military operations in the Taiwan Strait area.

China may have "cooled" the situation in the South China Sea to focus on the higher-priority concerns about Taiwan. Since then, however, Beijing's stance has stiffened. The Chinese have agreed to settle the disputes peacefully "through bilateral negotiation"—as long as the parties understand that China holds "indisputable sovereignty over the South China Sea and adjacent water."[62] Beijing has been remarkably consistent in this posturing: offering negotiation but insisting there is nothing negotiable about South China Sea sovereignty issues.

The Declaration (Code) of Conduct championed by Indonesia, Malaysia, and the Philippines and signed by China and the ten members of the Association of Southeast Asian Nations (ASEAN) in 2002 signaled a cooling of both rhetoric and military measures in the South China Sea.[63] The signatories promised to pursue diplomatic solutions to territorial disputes. The code includes five main provisions, the three most important of which are:

- The Parties reaffirm their respect for and commitment to the freedom of navigation in and over-flight above the South China Sea as provided for by the universally recognized principles of international law, including the 1982 UN Convention on the Law of the Sea.
- The Parties concerned undertake to resolve their territorial and jurisdictional disputes by peaceful means, without resorting to the threat or use of force, through friendly consultations and negotiations by sovereign states directly concerned, in accordance with universally recognized principles of international law, including the 1982 UN Convention on the Law of the Sea.
- The Parties undertake to exercise self-restraint in the conduct of activities that would complicate or escalate disputes and affect peace and stability including, among others, refraining from action of inhabiting on the presently uninhabited islands, reefs, shoals, cays, and other features and to handle their differences in a constructive manner.

To date, the declaration has been honored largely in the breach, although the attendant workshops have developed technical working groups (TWGs) to investigate specific areas of contention, with groups of experts' meetings reporting to the TWGs on specific issues. Dozens of meetings have been held, most recently in Beijing in July 2009, and every ASEAN member and claimant state except Taiwan has hosted at least one session.[64]

Despite Beijing's accession to the code, China's policy remains based on Qian Qichen's uncompromising speech at the 1999 ASEAN conference, in which he made six points:

1. China has indisputable sovereignty over the Spratly Islands and adjacent waters.

2. China is willing to hold peaceful talks with concerned countries to resolve disputes properly, in accordance with the principle of national defense law and modern maritime law.
3. China's proposal to "shelve disputes and facilitate joint development" is the most realistic and practical way to resolve the Spratlys dispute.
4. China is willing to hold bilateral consultations with claimant states, considering it inappropriate to hold multilateral talks at an international conference.
5. China has always attached great importance to safety and freedom in international lanes in the South China Sea and believes there should be no problems in this regard.
6. The Spratly disputes do not concern the United States at all, and it has no reason to interfere.

Additional agreements followed. China and ASEAN signed a Treaty of Amity and Cooperation in 2003 promising to form "a strategic partnership for peace and prosperity."[65]

In September 2004 China and the Philippines signed the Joint Marine Seismic Undertaking in the South China Sea, agreeing to exchange the results of seismic testing of the South China Sea ocean floor. In March 2005 Vietnam joined this agreement, renamed the Tripartite Agreement for Joint Marine Seismic Undertaking in the Agreement Area in the South China Sea. The agreement is among the respective national energy companies, however, and is not a formal treaty. By supporting the agreement, Manila essentially surrendered its South China Sea rights—perhaps unavoidably, given the lack of a credible Philippine military or economic deterrent to Beijing's claims.[66] The agreement was scheduled to end in 2008; while an extension has not been announced, the diplomatic process has continued.

Chinese officials consistently insist, first, that China has indisputable sovereignty over the South China Sea islands and their adjacent waters; second, that the Paracel Islands are excluded from any discussions under the code of conduct or the agreements with the Philippines and Vietnam; and third, that while it will participate in discussions focusing "on issues concerning East Asian cooperation in the financial, scientific-technological, and agricultural sectors," China's South and East China seas sovereignty claims are not subject to discussion. Beijing's attitude was supported by Admiral Liu Huaqing, the most notable PLAN commander, who argued in the 1980s that "whoever controls the Spratlys will reap huge economic and military benefits."[67]

Beijing has modified its previous insistence on bilateral "negotiations" but continues to insist that China holds complete sovereignty over the Paracel and Spratly islands. No resolution of the South China Sea territorial disputes appears in the offing in 2010, short of the other claimants agreeing to China's sovereignty throughout the sea.

Meanwhile, in parallel with its rhetoric, Beijing continues increasing the strength and capability of its naval presence in the South China Sea islands. The January 1995 Mischief Reef incursions were not pressed immediately, as noted above, but since early 1998 China has expanded its presence on these rocks, using them to build the artificial island that now constitutes a minor naval base. Similar increases in capability have been made on other Chinese-occupied land features in the South China Sea.

Beijing is able to pursue its two-track policy of diplomacy and increased military presence because it is the most powerful Asian military force in the South China Sea. Some of the regional states field formidable naval and air forces, but none of them compares individually with the PLAN or the PLA Air Force (PLAAF). Although united ASEAN naval and air forces could counter the Chinese military, the member states are unable to cooperate to that extent. Furthermore, the general mind-set among the ASEAN states, exemplified by Malaysia, is to act as if China is not a threat.

Beijing is also succeeding in the South China Sea because the only nation that could successfully curtail its efforts, the United States, is maintaining a hands-off policy. The U.S. position has been to urge peaceful resolution of the area's territorial disputes, insisting only that freedom of navigation not be restricted. Beijing says that it has no intention of interfering with navigation, but its advocacy of expanded sovereignty rights within its claimed EEZ, adherence to straight baselines, and policy of interfering with U.S. surveillance ships and aircraft belie that claim. China has also warned the ASEAN states against conducting military exercises with U.S. forces.[68]

Beijing's status among the other regional nations was summed up by Vietnam's ambassador to the United States, Le Cong Phung, in September 2009, when he explained that his country has to be realistic about the size and power of China: "The Paracels historically belong to Vietnam, . . . but China has the power."[69]

EAST CHINA SEA

China's maritime territorial disputes with the Republic of South Korea (ROK) and Japan include issues similar to those in the South China Sea but are much simpler. Disputes with the ROK have been focused on fisheries; the area's seabed energy resources lie well within Beijing's continental shelf in the Yellow Sea. Fisheries remain a vexatious issue, but China has reached a series of agreements with both Koreas and with Japan to arrive at an equitable division of the area's biological resources.[70]

Much more contentious are China's disputes with Japan over seabed petroleum resources in the East China Sea, prominently including the Chunxiao (Shirakaba) gas field. Despite a June 2008 agreement to develop the disputed areas near Chunxiao jointly, both countries were drilling independently in their claimed areas in 2009. The Sino-Japanese disagreement lies in the delineation of the two nations' rights under UNCLOS, because the distance between them is less than the 700 miles required for each to claim maximum continental shelf limits. Beijing insists that its continental shelf extends to a point close to Japan, while Tokyo wants a median line between the two countries to divide their waters. The 2008 agreement has not been followed by implementing negotiations, a situation described by one observer as "a security tinderbox."[71]

As troublesome as are the seabed issues, the more dangerous dispute between Beijing and Tokyo concerns the sovereignty of the Diaoyu/Senkaku Islands, five rocks and three small islands with a total area of three square miles. Neither country has shown any willingness to compromise; indeed, compromise seems inapplicable to such a fundamental sovereignty disagreement. The situation is made more serious by the U.S. interpretation that its mutual defense treaty with Japan includes the islands.[72]

Beijing's policy in the East China Sea is similar to its strategy in the South China Sea: it is maintaining a rigid position on the sovereignty of the islands but willing to discuss peripheral issues of territorial usage. Meanwhile, China insists on is own definitions of sovereignty, which augers ill for diplomacy resolving territorial disputes in either of these seas. The situation has given rise in recent years to incursions by Chinese surveying ships, as well as PLAN submarines and combatant vessels, into Japan's EEZ. Tokyo consistently protests these cruises, and Beijing as consistently dismisses the protests, claiming that the waters are really part of China's EEZ. This reflects a degree of hypocrisy in Beijing's position, since some of these incursions have occurred in areas of Japan's EEZ not disputed by China.

Tokyo often deploys tactical aircraft and armed coast guard ships in response to incursions by Chinese warships—both surface and submarine—and (nominally) civilian research vessels, thus creating opportunities for incidents and accidents that threaten unintended escalation to armed conflict. The United States, because of its mutual defense treaty with Japan, would almost certainly be drawn into such events.[73]

Beijing's inflexibility over its maritime territorial claims is influenced by China's increasing dependence on offshore energy resources. But this forms just one element of China's enormous dependence on the sea-lanes for the import-export trade that lies at the heart of its economic well-being. Unquantifiable but perhaps just as important a driver in Beijing's attitude and policies respecting maritime disputes are national pride and extreme sensitivity to sovereignty issues. These economic, historical, and nationalist elements all contribute as well to China's determination to deploy a Navy capable of operating effectively in the twenty-first century in defense of its maritime interests.

Varyag, an aircraft carrier acquired from Russia and since renamed *Shi Lang*, en route to China. (U.S. Navy)

Shang-class nuclear-powered submarine. (Courtesy of Mr. Richard D. Fisher)

Jin-class nuclear-powered ballistic missile submarine. (Courtesy of Mr. Richard D. Fisher)

Song-class submarine (Chinese built) moored in Hong Kong. (U.S. Navy)

Kilo-class submarine, acquired from Russia. (U.S. Navy)

Sovremenny-class guided missile destroyer, acquired from Russia. (Courtesy of Mr. Leo Van Ginderen)

Luhu-class guided missile destroyer. (Courtesy of Mr. Leo Van Ginderen)

Luhai-class guided missile destroyer. (Courtesy of Mr. Leo Van Ginderen)

Luyang I–class guided missile destroyer. (Courtesy of Mr. Charles Au)

Luyang II–class guided missile destroyer. (Courtesy of Mr. Charles Au)

Luzhou-class guided missile destroyer. (Courtesy of Mr. Charles Au)

Jiangkai-class guided missile frigate. (Courtesy of Mr. Leo Van Ginderen)

Jiangwei-class guided missile frigate. (Courtesy of Mr. Leo Van Ginderen)

Houbei-class missile boat. (Courtesy of Mr. Charles Au)

Yuzhao-class amphibious assault ship. (Courtesy of Mr. Charles Au)

Fuqing-class oiler. (Courtesy of Mr. Leo Van Ginderen)

Fuchi-class oiler/stores ship. (Courtesy of Mr. Leo Van Ginderen)

Peace Ark hospital ship. (Courtesy of Mr. Charles Au)

CHAPTER 3

China's Maritime Economic Interests

The Chinese Communist Party (CCP) believes that China's economic well-being is essential to the party's continued rule—that China's popular satisfaction and national coherence require continuing economic well-being. The importance of the maritime arena is increasingly crucial to that progress.

The world's best-known classic strategists, Karl von Clausewitz and Sun Zi, did not write about maritime power as such, but their strictures about matching power to policy underlie the value China's leaders place on a modern, effective Navy. The PLAN's value as an instrument of statecraft is linked directly to maintaining and defending China's maritime stakes: the concentration of the nation's economic enterprises in its coastal regions, its dependence on one of the world's largest fleets of merchant ships and the world's second-largest ship-building capacity, its massive seaport infrastructure, its dependence on riverine and coastal maritime commerce, and the increasing national dependence on offshore fisheries and other natural resources, especially oil and natural gas.

Beijing highlighted traditional marine industries in 1958 in the "Comprehensive Investigation of the China Near-Sea Environment and Resources," which led to the establishment of the State Oceanic Administration in 1964. During the 1990s Beijing published a National Ocean Development Plan and China Ocean Agenda 21, which were succeeded in 2000 by the National Outline for the Development and Planning of the Marine Economy and several other regulations, including laws addressing environmental protection and maritime scientific research.

Maritime priorities were emphasized in the State Council's National Maritime Economy Development Plan of 2003, the State Development and Reform Commission's Plan for National Economic and Social Development of 2006, and the State Council's Outline of the National Maritime Enterprise Development Plan of 2008. These have been supported by oceanographic research projects and the National Maritime Science and Technology Development Plan for the Eleventh Five-Year Plan, which began in 2006.[1]

China estimated the production value of its maritime industries in 1978 as approximately US$878 million; the 2008 estimate was $439 billion, an increase from less than 1 to 9.8 percent of China's GDP.[2] The maritime resource perhaps most important to the Chinese people is the fisheries from which they draw much of their daily nutrition. The most reported on and politically prominent maritime resource, however, is the offshore energy fields from which China draws an ever-increasing percentage of its daily petroleum needs.

China has developed significant energy resources in national waters that are for the most part undisputed: coastal waters, the Bo and Yellow seas, parts of Beibu Bay, and the northern South China Sea. Two potentially valuable areas, however, the East and South China seas, are very much in dispute.[3] China is the world's fifth-largest investor in offshore minerals recovery, and the China Association for Science and Technology describes the increasing requirement for energy as one of the "five challenges" for the twenty-first century.[4] The nation increasingly relies on imported oil and natural gas supplies. China currently imports more than 50 percent of its oil from abroad, an amount forecast to increase to 75 percent by 2030.[5] The bulk of this oil arrives by sea, primarily from the Middle East and Africa, over very long sea lines of communication (SLOCs). The value of offshore resources will continue to increase for China as its population—the world's largest at 1.3 billion—continues to grow and its economy continues to expand.

Beijing is moving on several fronts to ensure that its burgeoning economy remains supplied with sufficient energy. First is a concern to take full advantage of the strategic "security blanket" provided by the world's third-largest coal reserves, which provide at least 70 percent of China's daily energy needs and the use of which has increased 129 percent since 2000. Coal, however, has troubling environmental and health effects, and the government has been struggling for more than a decade to gain firm control of the industry.[6] Furthermore, promising technologies, such as gasification and liquefaction at the mouth of coal mines, are proving difficult. Second is the availability of offshore petroleum supplies. In addition to oil and gas, a future source of seabed energy may be methane hydrate, a semiliquid form of fossil fuel that is likely abundant in seabeds around the world, including those of the South and East China seas. The technology to recover methane hydrate efficiently remains under development, however, primarily because of the depth (more than 600 m) at which it lies below the ocean floor, the pressure under which it is found, and the problem of liquefying it for extraction.[7] A third source of future energy is represented in the investigation and use of non–fossil fuel sources of energy, primarily nuclear power but also hydroelectric, wind, tidal, and biomass-fueled power.[8] Oil imported from other nations is the fourth source; fifth is the large-scale campaign now under way to buy foreign oil fields, or at least their product.

China is the world's fifth-largest oil producer, with an annual output of 164 million tons. Approximately 85 percent of China's indigenously produced oil comes from onshore sources, with the Daqing fields in the northeastern provinces providing one-fourth of all indigenous production. These fields have peaked, however, and will decline in future years. One expected major source, the Tarim Basin in northwestern China, has been disappointing.

Faced with peaking domestic production and explosive growth of domestic demand, China became a net importer of petroleum in 1993 and now imports at least half of its oil, with 80 percent of imports arriving by sea. The demand for imported oil is increasing as industrialization continues, and probably will grow by as much as tenfold, assuming China's economic growth continues at an annual high single or double digit rate. China's oil demand increased more than 800,000 barrels per day in 2009, or about 32 percent of the world oil demand growth for the period.[9]

China has seized on offshore drilling as one way to make up for the shortages in its onshore energy sources. The process of exploration, discovery, and recovery of offshore petroleum reserves is lengthy and complex, however, as is getting the product to market economically. Those factors have resulted in extensive participation by foreign oil companies.

Exploiting maritime energy reserves is further complicated for China by disputes with the two Koreas and Japan over the territory China claims on the continental shelf in the Yellow and East China seas. Taiwan does not dispute Beijing's maritime sovereignty claims, but its self-proclaimed independence poses de facto challenges. Vietnam, the Philippines, Brunei, Indonesia, and Malaysia also claim some of the potential reserves that Beijing claims in the South China Sea.

Recovery of offshore resources is controlled by the state. Beijing reorganized this sector in the mid-1990s, promoting three state oil companies to the ministerial level directly under the State Economic and Trade Commission. These national oil companies are the China National Petroleum Corporation (CNPC), the China National Petrochemical Corporation (Sinopec), and the Chinese National Offshore Oil Corporation (CNOOC). China's oil company officials were concerned about maintaining their strong international competitive position after China joined the World Trade Organization, since WTO membership should force Beijing to remove the protective fence it has built around its oil industry; this has not been a problem.

Maritime fields are currently providing almost 10 percent of China's oil production and will soon provide more; offshore oil and gas production increased by about 20 percent annually between 2000 and 2005. Offshore exploration and production have focused in the Bo Sea, the Pearl River delta, and the East and South China seas.

The East China Sea also contains significant petroleum reserves, with production dating from 1998. These fields are especially bothersome because Japan claims them as well and is also drilling in the area.[10] Farther south, the area off the Pearl River estuary (near Guangzhou) may produce almost 30,000 barrels per day when it reaches full capacity. Finally, the South China Sea is currently producing oil or natural gas from its northern areas in the Gulf of Tonkin, near Hainan Island, along the Vietnamese coast, and along the Indonesian islands.

Natural gas is China's second-largest maritime source of fuel, with 80 trillion cubic feet (Tcf) of proven natural gas reserves in 2008. Natural gas provided just 3 percent of China's energy requirements in 2005, and the country became a net natural gas importer for the first time in 2007. Beijing aims to double domestic consumption by 2020, which will require increasing imports primarily by purchasing liquefied natural gas (LNG) from foreign sources as well as continuing its ambitious program of pipelines to bring in natural gas from Russia and the central Asian states. The South China Sea is a major source of this clean-burning, high-quality form of energy, with four separate Chinese fields identified. The nation's first natural gas liquefaction terminal is under construction near Shenzhen in anticipation of the South China Sea's yield.[11]

One valuable find being exploited is the Yacheng 13-1 field, China's largest offshore natural gas field and by 2007 Hong Kong's primary source of energy. This field also exemplifies the role of foreign companies in China's energy sector. British Petroleum and Kuwait Foreign Petroleum Exploration Company provide 34 percent and 15 percent, respectively, of its operating funds, with CNOOC providing the remaining 51 percent. Another major South China Sea natural gas field, the Liwan 3-1-1, is operated by Husky Energy and CNOOC.[12]

Beijing's reliance on offshore petroleum and natural gas reserves makes their defense a national security issue, and clearly a concern for the PLAN. These energy sources are located throughout China's continental shelf, extending more than 2,160 nm from Korea to Vietnam. The shelf is legally delineated by the 110-fathom (200-meter) curve, which lies 68–243 nm from China's coastline. China thus possesses a huge continental shelf of approximately 463,500 square miles—an extensive area for PLAN attention.

NATIONAL POLICY

Despite efforts in the 1990s to reduce significantly the country's reliance on coal, China continues to depend on that and other fossil fuels for most of its energy needs. Concern about increasing imports has been periodically exacerbated by problems with domestic energy production, such as the 3.3 percent drop that occurred in 1998 and the 9.6 percent drop in November 2008. In the first instance, Chen Geng, deputy director of the State Petroleum and Chemical Industries Bureau, cited increased energy demand when he listed several corrective steps with international and maritime implications:

1. China will continue to exploit domestic and overseas natural gas reserves, to include pipelines with Russia.
2. "Technical innovation" will increase recovery of China's petroleum assets. This effort includes a nationally directed program of "science and technology projects" to increase oil and gas development in the twenty-first century. The Bo Sea fields were cited for increased production as a result of technologically advanced methodology.[13]
3. The domestic pipeline network is being expanded to speed up energy distribution, especially natural gas.[14]
4. Beijing is building a national strategic reserve program to stockpile fuel in case of emergency.
5. China has been seeking additional overseas petroleum resources, including in central Asia, Russia, Africa, and Latin America, in addition to the Middle East.[15]

6. The national oil companies have been authorized to increase their profit limits.
7. The national oil companies have been given more freedom to attract foreign investors.

This plan has been effective in the twenty years since its promulgation, both in allowing China access to increased energy resources and in giving freer play to international market forces in the energy industry. It is accompanied by a declared goal of increasing domestic refining capacity by 25 percent by 2010.[16]

Hence, the early 1999 decision to increase state-directed exploration efforts in offshore areas, especially those thought to contain significant natural gas deposits, has been extremely active, with CNOOC dominating the effort. Promising fields in the South and East China seas and the Yellow Sea are being exploited, in almost every case with the involvement of foreign companies. CNOOC, for instance, has announced eight major new discoveries in offshore reserves since 2000, increasing the company's proven oil reserves to 1.6 billion barrels (bbl), and plans to double oil production in the Bo Sea alone, which is expected to produce more than one-half of China's indigenous domestic oil by 2015.[17]

OFFSHORE OIL FIELDS

Seven ocean basins are wholly or partially contained within China's continental shelf; from north to south they are the Bo Sea, North Yellow Sea, South Yellow Sea, East China Sea, Pearl River delta, Beibu (Tonkin) Gulf, and South China Sea basins.[18] Petroleum fields have been found in all of these basins, and the nation's continental shelf has yet to be fully explored.

The Bo Sea fields currently are China's most important offshore energy resource area, with annual production of 15.3 million bbl of oil and 367 million cubic meters of natural gas. In May 2007 PetroChina announced discovery of the Nanpu field, with proven oil reserves of at least 3.2 billion bbl, in addition to the previous estimate of 1.2 billion bbl for the Bo. Company officials began developing this field in June 2007 and hope to achieve daily production of 200,000 bbl by 2012.[19] The East China Sea is another significant source of petroleum products, especially natural gas. Discoveries indicate reserves of approximately 150 billion cubic meters, which are already providing the primary energy source for Shanghai and "major industrialized cities" in Zhejiang Province.

Foreign companies continue to play a significant role in many, perhaps most, of China's efforts to recover offshore energy. Since 1979 Beijing has "cooperated" with more than fifty foreign companies in exploring for offshore petroleum and has signed more than 130 contracts with more than seventy oil companies from eighteen countries in joint development efforts, with total foreign investments of US$6.4 billion.[20]

Beijing is allocating a very significant portion of a crucial economic sector to foreign companies. Several of them are registered in the United States, which of course maintains the strongest naval presence in East Asia. Hence, the calculus of a Sino-American crisis could involve the United States planning the evacuation of American oil company employees on a Chinese-owned oil platform located in international waters being defended by PLAN warships. This would not be a comfortable scenario for either navy.

South China Sea

The South China Sea is one of China's two contested areas of known energy reserves. The sea is surrounded by seven other nations, most of whom claim part or all of the sea's resources.[21] Estimates of the petroleum reserves in the South China Sea range from Beijing's wildly optimistic 213 billion bbl (105 in the area of the Spratlys) to a U.S. estimate of 28 billion bbl (2.1 in the Spratlys). A similar range of estimates exists for natural gas reserves, about which the Chinese are also optimistic, offering an estimate of more than 2,000 Tcf, while the U.S. estimate is a more modest 266 Tcf.

Natural gas is the most abundant proven hydrocarbon resource in the South China Sea—60–70 percent according to the U.S. Geological Survey— but the most abundant areas are already being exploited by China, Taiwan, Vietnam, Thailand, Malaysia, Indonesia, Brunei, and the Philippines. In April 2006, Husky Energy—working with CNOOC—announced a find of proven natural gas reserves of nearly 4–6 Tcf near the Spratly Islands.

The enormous Chinese estimate makes the Spratly Islands and surrounding waters an enticing prize to Beijing, despite the fact that no significant oil or natural gas has been discovered in the area after decades of exploration dating to the mid-1930s. China's belief in the apparently exaggerated estimates is more important than their dubious accuracy, since such high expectations might lead to the allocation of very significant national security resources to protect its South China Sea sovereignty claims. Beijing's ability to garner those resources rests to a degree on the ability of its Navy to enforce its national claims.

Total oil production from the South China Sea in 2008 was more 6 million bbl per day, from proven reserves of approximately 28 billion bbl. Natural gas production in 2008 was 8.3 bcf per day, with significant growth expected during the next decade. Almost all of this production has come from the uncontested northern area of the South China Sea. Despite several decades of exploration, there are no proven oil reserves in the Spratly or Paracel islands, and analysts disagree on the presence (and recoverability) of petroleum reserves in these areas.[22]

Indonesia claims the natural gas–rich fields offshore of the Natuna Islands, which have an estimated 46 Tcf of recoverable reserves. Despite its counterclaim to a large part of these waters, China has not objected to continued Indonesian exploitation of these fields, perhaps representing Beijing's preference for diplomacy over military force.

The most important Philippine energy fields are the Malampaya and Camago natural gas reserves, which lie in waters also claimed by China. These two fields may contain as much as 4.4 Tcf of reserves; the Malampaya field also contains an estimated 150 million bbl of oil, but exploitation had not begun as of mid-2009. As with Indonesia, Beijing has not objected to continued Philippine development of the fields.

Malaysia depends heavily on natural gas fields located offshore of Sarawak, in waters also claimed by China; Beijing had not objected to their development as of mid-2009. Brunei has, however, and Malaysia and Brunei are currently disputing ownership of oil fields offshore of Sabah discovered in 2002 and 2004 (by Murphy Oil and Shell Malaysia, respectively).

Beijing's 1992 territorial law brings it into direct contention with the other claimants to South China Sea resources.[23] PLAN forces have regularly deployed to the Paracel Islands since the early 1970s, and to the Spratly Islands since the early 1980s. A military presence had been established on six of the islands by 1989.

OIL IMPORTS AND EXPORTS

In addition to using foreign investment and technological know-how to extract energy from offshore reserves, Beijing is pursuing an active campaign to secure energy supplies from international sources. In 2009 China took advantage of the economic downturn and lower asset values to step up its global acquisitions and financing of energy resources in several countries. China in the past decade has finalized loans for oil deals with Russia, Brazil, Venezuela, Kazakhstan, and Ecuador; and has reportedly agreed to multi-billion-dollar loans to Turkmenistan, Russian companies, Brazil, Venezuela, and Kazakhstan. China's overseas equity oil production grew from 760,000 bbl/day in 2007 to 820,000 bbl/day in 2008, approximately 29 percent of China's total oil production in 2008.

Beijing reportedly held international assets in twenty-nine countries by the end of 2008, with oil production from Southeast Asia, central Asia, Russia, the Middle East, Africa, and Latin America. The CNPC holds oil concessions in Canada, Kazakhstan, Venezuela, Peru, Sudan, and Iraq. Investments also have been made in the petroleum production industries of Bangladesh, Burma, Colombia, Ecuador, Indonesia, Iran, Iraq, Malaysia, Mexico, Mongolia, Nigeria, Pakistan, Peru, Papua New Guinea, Thailand, and Venezuela. Crude oil imports in 2008 came primarily from Southwest Asia (50 percent), sub-Saharan Africa (30 percent), and Southeast Asia (3 percent). These ratios held true for the first half of 2009; the two largest sources of imported oil were Saudi Arabia and Angola, both located at the end of very long SLOCs.

Despite Beijing's campaigns to secure energy supplies around the world, the Middle East remains China's primary source of overseas oil, in part simply because these countries contain the world's largest proven petroleum deposits (65 percent of the global total) and offer the world's lowest recovery cost, one-tenth of that in China.[24] A 1999 report by China's Strategy and Management Society emphasized the security aspects of this relationship, urging that China adjust its policies in "political, diplomatic, economic, and trade fields" to ensure that "Middle East oil will be provided to China for a long time to come."[25] Beijing maintains this prioritization in 2010.

Extensive foreign investment in its energy sector exposes China to foreign influence, an important factor because energy resources are at the heart of continued economic growth, which in turn directly affects regime legitimacy. WTO membership may further increase dependence on imported oil because it will then be even less expensive than the domestically produced product.[26]

Relying on foreign sources of energy also creates strategic problems for China. Russia is severely troubled by demographic and economic problems and corruption. Furthermore, recovery of the huge reserves of oil and natural gas in Siberia poses significant financial and technological difficulties. Central Asia is beset by political uncertainty, lack of infrastructure, and high costs of doing business. The Middle East and Africa are politically complex, to say the least, and present unreliable dictatorships, religious and ethnic fault-lines, and political hotspots.

ALTERNATIVE ENERGY SOURCES

China is pursuing non–fossil fuel sources of energy—including hydropower, solar, wind, geothermal, tidal, and biomass sources—with some success. Commercial nuclear power was inaugurated in 1990 and its use is growing, although at a slow pace. Eight new plants were under construction in 2009 and eight more were planned, with a 2014 completion date set for the largest. Despite this ambitious program, nuclear power provided only 1 percent of the nation's electricity in 2009, and will provide no more than 4–6 percent in 2020.[27]

China has been the world's largest producer of hydroelectric power and the fifth largest producer of wind power since 2007. Regardless of the energy's source, however, it must be distributed. China's economic imbalance, with energy consumers concentrated in the eastern region of the country and primary energy sources located in the northeast and northwest, exacerbates the power distribution problem for Beijing. Massive reorganizations of this sector instituted since 2002 have had decidedly mixed results.

FISHERIES

China has led the world since 2004 in the fisheries industry, another vital offshore resource, with 16.9 million tons harvested in 2004 and approximately 8 million fishermen operating almost 300,000 motorized fishing vessels. The South China Sea is rich is this resource but is in danger of being "fished out."

Fisheries are under the aegis of the Ministry of Agriculture, which includes three important bureaus. The International Cooperation Department coordinates participation in various treaties and management conventions. The Fisheries Bureau manages the commercial fishing industry, including the stocks, fishermen's welfare, and supporting universities. The Fisheries Law Enforcement Command (FLEC) is responsible for enforcing fisheries regulations through a large fleet of patrol boats operated by the Agriculture Ministry, but is clearly failing to do so. The FLEC is responsible for "protecting Chinese fishing vessels and personnel, resolving disputes in fishing activities, preventing illegal fishing, and protecting maritime resources." ASEAN is also addressing the issue of conserving Southeast Asian fish stocks, but with little success to date.[28]

Beijing worked actively with the UN to develop its 1995 Fish Stocks Agreement, aiming to prevent areas from being overfished, and has since undertaken independent action to conserve fisheries. Beijing's 1999 plan of "zero growth" for fishing was not successful; a series of annual fishing bans followed, but with few tangible results.

China implemented EEZ Fishery Agency patrols in February 2009. Their effectiveness in the South China Sea has been limited by the lack of international cooperation, although Taiwan appears to be cooperating. Furthermore, Beijing's fish conservation efforts are not welcomed in China's coastal provinces, whose people rely heavily on ocean resources. The most recent ban in the South China Sea began on 16 May 2009, with eight Fishery Bureau ships patrolling more than 128,000 km^2. Vietnam lodged protests against this ban, but China insisted on its "firm attitude" to limit fishing activities.[29]

China has been involved in continuing significant fishing disputes with Russia, Japan, North Korea, South Korea, Taiwan, the Philippines, Indonesia, Vietnam, and Thailand. Some of these problems have threatened to turn into a "cod war" reminiscent of that between Iceland and Great Britain in the 1970s. None of the clashes has so far directly involved the PLAN.

China and Japan signed a bilateral fisheries treaty in 1997 but did not agree to implement it until May 2000. The treaty establishes a "fisheries zoning line" at 127°30' east longitude in the East China Sea. Six hundred Chinese boats a year will be allowed to fish east of this line. Even before the implementation date, Beijing announced that its fishery administration fleet—not the PLAN—would be responsible for enforcing the treaty.

China has also negotiated a series of agreements with South Korea to conserve Yellow Sea fisheries and to continue the Yellow Sea Marine Ecosystem Preservation Project begun in 1991. The Maritime Safety Administration (MSA) and the South Korean Ministry of Maritime and Fishery also agreed at the Second Sino-Korean Sea Safety Cooperation Meeting in May 2000 to "deepen their understanding of each other's safety rules [to] facilitate bilateral trade." A fisheries agreement is under negotiation, with talks ongoing.[30]

SHIPPING

The PLAN has a strategic interest in the defense of oceanic trade in view of China's large and growing dependency on foreign trade and energy sources, and its rapidly growing merchant marine. As much as 50 percent of China's economy depends on foreign trade, about 90 percent of which is transported by ship. This reflects the economic benefit of using maritime transportation; it is cheaper to ship a ton of coal five thousand miles by sea than three hundred miles by rail, for instance. China's long coastline, thousands of islands, and important rivers make sea transport attractive.[31]

China's merchant fleet calls at more than six hundred ports in more than 150 countries. As of 2006, China (including Hong Kong) flagged almost twice as many merchant ship tons as the next-largest fleet in Asia. Chinese ports also led the world in container traffic. The maritime environment directly impacts China's serious and increasing resource problems, especially energy and food, the reliability of which depend on the sea. China relies on tankers for almost all its crucial oil imports and annually imports millions of tons of grain by sea.[32]

Beijing has been particularly concerned about the low number of tankers sailing under the Chinese flag, many of them too small for profitable employment on the long SLOCs to the Middle East. In 2006 Beijing ordered a shipbuilding program that would raise the percentage of seaborne oil imports from approximately 10 percent to 60–70 percent by 2020.[33] This apparently appeals to China's leadership from an economic perspective, but from a military view of energy security it makes little sense to increase the number of Chinese-flagged tankers because doing so very significantly eases the "identification-friend-or-foe" problem for intercepting naval vessels.

Ships are and will likely remain the most cost-effective means of transporting oil: the cost of transporting one barrel of oil over a distance of 1,000 km (540 nm) was estimated in 2007 to be $0.163 by tanker, $0.793 via pipeline, and $7.190 by train. This is one reason why Beijing has established the ambitious goal of becoming the world's number-one shipbuilder by 2015. China recently passed Japan in tonnage built but will have to increase its production by 50 percent if it is to overcome South Korea, the world's leading shipbuilder.[34]

China's continuing dependence on Middle Eastern oil requires Beijing to make "appropriate arrangements and preparations in the political, diplomatic, economic, and even military aspects," and to take measures to "guarantee unimpeded passage through the international oil routes." Finally, "militarily speaking, China must make necessary arrangements for the safe supply of energy for itself." The PLAN's role in this mission is obvious, although the threat to be countered is difficult to discern: there are very few incidents of maritime terrorism on record; piracy is a localized phenomenon; and the internationalization of the energy market would make any attempt to interrupt the flow of oil to China quite difficult.[35]

SLOC defense is the PLAN mission most directly tied to energy security. The Navy must safeguard sea-lanes in the territorial waters China claims, which requires an effective naval force in the Yellow Sea, the East China Sea west of the Japan-Philippines line, and in the South China Sea. The PLAN may possess the assets to defend its coastal SLOCs—those within 100 nm of the mainland—but the next level of SLOC protection includes sea-lanes that extend throughout East Asia from the Sea of Japan to the Andaman Sea west of Malacca. The PLAN is not capable of defending these regional SLOCs in 2010.[36] Long-range SLOCs include sea-lanes throughout the East China Sea and South Asian waters, including the Indian Ocean, the North Arabian Sea, and perhaps even the Persian Gulf and Red Sea. The PLAN has little ability to defend SLOCs west of Malacca or in other distant areas, and there is little evidence that Beijing is taking significant actions to improve this capability.

PLAN operations in the Indian Ocean may not be tasked to a specific fleet, but the South Sea Fleet's area of responsibility (AOR) includes the eastern approaches to the Indonesian straits—Makassar, Sunda, Lombok, and Malacca—that control the SLOCs into the Indian Ocean. China's primary maritime concern west of Malacca is maintenance of the Indian Ocean SLOCs vital to China's international trade, highlighted by oil imports from the Persian Gulf.[37]

Chinese policy analysts often refer to the "Malacca dilemma" to indicate China's unacceptable reliance on energy imports that must transit that choke point, based on the fact that in 2008—seven years ahead of a 2004 estimate—75 percent of China's energy imports originated in the Middle East and Africa and were shipped across the Indian Ocean and usually through the South China Sea. In mid-2004, for instance, an article in the government's *China Youth Daily* stated that "it is no exaggeration to say that whoever controls the Strait of Malacca will also have a stranglehold on the energy route of China."[38] Even more extreme is the statement by noted hardliner Zhang Wenmu of the University of Aeronautics and Astronautics, who argued that "China's dependence on international energy imports is rapidly changing from a relationship of relative dependence to one of absolute dependence. . . . China is almost helpless to protect its overseas oil import routes."[39] Various projects have been designed to reduce China's reliance on the Malacca Strait, most notably proposals to build a pipeline across the Kra Isthmus or from the Andaman Sea through Burma to Yunnan Province. The former is unlikely to occur because of natural and political problems; construction of the latter has been announced and apparently is in progress.[40]

While straits between the Indian Ocean and South China Sea are the primary means for energy from Southwest Asia and Africa to reach Northeast Asia, the role of the Malacca Strait is exaggerated. In fact, as of 2009, China imports no more than 10 percent of its daily energy needs through the South China Sea straits.

CONCLUSION

Barring some massive petroleum discovery, China's dependence on imported oil and natural gas will continue to increase annually and China will remain a net energy importer. This in turn will increase the importance of the SLOCs over which petroleum products flow. None are more important than those that cross the Indian Ocean, and none are longer or pose a more difficult problem for a maritime planner. The PLAN is not capable of maintaining even a presence in these farflung SLOCs, let alone controlling them. Beijing will not be able to rely on the Navy to protect its vital SLOCs unless the PLAN is expanded and improved dramatically. There is no evidence of that occurring, however, which means that China will have to continue its current diplomatic and economic policies to ensure a steady supply of energy resources.

Conserving and maintaining adequate fisheries is a complex international situation. The PLAN can play an enforcing role in the Yellow, East China, and South China seas, but Beijing to date has relied on diplomatic, economic, and international environmental conservation efforts, with a strong Coast Guard presence, to ensure obtaining its fair share of diminishing ocean protein.

The PLAN has played a slight role in China's very significant efforts to garner offshore resources. The Navy does have an active oceanographic research program in cooperation with the State Oceanographic Administration, with major implications for commercial application. It has conducted extensive surveying operations on China's continental shelf, for instance, albeit more likely for operational reasons such as preparing for submarine and ASW operations than for finding resources. Nonetheless, the PLAN's presence in China's claimed territorial waters underlies the sovereignty that allows China to benefit from the sea's resources.

China has developed a series of "marine high-technology" plans devoted to both military and civilian economic ends. A notable example is the 863

Program, instituted in 1996 for its "far-reaching strategic significance for protecting China's maritime rights and interests, developing a marine economy, furthering marine S&T development, and building a stronger China." The project focused on technology-intensive maritime territorial investigations, marine petroleum exploration and development, bioresources development, and marine environmental surveillance and warning. Particularly highlighted was "marine detection technology," including navigation and positioning systems; shipborne radar and GPS; and various sensor technology, including satellite optical, electronic, acoustic, and bottom-array systems.[41]

China today is among the nations most dependent on the oceans for food, energy, and trade. Chinese strategists have described four vital sea-lanes for their nation, one in each cardinal direction. The "western SLOC," which runs from the Indian Ocean through the Malacca Strait and the South China Sea before reaching China, has been described as "China's 'lifeline' of economic development" because it carries approximately 75 percent of the nation's oil imports.[42] This dependence places the PLAN in a position of major responsibility for the nation's security and well-being. The next two chapters focus on the Navy's organization and ability to fulfill that responsibility.

CHAPTER 4

PLAN Establishment

PLA personnel reductions over the past twenty years have affected the Navy less than they have the Army, reflecting Beijing's analysis of China's national security situation. The Army continues to command the highest percentage of manpower in the PLA, however—approximately 70 percent of the total, with the Navy scoring just 12 percent.[1] Although the PLAN remains the smallest of China's conventional armed services, it may be exerting influence in PLA policy determination out of proportion to its size. The PLAN receives a share of the PLA budget out of proportion to its percentage of PLA personnel. China's 2004 Defense White Paper notes that PLA budget priority is being given to the Navy, the Air Force, and the Second Artillery "in order to strengthen the capabilities for winning both command of the sea and command of the air, and conducting strategic counterstrikes." The PLA budget also includes specific allotments to the Central Military Committee; Ministry of Defense; General Staff, Political, Logistics, and Armaments departments; Academy of Military Science; and National Defense University.[2]

PLAN BUDGET DETERMINATION

As noted earlier, analyzing and understanding China's military capabilities is made difficult by a lack of transparency regarding the administration and priorities of those services. In no case is the process more hidden than that of defense budget allocations. First, even when data are available, understanding their importance is complicated by the oft-quoted caution that "there are three kinds of lies: . . . lies, damned lies, and statistics."[3] Second, Beijing has more than one way of describing the resources it puts into its military budget. "Defense budget" is not a commonly used term in China; "defense expenditure" or "military expenditure" is more common and can cover many categories of spending. Third, the Ministry of Finance categorizes allocations as either central or local which complicates understanding the budget process. In some cases, naval costs—including some naval militia operations—are borne by provincial or municipal bodies, or even come from the commercial sector. Fourth, clear definition is often lacking for various defense spending categories such as research and development, capital construction, and some personnel accounts, including retirement and demobilization costs. Fifth, while the Navy is undoubtedly receiving a degree of priority in PLA defense allocation, the degree to which this has resulted in a meaningful shift of strategic emphasis from continental to maritime concerns is still not clear.

The Navy's budget process itself involves a number of steps. First, the service's leadership formulates its request from among several categories. These include the following:

- Personnel covers pay and other financial benefits to naval personnel, including rations, uniforms, pensions, and possibly some demobilization compensation; this category also includes civilian employees.
- Education and training includes all three (North Sea, East Sea, and South Sea) fleets' shore-based training establishments; enlisted recruit and new officer training; naval academies and other naval colleges; and possibly the PLAN's share of the operating costs of some joint schools.
- Operations and maintenance funds everything from fuel to spare parts for the ships, submarines, aircraft, Marine Corps, coast defense, and other units under PLAN command; also included are meteorological-oceanographic support and shore-based communications systems.
- Research and development (R&D) is largely conducted and funded on a centralized basis, although the PLAN has an in-house R&D establishment for addressing Navy-specific areas such as antisubmarine warfare (ASW).
- Procurement, which may not include systems and platforms obtained directly from foreign states by the central government, forms one of the major elements of Navy spending, particularly in view of the increased emphasis on procuring indigenously produced equipment from China's expanding and modernizing military-industrial complex.

- Construction focuses primarily on naval base and other facilities construction, ranging from piers to warehouses to personnel housing and recreation facilities; the Navy's fuels systems, including storage, pipelines, and pumping facilities comprise another important line item in this category.
- "Civil sector" is an unclear category but probably includes PLAN funding for naval militia and reserve units; it may also include some naval financial support for the conscription process.[4]

The budget process remains opaque. It may be based on the PLAN's five operational forces—surface vessel, submarine, aviation, coastal defense units, and the Marine Corps—or it may rely primarily on inputs from the three operating fleets and type commanders. What is certain is that China's booming economy of the past thirty-five years has allowed the PLAN to garner increasing resources.

PLAN LEADERSHIP

PLA commanders should be important participants in determining China's national security policy prioritization, but the "commanding heights" of that effort are jealously guarded by the Chinese Communist Party (CCP) leadership. Lack of PLA participation at this level was ameliorated only in 2004 when the commanders of the Navy, the Air Force, and the Second Artillery were appointed to China's eleven-member Central Military Commission (CMC). The CMC is China's senior military body, although it is headed by the CCP chairman.

Those appointments were a signal change for the leaders of China's military services, but the same has not been true for senior PLAN political officers, who may have little naval experience. For instance, a series of leadership changes in July 2008 included the retirement as PLAN political commissar of Hu Yanlin, whose prior career had been spent in the Air Force; the appointment as the Navy's deputy political commissar of Fan Yinhua, who had spent his previous tours in the Army; and the transfer of Xu Jianzhong from an Army billet to become director of the Navy's political department.[5]

Given the continued domination of China's military by the Army—whose officers serve as the commanders of China's seven military regions (MRs)—the Navy commander's ability to influence national security policy likely depends to a significant degree on personality and length of service. The PLAN commander normally is a vice admiral when appointed to his position and is promoted to admiral at some point in his tenure. Three of the coastal MR commanders have a Navy deputy commander responsible for the employment of PLAN forces. These deputies may exert influence beyond that responsibility, depending on personal relations with their MR commander.

The heads of the PLA's four general departments are senior in rank to the service commanders and probably dominate them in the national security policy process. These officers—heading the General Staff Department (GSD), General Political Department (GPD), General Logistics Department (GLD), and General Equipment (or Armaments) Department (GED)—are collocated in Beijing with China's civilian leaders and control most of the resources allocated to the defense establishment. Each department forms a complex bureaucracy, of course, within which resident officers wield various degrees of influence.[6]

The Navy is subject to the Leninist character of China's military: the PLA retains a system of political commissars paralleling its operational commanders, and party committees are involved in decision making throughout. Just as the PLAN commander has a political commissar counterpart of equivalent rank, so the captain of a warship has a political commissar counterpart. This system is aimed at ensuring constant CCP presence throughout the Navy chain of command. Onboard ship, for instance, each department, division, and even work center includes a party committee or at least a representative. Although not necessarily a trained CCP commissar, this individual is usually a member of the CCP and is expected to function as its representative during the ship's daily work.

This may mean that in even a small work center aboard ship—the electronic warfare center, for example—one of the four to six enlisted personnel assigned will be designated the CCP representative and will report up the party chain of command to the ship's senior commissar, who usually holds the same rank as the ship's commanding officer. The PLA's Revised Routine Service Regulations define the relationship for multiship organizations: "The commander of a regiment (brigade) [or destroyer squadron, for instance] and the [unit's] political commissar are the senior officers of the regiment (brigade), and they are jointly responsible for the work of the entire regiment (brigade)." The same relationship exists up through the military region and service levels, and down to the individual ship.

Formally trained shipboard political commissars are supposed to be operationally proficient as well so that they can provide realistic decision-making advice to the operational commander. A number of deputy commanders are appointed at senior levels, such as fleet and base commands, including six deputies at PLAN Headquarters and six in each fleet. Each deputy has a specific responsibility—for logistics and armament, perhaps—and for overseeing the various branches, such as surface, aviation, subsurface, and coastal defense arms. In the South Sea Fleet, a deputy political commissar is assigned responsibility for the Marines.

NAVY HEADQUARTERS

The Navy commander is headquartered in Beijing; his political officer usually matches him in rank.[7] Three vice admirals serve as deputy commanders, and two deputy political officer billets are filled by a vice and a rear admiral, with the latter serving also as PLAN inspector-general. Departmental responsibilities, and perhaps the degree of influence each wields over general Navy policies and trends, were redefined in 2009.[8] There are four departments in PLAN Headquarters; the Headquarters and Political departments are headed by vice admirals and the Logistics and Armament departments are headed by rear admirals.

The primary tasks of the Headquarters Department are to "increase combat capability" through emphasizing "military training" and to ensure that the Navy is administered "according to law." Four specific tasks are to (1) emphasize standardization in operations; (2) strengthen the Navy's legal system; (3) "prevent . . . major safety problems"; and (4) "promote naval standardized construction" and improve training to include "deepening preparations for military struggles" by (a) accelerating training reforms; (b) training in "a complex electromagnetic environment"; (c) emphasizing training in basic techniques and tactics; (d) improving the quality of the Navy's academies and schools; and (e) improving the "organization and leadership" of training.

The Political Department manages Navy personnel, including promotion boards—a primary source of power within the PLAN. This department is charged to "make new and higher requirements on political work," focusing on six points: (1) "uplifting the banner of the patriotic spirit [of] socialism with Chinese characteristics"; (2) "constantly deepen[ing] the political work of preparation for military struggles"; (3) "strengthen[ing] the building of party committees"; (4) advancing the "strategic personnel project"; (5) "intensify[ing] grassroots construction"; and (6) "strengthen[ing] construction among political organs and political cadres."

The Logistics Department includes offices of Supply, Finance, Ordnance, Civil Engineering, Transportation, and Medical (Hospitals and Public Health). It is directed to "deepen logistics preparations for maritime military struggles," to include bettering personnel living support, while emphasizing "war readiness training."

The Armament Department includes offices for Development, Construction, and Repair, each containing bureaus for surface, subsurface, and aviation systems. There are also Equipment Technology, Equipment Repair, and Science and Technology offices, as well as the Center for Equipment Feasibility (probably within the Navy Equipment Research Agency). The department also manages the Underwater Ordnance Testing Ground offshore of Shanghai and the missile and gunnery testing ranges off the Liaodong Peninsula. This department is responsible for full-life acquisition and maintenance of arms equipment and systems. It is specifically assigned six work areas: (1) activate "integrated armament construction"; (2) "gradually construct a blue water defense combat armament system"; (3) "firmly establish a material foundation [of new weapons and equipment] for transformation work"; (4) deepen "integrated military-civilian support"; (5) improve "armament management by the troops" to ensure operational readiness; and (6) increase military-civilian "competitive procurement of armaments" and "integrated equipment repair support mechanisms."[9]

This list is rather general, but it does indicate PLAN leadership concerns. There is a clear emphasis on improving management and leadership, and on training and educating personnel to prepare for actual warfare, with a focus on regulation and law. Almost certainly contributing to this focus are incidents of corruption and inconsistent training and administrative practices, which have led to inconsistent operational results and concern for the PLAN's readiness to complete assigned missions successfully.

This departmental structure is modified at fleet and lower levels. Each of the PLAN's three fleets has two major departments, Headquarters and Political. The naval bases, however, follow Beijing's lead and have four major departments: Headquarters, Political, Logistics, and Armament, as do naval garrisons. Seagoing flotillas are organized under Headquarters, Political, and Logistics departments.

THE PLAN'S ROLE

The Navy's leadership has become both more professional and more responsible since the 1980s. The commander in 2000, Admiral Shi Yunsheng, had risen rapidly to that position after service in senior positions in the North Sea and South Sea fleets, including command of the Naval Aviation (PLANAF) forces that participated in the 1988 battles against Vietnam in the South China Sea. He was the first naval aviator to command the Navy. Shi's removal from office in 2003 following loss of the Ming 361 submarine crew was probably due to the PLAN's unsatisfactory overall performance rather than to any personal failing. That the problems lay more in the administrative than the operational or political reliability categories did not prevent his dismissal, and in fact indicate an increasing sense of professionalism and responsibility in the PLAN.[10]

Shi's successor was Admiral Zhang Dingfa. Zhang may have simply been deemed the best choice available to command China's Navy, but he did possess specific qualities for the job at that time: a submariner following the loss of a submarine, particular experience as an engineer, and well suited to command a PLAN that has come to rely on the submarine as its "capital ship" in the event of war fighting in a Taiwan scenario, which is likely to feature U.S. naval intervention.

Zhang Dingfa died of cancer after three years as Navy commander, but not before initiating the reorganizational steps deemed necessary by the loss of the Ming 361. These included changing the chain of command to ensure better accountability for maintenance activities, realigning headquarters-base-garrison responsibilities, and emphasizing realistic training for ships' personnel. Zhang's successor in 2007, Admiral Wu Shengli, is a surface warfare officer who has continued these reforms.

The PLAN commander has to wear more than one hat. First, as the senior officer in the Navy, he is responsible for directing the operational tasking of the force in accordance with the determination of national security objectives. The most important facet of this responsibility is ensuring that the PLAN is ready to fulfill its role in situations ranging from combating piracy to preparing for various operational options regarding Taiwan.

INTERNATIONAL DEPLOYMENTS

It is up to the Navy commander to gain authorization from the national policy-making apparatus for missions the Navy wants to execute—such as multiship deployments to foreign nations—by presenting such missions as beneficial to China. These tasks historically have focused on the mission of "presence," using the Navy as a vehicle of national prestige and diplomacy. In December 2008, however, the PLAN was directed to execute its first operational mission overseas when it dispatched a three-ship task group to the Gulf of Aden to participate in the UN-sanctioned effort to suppress piracy.

Diplomatic missions typically involve careful preparations. These begin in Naval Headquarters in Beijing in late October or early November, when the CMC decides on PLAN ship visits for the coming calendar year. PLAN Headquarters or fleet commanders nominate countries for visits they think will support national goals and further PLAN capabilities. The nominations are submitted to the First Office of the Ministry of Defense for vetting, and if approved there, to the CMC for approval. Once national approval is gained, ship selection and preparation are the responsibility of the Navy offices and fleet headquarters designated by PLAN Headquarters.[11]

RESOURCE ACQUISITION

The Navy commander represents his service in the resource allocation process—that is, in PLA and Ministry of Defense budget battles. His personal effectiveness in this role is not easily quantifiable but is central to his service's success in the modernization and equipment acquisition programs that directly affect PLAN capabilities.

In addition to major acquisition programs, the Navy commander leads his service in the intra-PLA struggles and debates over personnel allocation and joint command assignments, and determines to a degree the PLAN's status within military and even governmental priorities.

EDUCATION

The organizational changes that have taken place since Shi assumed office in 1997 may be as significant as the PLAN's equipment modernization. The changes seem to have intensified following Shi's forced departure from office in 2003. The training and education establishment has been streamlined in areas ranging from officer accession to ship's crew training, including a reduction in the number of PLAN officer academies.

The PLAN has also been subject to the general overhaul of PLA service academies that has taken place since the late 1990s and has established a system of ROTC-like units.[12] In Wuhan, for example, the former Navy Engineering Academy and Navy Electronics Engineering Academy were merged into the Navy Engineering University. The new school, established in June 1999, reportedly awards undergraduate degrees and has graduate programs in thirty-five subjects offered by thirteen departments that focus on the advanced technological areas applicable to the putative revolution in military affairs; they include warship kinetic engineering, electronic information and naval arms engineering, and command and electronic warfare engineering.[13] This is a clear example of the Navy's participation in the PLA-wide campaign to follow the government's direction to ensure that academy education contributes to "strengthening the military through science and technology."[14]

The Navy also operates its own academic research institute (the Naval Research Institute, or NRI) and equipment research institute (the Naval Equipment Research Academy, or NERA) in Beijing, which are under the direction of the Navy commander. The NRI focuses on strategic and doctrinal issues. The NERA conducts studies relating to future technology developments in fields such as maritime warfare; information; nanotechnology; and aerospace, precision guidance, and stealth technologies; with application to ship-aircraft operations and over-the-horizon (OTH) guided missile employment; as well as electronic, underwater information, and maritime blockade warfare.

Shipboard Training

Prior to the 1980s ship's crews were educated almost entirely aboard ship. Since then, however, the PLAN has created more centralized schools to facilitate teaching personnel how to operate modern systems. These new schools and training centers are operated by each fleet's naval base commands, and include institutions to teach engineering, surface warfare, ship handling, aviation operations, submarine warfare, and medical operations, in addition to addressing specific equipment systems.[15]

The PLAN school structure apparently remains strongly oriented toward individual ship performance, with personnel only rarely reporting to a new ship after being sent to school by their previous vessel.[16] There seems little doubt, however, that China's naval education system has been much strengthened since the fleet acquired new submarines and surface combatants at the beginning of the twenty-first century. The loss of the Ming 361 in 2003 and a possible fire in another Ming-class submarine in the South China Sea in 2005 must have dramatically highlighted the need to improve personnel performance and qualifications.[17] The PLAN now fields platforms and systems that require highly intelligent operators and maintenance personnel. Successful twenty-first-century maritime conflict demands integrated systems and joint efforts. Naval personnel are believed to need extensive, continuing training on their equipment; the intellectual prowess and skill necessary to operate it; and thorough knowledge of doctrine.

Perhaps most important, effective force modernization requires an NCO corps of individuals who are both professionally competent and committed to a long-term career in the PLAN. This is a goal toward which the Chinese Navy has been moving slowly; the more systematic approach to shipboard and shore-based training should prove a useful vehicle for helping to create this corps of enlisted careerists.

LOGISTICS

The PLAN has been striving to improve its support infrastructure since at least the mid-1990s, about the time Shi Yunsheng became Navy commander and emphasized the importance of logistics. Shi devoted considerable attention to improving the Navy's General Logistics Command and launched a campaign to build a "modern logistic support system," to include oil and water supply systems for the fleet as well as modernizing the fleet of surveying, salvage, transport, and hospital ships.[18]

One step in that direction was a change in the character of the Navy's bases in 2003. Naval bases lost their responsibilities for operational units but assumed the logistics duties previously assigned to the fleet-level logistics departments, which were abolished. The result of this reorganization would seem to shift more of the direct operational responsibility to the fleet commanders while also giving them direct command of the bases in their respective areas of operation (AORs).

Ship maintenance has become a high priority since 2003, as has improved support for equipment maintenance. Key to this effort has been a centralization of Navy supply and spare parts services, a difficult task for any Navy and one with which the PLAN reportedly is making slow progress.[19]

The Navy has also been working to implement the PLA General Logistics Department's plan to establish a joint logistics service to improve the timeliness and effectiveness of PLA logistics, even extending to privatization of some parts of the system. This plan includes creation of joint "naval-air-ground rapid-response logistics units," while the Navy remains responsible for specific requirements linked to operations at sea, such as underway replenishment, providing shipboard-specific supplies, and harbor facilities.[20] Naval base structure has been reorganized to improve provisioning, repair and maintenance, medical care, and technical systems support of naval units and activities both afloat and ashore.

NATIONAL MILITARY POLICY

The PLAN commander is expected to wear a joint (or "purple," in U.S. parlance) hat as a senior member of China's military hierarchy. The importance of ensuring the close coordination of efforts by all services to implement joint warfare was brought home to the PLA by the allied forces' victory in operation Desert Storm in 1991. To further joint operation the commander must either be prepared to sacrifice Navy priorities within PLA plans that may be dominated by ground force officers, or be clever enough to ensure that the PLAN receives the share of defense resources necessary for continued modernization of the fleet and professionalization of its personnel.

This role is more complex for senior PLAN officers than for their foreign counterparts because of the relationship between the CCP and the PLA. The modernized Army must still be a "party Army." "Red" versus "expert" is too stark a phrase to use—there is no reason why a military member cannot be both politically reliable and professionally competent—but increasing military professionalism is clearly one of Beijing's goals and is not likely facilitated by the continuing emphasis placed on ensuring an ideologically oriented military loyal to the CCP. In other words, service commanders in China must not only be "purple," they must also be "red," since the PLA remains a Leninist force, in the sense of being populated with political officers (commissars) who are in rank co-equal with their operational counterparts.[21] In practice, these relationships are likely to be personality dependent to a significant degree at the unit level and more formal at senior levels of the naval hierarchy.[22]

The PLAN commander represents China in his relations with foreign navies. Navy commander Admiral Wu Shengli traveled to the United States in 2007 and to India and Japan in 2008. Such trips enable commanders to investigate future possibilities for PLAN modernization but are also responsive to tasking from the CMC.[23]

Evaluating a PLAN commander's effectiveness is difficult given the opaqueness of PLA Headquarters. The Navy commander also has to function in the shadow of Liu Huaqing, who retired in 1997 as CMC vice chairman after previously serving as the first Navy commander with the power to change PLA priorities. Liu certainly wore "purple" and "red" hats, but more than two decades later he remains the "father of the modern PLAN." No relatively junior Chinese Navy commander can expect to have Liu's stature or his personal relationship with China's president and range of experience in the PLA. Michael Swaine's 1997 description of the PLAN "behaving as a quasi-independent bureaucratic actor ... pushing for a greater recognition of its institutional viewpoint in the senior levels of the PLA leadership, with significant success ... as the major ... proponent of the creation of a technologically sophisticated, operationally versatile blue water force" remains valid, as does his caveat that the "pace and direction of naval modernization remains a major subject of debate" among PLA leaders, with the PLAN viewpoint "often challenged by the ground forces orientation of the GSD."[24]

PLAN FORCE STRUCTURE

The 1998 PLAN force structure instituted by Admiral Shi Yunsheng remained in place in 2009 under Admiral Wu Shengli. The PLAN is divided into five "major arms systems": naval surface vessel units, naval submarine units, Naval Aviation units, naval coastal defense units, and the Marine Corps.[25] "Missions" are crucial to force structure organization. A useful list of naval missions includes: maritime diplomacy, domain maintenance, maritime presence, sea control/sea denial, deterrence, tripwire, and power projection. These missions are translated in the *Chinese Naval Officer's Manual* into operational-level duties for the various PLAN warfare communities.

The surface fleet is responsible for attacking enemy warships (ASUW), antisubmarine warfare (ASW), amphibious warfare (AMW), coastal defense, maritime surveillance, mine warfare (MIW), merchant ship convoys, search and rescue (SAR), and logistics.

The submarine force is responsible for strategic nuclear strikes, interdicting enemy logistics, attacking enemy naval bases and coasts, maritime patrol and reconnaissance, MIW, logistic lift, and SAR.

Naval Aviation's responsibilities include ASUW, attacking enemy naval installations, defending PLAN surface and submarine forces during offensive operations, AMW and antiair warfare (AAW), maritime reconnaissance, ASW, MIW, early warning, communications, SAR, and logistic lift.

Finally, the Marine Corps is assigned AMW, forward base seizure, and coastal defense.[26]

PLAN HEADQUARTERS ORGANIZATION

The most significant of the departments located in Beijing is the Headquarters Department, because the PLAN's operational chain of command passes through it.[27] A senior captain directs each of the five "offices" under the Headquarters Department. The most significant of these is the General Office, which includes the following divisions: Military Strategic Studies, Political-Military Affairs, Operations, and the military assistants to the PLAN commander and the PLAN political commissar.

The Operations Office oversees the three operational fleets: the North Sea Fleet, the East Sea Fleet, and the South Sea Fleet, each commanded by a vice admiral. The Intelligence Office is organized around regional intelligence divisions—that is, Western Hemisphere, Europe, Asia, West Asia, and Africa—plus a General Planning and Secretarial Division. The Training Office administers the PLAN's surface warfare, submarine, aviation, and engineering academies. Finally, the Military Affairs Office has responsibility for doctrine, regulations, and publications.

GEOGRAPHIC FLEET ORGANIZATION

The three fleets are similarly organized, with each assigned three air divisions of approximately thirty-six aircraft each. An air division typically comprises four air regiments, which in turn comprise four air groups.[28] A fleet's aviation assets include land-based and seaplane patrol planes, and bomber, fighter, rotary-wing, transport, and support aircraft. The fleet air commander is operationally responsible to his fleet commander, and since the recent disestablishment of the Beijing Naval Aviation headquarters, likely also receives admin-

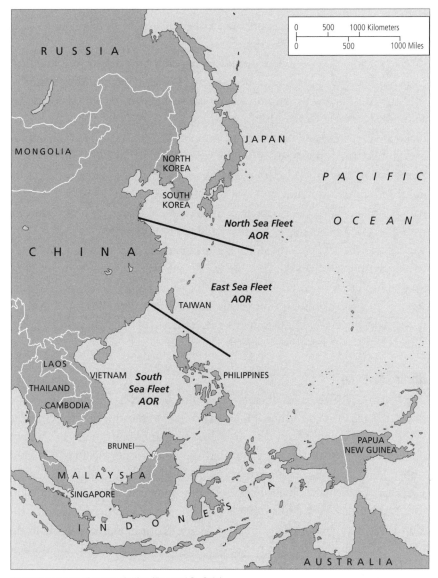

PLAN fleet areas of responsibility. (Bernard D. Cole)

istrative support from his fleet commander. The old Naval Aviation offices at Liangxiang Airfield, near Beijing, may still provide Navy-wide engineering, maintenance, supply, and training guidance.

In addition to its aviation arm, each fleet includes senior captains as type commanders of the surface forces, service force, and submarine flotillas, all organized in squadrons of the same ship type. These flotilla commanders report directly to the fleet commander; the small-craft flotilla commanders report to the local naval base commander.

Surface forces in each fleet include large combatants (destroyers and frigates), small combatants (patrol boats), amphibious transports, mine warfare craft, and miscellaneous support ships.[29] Each of the three fleets also includes a Combat Support Vessel Flotilla to which is assigned that fleet's replenishment-at-sea (RAS) and other logistics support vessels, and at least one speedboat flotilla. The support vessel flotillas were organized in 2004 and represent a significant step in PLAN modernization. Establishing dedicated logistics units will almost certainly increase the efficiency of the logistics functions within China's Navy, most notably in the mission of underway replenishment, with direct improvements in the Navy's ability to project power at sea.[30]

Each of the PLAN's three fleets is assigned naval bases and subordinate naval garrison commands. These are important organizations with extensive geographic areas of responsibility: they provide "hotel" and other logistics services to fleet operating units, including training and education, maintenance, and general administrative support. Each of the approximately ten PLAN bases oversees at least one garrison.[31]

North Sea Fleet

The North Sea Fleet is headquartered at Qingdao and has primary bases and associated garrisons at Lushun, Huludao (in charge of testing ranges), Qingdao (Weihai), and Lianyungang. This fleet also commands one of the PLAN's two major submarine bases, at Qingdao. Garrisons and smaller facilities, including shipbuilding facilities, are located at Dalian, Weihai, Qingshan, Lianyungang, Lingshan, Dahushan, Changshandao, Liushuang, Yushan, and Dayuanjiadun. The North Sea Fleet's AOR extends from the Korean border (marked by the Yalu River) to approximately 35°10' N, an area corresponding roughly to the Shenyang, Beijing, and Jinan MRs. The AOR's coastline is divided into nine coastal defense zones.

The Qingdao shipyard, on the Shandong Peninsula, has long specialized in constructing small patrol craft and landing ships, while the facility at Lushun has built Yushu-class landing ships in recent years.[32] Naval Aviation facilities are located at Liangxiang, Luda, Qingdao, Jinxi, Jiyuan, Laiyang, Jiaoxian, Xingtai, Laishan, Anyang, Changzhi, and Shanhaiguan. This fleet also oversees various weapons and sensor test ranges in the waters off the Liaodong Peninsula.

The North Sea Fleet's forces include three submarine flotillas: the 1st (Nuclear), 2nd, and 12th; the 1st Destroyer Flotilla; 1st Landing Ship Flotilla; 1st and 6th speed boat flotillas; and four sub-chaser squadrons. Also assigned are the 1st Operations Support Vessel Flotilla, one minesweeper squadron, and the Bo Sea Training Flotilla.[33] Additionally, the North Sea Fleet—and probably the East and South sea fleets as well—is assigned a Hydrographic Surveying and Charting Ship Squadron divided into two divisions: one of surveying and charting ships, and one of reconnaissance vessels.[34]

As is the case with all three fleets, the North Sea Fleet's command structure replicates that of PLAN Headquarters in Beijing. Each fleet commander also serves as deputy commander of the matching MR. A vice admiral commands the fleet and serves as the Shenyang MR deputy commander, but his authority during wartime is unclear: would he function as a true joint deputy commander or merely be the deputy in charge of naval forces?[35]

The fleet's political commissar is a vice or rear admiral. Command relationships within the MRs during peacetime are complicated by the PLAN and PLAAF commanders' dual chains of command: administrative and operational, with the MR commander—invariably a ground forces officer—not in control of both chains.

Command relationships are theoretically clarified during wartime, when the MR forms a "front," as did the Beijing and Shenyang MRs during the 1979 Vietnam incursion. Two fronts were established in that case, with the CMC sending representatives to the Northern Front, formed with the Shenyang and Beijing MRs, and the Southern Front, formed by the Chengdu and Guangzhou MRs. Officers provided from Beijing headquarters staffs augment the front's command structure. These officers are empowered to relax or sustain constraints on the MR commander's freedom of action: in the 1979 case, these included the distance he could move forces into Vietnam and the degree to which "hot pursuit" could be effected.[36] Despite the recent advances in material, systems, and procedures, the PLA seems to have only marginally decentralized this inherently rigid system of command and control. It obviously meets PLA requirements, but it may not prove suitable in a twenty-first-century wartime environment at sea.

The North Sea Fleet has three rear admirals as deputy commanders and three more as deputy political commissars; the fleet aviation commander is also a rear admiral, as are the commanders of the Lushun and Qingdao naval bases. The garrisons at Dalian and Weihai are commanded by senior captains.

East Sea Fleet

The East Sea Fleet is headquartered at Ningbo, with other major bases at Shanghai, Zhoushan, and Fujian (Fuzhou). Garrisons and lesser facilities are located at Chenjiagang, Dinghai, Wusong, Xinxiang, Wenzhou, Sandu Bay, Xiamen, Quandao, and Xiangshan (submarines). The fleet's AOR reaches from approximately 35°10' N southward to 23°30' N, corresponding roughly to the Nanjing MR. Its coastline is divided into seven coastal defense zones.

The East Sea Fleet's AOR contains China's most important naval shipyards. No less than five significant shipbuilding facilities are located at Shanghai (for surface ships), with another at Wuhan (for submarines). The Wuchang shipyard, located six hundred miles up the Yangtze River at Wuhan, is one of China's most important producers of conventionally powered submarines. The Jiangnan shipyard began building warships in 1865 when it was founded by the British. In fact, that yard built Yangtze River gunboats for the U.S. Navy in the 1920s.[37] It currently produces China's newest destroyers, such as the Type-052C, as well as submarines, frigates, and several classes of large auxiliary vessels.

Second in importance only to Jiangnan is the Hudong shipyard, which has been building the PLAN's newest classes of frigates as well as new Fuchi-class underway replenishment ships. A third major shipyard in this AOR, at Honghua, was founded in 1926. It is a large commercial shipbuilding enterprise but has also been the PLAN's primary source of amphibious warfare ships. Another Shanghai area shipyard, the Qiuxin, is much smaller but has been building China's latest class of minesweeper, the Type-082.

East Sea Fleet Naval Aviation facilities are located at Ningbo, Shanghai, Luqiao, Shitangqiao, Danyang, and Daishan. This fleet's AOR does not appear to include a major submarine support base, indicating that the PLAN's newer submarines are homeported with the North Sea and East Sea fleets; this in turn indicates primary concern with submarine employment in northern areas—possibly against Japan and the United States, and in the East China and Philippine Seas.

Assigned forces include the 22nd and 42nd submarine flotillas (which include all twelve Kilo-class boats), 3rd and 6th destroyer flotillas, 3rd and 8th frigate squadrons (which probably report administratively to the destroyer flotilla commanders), the 5th Landing Ship Flotilla, 16th and 21st speed boat flotillas, four sub-chaser squadrons, and a Navy Reserve minesweeper squadron. The East Sea Fleet also counts the 2nd Operations Support Vessel Flotilla, which includes one old and one new replenishment-at-sea ship and perhaps two hundred small patrol and auxiliary craft, including those that patrol the Yangtze and other riverine waters.

The East Sea Fleet is commanded by a vice admiral who serves as a deputy commander of the Nanjing MR; its political commissar is also a vice admiral. The three deputy fleet commanders are rear admirals, as are the three deputy political commissars. The fleet aviation commander is also a rear admiral. Base commanders for Fujian, Shanghai, and Zhoushan are rear admirals, while the Xiamen Naval Garrison is probably commanded by a senior captain.

South Sea Fleet

The South Sea Fleet is headquartered at Zhanjiang, with other major bases at Guangzhou (Shantou), Zhanjiang (Beihai), and Yulin (Xisha). Garrisons and lesser facilities are at Hong Kong, Haikou, Shantou, Humen, Kuanchuang, Tsun, Mawai, Beihai, Pingtan, Sanzhou, Tang Chian Huan, Longmen, Bailong, Donguon, Baimajing, Xiachuandao, and Xisha (in the Paracel Islands). The fleet's AOR stretches from approximately 23°30' N to the Vietnamese border, equating to the Guangzhou MR, and its coastline is divided into nine coastal defense zones.

Two naval shipyards of note are located in this fleet's AOR. The Guangzhou yard has recently concentrated on commercial shipbuilding, although it produced one of the Fuchi-class oilers. More significant is the Huangpu shipyard, also located at Guangzhou, which has recently built some of the PLAN's newest frigates. Sanya, the new submarine base on Hainan Island, falls within the South Sea Fleet's AOR.

Naval Aviation facilities are located at Lingshui, Foluo, Haikou, Sanya, Guiping, Jialaishi, and Lingling. The fleet is also responsible for the South China Sea, with significant support facilities on Woody Island and on Fiery Cross, Lincoln, and Duncan reefs. The fleet's AOR includes the contested Paracel and Spratly islands and the Macclesfield Bank, which explains the presence at Lingshui, on Hainan, of the PLANAF's long-range B-6 "Badger" aircraft. The base on Woody Island (Xisha) in the Paracels is the only South China Sea facility capable of supporting tactical aircraft.[38]

The South Sea Fleet is home to the PLAN's newest guided-missile destroyers and, more significant, the new submarine base at Sanya, on Hainan Island, which is homeport to the 32nd Submarine Flotilla of conventionally powered (Ming-class) submarines; another flotilla has probably been created to host the new nuclear-powered submarines assigned to the base at Sanya. The fleet includes the 2nd Destroyer Flotilla; and 1st, 2nd, and 18th frigate squadrons; 2nd and 6th landing ship flotillas; 11th and 26th speed boat flotillas; four sub-chaser squadrons; one MIW squadron; and more than two hundred patrol and auxiliary craft, including those based at Hong Kong and on the MR's rivers. Additionally, the fleet includes the 3rd Operations Support Vessel Flotilla, which includes two of China's five major replenishment-at-sea ships, the *Nancang* and the *Weishanhu*, and the majority of China's newer amphibious ships, including all seven of the Qiongsha-class troop transports, ten of the fifteen Yuting- and Yukan-class LSTs, and all four of the Yudao-class LSMs.[39]

The PLAN's Marine Corps is stationed in the South Sea Fleet's AOR. It is composed of two multiarm brigades of approximately 6,000 personnel each, organized into 750-person battalions. This force includes infantry, artillery, armor, engineer, communications, antichemical, antiarmor, and amphibious scout personnel. The Corps' primary mission is amphibious warfare; its anticipated operating theater is the South China Sea and possibly islands occupied by Taiwan. The Marine Corps reports operationally through the South Sea Fleet commander but is administratively responsible to PLAN Headquarters in Beijing for training, equipment, strategic planning, personnel, and policy. Furthermore, the Marine Corps is designated as part of the PLA's rapid reaction force and during crises would likely be tasked directly by the CMC.

The vice admiral commanding the South Sea Fleet serves as the Guangzhou MR deputy commander; another vice admiral is the fleet political commissar. The three deputy commanders are rear admirals, as are the three deputy political commissars. The fleet's Naval Aviation forces are commanded by a rear admiral; the Marine Corps brigades by captains or senior captains. The fleet's naval bases at Guangzhou, Zhanjiang, and Sanya are commanded by rear admirals, while the naval garrisons at Shantou and Xisha are commanded by senior captains.

The recently expanded base at Sanya, at the southernmost point of Hainan Island, is notable as the apparent homeport of China's newest nuclear-powered submarines, including the Type-094 Jin-class SSBNs. This base has modernized piers for surface ships, an apparent degaussing range, and underground tunnels deep enough to berth submarines.[40]

NAVAL AVIATION

Organization of the Chinese Naval Aviation branch was decreed by the Central Military Commission on 06 September 1952, and it reportedly began shipboard operations in January 1980. The branch includes approximately eight hundred aircraft organized in nine operational divisions, each composed of two or three regiments of twenty-four or twenty-five aircraft each. Several independent regiments carry out special tasks. While Naval Aviation historically has not kept pace with PLAAF aircraft acquisitions, some air-to-air refueling exercises have been conducted at relatively long intervals, notably by the South Sea Fleet air arm, albeit more than a year after the PLAAF first conducted these operations.[41]

The chain of command from Navy Headquarters runs through the Headquarters Department to the three operating fleets; until October 2003, Naval Aviation had a headquarters in Beijing, where its commander, a vice admiral, was responsible for his force's aircraft and approximately 25,000 personnel. In the 2003 reorganization, the Naval Aviation staff in Beijing was demoted to a second-level department within the Navy's Headquarters Department. Naval Aviation's command structure is now tied more directly to each of the three fleet commanders, albeit with political commissars nominally co-equal with each aviation flag officer.[42]

Each fleet's Naval Aviation headquarters has four primary departments: Headquarters, Political, Logistics, and Equipment. While this nominally gives each fleet commander a readier grasp on employing his aviation assets—one report indicates that the reorganization was made so that "integrated command of ships and aircraft will become a reality"—it raises several questions.[43] How efficient is the centralized Naval Aviation supply system? Are all fleet aviation arms treated equally by Beijing? Are the different fleet aviation branches held to Navy-wide standards through a system of centralized standards and inspections; and if so, which organization sets and enforces those standards?

One important but unclear relationship is that between Naval Aviation and Air Force components. In time of war, for instance, do Naval Aviation units "chop" to the PLAAF commander for tasking? Are Naval Aviation units solely responsible for the defense of naval bases and other facilities, or can they call on the PLAAF assistance? Or are the two air components in the midst of the same command-and-control imbroglio that dogged the American military for so many years? The preliminary, general response to these questions is that although overwater flights have now become routine for the PLAAF, joint flight operations between the two "air forces" are still few.

One of the factors in this situation is the organization of China's coastal air defenses. Another is the way the PLA has assigned coastal air defense missions. From north to south along China's coast, air defense is assigned by the proximity of airfields rather than by service. The North Sea Fleet's aviation contingent has the responsibility from its northern border down to about the Shandong Peninsula; the PLAAF then assumes air defense responsibility to a point south of Shanghai, although that city is located in the heart of the East Sea Fleet's AOR. Naval Aviation resumes air defense responsibility for a brief stretch south of Shanghai, but the Air Force then has the air defense mission for most of Fujian Province's coastline, which places it on the front line of the Taiwan Strait. The PLAN resumes air defense for most of the South Sea Fleet AOR, including the South China Sea.[44]

This system, based on geographical sectors rather than service capability or doctrine, indicates not only that joint maritime flight operations are not routinely employed, but that joint doctrine for such operations has not been systemically developed by the two "air forces." Indeed, PLAAF operations over water likely concentrate on classic air intercept and pursuit operations, while PLANAF operational doctrine concentrates on fleet support missions such as surveillance and ASW.

COAST GUARD

Sun Zhihui, the director of China's State Oceanic Administration, described his nation's "coast guard" situation as "chaos in management," noting that "China Marine Surveillance is responsible for 'marine surveillance and monitoring within sea areas'; the Ministry of Transportation takes charge of handling 'maritime affairs'; the Ministry of Agriculture is in charge of 'fisheries'; and the Ministry of Public Security takes care of 'coastal defense.' Sometimes, a dispute between China and another country cannot be handled by one department alone." Sun also noted, however, that China had "combined ocean satellites with marine surveillance aircraft, ships, floats and shore stations together to establish a security system for *both military and civilian* purposes for the sea areas under the jurisdiction of China [emphasis added]." This latest development followed the change in 2006 "from irregular to regular" marine patrols.[45]

All of China's maritime auxiliary forces are uniformed, and some of them are armed, but most consider their mission to have a police rather than a military character.[46] China's Coast Guard (CCG) does not fulfill the same role as most other coast guards; it was formerly the Border Control Department (BCD), one of the major departments of the People's Armed Police (PAP). The CCG operates patrol vessels ranging in displacement from 150 tons to a 1,000-ton ship launched in 2006; the BCD has also received a few decommissioned Jianghu-class FFGs from the PLAN.

Although the hulls of BCD cutters are marked "Maritime Police," they have since 2006 carried "China Coast Guard" as well. Finally, the BCD is "in charge of administering social order of vessels along the coasts" with orders to "strictly abide by law-enforcement procedures [and not] to levy fines which are beyond their authority, or which are too excessive."[47] The PAP also operates China's Customs Service vessels, although these vessels are subordinate to the Customs Service.

The Maritime Militia was organized in the early 1950s as part of the effort to defend China's fishing fleet and coastal trade against depredations by KMT naval forces. The militia at that time consisted largely of fishing trawlers armed with machine guns and hand-held weapons; they were controlled by local CCP branches and when on a mission carried party representatives.[48] The Maritime Militia in 2010 is quite active; a military analyst at the PLA's Academy of Military Science noted "four supporting roles for the PRC coastal militia" in 2003: "maritime reconnaissance and warning," "information support," assist with civilian craft in "maritime supply security," and "maritime camouflage and feint."[49] The militia's ability to operate with the PLAN is problematical.

Other "coast guard" functions—including maritime safety, rescue and salvage, and environmental protection—are the responsibility of other national organizations as well as provincial and municipal bureaus that regulate riverine and coastal waters. The State Oceanographic Administration (SOA) is responsible for research and environmental protection, including enforcement of the Marine Environmental Protection Law of the PRC, passed in December 1999.[50] This law assigns responsibilities as follows:

- State Environmental Protection Administration (SEPA): a supervisory and managerial department for national environmental protection work.
- State Oceanographic Administration: supervision and management of the marine environment and organization of investigations, monitoring, lookout, evaluation, and scientific research of the marine environment.

- Maritime Safety Administration (MSA): supervision and management of nonfishing and nonmilitary shipping pollution of the marine environment.
- State Fishery Administration: supervision and management of pollution to the marine environment by nonmilitary ships inside fishing port waters and fishing boats outside fishing port waters.
- Military Environmental Protection Department: supervision and management of pollution to the marine environment by military ships and boats.[51]

The MSA, organized in the late 1990s, is charged with supervising the "management of navigation marks, the surveying of sea-routes, and the inspection of ships and maritime facilities," with a special focus on shipboard safety. It is described as "an important law enforcement force in the transport system" because it has responsibilities to manage maritime transport systems and "comprehensively promot[e] the administration within the law," but it actually focuses on regulatory functions. It has been assigned development objectives for 2010 and 2020. Its AOR includes China's EEZ "and other jurisdictional seas," to include navigable rivers. Water traffic safety supervision generally aims to achieve "navigable ships, competent seafarers, safe and open waters, effective controls, [and] quality services." Specific objectives are: (1) to make navigation safer, waters cleaner, and transportation easier; (2) to meet the requirements of "professional staffs, state of the art equipments, skillful operations, in order to offer dependable responses in critical events"; and (3) to provide for future improvements in these areas.[52]

The MSA's 2010 goal is to establish an effective "modern maritime supervision system," to include significantly shortening its response time for supervising maritime traffic safety, enforcing maritime laws, and ensuring environmental enforcement and cleanup in "coastal and inland marine areas." MSA objectives for 2020 are described as establishing "a modern multifunctional maritime safety supervision system with all weather capability and quick response," with improvements in reducing accidents, safety violations, and environmental problems. Throughout these plans are emphases on improving personnel performance, digitized procedures, and matching international standards. The MSA operates a fleet of buoy tenders and regulates shipbuilding.

The MSA has maritime rescue teams equipped with boats and helicopters. Ship salvage responsibilities were reorganized in 2006 and are carried out through the China Rescue and Salvage Bureau (CRSB). The CRSB is divided into two branches: the rescue arm is government funded and operates a fleet of rescue boats and helicopters; the salvage arm operates major salvage vessels with deep-dive capabilities and operates on a fee-for-service basis.[53]

The most military coast guard organization is the China Marine Surveillance service (CMS). Although administratively subordinate to the SOA, the CMS is responsible for coordination with the PLAN. The CMS was created on 19 October 1998 in its present form, although parent organizations existed as long ago as the mid-1960s. The CMS is responsible for enforcing laws and order within China's territorial waters, EEZ, and shore; protecting the maritime environment, natural resources, navigation aids, and other facilities; and carrying out maritime surveys. The CMS is also capable of carrying out SAR missions.

The CMS employs boat and aircraft to conduct "regular patrols and inspections in China's coastal waters and shorelines." Its missions include prevention of "illegal dumping of wastes into the sea" by ships and onshore facilities. CMS vessels also conduct patrols in disputed East China Sea waters to emphasize China's sovereignty claims.

The CMS is a paramilitary organization, with regional headquarters in Qingdao (covering the Bo and Yellow seas), Shanghai (covering the East China Sea), and Guangzhou (covering the South China Sea). Each regional headquarters has three marine surveillance flotillas, an aviation unit, and a number of communications and logistics support units. CMS personnel wear a blue-and-white uniform and receive some military training; the officers are offered commissions in the PLAN Reserve. The CMS had ninety-one patrol vessels and four aircraft assigned as of the end of 2005, operating with 11 provincial, 50 municipal, and 170 county marine surveillance units across China's coastal region; however, these units' connectivity and coordination capabilities are uncertain.[54]

The CMS is closely associated with the PLAN, and that service apparently is trying to gain closer control over CMS operations. An October 2008 report, for instance, announced that China's "marine surveillance force" was to become a "PLA Naval Reserves Unit." The report described the CMS as "a quasi-military marine law enforcement force" with a mission of "patrolling and overseeing" China's "territorial waters (including the coastal rim)."[55] CMS units have been responsible for the several harassment incidents involving U.S. surveillance ships in the East and South China seas.

At least three such significant incidents have been reported since 2001, when USNS *Bowditch* was intercepted by Chinese vessels in the Yellow Sea.

In March 2009 USNS *Impeccable* was similarly interfered with in the South China Sea, and USNS *Victorious* was harassed while conducting surveillance operations in the Yellow Sea. The Chinese ships involved were manned by personnel in civilian clothing and did not fly PLAN ensigns; they likely were CMS vessels operating under PLAN direction.[56]

Finally, the Coastal Regional Defense Force, which is probably part of the Naval Coastal Defense System, includes a system of coastal observation posts spread along China's coastline, coastal cruise missile and artillery sites, coastal patrol-boat squadrons, and a network of coastal radar and communications stations.[57]

COAST DEFENSE FORCES

The Navy's coastal defense force numbers approximately 25,000 personnel and is designed to form the first line of defense against amphibious and air attack from the sea. These troops operate a variety of artillery, missile, and sensor systems, but their capability as a twenty-first-century force is problematic. The coastal defense troops were important in the PRC's early years, during the Taiwan Strait crises of the 1950s and during the 1960s–1980s, when they were focused on defending China's coast from a possible Soviet amphibious attack. The principal coastal defense weapons were artillery and early-generation cruise missiles, primarily the HY-2 coast-launched antiship missile, a version of the Soviet SS-N-2 Styx. Since the 1990s the coastal defense forces have received more advanced antiship and antiaircraft missile systems, drawing on dual platform systems such as the C-802 Ying Ji-2 Saccade, a Chinese modification of the French Exocet missile system.[58] Construction of updated coastal defense infrastructure—including piers, monitoring stations and centers, and auxiliary facilities—has apparently been under way since 2004, possibly as part of the PLAN's post-2003 new look.

CONCLUSION

Missing from this discussion is a crucial element required to understand how the PLAN command structure functions from commander down to the individual operational unit: an understanding of the linkages among the Navy's bureaucracy and operational forces. How, for instance, does the headquarters

Training Department in Beijing track and evaluate the effective implementation of its annual training objectives? A system of regular inspection visits to the lower-echelon units, from fleet to ship levels, seems likely, but evidence is spotty.

To all appearances, however, the PLAN today is logically organized with an emphasis on maintaining and improving its operational forces. Its basic organization is a mixture of geographic and mission-oriented commands typical of large navies. The three operational fleets are organized along lines that are geographic, but also oriented toward historic and potential threats to China. The fleet is supported by a dynamic maintenance and technological structure, and by the world's most impressive developing system of shipyards.[59]

The North Sea Fleet faces a complex theater involving Russia, Korea, and Japan. The East Sea Fleet's AOR focuses on Taiwan but also includes the Diaoyu Islands and the disputed sea bottom resources of the East China Sea. This fleet is the focus of the Navy's planning and execution responsibility for naval action against Taiwan. While the fleet's assets are inadequate to execute any significant action against Taiwan, it would be reinforced by aircraft, surface ships, submarines, and other resources from its sister fleets in time of crisis. Historically, China's naval organizational paradigm has been based on geographically discrete operational fleets, as indeed it is today. This led to disaster in the late-nineteenth-century wars against France and Japan, when the fleets were administered and operated as discrete units, but Beijing appears to have adopted policies that will prevent a recurrence.

The South Sea Fleet also faces a complex operational situation, with its AOR including the South China Sea's operational and political problems. These include not only the disputed land features of that sea—mainly the Paracel, Spratly, and Natuna islands and the Macclesfield Bank—but also the international problems of piracy and terrorism at sea that threaten the security of the Malacca and other Indonesian straits through which so much of China's merchant traffic passes.

The PLAN's headquarters organization in Beijing is unremarkable, reflecting the usual requirements for administering a large maritime force. Where it perhaps differs is in substance rather than process, given the ideological coloration to China's national security policy determination. The PLAN's commander holds the same substantive rank as his organizational contemporaries, the PLAAF and MR commanders. Since the current trend of appointing experienced professional naval officers to command the PLAN was instituted in 1992, the Navy's commanders appear to have been effective, even to obtaining a disproportionate share of the PLA budget for the Navy. In fact, China's 2004 Defense White Paper stated baldly that budget increases were focused on enhancing "the development of [the PLA's] operational strength with priority given to the Navy, Air Force and Second Artillery Force."[60] Shi Yunsheng was the first in this chain and also can claim credit for initiating the continuing improvements in education and training; maintenance and fleet support; and, most important, the ability of the force to attain its strategic objectives.

China's Navy has evolved slowly since it was founded sixty years ago as the East China Force in reaction to the continuing KMT threat from Taiwan and other offshore islands. The PLAN soon evolved into today's geographically delineated fleets. The relative strengths of the North, East, and South sea fleets have not varied startlingly over time, and changes are discernible during various periods when Beijing identified national security threats from the United States, the Soviet Union, Taiwan, and the South China Sea. Heightened concerns about India would likely result in a similar shift in emphasis, with the South Sea Fleet receiving more modernized ships and aircraft, and expanded shore facilities as it gained stature in comparison to its eastern and northern sisters. In fact, the South Sea Fleet has provided most of the forces for the PLAN's deployments to the Gulf of Aden.

China's fleet organization is, however, marked by some interesting factors. First, the different fleets have also been assigned responsibility for specific platforms, such as submarines or amphibious ships, probably either for reasons of assigned missions or for ease of maintenance and operation. Second, although the relationship between the training department in the Beijing headquarters and those of the three fleets is not clear, indications are that the fleet departments feel free to modify doctrinal guidance from Beijing. This might enhance individual fleet training, but it raises questions about operational commonality among the three fleets. Third, concentrating all ships of a class in the same fleet simplifies maintenance, training, and support in general of that class, but it has the potential to reduce the usefulness of those ships if they have to be assigned to a different fleet. Again, the issue of fleet interoperability and standardization is not clear.

Currently, all three fleets appear to be receiving their share of new PLAN ships and aircraft. This is to be expected given the strategic priority of the Taiwan and South China Sea issues, as well as those of the East China Sea. Nevertheless, the presence of the very strong, modern Japanese Maritime Self-Defense Force means that China will be cautious about diverting too much strength from the North Sea Fleet. In the near term, the three fleets should remain balanced, with each deploying the surface, submarine, and aviation assets required to accomplish its tasking. Competition for resources between the fleets and within the fleets among the surface, submarine, and aviation branches will also continue, but so will firm national direction.[61]

The Navy's organization is determined to a significant extent by the threats to China's national security that the service is expected to counter, as well as by its ships and aircraft. The goal is maximum effectiveness of these units, inevitably modified by other factors, including geography, perceived threats, and domestic political considerations. PLAN organization will change, furthermore, as the Navy grows and modernizes—as new ships and aircraft are deployed.

CHAPTER 5

Ships and Aircraft of the PLAN

The PLAN has for the past two decades focused on modernizing its ships, submarines, and aircraft. This chapter surveys the Chinese Navy's progress from obsolete Soviet ships to near-state-of-the-art warships and evaluates PLAN platforms across the primary naval warfare areas.

Three types of naval warfare predominate. The first is antisurface warfare (ASUW), operations conducted to detect, localize, target, and attack surface ships. ASUW missions are typically carried out with radars, guns, missiles, or torpedoes, but may also be carried out by submarines, aircraft, or shore batteries.[1] Second is antisubmarine warfare (ASW), conducted by submarines, aircraft, and surface craft to detect, localize, target, and attack submarines. ASW is typically carried out with sonar, depth bombs, and torpedoes: tube- or air-launched, or assisted by rockets. The third primary warfare area is antiair warfare (AAW), conducted to detect, track, target, and attack manned aircraft and unmanned air vehicles. Radar, missiles, and guns are the usual means of conducting AAW. It is assigned to aircraft, surface vessels, and shore batteries.

Less prominent naval warfare areas include amphibious warfare (AMW), operations to move ground forces ashore, usually with small seaborne landing craft, air-cushion vehicles, helicopters, or vertical take-off and landing fixed-wing aircraft. Navies typically have marine corps for this mission, but the PLA also has Army divisions stationed in Fujian and Guangdong provinces dedicated to the amphibious mission. Within AMW are several subsidiary missions, ranging from a full multidivision assault against an opposed beach to small raids conducted by special operational forces. Mine warfare (MIW) utilizes sonar, unmanned underwater vehicles, divers, and trained mammals to install and remove mine fields. MIW is conducted by aircraft, surface ships, and submarines. Information warfare consists of information operations, operational security, psychological operations, deception, and electronic warfare (EW). EW in turn includes operations to utilize the electronic spectrum for detection and warning while denying an opponent the ability to do so.

From its inception in 1950, when it commissioned its first patrol boats, small combatants (frigates and corvettes), and submarines, China's Navy has depended on Soviet/Russian platforms and technology. This dependence continues to a much lesser degree, although in the early 2000s China acquired from Russia four *Sovremenny*-class guided-missile destroyers (DDG), twelve Kilo-class conventionally powered submarines (SS), and twenty-four Su-30MK2 aircraft for maritime interdiction. Less easy to assess is the engineering and technical assistance that Moscow is almost certainly continuing to provide to Beijing's naval modernization efforts, such as in the design and construction of the new nuclear-powered Type-093 attack (SSN) and Type-094 ballistic missile submarine (SSBN) classes that China is building.[2]

During the past twenty years the PLAN has added to its ranks approximately 38 conventionally and 5 nuclear-powered submarines—2 or 3 of them SSBNs; 15 DDGs; 16 guided-missile frigates (FFGs); more than 50 patrol craft capable of firing cruise missiles; at least 1 Yuzhao-class landing platforms dock (LPD); 24 landing ships tank (LSTs); and 2 replenishment-at-sea (RAS) ships. This has been a steady, moderate program of naval modernization, but it has accelerated since 2000, when all of the 4 nuclear-powered and 22 of the conventionally powered submarines have been commissioned, as have 10 DDGs and 6 FFGs, all of the 26 amphibious ships, and at least 40 (Houbei-class) missile patrol boats. In the first decade of this century, China has led the world in submarine construction, building almost three boats per year (Table 1).[3]

Except for submarines, China remains far behind the United States in terms of fleet modernization. By the end of 2010 the latter will have built 7 nuclear-powered submarines, 2 nuclear-powered aircraft carriers, 33 DDGs, 2 FFGs, 2 amphibious assault ships, 8 LPDs, and 9 RAS ships.[4]

Chinese naval analysts have recently emphasized the value of technological advances, including a shift from a "platform-centric to [a] network-centric . . . strategy based on the speed of command."[5] This follows the U.S. Navy doctrine that fleet operations are most effectively conducted not by individual ships acting on the basis of their own sensors; weapons; and communications, command, and control systems, but by groups of ships operating as members

Table 1. THE PLAN 1955

Ship Type	Number	Source
Light cruiser	1	ex-KMT *Huang* Ho
Destroyers	2	ex-Soviet *Gordy*
Frigates	12	ex-Japan/U.K.
Gunboats	16	ex-U.S./U.K./Japan
Minesweepers	2	ex-U.S.
Landing craft	4 LST/28 LSM	ex-U.S.
Supply ships	4	ex-U.S.

of a cooperative network. The ships, aircraft, and even shore stations will be linked by computers and will operate in a coherent network-centric environment, passing information back and forth and functioning as an integrated entity.

Until about 2005, however, the PLAN was still very much "platform-centric," almost wholly dependent on individual ship and aircraft operations with only rudimentary radio and data-link coordination. As the first decade of the new century comes to an end, China is deploying ships capable of operating in coherent naval task forces able to project power on the seas. These new platforms are the beginning of the first really modern navy that Beijing will deploy as an instrument to deter Taiwan, thwart U.S. intervention, and secure China's territorial claims in the East and South China seas, as well as other maritime missions characteristic of a global power (see Tables 2–7).

Air power is crucial to naval power, and Chinese officers have long expressed interest in acquiring aircraft carriers. Many reports of PLAN carrier construction were published during the final quarter of the last century; none were accurate, but President Jiang Zemin may have given the Navy permission to begin carrier design in the mid-1990s.[6] While Zhang Guangqin, a senior shipbuilding official, denied in June 2005 the report that China was building an aircraft carrier in Shanghai, in October 2006 a senior officer in the PLA

Table 2. THE PLAN 1960

Ship Type	Number	Source
Destroyers	4	ex-Soviet *Gordy*
Frigates	16	ex-Japan /U.K.
Gunboats	27	ex-U.S./U.K./Japan
Minesweepers	17	ex-U.S.
Submarines	26	Ex-Soviet W/S/M-V
Landing craft	12 LST/28 LSM	ex-U.S.
Supply ships	3	ex-U.S.

Table 3. THE PLAN 1970

Ship Type	Number	Source
Destroyers	4	ex-Soviet *Gordy*
Frigates	16	4 Jiangnan/4 ex-Soviet Riga 8 ex-Japanese
Missile boats	10	ex-Soviet Osa/Komar
Minesweepers	25	20 ex-Soviet/5 ex-U.S./U.K.
Submarines	35	ex-Soviet G/W/R/M-V
Amphibious craft	20 LST/29 LSM	ex-U.S.
Supply ships	8	ex-U.S.

Table 4. THE PLAN 1980

Ship Type	Number	Source
Destroyers	11	7 Luda/4 ex-Soviet *Gordy*
Frigates	16	5 Jianghu/2 Jiangdong/5 Jiangnan/ 4 ex-Soviet Riga
Missile boats	161	OSA/Komar (Soviet design)
Minesweepers	17	Soviet design T-43
Submarines		
SSN	2	Han
SSB	1	Golf (Soviet design)
SS	84	2 Ming/62 Romeo+20 Whiskey (Soviet design)
Amphibious vessels	43	
LST	15	ex-U.S.
LSM	21	2 Yuling; 19 ex-*U.S.*
Supply ships	~40	PRC-built/ex-*U.S.*

General Armament Department, Lieutenant-General Wang Zhiyuan, stated that "the Chinese army will study how to manufacture aircraft carriers so that we can develop our own.... [They] are indispensable if we want to protect our interests in the oceans." A similar statement was made six months later by a senior PLAN admiral, and then by China's defense minister, General Liang Guanglie, who reportedly stated in March 2009 that China intends to build aircraft carriers.[7]

China in 2010 does not have any aircraft carriers in commission or under negotiation for foreign purchase, although it has acquired four second-hand carriers in the past forty years, the first being the former HMAS *Melbourne*, purchased from Australia in the 1970s. The ship was eventually scrapped, but only after Chinese engineers had measured the hulk and learned what they could about carrier construction.

Table 5. THE PLAN 1990

Ship Type	Number	Source
Destroyers	14	14 Luda
Frigates	24	24 Jianghu
Missile boats	~160	Houku/Huangfeng (Soviet design)
Minesweepers	16	T-43
Submarines		
SSN	5	Han
FBM	1	Xia
SSB	1	Golf (test platform)
SS	~44	4 Ming/40 Romeo
Amphibious vessels		
LST	7	Yukan
LCU	31	Yuling
AP	6	Qiongsha (2 hospital ships)
Fleet auxiliaries	~24	
RAS-capable logistics	3	2 Fuqing/1 ex-Soviet *Nanyang*

Three ex-Soviet carriers, *Minsk, Kiev,* and *Varyag,* have also been purchased by Chinese companies, supposedly for conversion to casinos. *Minsk* and *Kiev* are decrepit hulks; as two of the Soviet Union's first carriers they were inactive for several years before being sold to Chinese interests.[8] *Varyag* is equipped with a "ski jump" bow to facilitate fixed-wing aircraft operations. Its construction began in a Ukrainian shipyard in 1985 and stopped in 1992, a year after the 1991 collapse of the Soviet Union. The ship lacked engines when acquired by China in 2003. The partially completed ship had by 2010 been under shipyard care in China for approximately eight years, apparently being prepared for active service, most likely as a training platform for PLAN pilots. Renamed *Shi Lang* in 2008, the carrier was moved to a new dry dock in mid-2009 and may be receiving engines to make it operational.[9]

Table 6. THE PLAN 2000

Ship Type	Number	Source
Destroyers	21	2 *Sovremenny*/1 Luhai/2 Luhu/16 Luda
Frigates	41	10 Jiangwei/31 Jianghu
Missile boats	~98	4 Houjian/24 Houxin/ 70 Houku/Huangfeng
Minesweepers	16	T-43
Submarines		
SSN	5	Han
FBM	1	Xia (not operational)
SSB	1	Golf
SS	~57	4 Kilo/1 Song/ 21 Ming/~31 Romeo
Amphibious Vessels		
LST	12	5 Yuting/7 Yukan
LCU	31	Yuling
AP	6	Qiongsha (2 as hospital ships)
Fleet auxiliaries		
RAS-capable logistics		

Statements by senior Chinese military leaders, the work being performed on *Shi Lang*, and Beijing's negotiations to procure carrier-compatible aircraft, the Su-33, from Russia all indicate that the PLAN will almost certainly deploy at least one large, air-capable ship within the decade.[10] There also is some evidence that the PLAN has conducted training in simulated carrier operations for pilots and relatively senior officers.[11] Press reports about a PLAN carrier usually describe a 40,000–50,000-ton ship, perhaps similar to the French-built *Charles de Gaulle*.[12]

While China almost certainly continues to receive technical advice from Russian naval architects and engineers experienced in aircraft carrier design and construction, the ships will be constructed in China for reasons of control and national pride. Further, none of the non-American shipyards with experience

Table 7. THE PLAN 2010

Ship Type	Number	Source
Aircraft Carriers	1	*Shi Lang* (ex-*Varyag*)
Destroyers	26	4 *Sovremenny*/2 Luzhou/ 4 Luyang/1 Luhai/ 2 Luhu/13 Luda
Frigates	51	8 Jiangkai/14 Jiangwei/29 Jianghu
Missile boats	~79	~50 Houbei/5 Houjian/24 Houxin
Minesweepers	20	16 T43/4 Wosao
Submarines		
SSN	~5–6	3–4 Han/2 Shang
FBM	~5	1 Xia/~4 Jin
SS	~51	3–4 Yuan/12 Kilo/14 Song/21 Ming
Amphibious vessels		
LPD	1	*Kunlunshan*
LST	26	19 Yuting/7 Yukan
LCU	31	Yuling
AP	4	Qiongsha
AH	1	*Peace Ark*
Fleet auxiliaries	~19	Various
RAS-capable logistics	5	2 Fuchi/2 Fuqing/ 1 ex-Soviet *Nanyang*

constructing large (more than 50,000 tons displacement) aircraft carriers—
the Chenormorsky facility in Ukraine and Russian yards in Severodvinsk and
Saint Petersburg have engaged in carrier construction since 1992.

The PLAN has been able increasingly to rely on China's indigenous shipbuilding industry. Older Chinese-built combatants were based almost entirely
on Soviet designs. The Luda-class DDG, for example, was a 1960s copy of the

Soviet 1940s Kotlin-class destroyer. The newer 1990s Luhu-class DDG is a modernized version of the Luda, and the even newer Luhai is simply a larger Luhu.

Before 2000, only the three Song-class submarines, nine Jiangwei-class FFGs, twenty-five Houxin- and Hojian-class missile patrol boats, and two Fuqing-class RAS ships were indigenously designed and constructed—and even these relied heavily on foreign designs, engineering, weapons, and sensor systems. China's own Navy Weapons Assessment Research Center reported in 1990 that it had "gathered and translated" more than five million words "from foreign naval materials" since its establishment in 1983 and had written "sixty-six investigative reports on foreign vessels."[13]

A similar dependence on foreign designs previously marked the PLAN's submarine fleet; the single Xia-class fleet SSBN, a copy of the Soviet Yankee class, conducted a successful missile-firing exercise in 1988 but was never a successful operating unit.[14] The Song class is the first all-Chinese boat, although it apparently incorporates German-designed diesel engines and French hull construction and sonar technology.[15] The conventionally powered Type-39A (Yuan) submarine, which may be the first Chinese boat to include air-independent propulsion (AIP), bears some exterior resemblance to the Soviet-designed Kilo class but nonetheless demonstrates China's ability to build state-of-the-art conventionally powered submarines.[16]

The same advances in the design and construction of Chinese submarines are reflected in the PLAN's newest surface combatants. Since 2003 the Navy has acquired three new classes of DDGs: the Luzhou, Luyang I, and Luyang II. The Navy is also acquiring the Jiangkai- and Jiangkai II–class FFGs, which, while significantly less capable than the DDGs, exhibit the most "stealthy" characteristics of any PLAN ship. These FFGs bear a striking resemblance to the French-designed La Fayette–class ships deployed by Taiwan. These ships were likely designed to operate primarily in littoral waters, but they have been apparently performing very well during extended operations in the Gulf of Aden. The new FFGs appear to incorporate towed sonar arrays, which would significantly increase their ASW capability.[17]

A particularly interesting addition to the PLAN's surface force is the Type-022 (Houbei) missile craft. These ships feature a wave-piercing catamaran hull that provides an unusually seaworthy platform for cruise missiles. That this hull form was copied from a commercial vessel purchased from Australia does not detract from China's accomplishment in producing dozens of a relatively inexpensive combatant that might prove very threatening to much larger naval vessels.

A similar pattern pertains to the PLAN's amphibious force, which although not expanding its troop-carrying capability significantly during the past decade—approximately one mechanized division—has been significantly modernized.[18] The new LSTs and LPDs appear to be straightforward copies of Soviet LSTs and the U.S. *San Antonio*–class LPD, respectively.

Few ships are more important to increasing the power-projection capability of a fleet than those capable of replenishment at sea. China has added just two RAS ships, the Fuchi class, since 2000. These are the first PLAN support ships capable of simultaneously providing destroyers and frigates with fuel, provisions, and ordnance.

In sum, in addition to significant aircraft modernization, fleet acquisitions since 2000 reflect the dramatic increase in Chinese shipbuilding capability during the past two decades, especially in the technologically challenging field of submarine construction.[19]

THE PLAN IN 2010

The Navy entered the twenty-first century with ambitious plans. Foreign purchases and Chinese-built ships are adding to its size, and modern technology is adding to its efficiency.

Submarines

The PLAN by 2000 had signaled its intention to deploy a large force of modern submarines as its featured platform. It already maintained a large if mostly old submarine force, but modernization was well under way. The bulk of its undersea force was composed of thirty to forty improved versions of the 1950s Soviet-designed Romeo-class submarine. These boats have only rudimentary ASW capability and have seldom been seen at sea since the 1990s, possibly because of a lack of trained crews; their number was down to eight in 2009, and the entire class should be inactive by the end of 2010.[20]

China built nineteen Ming-class submarines, an improved Romeo design; most are based in the North Sea Fleet. The PLAN then improved on this class, adding the Song-class conventionally powered submarine to its force; thirteen of these boats were in commission in 2009. China underwent an interesting "learning curve" with this class; the first two boats suffered from design flaws so serious that they were essentially rebuilt and the basic design changed in significant ways. These are nevertheless capable submarines with design features incorporated from the Kilo class, and they are capable of submerged launch of C-801A antiship cruise missiles (ASCMs).[21]

Twelve Russian-built Kilo-class submarines have been acquired since the late 1990s. Two of them are the "export" model, but the other ten are the quieter and more capable design produced for the Russian Navy. The later versions acquired by the PLAN are much more capable than the original ships of this class. They are heavily armed with torpedoes or mines—up to eighteen of one or the other—and the final eight acquired can fire the Russian SS-N-27B Klub-s supersonic antiship cruise missiles while submerged.

These and other submarines require proper maintenance and well-trained crews to operate to full capability, and the PLAN has experienced shortfalls in these areas. Maintenance for the Kilos appears to be a problem. Crew training has not gone well. Serious problems with the propulsion batteries developed but may have been overcome; the previous need for the submarines to return to Russia for all but routine maintenance has apparently eased. That the PLAN has been slow to improve its maintenance practices is reflected in the report that a modern maintenance management system apparently was begun only in 2008.[22]

The PLAN has been focusing on the Song class as its primary conventionally powered submarine, but at least five or six Yuan-class boats had been launched by 2009. The Yuans were first thought to incorporate an AIP module but may lack the necessary hull capacity for this innovation. With or without AIP, they represent China's attempt to apply construction lessons learned from the Kilos acquired from Russia as a model for future submarine developments.[23]

AIP has long promised to revolutionize conventional submarine capabilities by extending maximum submerged operating time from the Kilo's four days to at least fourteen days. AIP systems fall into two broad categories: fuel-burning heat engines, which reuse a combination of oxygen and the products of engine combustion, and electrochemical engines, which transform chemical energy into electrical power by using hydrogen and oxygen.[24]

A notable feature of China's new submarine construction programs has been expanded use of nuclear propulsion. One former PLAN commander claimed that "the development of nuclear-powered submarines is the chief objective of this century." The PLAN has two active building programs to replace its six old nuclear-powered submarines, the Xia-class SSBN and five Han-class SSNs.[25] These vessels were built in China with Soviet design influence but have not been entirely successful. The Xia has seldom been seen at sea, while the Hans—probably just three are operational—are relatively noisy and have suffered frequent engineering problems.[26]

China's new class of SSNs, designated the Type-093 (Shang class), and a new SSBN, designated the Type-094 (Jin class), almost certainly rely on Russian design and engineering assistance provided by St. Petersburg's Rubin Central Design Bureau. Two of the Shangs had been launched by the end of 2008, following an unusually lengthy construction process; additional submarines of this class are not known to be under construction, indicating that China is building a follow-on class of SSNs.[27] At least three Jins were in commission in 2010, but full operating readiness reportedly is pending resolution of reactor problems and final development of the boat's main battery, the JL-2 ICBM. Twelve of these missiles are estimated to form the main battery of the new SSBNs. Their missile service-entry date is given by the U.S. Department of Defense as 2010; they have a range of approximately 4,000 nm.[28]

These multiple building programs attest to the very significant changes in the composition of China's submarine force during the past two decades. Furthermore, the PLAN is improving its submarine weaponry. Wire-guided and wake-homing torpedoes purchased from Russia provide very capable weapons that are difficult for surface ships to counter. Beijing has also reportedly purchased Soviet-designed rocket-propelled torpedoes from Ukraine that take advantage of supercavitation to reach speeds unprecedented for underwater bodies.[29]

Surface Combatants

The most numerous and largest ships in China's Navy are its surface combatants, described as the "vital" or "main" PLAN component. As recently as 2001 a senior Chinese naval officer described even the newest warships as only "on a par with foreign warships of the 1980s."[30] The PLAN in 2010, however, is deploying ships that are suitable for twenty-first-century multimission task groups.

The direct acquisition of Soviet combatants in the 1950s and an indigenous shipbuilding industry capable of producing copies of Soviet models in the 1960s and 1970s represented the first era of PLAN growth. The second was marked by acquisition of the *Sovremenny* class from Russia and construction of the Luhu and Luhai classes. China moved into its most significant period of naval surface ship modernization after the turn of the twenty-first century with indigenous construction of three new classes of DDGs. China has initiated several active surface combatant acquisition programs since the mid-1990s. While one notable program brought Soviet-designed *Sovremenny*-class DDGs to the PLAN, all other classes were indigenously designed and produced, albeit with significant reliance on Russian and other Western technology and systems.

The four *Sovremennys* arrived between 1999 and 2006; all are assigned to the East Sea Fleet. Probably purchased for $420 million each, the *Sovremennys* are capable warships designed by the Soviet Union in the early 1970s for surface warfare.[31] Their primary armament is the formidable Moskit (or Sunburn) ASCM, specifically designed to attack U.S. aircraft carriers and their escorting Aegis cruisers. Each *Sovremenny* carries eight Moskits, with no reload capability while the ship is at sea. The Moskit has a range in excess of 87 nm and carries a large 661-pound conventional warhead. The missile's lethality results for the most part from its speed and flight profile: following launch to a probable altitude of several hundred feet, the missile quickly descends to "sea-skimming" altitude—below 66 feet above the surface. As it closes the target, the Moskit accelerates to a speed as high as 2.5 Mach. This final part of the flight profile is complicated by the missile's ability to conduct radical evasive maneuvers, possibly "a series of sharp S-shaped maneuvers, with overload as much as 15 Gs," to complicate the fire-control solution for the target's defensive systems.[32] Forty-eight Moskits had been delivered to China by 2001.[33]

The *Sovremenny* is also capable of firing the Moskit's successor, the Yakhont, which has almost twice the range—162 nm—but a smaller warhead (441 pounds).[34] Beijing has apparently not purchased the Yakhont for the *Sovremennys*, possibly preferring to invest the cost in air- or submarine-launched versions of this potent weapon.

The *Sovremenny*'s capabilities in other warfare areas are much less formidable. Its only AAW missile system fires the SA-N-7 "Gadfly." Although superior to any previous PLAN AAW system, this is essentially a "point defense" system, since its maximum range of 13.5–15 nm is too short to allow significant area air-defense coverage. Four 30-mm rapid-fire guns provide even shorter-range air defense.[35] The *Sovremenny*'s ASW capability is equally unimpressive, incorporating a medium-frequency, hull-mounted active sonar and a weapons suite composed of torpedoes and mortars. The ship's most significant ASW system is its Ka-28 helicopter, which is equipped with surface search radar, dipping sonar, and other submarine detection systems, and is armed with torpedoes; this aircraft may also serve as a source of over-the-horizon targeting (OTH). The ship is capable of embarking just one of these aircraft, and China has acquired only four of the ASW versions of this helicopter. Aircraft utility is severely limited by the ship's lack of a helicopter hangar and attendant maintenance facilities.[36]

These weaknesses in AAW and ASW do not detract from the *Sovremenny*'s potent ability to attack surface ships but do highlight the fact that it was not designed by the Soviet Union to operate alone. *Sovremenny*s were intended to serve as one element in a multimission task force; the PLAN will have to orchestrate wartime operations very carefully to prevent the *Sovremenny*s' quick destruction by aircraft or submarines.

China's first DDG was the Luda-class ship, which joined the fleet in 1971. No more than twelve of these ships remain in commission, and the class is being retired. Some Ludas have served as test platforms for new combat systems, including helicopter flight decks and hangars. The class was severely restricted in war-fighting capability, lacking adequate electrical-generating systems, sufficient air conditioning, an AAW missile system, and combat information centers (CICs) to coordinate war-fighting efforts. The Ludas also had the typically limited PLAN ASW suite: medium- or high-frequency hull-mounted sonar; Soviet-designed mortars/depth charges; and (in this case, Italian-designed) torpedoes. This detail is noteworthy because most PLAN warships continue, forty years later, to follow this model of limited AAW and ASW capability.

However, the Ludas also set the continuing standard of relying on ASCMs as PLAN warships' main armament, in their case armed with the Hai Ying–2 (HY-2) system with a range of 51 nm. Even this old missile system still—in 2010—poses a significant danger to the most modern combatant.

The PLAN took a significant step forward in the mid-1990s with the Luhu-class DDG. Only two of these ships were built, but they were China's first gas turbine–powered warships. Although the Luhu represents only incremental advances over the Luda across the spectrum of naval warfare capabilities, it is China's first warship designed from the keel up with a CIC and true multimission warfare capability—the hallmark of a post–World War II combatant.

The two ships of this class, *Harbin* and *Qingdao*, are equipped with many foreign-designed systems: the gas turbine engines and super-rapid-blooming off-board chaff (SRBOC) dispensers were purchased from the United States; the Crotale AAW missile system, Tavitac combat integration system, and Zhi-9A helicopters are French designs; the four automatic 30-mm Gatling guns of the close-in weapons systems (CIWS) offering short-range air defense appear to be Dutch in design; the ships' ASW torpedoes are Italian; and the

ASW mortars and 130-mm guns are Soviet-designed systems.[37] The ships' main battery is the 22-nm-range C-801 surface-to-surface missile (SSM); a logically designed combat direction center enhances the Luhu's combat effectiveness. ASW capability remains poor, based on a hull-mounted, medium-frequency sonar.

The small size of the Luhu class may be due in part to China's having acquired only five LM-2500 marine gas-turbine engines from the United States, but it also represents the PLAN's standard ship construction paradigm of building a succession of classes, each with one to four ships, to more rapidly incorporate advances in foreign system purchases and increases in indigenous construction capabilities. Hence, the Luhus, each equipped with two of the LM-2500s, were succeeded by the Luhai-class DDG in 1999, powered by gas turbine engines acquired from Ukraine.

The single ship of the Luhai class, named *Shenzhen,* is significantly larger than the Luhus, displacing 7,940 tons to their 4,200, but with the same dependence on foreign-designed/produced systems. *Shenzhen* is armed with the C-802 SSM, similar to the C-801 carried by the Luhu but with a greater range (66 nm). AAW defense is similar to the Luhus'—the Crotale AAW missile system and Gatling guns—as is the ASW suite: medium-frequency sonar, torpedoes, mortars, and the capability to embark two Ka-28 helicopters.

Shenzhen's larger size may have been dictated primarily by the need to install Ukrainian-built gas turbine engines, which are larger than the Luhus' LM-2500s, but the additional volume offered valuable room and stability for modernization with improved weapons and sensor systems. This process apparently has not occurred; rather than updating *Shenzhen's* systems, the PLAN has continued its practice of installing newly acquired or produced systems on new ship classes. Hence, *Shenzhen* remains a one-ship class of combatant, which complicates its maintenance and supply support.

China's new DDG classes began with the Luzhou class, or Type-51C, sometimes referred to as the Luhai II class. The first ship in this class is *Shenyang* (DDG 115), launched in 2003 and commissioned in 2004. The second class member is *Shijiazhuang* (DDG 116), also launched in 2003 but commissioned in 2005. These ships probably use a combined-diesel-or-gas-turbine (CODOG) propulsion plant, with French-designed diesel engines for cruising and Ukraine-built gas turbines for higher speeds, although steam propulsion is also possible.

The ship's formidable AAW system is built around the Russian SA-N-20 Rif-M missile, the naval version of the S-300. Acquired by China in 2002, this twenty-year-old missile system remains formidable, with an 81-nm range and top speed of Mach 6. *Shenyang* and *Shijiazhuang* are equipped with six eight-cell, revolving vertical launching systems (VLS), two aft of the gun mount forward of the superstructure, and four aft, just forward of the ship's flight deck. The ships have a capacity of forty-eight missiles but probably carry a normal load of forty-one or forty-two, because typically one cell in each launcher is left empty for maintenance and at least one test missile is carried. Furthermore, VLS launchers are not designed to be reloaded at sea. Both ships have been assigned to the North Sea Fleet.

The Luzhous are also armed and equipped to participate in ASUW and ASW mission areas. Most potent are the eight indigenous C-602 SSMs with which the class is armed. This missile relies on active radar homing, approaches its target in sea-skimming mode at a speed of Mach 0.9, and carries a conventional 364-pound warhead. The ship's other ASUW weapon is a French-designed, single-barrel 100-mm gun that fires up to 90 rounds per minute in fully automatic mode. The Luzhou is also armed with two Gatling guns designed as a last-ditch (maximum range of 3 km) defense against incoming aircraft and missiles.

The Luzhou class exhibits the typically limited PLAN ASW capability, depending on a medium-frequency, active/passive sonar and torpedo tubes. Its primary ASW weapon should be the helicopter it is capable of embarking, but the lack of a hangar limits this aircraft's operations. For operations in a modern electromagnetic environment, the ship is equipped with chaff/decoy launchers and has active ECM capability.[38]

Joining the fleet contemporarily with the Type-51C are the two Luyang ship classes, the Type-52B and Type-52C, displacing approximately the same 7,000 tons as the 51C (compared with the *Sovremenny*'s 8,000 tons). The Luyangs' engineering plants are similar to the 51C's. The 52B seems designed to focus on the ASUW mission, although also equipped with short-range AAW capabilities. The two ships of this class, *Guangzhou* and *Wuhan*, were both commissioned in 2004 and are assigned to the South Sea Fleet. They appear to be the Chinese version of the Soviet *Sovremenny*-class DDGs, intended as a multimission naval task group's primary ASUW platform. Their main battery is the same box-launched C-803 SSM found on the 51C, but they carry sixteen missiles instead of eight. The 51B is also armed with a relatively short-range AAW missile, the Russian SA-N-12 (Grizzly), a subsonic, semiactive-radar-guided weapon with a maximum range of less than 20 nm.

The Luyang I can be armed with forty-eight SA-N-12s fired from Russian-designed missile launchers, but the normal load is probably forty-four to allow for maintenance and test missiles. Again, these missiles cannot readily be replenished at sea. These ships also carry the same single 100-mm gun and two CIWS gun mounts as the 51C. They are no more formidable as ASW platforms, although they are armed with Russian-designed multibarrel ASW mortars, as are most PLAN combatants (but not, apparently, the 51Cs), and are equipped with hangars for the helicopters they operate from their stern flight deck. They may also be equipped with towed sonar arrays.

The two Type-52C DDGs, *Lanzhou* and *Haikou* (hull numbers 170 and 171), appear to be built on the same hull as the 52B and equipped with the same propulsion plant, guns, ASW, and ECM capabilities. However, their primary mission is AAW; the ships' most notable topside feature is an Aegis-like phased-array radar system. This class can operate two helicopters rather than the one of the 51C and 52B. This increased capability is likely due more to a technologically advanced CIC than simply to a larger hangar.

The Type-52C is armed with the Hai Hongqi (HHQ-9) AAW missile system using forty-eight fixed VLS cells—thirty-six forward and twelve aft of the ship's superstructure. This missile system began in the early 1980s as an attempt to emulate the U.S. Patriot system. Its further development has included borrowed Russian technology, but it is a Chinese design, although installed only on the two ships of the Luyang II class. It has a range of 54 nm, flies at Mach 3, and relies on semiactive radar homing. The Type-52C also has a very capable ASUW suite composed of eight C-602 SSMs in two cylinder-shaped launchers amidships. Each of these subsonic, semiactive-radar-homing missiles features both inertial and GPS-assisted guidance systems and has an impressive 151-nm range. Both Luyang and Luzhou classes feature the Russian MR331 Mineral-ME (NATO designation Band Stand) fire-control radar. This impressive system provides targeting for the antiship missile and for the main gun. It may be capable of OTH targeting, and also has been installed on Jiangkai II frigates.

Two significant features in these new ship classes evidence China's limited ability to build modern warships. First, they still depend on foreign designs in almost all areas, from propulsion plants to the mast-top sensors and embarked aircraft. The PLAN's apparent inability to procure indigenously designed and produced gas turbine engines is especially curious. An important question relates to the fact that all six of the vessels in these three new combatant classes, especially the Type-52C, depend on command and control facilities significantly in advance of their predecessors. The Luhu- and Luhai-class warships depend on a version of the French Tavitac system to monitor and control their sensors and weapons; the newer classes no doubt possess a more capable CIC to coordinate and integrate their longer-range systems.

Second, command and control information management remains problematical, although "link" systems allow coordinated operations both among ships and between the ship and its embarked helicopter. However, it does seem clear that the PLAN, even in its newest ships, has yet to demonstrate the command and control capability necessary successfully to conduct net-centric operations in a twenty-first-century maritime battlespace.[39]

The fact that both Type-51Cs are assigned to the North Sea Fleet, the Type-52Bs to the East Sea Fleet, and the Type-52Cs to the South Sea Fleet indicates that Beijing has chosen to increase its war-fighting capabilities across the entire force rather than concentrating its newest ships in a single fleet, presumably to be used against a single, specific mission objective, such as Taiwan.

Beijing's future combatant construction plans are uncertain. It is not clear if the PLAN has settled on one or more of these three new combatant designs as harbinger(s) of large classes, or whether the service will continue with its traditional practice of building new ship classes from the keel up to incorporate the incremental advances in propulsion and weapon-systems technology that are characteristic of advances in maritime warfare capabilities. Whether these three classes—51C, 52B, 52C—are class-setters or evolutionary units, they signal the PLAN's "arrival" on the seas of twenty-first-century naval warfare.

Frigates are smaller versions of destroyers, usually designed for more limited missions and perhaps for operations at lesser ranges from homeport. The PLAN's newest frigates are the Jiangkai I– and Jiangkai II–class FFGs, which augment the Jiangwei class, of which two or three subclasses were built. The first Jiangwei was commissioned in 1991; eight more have since joined the fleet. At 2,250 tons displacement, this ship is a capable escort, although much smaller than China's 7,000-ton destroyers. The Jiangwei I subclass is armed with the C-801/2 SSM and Hongqi-61 (HQ-61) AAW system. This latter missile is a Chinese-built point-defense weapon with a 7.5-nm range, apparently reverse-engineered from the Crotale system. The Jiangwei II subclass differs in substituting the Crotale for the HQ-61—apparently because the indigenous copy proved unsatisfactory. Additional air defense is provided by Gatling guns and SRBOC launchers.[40]

The Jiangweis are powered by German-designed diesel engines and have the typical PLAN ASW suite—a hull-mounted medium-frequency sonar and ASW mortars—but lack torpedoes. They embark a single French-designed Z-9A helicopter and have well-ordered combat direction centers equipped with the Tavitac combat integration system.

The Jiangwei class represented a significant step forward from the older Jianghu-class frigates. Twenty-eight Jianghus were commissioned between the mid-1970s and 1996. They are diesel-powered and armed with four HY-2 SSMs for surface warfare, but have neither AAW missiles nor Gatling guns. Their ASW suite is limited to a hull-mounted, medium-frequency sonar, mortars, and depth charges. These ships lack torpedoes and helicopters, except for *Siping*, which was converted as a test ship for a flight deck for a Z-9A helicopter, Italian-built ASW torpedo tubes, and two Gatling gun installations.[41]

The Jianghu's numerous portholes indicate a lack of air conditioning, which would adversely affect the performance of onboard electronic equipment during operations in tropical or subtropical waters. The ship's most serious shortcoming, however, is the lack of a CIC in most units of the class. A warship lacking this most basic element of system integration—installed in U.S. ships during World War II—is essentially unable to operate in a modern naval environment. A few of these frigates have been converted to coast guard missions.

The PLAN's origin as a coastal defense force and early Soviet influence included reliance on relatively small warships, usually displacing less than 1,000 tons. In the mid-1960s China began building and deploying larger frigates (the Jianghu class) and destroyers (the Luda class), both armed with SSMs and both multimission-capable to a degree. Currently, the PLAN includes more than one hundred small gun- and torpedo-armed patrol boats of various types. Between fourteen and thirty Chinese versions (Houku class) of the old Soviet-designed Osa/Komar-class patrol boats firing SSMs with a 25- or 45-nm range are also maintained, but these boats are likely in reserve and have been replaced by more capable Chinese-built missile boats. Among these are eight Huangfeng-class, twenty-two Houxin-class, and seven Houjian-class boats. All these classes are armed with 25-nm C-201 or C-801 SSMs. They are coastal craft, with the Houjians homeported in Hong Kong but capable of operating in the South China Sea and the waters around Taiwan in calm to moderate weather.

Much more formidable is China's newest class of small combatant, the Houbei-class catamarans, which the PLAN began building in 2004; at least forty were in commission or under construction in 2009. They are small, displacing just 250 tons, but remarkably seaworthy because of their wave-piercing hulls, apparently copied from an Australian design. This warship's development is an example of the difficulty of controlling undesirable exports to the PLA in an era of increasing dual-use technology. The AMD

Marine Consulting Company of Sydney reportedly formed a joint venture in Guangzhou, Sea Bus International, to design and build commercial craft; their basic hull design was then copied by the PLAN in the Houbei class.[42]

China may acquire as many as one hundred of these boats to replace the numerous classes of older patrol craft, most of which are obsolete. The Houbeis are each armed with eight C-803 SSMs. If the Houbeis are equipped with a data link capability, they present the PLAN with a new capability to deploy anti–surface ship barriers in littoral waters that would essentially be immune from submarine attack and that would, given the craft's small size, high speed (45 knots), and potential numbers, offer a difficult target to attacking aircraft.

Mines are the most cost-effective means of naval warfare, especially in littoral waters; hence, it is not surprising that China, with its self-proclaimed defensive maritime strategy, has made a large investment in mining capability. It is surprising that the PLAN has not made a concomitant investment in the mine-hunting and -clearing mission. The PLAN maintains only one dedicated minelayer, although almost any naval surface ship—as well as most merchantmen and fishing trawlers—can deploy mines if the appropriate equipment is installed and requisite training conducted. China also has a small, old mine-clearing force, based on forty Soviet-designed T-43 oceangoing and four coastal minesweepers (twenty-six of the former in reserve, as are forty-six remote-operated minesweepers).

Only in 2004 did China commission a new minesweeper design, the Type-821 *Houqiu*. This ship uses the nonmagnetic glass-reinforced plastic (GRP) construction technology first employed by several European navies in the late 1970s and long common among other forces, including the U.S. Navy. It apparently remains a one-ship class.[43]

The PLAN's inventory may include as many as 100,000 mines, but the majority are probably older models.[44] Despite its apparent lack of resources dedicated to modernizing its minesweeping force, China is devoting significant attention to acquiring the most modern and lethal maritime mines. This probably reflects Beijing's focus on employing maritime mines to defend against potential U.S. submarine operations in Chinese littoral waters. The Soviet Union employed mines in this fashion, primarily as a means of defending the safe havens ("bastions") within which they operated their ballistic missile submarines during the latter part of the Cold War.[45] Should China indeed utilize its expanded naval base at Sanya, on Hainan Island, as the sole homeport for its new Jin-class SSBNs, it might indicate that, first, Beijing had adopted a bastion strategy for its maritime strategic deterrent force, and, second, would likely be utilizing extensive defensive minefields to defend its bastion, presumably in the northern South China Sea or the Bo Sea.

The PLAN earned its first laurels engaging the Taiwanese Navy among the islands of China's coastal waters in the early 1950s, actions that centered on launching or repelling amphibious operations. Despite this experience, the PLAN during the past sixty years has not constructed a large amphibious force. Since 2000, its shipbuilding program has been directed at modernizing the amphibious force, but not at significantly expanding its capacity: the PLAN is still limited to transporting approximately one mechanized division of fully equipped troops.[46]

China has built more than twenty new LST and smaller LSM (landing ship mechanized) ship classes since 2000, all capable of landing troops and equipment directly on a beach, over a bow ramp, and all equipped with a flight deck. This is a minimally aviation-capable feature, since all of these ships lack hangars or aviation maintenance facilities. The new amphibious force includes several classes, headed by the twenty Yuting I– and Yuting II–class LSTs, displacing 4,800 tons and capable of embarking 250–300 troops and ten to twelve tanks; they also have small well decks for the interior docking and loading of landing craft but are slow (14-knot) ships powered by French diesels currently manufactured in China.[47]

The Yutings supplement the seven ships of the older Yukan-class LSTs. These 4,100-ton, 14-knot ships can embark 200 troops and ten tanks; they entered service between 1980 and 1995. The PLAN's newest LSMs are the ten ships of the Yunshu class, 1,850-ton vessels capable of carrying six tanks at 14 knots, all commissioned in 2004—one of the rare cases of China mass-producing a single ship class nearly simultaneously.

Ten more landing craft, categorized as landing craft, utility (LCU), were built at about the same time (2003); the Yubei-class craft displace 1,200 tons and can carry twelve tanks. In addition to these thirty-seven relatively new, large amphibious ships, the PLAN operates hundreds of smaller landing craft designed to carry troops ashore from larger transports operating offshore.

The most impressive surface ship built by the PLAN to date is another amphibious ship, similar in design, size, and apparent capability to a U.S. *San Antonio*–class LPD. This *Yuzhao*-class (Type-071) vessel, *Kunlunshan*, displaces approximately 18,000 tons and has both a very large well deck capable of holding four air-cushion landing craft (ACV) and a flight deck capable of handling two large helicopters, as well as a hangar. *Kunlunshan* is powered by the combined-diesel-and-diesel system of twin diesel engines driving a single shaft that increases engineering plant reliability. Although relatively lightly armed, with just a single 76-mm gun and four 30-mm CIWS, it is by far the most impressive air-capable warship that China has developed. Perhaps as important as its combat potential, however, is the ship's ability to conduct military operations other than war; as China looks beyond a Taiwan scenario, *Kunlunshan* offers a platform for humanitarian operations similar to the 2004 post-tsunami and other relief efforts that the United States has been able to conduct throughout the Asia-Pacific region.

The PLAN includes numerous supply and support ships, but only five of them are capable of underway replenishment at sea. Each of the three fleets is assigned one or two of these small ships, which are quite old. One of the two Fuqing-class oilers is assigned to the North Sea Fleet; the second is assigned to the East Sea Fleet. These thirty-year-old ships were indigenously built, displace 21,740 tons fully loaded, and are equipped with four modern liquid-transfer stations—two to port and two to starboard—and a flight deck. Their lack of a hangar means they are unable to embark a helicopter for an extended period. The Fuqings can each transfer no more than 11,000 tons of fuel and very little cargo.

The South Sea Fleet deploys the larger, Russian-built oiler, the *Nancang*; this 37,000-ton displacement ship has four liquid and two solid-stores transfer stations and a small hangar in addition to a flight deck. *Nancang* can provide approximately 20,000 tons of fuel and 3,000 tons of cargo.[48] The ship began construction in the Soviet Union in 1989, was completed at Dalian, and joined the PLAN in 1996. It is propelled by a diesel engine power plant, as are the two Fuqing-class oilers.

An indication that China is contemplating deploying a PLAN capable of extended operations is the decision early in the current decade to build additional underway replenishment ships. Two Fuchi-class oilers joined the fleet in 2005, one each to the East Sea and South Sea fleets. These are relatively small, displacing 22,000 tons and able to provide just 10,400 tons of fuel. The Fuchis do have both flight deck and hangar, and so are able to embark a helicopter full time.[49]

Thus, China has been slow to increase its Navy's ability to remain at sea for extended periods. Only two of the PLAN's five oilers are less than twenty years old, and only one (*Nancang*) is capable of providing more than a single major fueling to a task group composed of four or more ships. This indicates that at least the logistic focus of maritime thought in Beijing remains on Taiwan and other regional situations such as the East and South China seas.

The PLAN also includes five much smaller cargo ships (4,300–8,800 tons displacement), and several dozen small tankers, many of them in the merchant fleet but apparently available for Navy tasking. The latter displace from 530 to 2,300 tons; while neither designed nor equipped for underway replenishment, they could serve in a crisis as refueling platforms for operating ships, either by refueling at anchor or by being equipped for the relatively undemanding process of stern refueling, as opposed to the more challenging alongside refueling procedure.

The Navy deploys several other auxiliaries, including twelve submarine support ships and a small repair ship (converted from an old U.S.-built LST), as well as two dozen oceangoing tugboats. Troop transports include four Qiongsha-class ships, each capable of embarking four hundred troops and all stationed in the South Sea Fleet. A notable recent addition to the PLAN's auxiliary forces is China's first dedicated hospital ship, the Type-920 named *Peace Ark*, commissioned in 2008. This 23,000-ton ship appears to have been constructed on a Fuchi-class oiler hull; it has a flight deck and large helicopter hangar.[50]

Beijing continues to deploy a robust fleet of survey and research ships, led by two 25,000-ton Yuanwang-class "space event" ships commissioned in 2007 and 2008; these augmented four 18,000-ton ships that entered service between 1979 and 1999 to support China's space program.[51] An additional fifty or so ships serve multiple purposes, from exploring the ocean floor to intelligence gathering. The most modern are the two flight-deck-equipped Wuhu-class surveillance ships launched in 1997. Some of these research vessels are operated for the Academy of Sciences; approximately two dozen others are assigned to the Ministry of Communications or the Hydrographic Department. Additionally, a large number of fishing trawlers may be used for offshore surveillance as part of the Maritime Militia, but their ability to operate with the PLAN in terms of personnel training and augmentation requirements, command and control capability, and armaments is not clear.

Ballistic Missiles

The Navy's role in China's national nuclear deterrent force was limited to its single Xia-class SSBN, with its twelve Julang-1 (JL-1) intermediate-range ballistic missiles, until well into the first decade of this century. The JL-1, a solid-fuel, nuclear-warhead missile with a range of 1,900 km, took sixteen years to develop and deploy. The Xia has never served as an operational fleet unit.

More formidable by far is the new Jin-class (Type-094) SSBN China began constructing in the early 2000s. Two of these boats have been launched and possibly underwent sea trials in 2008, with three others under construction. The Jins are armed with the JL-2 ICBM.[52] This new class of submarines, with its new missiles, will provide China for the first time with a viable sea-based nuclear deterrent. As noted earlier, Beijing seems to be opting for a bastion (safe-haven) rather than a patrolling operating strategy for this leg of its deterrent force. That leg is much more secure but also much more expensive than the land-based DF-31/31A missiles, which are road-mobile, solid-fuel weapons.

Naval Aviation

The PLAN's own "air force," Naval Aviation, is one of the world's largest naval air arms, consisting of approximately twenty-seven regiments, each with twenty-four to twenty-five aircraft. Total Naval Aviation strength is uncertain but numbers approximately eight hundred aircraft spread among the three operating fleets.[53] Since it was formed in 1952, Naval Aviation has been a "poor cousin" to the PLAAF when it comes to acquiring new aircraft.

Naval Aviation began flying Su-30s acquired from Russia in 2004, for instance, after the PLAAF had already been flying them for three years. The naval air force still relies on several hundred F-6, F-7, and F-8 fighter-bombers as front-line tactical aircraft, in addition to its twenty-four Su-30s.[54] Naval Aviation missions nominally include fleet air defense, at-sea reconnaissance and patrol, ASW, electronic countermeasures, transport, mine-laying, rescue, and vertical assault. The PLAN's surveillance aircraft include four SH-5 amphibians and four maritime versions of the Soviet-designed Y-8 (AN-12) transport, which are capable of rudimentary ASW operations. The naval air force also flies approximately twenty B-6 (Soviet-designed Tu-16) aircraft capable of launching ASCMs.

The most serious aviation shortfalls are in effective fixed-wing ASW aircraft, tankers, and airborne warning and control aircraft (AWACS). Naval Aviation did not conduct its first air-refueling mission until 2000.[55] The PLAAF has been acquiring AWACS, but at a slow rate. Perhaps because of cost and mission assignment, the PLAAF retains priority for receiving and training in these capabilities.

Another important modernization issue is selecting a long-range strike aircraft to replace the B-6, although the latter will probably not be completely phased out for several years. In fact, approximately twenty of these airframes have been converted to carry the very capable C-801 ASCM. Naval Aviation may view the Su-30 as the B-6's successor, although it also flies the JH-7B, a strike aircraft that was under development for more than a decade and can carry two to four C-801 ASCMs.[56]

Helicopters (helos) are the most important element within the Navy's aviation arm. The Navy's first helos were twelve French-built Super Frelon AS321s delivered in 1977–78. France agreed to Chinese production of these helos as the Z-8, intended primarily for ASW, but it was not until 1994 that China had created the infrastructure to begin manufacturing these aircraft. As many as fifty-four have joined the fleet; they are able to operate from almost all PLAN auxiliary and combatant surface ships with flight decks not equipped with the recovery system installed on the newest ships; on those, the Z-8 may conduct only hover operations. Some of these aircraft are equipped with dipping sonars and remain the PLAN's premier ASW helicopter.

Other helicopters in the PLAN inventory are also copies of French or Russian designs. The Eurocopter AS.565 Dauphin is built in China as the Z-9 with a primary mission of ASW; the 2010 inventory exceeds thirty airframes. Acquisition of the four *Sovremenny*-class DDGs from Russia in the late 1990s was accompanied by the purchase of eight Ka-28 helos, four of them specifically equipped for ASW. As many as thirty-four of these very capable multi-mission aircraft may be in operation by the end of 2010.[57]

The Z-9 is the PLAN's most ubiquitous helo and is capable of operating from all flight-deck-equipped ships. The latest models are equipped with dipping sonars and may also serve as a data link between missile-firing warships and the C-802 SSM when attacking OTH targets.[58]

China has acquired the French SAMAHE landing and traversing system for its two Luhu- and some of its Jiangwei-class combatants; a similar system appears in pictures of the Jiangkai-class FFGs and may also be installed on the newer Type-52B and Type-52C classes. Without such a system, shipboard helo operations are significantly restricted by weather and by the weight of the helo.[59]

China's most formidable naval weapon systems are its ASCMs—air, surface, and subsurface launched. Table 8 summarizes the ASCMs currently in use. China's indigenous cruise-missile development program dates back to the late 1950s, before which the PLAN had been operating SS-N-2 Styx SSMs provided by the Soviet Union. Later purchases of French-built Exocets provided an additional model for Chinese designers. Long-range—more than 100 nm—ASCMs have been developed and are deployed on submarines.

Despite a degree of continued dependence on foreign-origin systems, China has developed the capability of designing and manufacturing cruise missiles with close to state-of-the-art features, including supersonic speed, complex maneuvers, and submerged-submarine-launch capability.

The PLAN's short- to medium-range SSMs include the Shangyou-1A (SY-1A), a version of the Soviet-built Styx, with a range of 51 nm. This missile has been widely exported and will remain in service as long as do Luda destroyers, Jianghu frigates, and older missile patrol boats. Its successors, the C-801 and C-802, have ranges of 22 and 65 nm, respectively, and are similar to Exocet models. They are in service on later Jianghu and Luda models, on Jiangwei frigates, Luhu and Luhai destroyers, and newer (Houjian- and Houxin-class) missile patrol boats. At least three of the Han-class submarines may have been modified to launch either the C-801 or C-802 while submerged.

The most formidable maritime ASCM is the Russian-made SS-N-22 Sunburn (carried by China's four Russian-made *Sovremenny*-class destroyers) and the SS-N-27 Sizzler (carried by eight of China's twelve Russian-made Kilo-class submarines). French technology has also provided the PLAN with SSMs of the Exocet family, some of which have been reverse engineered; one is the C-801 series, the most advanced of which arm the PLAN's newest surface combatants. These provide China's indigenously constructed submarines of the Song and possibly the Yuan and Shang classes with SSMs that can be launched from a submerged platform. China's fixed-wing naval aircraft are all shore based, and those designed for attack—the A-5, FB-7, Su-30, and B-6—are all capable of launching cruise missiles against surface ships.[60]

Additionally, China has developed land-attack cruise missiles that can be fired from land bases, land-based aircraft, or submarines to attack shore targets, including air and naval bases. The most capable of these is the Dong Hai 10, reportedly capable of carrying a 1,100-pound warhead over a range of 810 nm, with an accuracy of a 33-foot circle error probable (CEP).[61]

China's most formidable maritime missile, the shore-based antiship ballistic missile, probably is not directly controlled by the PLAN. This addition to China's arsenal, which may be operational within a few years, requires significant technical advances to allow Second Artillery crews to target ships maneuvering at sea, specifically, the ability to redirect a ballistic missile or provide terminal homing, perhaps on a continuing basis, after it has reentered the atmosphere.[62]

Table 8. CHINESE ANTISHIP CRUISE MISSILES

Designation	Range	Mach	Warhead	Altitude	Guidance	Remarks
C-101 (HY-3)	50 km	2.0	400 kg	300 m	Active radar	On older ships
C-201 (HY-2)	70 km	.9	513 kg	30–100 m	Active radar	Soviet Styx
C-202 (HY-4)	135 km	.85		70–200 m	Active radar	Silkworm; air-launched
C-301	100/200 km	2.0	510 kg	100–300 m cruise/ 7–50 m homing	Active radar	Coast defense
C-601/C-611	25–100 km/ 220 km	.9	510 kg	30–100 m	Active radar	Air-launched
C-602	50–280 km	.7	300 kg	30 m cruise/ 8–10 m homing	Active radar	Ship- or coast-launched
C-701	15 km	.8	30 kg	50 m cruise 5 terminal	Television	Air-launched
C-801 (YJ-1)/ YJ-8	45 km	.9	165 kg	255 m	Active radar	"Chinese Exocet": surface-, air-, submarine-launched versions
C-802 (YJ-82)	15–120 km	.9	165 kg	20–30 m cruise 5–7 terminal	Active radar	Coast-launch version available
SS-N-22	160 km	2.5	300 kg	20 m	Active radar	Complex terminal maneuvers

CONCLUSION

The Chinese Navy in 2000 was a modernizing force, but one still severely limited in several warfare areas. Its submarine force was the exception, although composed mostly of old boats. But that situation has now changed. In fact, the PLAN in 2010 is developing into a maritime force of twenty-first-century credibility in all warfare areas—even if marginal in AAW, ASW, and force integration.

The surface combatant force has also made major strides in the past decade, now mustering its first area-AAW defense destroyers and more capable ASW ships. China is still apparently following its pattern of building successive classes of ships, each numbering in the high single digits; the next destroyer class is reportedly well into the design process and will represent a significant increase in size, perhaps displacing more than 10,000 tons, which will match the size of the U.S. *Arleigh Burke*-class destroyers.[63]

The numbers of state-of-the-art ships, submarines, and aircraft it fields do not yet give the PLAN the ability to dominate East or South Asian waters, certainly when measured against the U.S. Navy or even the Japanese Maritime Self-Defense Force or the Indian Navy. However, measuring total naval forces against one another is not particularly useful in strategic operational terms; what is more meaningful is a Clausewitzian measure: how much (and, we might add, how effective a) naval force China can deploy against a given objective at a time of Beijing's choosing. Whether this mission concerns Taiwan or an East or South China Sea objective, it seems fairly certain that China will be able to seize the initiative when employing its new Navy.

CHAPTER 6

Personnel, Education, Training, and Exercises

Discussion of PLAN modernization typically focuses on hardware—new ships, submarines, missiles, and airplanes. That technological emphasis is understandable, but it too often overlooks the key factor in naval effectiveness: the people who maintain and operate the hardware. China's Navy in 2010 includes approximately 290,000 personnel. This equates to 12.6 percent of China's total military personnel, including the Marine Corps but not including the People's Armed Police, reserve forces, and militia.[1] The size and capabilities of the "maritime militia" are difficult to ascertain, especially in view of Beijing's recent, probably successful campaign to rationalize the organization of the country's various coast guard–type organizations into a national Coast Guard. This chapter addresses the human factor in the Chinese Navy. The PLAN remains an overwhelmingly male-dominated organization, although women play a role in shore administration and training billets.

Addressing the Central Military Commission (CMC) in 1999, President Jiang Zemin stated, "We must [develop] high-quality talented military people." Beijing emphasized its concern with military training in China's 2008 Defense White Paper, which prioritizes the creation of "a scientific system for military training in conditions of informationization" as part of "attaching more importance to Military Operations Other Than War (MOOTW) training in counter-terrorism, stability maintenance, emergency response, peacekeeping, emergency rescue and disaster relief."[2]

The Chinese Navy has followed this directive during the past decade of modernization. Advances in personnel education and training, accompanied by advanced individual and unit exercising, were especially spurred by the loss of the crew of the Ming 361 submarine in 2003. The deaths of the seventy personnel onboard were almost certainly due to inadequate training, with shoddy equipment maintenance apparently contributing to the tragedy.[3]

One result of the accident was a major leadership turnover in the PLAN, including the dismissal of the service's commander and political commissar; the commander and political commissar of the North Sea Fleet, of which Ming 361 was a unit; and at least eight other senior officers, including the commander of the Lushun Naval Base, who were apparently held responsible for the maintenance work performed on the submarine shortly before its loss. Of note is that the succeeding PLAN commander, Vice Admiral Zhang Dingfa, was a career submarine officer. Zhang's appointment suggests both CMC dissatisfaction with accepted Navy practices under the command of Admiral Shi Yunsheng, an aviator who had served for almost seven years as PLAN commander, and concern about ensuring the capability of China's submarine force to serve as a primary military instrument in the event of a security confrontation with the United States over Taiwan's status. It is also significant that in 2004 Zhang was selected as a member of the CMC, the first PLAN commander so appointed.[4]

An assessment of current PLAN education, training, and exercise practices indicates that the Navy's leadership has implemented extensive "lessons learned" from the Ming 361 accident and other incidents that have occurred during post-1980s operations. One step involved realigning the operational and maintenance responsibilities of the Navy's shore establishment. Discussions with senior PLAN officers indicate that these changes, while not always welcomed by shipboard officers, have regularized, centralized, and probably improved Navy-wide maintenance, supply, and training paradigms.[5]

PLA study of U.S. military operations since 1990 has influenced a thorough revision of Chinese training objectives and methods. In 1996 Prime Minister Li Peng stated that China must strengthen "the Army through technology, enhance research in defense-related science [and develop] arms needed for defense under high-tech conditions." Success in this policy—amounting to the transformation of China's military-industrial complex—was noted in 2003, when the director of the General Arms Department (GAD), General Li Jinai, described "marked improvement in national defense scientific research and in building of weapons and equipment," adding that "the past five years has been the best period of development" in China's history.[6] Revised training regulations issued in 2002 replaced the 1990 version; the new regulations emphasize standardized training relying on science and technology to prepare for "modern warfare."

The PLAN plans its training and exercise year from the Outline of Military Training and Evaluation (OMTE) issued by the PLA General Staff Department's (GSD) Military Training and Service Arms Department in Beijing. According to the PLAN Dictionary, the OMTE provides guidance for use by each branch and vessel class in the Navy, ranging from "Units for Each Class of Naval Submarine and Surface Vessel" to shore-based "Chemical Defense Units and Elements." The outline delineates procedures for drafting training plans, organization, and assessment.

The current OMTE, which went into effect in January 2009, emphasizes that training must be "scientific," and focuses on developing operational proficiency at the tactical level, on combined arms tactics, and individual and unit training before addressing joint training.[7] MOOTW are prominently featured, an element of direct concern to the Navy in view of China's relative inability in the past to respond to foreign disasters such as the 2006 tsunami that struck Southeast Asia.

It also directs the PLA to follow standardized training practices accompanied by a four-tier examination and appraisal system. GSD direction for PLA training emphasizes training in a "complicated electromagnetic environment," with six specific objectives:

1. Emphasize fundamentals to "all-roundly and strictly train troops in line with the new OMTE." The ability to command and think strategically by "the leading bodies should be intensified," as should the study of operations and "use of new equipment" with an emphasis on maximizing "the combat effectiveness of new equipment."

2. Train (scientifically) in compulsory subjects including "planning . . . and exercise on joint commanding, and research in MOOTW."

3. Joint training and the "comprehensive integration" of operational units and the "systematic operation capability of the PLA under information-based conditions."

4. Continue to reform "military base training, simulated training and online training," with a focus both on training in a "complicated electromagnetic environment" and "trans-regional" training.

5. Increase the reform of academy education with emphasis on the "cultivation of commanders for joint operations [in a] complicated electromagnetic environment and [for] MOOTW."

6. Increase training support, with a focus on the "construction of information-based training conditions," in an "information-centric" and "complicated electromagnetic environment."

This OMTE represents more continuity than change from the previous training plan, which also emphasized training under "informatized conditions" and a "complex electromagnetic environment." That plan's eight objectives also included the regularization and accurate assessment of training; realistic training in specific operational and tactical tasks, including "various kinds of security threats" and "diverse military tasks"; "basic and integrated training" to include new equipment operation and maintenance; command and staff training, including MOOTW; joint training; prevalence of OMTE training objectives in civilian officer candidate education programs; and increased training support.[8]

China's 2008 Defense White Paper also addresses the "strategic project for talented people," highlighting the "training of commanding officers for joint operations and high-level technical experts." It was followed in April 2008 by the CMC's "Opinions on Strengthening and Improving the Officers' Training Work of the Armed Forces." Interestingly, this directive addressed linking "institutional education" with operational training.

The consistent emphasis on preparing to operate under conditions of information warfare, including a "complicated electromagnetic environment," and the focus on joint warfare evince what the PLA believes are vital lessons learned from its observations of recent U.S. operations and a conviction that the United States is the opponent it is most likely to face in the near future. These concepts are sometimes included under a general training rubric, such as the 2009 report of officers of all three PLA services "drilling on joint operations . . . under informatized conditions."[9]

PLAN MANNING LEVELS

The PLAN was organized in 1950 with an initial strength of 450,000 personnel but soon began declining in size. By 1995 PLAN forces numbered approximately 270,000, about 9 percent of overall PLA strength. This number fell to 225,000 in 2001 following completion of the 500,000-person reduction in PLA manning announced by Jiang Zemin in 1997. The increase in personnel since then, to approximately 290,000, reflects the Navy's increased platforms and modernization. Probably one-half of this number is assigned to the operating forces.[10] Of the other half, Naval Aviation numbers 26,000 personnel and the Marine Corps, 12,000. The remaining 107,000 men and women include unknown numbers assigned to coastal defense units ashore, as well as to various schools and staff positions ashore.

A reduction of 700,000 personnel from the Army (reportedly not from the Navy or Air Force) was rumored in September 2009, as was a possible reduction in the number of China's seven military regions. In combination, this would indicate that most of the personnel reduction would come from the Army's officer corps, especially among those assigned to the regional and district headquarters that would be abolished.[11]

The PLAN's manning challenge is not numbers but the education and intellectual capability required of its personnel. Today's technologically intense naval systems require recruits with sufficient education and potential to learn how to maintain and operate complex engineering, sensor, and weapons systems. Despite fluctuations in overall naval strength during the past quarter-century, the PLAN has benefited from its personnel's increasing educational background and intellectual capability. Efforts have also been made to create a professional corps of noncommissioned officers (NCOs) with both leadership skills and the technical know-how to play the central role in the PLAN personnel system. The demand for skilled personnel has been exacerbated by inconsistent assignment policies in the PLAN. Although naval personnel tend to remain in the same fleet and even in the same homeport for long periods, there are no set terms for sea duty or shore duty. Assignments apparently are made based almost entirely on service needs. Even officers' tour lengths are not standardized; although most ship commanding officers are in command for three to four years, some tours have lasted seven years.[12]

If just 107,000 personnel are responsible for manning and supporting about two hundred significant surface ships and submarines, China has a personnel-to-ship ratio of roughly 535, about the same as the naval forces of Korea (525), Taiwan (480), and, Japan (470), and not much more than the U.S. Pacific Fleet's 430, indicating that the PLAN is utilizing its manpower efficiently.[13]

The Marine Corps is one arm of the PLAN that has not been down-sized. It consists of two augmented brigades of approximately 12,000 total personnel, one of which was converted from an Army division in the late 1990s. Interestingly, Marine Corps officers are drawn from the PLAN and are able to move back and forth between naval and marine units during their term of service.[14]

The PLAN recognizes that the evolution of Chinese military philosophy from Mao Zedong's original concept of manpower-intensive "people's war" to "revolution in military affairs" warfare has not reduced the importance of the human element in deploying combat-capable forces. Increased personnel expertise, in conjunction with technologically advanced systems, is described in the importance of "the organic integration of man and weaponry."

President Jiang Zemin stated in 2002 that "command and control is moving towards automation and is using C4ISR systems to integrate the weapons systems, combat platforms, and support equipment of the various services on the battlefield into an organic whole [on] land, sea, air, space, and the electromagnetic spectrum." President Hu Jintao expanded on this theme in 2009 on the eighty-second anniversary of the founding of the PLA, focusing on the necessity of civilian-military "integration" and "coordination" when he emphasized the direct relationship between economic prosperity and a strong military.[15] A recent PLA article notes that "human factors will be of primary importance" in a strong China. Jiang Zemin likewise argued that "manpower is a decisive factor in determining the outcome of war." His successor, Hu Jintao, has placed even greater emphasis on the centrality of personnel performance in military effectiveness as part of the Scientific Development concept.[16]

RECRUITING

The Navy faces tough competition attracting both officer and enlisted recruits because the best-qualified young high school and college graduates have attractive opportunities in the private sector.[17] The PLAN has been trying to reduce the percentage of recruits in its force from more than 80 percent to 65 percent. Pay has also increased steadily during the past decade, with as much as a 100 percent increase for some ranks in 1999–2000 and a further large (as much as 50 percent) increase in 2009.[18]

China's military conscription system targets males eighteen to twenty years old and females seventeen to nineteen years old. All male enlistees must have completed at least junior school; females must be high school graduates. Women college graduates may be twenty-four years old—and reportedly are judged on "their eloquence, artistic skills, and even their appearance."[19] Males up to the age of twenty-two may enlist if they have a college education.

The annual conscription process begins in August when the GSD conducts a two-day conference to determine the number of conscripts required. Navy requirements originate in the fleets, which report the number of required conscripts to PLAN headquarters. The figures are compiled at headquarters and sent to the GSD. The local People's Armed Forces departments (PAFDs), which establish liaison directly with local governments, then contact all draft-age males to register for military service.

Conscripts are supposed to be inducted equally from across China's population, but in practice two-thirds of conscripts reportedly come from rural areas. Individuals specifically exempted from registration include those who have been admitted to college, are medically or physically unfit, have been imprisoned, or face criminal charges. Bribery reportedly is not uncommon, both by unqualified youths who want to enlist and, more commonly, by those avoiding conscription. Following registration, the PAFD begins preselecting potential conscripts until it receives conscription numbers from the GSD, which also delineates conscription procedures. The PAFDs then instruct potential conscripts to report to a local induction center for physical, political, and psychological examinations.

The PLA apparently does not administer preinduction written examinations such as the U.S. Armed Forces Vocational Aptitude Battery to evaluate a conscript's qualification for specific military specialties. As PAFDs are composed primarily of personnel from the ground forces, recruitment teams from the PLAN are sent to selected regions to handpick their conscripts. For instance, a particular naval unit would be assigned to a specific area and would send two or three junior officers as a "selecting team" to that locality.

Although the PLA provides stipends for conscripts and their families, these are minimal allowances that are not attractive to individuals from more affluent areas of the country. Therefore, despite the recent emphasis on technology and education, the core of the enlisted force continues to be made up of young men from poor rural areas. Although four of the annual conscription orders issued from 2001 to 2005 note that conscripts recruited from rural areas should be high school graduates, most rural conscripts are intermediate school graduates with low degrees of technical proficiency.[20]

Enlistments have also been shortened from three years (for the Army) and four years (for the Navy and Air Force) to two years for all services as part of the 1999 overhaul of the enlisted rank structure codified in the Military Service Law of the People's Republic. The PLAN, however, still requires a three- or four-year obligation if the recruit is going to attend a technical training course before or immediately after reporting to his or her first operational unit. This policy illustrates the Navy's need for extensive technical training for many of its recruits.[21]

PLAN "boot camp" lasts approximately twelve weeks and focuses on physical training and basic military orientation. Recruits then either move on to their first duty assignment or receive further training. Enlisted training and education typically occur aboard the first operational unit or are conducted by a naval base command within one of the three geographic fleets. Each fleet command has a training directorate with responsibilities that likely include training standardization and prioritization. "Floating schools" exist in such specialties as engineering, medical, surface warfare, aviation, and submarine warfare. There is apparently no formal coordinating body among the three fleet training directorates, other than the chain of command from one fleet up to PLAN headquarters in Beijing and then back down to another fleet.

The PLAN does not have U.S.-style "type commanders"—admirals with large staffs dedicated to ensuring that ships and aircraft of a particular class or type are maintained and their personnel trained to meet Navy-wide standards of operational excellence. Each of the three geographic fleets apparently bears this responsibility.[22]

OFFICER ACCESSION

PLAN officers are assigned to one of five career tracks: military (line), culminating in operational command; political; logistics; equipment; or technical. The officer corps is managed by the General Political Department's (GPD) Cadre Department, which oversees all PLA officer promotion, assignment, and retirement issues. This organization has branches at the fleet, flotilla, squadron, base, and garrison levels. The PLAN's Political Department includes a Cadre Department that is responsible for all PLAN officer personnel issues.[23]

Currently, the PLAN finds new officers from one of three sources: high school students entering military academies, enlisted personnel applying to those academies, or civilian college students. Addressing the CMC in 1999, Jiang Zemin stated that China "must place education at academies and universities in a strategic position among our development priorities," and that "our goal [is] giving priority to developing military academies and universities."[24] This theme has continued under Hu Jintao, who succeeded Jiang in 2004 as CMC chairman. Hu delivered an important speech at the 2006 PLA training conference urging the acceleration of "innovation and reform in military training" to make it comprehensive, noting that "vigorously and satisfactorily conducting military training is beneficial for advancing comprehensive army building."[25]

The traditional source of new PLAN officers is its nine naval academies. They are headlined by the Naval Command Academy in Nanjing and the Wuhan-based Naval Engineering University. In 2004 the former Guangzhou surface ship department head school was reorganized to serve as the Naval Service Arms Command Academy with a program aimed at training inter-mediate-level command personnel in all the PLAN's branches.

Possibly in recognition of the problematic quality of the academies' educa-tion, the PLAN in the late 1990s began offering commissions to civilian university graduates "to cultivate more high-caliber officers for the Navy." More permanent steps were codified in the 2000 Decision on Establishing a Military Cadre Cultivation System Relying on General High-Level Education, and in the realignment of professional military education (PME) institutions described in China's 2004 Defense White Paper.[26]

The PLA's long-expressed desire to emulate U.S. Reserve Officer Training Corps (ROTC) programs to produce well-educated, technically oriented candidate officers has been implemented as the National Defense Student program, most prominently through agreements between MR headquarters and civilian universities by which the university receives compensation for producing military officer candidates.[27] The Guangzhou MR, for example, has an agreement with Wuhan University under which students who are selected by the PLA receive military training during summer and winter vacation periods in return for National Defense Program scholarships. The program is open to qualified undergraduate and graduate students who sign an agreement to join the PLA after graduation. In addition to their classroom work these students undergo limited military training, including some at-sea time for those destined for PLAN commissions. While the financial help provided is reportedly similar to that offered to U.S. ROTC students, the Chinese partici-pants do not wear uniforms on campus.

The program was expanded in late 2009 by a decision to extend to students at private colleges the opportunity to enter the PLA directly, with the govern-ment repaying approximately US$2,000 of the entrant's college costs. This innovation reportedly has been very popular—so popular, in fact, that either the statistics are inflated or the military is an unexpectedly fashionable recourse for students.[28]

Officer accession programs were redefined in October 2007 when the CMC issued the Regulations of the Chinese People's Liberation Army on the Admission Work of Educational Institutions, which govern the admission of high school graduates and enlisted personnel into military academies. Then, in

December 2007, the Ministry of Education and the PLA's GPD convened a conference on civilian university students destined for commissions. At that time, 117 colleges and universities hosted National Defense Program students. In addition, almost one thousand key middle schools across China had been selected as potential sources for these students.

The Navy is pursuing especially ambitious ROTC-type programs by establishing "science and technology cooperative ties" with more than one hundred colleges in twenty provinces and municipalities.[29] The focus of these civilian-sourced programs is clearly on increasing the number of naval officers with technical qualifications. A senior PLA officer confirmed that the "Chinese Navy plans to recruit about 1,000 officers from non-military universities and colleges yearly . . . in an effort to meet its need for command and technical talent," and predicted that these officers "will account for 60 percent of all naval officers by the year 2010."[30]

Two programs are currently in operation. The National Defense Scholarship program recruits students still in high school or in their first year of college. They receive financial support and undergo some military indoctrination prior to graduation. This program produced 600 officers in 2006 and is expected to produce more than 1,200 in 2010. The second program recruits civilian university seniors just before graduation.[31] The system of commissioning enlisted personnel has also been regularized so that "outstanding compulsory servicemen" are vetted for "political and ideological firmness, professional and technological competence, a high cultural standard, and a fine physical and mental quality."[32]

PLA and PAP military academies in total have sought as many as fifteen thousand entrants annually from graduating high school seniors, with the Navy giving priority to "outstanding student cadres" willing to volunteer for submarine service.[33] Applicants are required to take the nationally administered Unified College Entrance Examination, usually in late June. The military academies (and other "special schools") have first choice of the successful applicants, before the other universities select; student preferences are of secondary consideration. New cadets are admitted on a provincial basis, almost always to the service academy in or nearest to their native province.[34]

PERSONNEL RETENTION

The PLAN has difficulty retaining highly trained enlisted and officer personnel because China's rapidly growing economy offers attractive alternatives to sea duty and military discipline, particularly for the highly trained technicians the PLAN most wants to retain. At the end of the first enlistment, a sailor may reenlist for an additional three-year tour, followed by a succession of two four-year obligations, a five-year reenlistment, and finally a nine-year obligation. Total service is limited to thirty years or the age of fifty-five. To reenlist, the individual must (1) be devoted to the national defense cause; (2) be competent for the job; (3) possess a desired skill; (4) be a lower-secondary or higher school graduate; and (5) be physically healthy. In most cases the reenlistment volunteer remains and receives additional training at his or her original unit.

Prior to recent efforts to professionalize the NCO corps, the great majority of sailors left the Navy after fourteen to eighteen years, depriving the service of a mature, experienced body of senior NCOs. PLAN officers recognized this problem, and training reforms instituted in the late 1990s included the development of technically competent NCOs who are also effective leaders. This goal has continued to receive priority, with the latest reform plan announced by the CMC in July 2009. This plan aims to increase the NCO corps PLA-wide to approximately 900,000 personnel, with a new rank structure consisting of seven instead of the previous six steps, from corporal to master sergeant class one. The emphasis will be on training NCOs in technical specialties, with increased pay rates authorized.[35]

The 2008 Defense White Paper delineates a major PLA program for increasing personnel retention based on cash awards to individuals and to teams "which have made great contributions in scientific and technological innovation." Since 2007, RMB700 million (approximately $102.5 million) has been allotted to this program. Guidance for the awards is provided in the Provisions of the Armed Forces on Attracting and Retaining High-Level Specialized Technical Personnel issued by the CMC in July 2007, which describes measures to "attract and retain particularly leading scientists, first-rate personnel in specific disciplines and technical experts."[36]

Uniformed civilian employees form an important element of PLAN personnel and are included in the Navy's total active-duty numbers. They perform technical and specialist functions, mostly in schools, hospitals, and administrative centers, and may comprise as much as 25 percent of total PLAN active-duty strength.[37]

REGULATIONS AND STRUCTURE

The PLAN's rank structure is similar to that of other navies, except that the senior officer who heads the Navy usually begins his tour as only a vice admiral (two-star rank in the PLAN); typically he is promoted to the rank of full admiral (three stars) while in the billet. There is only one other flag rank active in 2010, that of rear admiral (one star). Other officer ranks are senior captain, captain, commander, lieutenant commander, lieutenant, lieutenant (junior grade), and ensign.

Enlisted draftee ranks run from seaman 2nd class to seaman 1st class after one year of satisfactory duty. Volunteer enlisted personnel, including draftees who reenlist after their initial tour of service, are ranked as petty officers grades 1–6. Petty officers grades 1 and 2 are "junior petty officers"; those in grades 3 and 4 are "intermediate petty officers"; and those who occupy grades 5, 6, and 7 are "senior petty officers." Promotion through the enlisted ranks is based on professional qualifications, time in service, and political reliability.[38]

This rank structure was overhauled in the 1999 reform of thirteen PLA regulations on military service. A particular target of the restructuring was the NCO corps, which was deemed "too narrow and . . . too small," especially in comparison with the "armed forces of some developed countries, a situation which is not conducive to winning local wars under conditions of modern technology." The new NCO corps continues to focus on promoting technicians but also promotes administrative, training, and operational specialists as well as some small-unit leadership positions.

The PLAN has continued to emphasize regularization of its procedures, a process reflecting an emphasis on "legal warfare" and formalization of civil-military relations in China begun in 1988 when the CMC set up a legal office and directed the services and regional commands to do the same. The Law of the People's Republic of China on National Defense issued in 1997 specifies that the CMC is responsible for enacting military regulations; this was followed in 2000 by the Law of the People's Republic of China on Legislation, which further defines the legislative authority of the CMC, services, and area commands. The National People's Congress had issued fifteen laws and related decisions on national defense by October 2008; additionally, the military command system, from State Council and CMC to service and area commands, had formulated more than three thousand military rules and regulations. Of particular relevance to the Navy is the program in which the crews of ships making foreign port calls study the United Nations Convention on the Law of the Sea (UNCLOS) and other applicable international regulations. Finally, in November 2007 Beijing established the National Committee for International Humanitarian Law for the purpose of enhancing the PLA's knowledge and capabilities to conduct international humanitarian operations, an assignment most pertinent to the Navy.[39]

Professional Military Education

The 1950 plan for organizing the Navy included schools to address command, submarines, fast boats, gunnery, aviation, joint service, political cadre, logistics, mechanical engineering, and naval engineering. The PLAN's school structure passed through four broad phases during the ensuing sixty years.

The first period lasted from 1950 to about 1960, when Moscow's influence was at its peak and the PLAN's curricula were based on the Soviet model. Curricula included the study of service regulations, ordinances, and rules; damage control; biological-chemical warfare defense; shipbuilding techniques; reconnaissance; navigation; gunnery; communications; electronics and counterelectronics; radar; and mechanical engineering.[40] A second, ill-defined period ensued in the late 1950s and early 1960s, during which the PLAN leadership tried to absorb the lessons of the Korean War, the advent of nuclear technology, and the unsettled leadership situation that surrounded the Peng Dehuai affair. The third period, marked by the Great Cultural Proletarian Revolution (GCPR), was as disastrous for naval professional education as it was for the PLA in general. The fourth period began after Deng Xiaoping returned to power in the late 1970s. Deng instituted significant reforms, which included reorganization and consolidation of the PLA education system. He stated in 1975 that "peacetime education and training should be considered a matter of strategic importance."[41] The founding of the National Defense University in Beijing in 1985 heralded the professionalization of military education in China.

The PLA initiated further major changes in the organization and curricula of its education system in 1998. These were undertaken by the CMC in the belief that "warfare is changing from a traditional mechanical war to an informatized one," and that the "key in competing for strategic initiatives in the new century [is] the establishment of a new military educational system." This passage is evidence of apparent PLA belief in and understanding of an ongoing revolution in military affairs (RMA): war by machine is being superseded by war conducted on the basis of controlling information. The CMC criticized the military academies for dispersing resources in too many colleges operating on too small a scale, as well as for their low training standards and unprofitability.[42]

Senior leaders also continue to address the importance of political reliability. Jiang Zemin's 1999 remarks about the importance of the PLA's academies emphasized selecting academy leaders "who are strong in politics and good at education." He also urged adequate funding for the academies "at the same pace as the increase in defense expenditures" and ensuring that teaching facilities and equipment "are ready to provide academies with new weapons and technical accoutrements."[43]

In April 2000 the CMC issued the Essentials for Reform and Development of Military Universities and Schools, which aims to define military education for the twenty-first century.[44] The plan applies to both military schools and civilian universities participating in officer candidate programs. The "essentials" specify three types of programs: undergraduate degree programs for officer trainees, continuing education in engineering for serving officers, and "reading-for-degree" and postgraduate courses, also for active-duty officers. Changes in military education have aimed at streamlining curricula and focusing them on the sciences and technology, consolidating schools, trying to ensure the applicability of the military educational system to current and future operational requirements, and emphasizing the ideological content of coursework. In a 2000 address at the NDU, for instance, General Zhang Wannian, the PLA's commander, repeatedly emphasized that the school "must consistently put ideological and political building in first place" and remain loyal to the CCP. Hu Jintao emphasized this point as the first of his "Four Historic Missions" in 2004.[45]

Jiang Zemin's speech to the fourteenth meeting of the PLA's Institutes of Higher Learning in 1999 summarized the direction that education of PLA forces was to take: "We must ... prove our armed forces' defense ability to cope with hi-tech local war. ... We should give priority to ideological and political buildup in all military work ... to ensure that [cadets] are really politically qualified. ... Military academies should ... boldly proceed with scientific and technological innovations; play a bigger role in ... promoting the transformation of scientific and technological achievements into combat forces; and actively provide knowledge, technology, and information service for armed forces' units and institutions." Jiang often stressed the importance of ideological education, as does his successor, Hu Jintao, and as do PLA leaders. The PLAN chief of staff, Admiral Su Shiliang, for example, stressed the importance of "ideology first ... to guarantee the party's absolute leadership" for the Navy.[46]

The educational reform program of 2000 remains a significant measure in the PLA's effort to modernize its educational system. The CMC stipulated in the reform measure that "evident improvement should be registered" by 2010, with an overall goal of having at least ten military academies "reach or approach the advanced national level"; some of the ten are expected "to reach or approach the advanced international level."[47]

Professional military education in China is formalized, well established, and required for officer promotions. The CMC stated as long ago as 1978 that "those who have not received training in military academies cannot be promoted."[48] Military schools teach professional subjects ranging from engineering and technical topics to international relations, but China's leaders believe that the proper ideological spirit is most important. Jiang Zemin has described this as the "two armings—arming the military with ideology and theory, and with high science and technology."[49] This continued twin emphasis on ideological reliability and technical competence illustrates the difficulty faced by a modernizing Leninist military.

The Navy has participated in the general overhaul of PLA service academies during the past decade. PLAN officer academies have been reduced in number and their curricula revised, demonstrating the Navy's participation in the PLA-wide campaign to ensure that academy education contributes to "strengthening the military through science and technology" and to supporting the CCP.[50] The Navy has four academies and an estimated annual throughput of five thousand sailors, marines, and officers. It also recruits about one thousand college graduates from prestigious civilian universities each year.[51] The first academy was established at Dalian in 1949 to train surface warfare officers; a second academy for this branch was opened in 1979 at Guangzhou.[52] Other PLAN academies are located at Qingdao for prospective submariners, and at Huludao for future naval aviators; the Naval Technical Aviation School was established in Qingdao in 1950. Naval engineering students may attend the Aviation Engineering College at Qingdao, the Navigation Engineering College in Yantai, or the Naval Engineering University in Wuhan. The PLAN Logistics Academy is located in Tianjin, and the Navy Medical Academy in Jiangsu. Finally, the Naval Political School for training political commissars is located in Dalian.

At midpoint in their career (as lieutenant commanders or commanders) naval officers are expected to attend the Naval Command School in Nanjing, which concentrates on courses in technical subjects but also addresses naval operations analysis, strategy, and campaign planning—all supported by a wargaming center.[53] This school maintains a "practice base" with the East China Sea Fleet, where students presumably apply their studies in an operational setting.[54]

The NDU is the senior and most important element in China's PME system. It is usually commanded by a full general and includes a strategic studies institute. Promotion in the senior ranks requires attendance at three of the courses offered by the NDU in Beijing—as captains or senior captains (two-year division commander course), as rear admirals (one-year group-army commander course), and as rear or vice admirals (three-month "capstone" course).[55] These programs received increased emphasis in 1994 with the CMC's directive to "focus training and education on high-tech conditions." This directive also linked higher education to officer promotion in the PLA. The campaign appears to be bearing fruit; recent statistics show that senior PLAN officers are both younger and better educated than their predecessors.[56]

Admiral Shi Yunsheng ordered the Navy in 1999 to build "a new education system" covering combat command tactics, engineering technology, logistic management, political work, and rank and file education. He wanted a "naval commander training system at four levels": technological, tactical, joint tactical, and campaign. Shi's successors, Admiral Zhang Dingfa and Admiral Wu Shengli in 2009, have continued that theme.[57]

This educational infrastructure is central to PLAN officer education en route to command and then to senior rank and positions. Shipboard officers must complete the appropriate course of instruction before assuming designated duties. Ship and aviation squadron commanding officers must satisfy educational requirements as well as demonstrate political reliability and operational expertise. Commanders must satisfy requirements at the technological, tactical, joint tactical, and campaign levels before taking command. The requirements involve both practical and theoretical examinations, including "a wide range of professional knowledge and skills on thirty-four professional and academic subjects."[58] The campaign to increase commanding officer qualifications—and by inference performance—was proclaimed, albeit perhaps extravagantly, in an October 2008 PLA claim that "100 percent of frontline captains of the Navy are graduates of specialized academies."[59]

Commanding officers are now subject to new evaluation standards: the Guideline of the Chinese People's Liberation Army for the Evaluation of Commanding Officers and supporting instructions issued in July 2008. These aim to evaluate commanders "in accordance with the requirements of scientific development."[60]

The Navy has moved to link classroom education and operational training to address combat command tactics, engineering technology, logistics management, political work, and enlisted education and training. Although detailed information about career progression in the PLAN is scarce, officers probably follow a path similar to their American counterparts: approximately ten years of commissioned service to reach the position of executive officer, and another three to five years to receive a commanding officer assignment at sea.[61]

Although the emphasis of recent revisions and innovations has focused on officer education, enlisted personnel have not been neglected. The most recent innovation established the All-Army Propaganda and Cultural Information Network, using Internet technology to enable centralized education among different bases and units. This system's ability to provide enlisted personnel with political education is another indicator of the leadership's concern with political reliability. Improved enlisted educational opportunities focus on technical capability but include officer accession programs as well.[62]

TRAINING

Crew training has traditionally occurred almost entirely on board ship, and this remains the focus of the PLAN's effort. Within the past decade, however, the PLAN has created more centralized facilities to teach personnel how to operate modern shipboard systems. These new schools/training centers are operated by each fleet's naval base commands to teach engineering, surface warfare, ship handling, aviation operations, submarine warfare, and medical operations in addition to addressing specific equipment systems.[63]

Navies typically follow one of two general training systems. The U.S. model maximizes the amount of training conducted under operational conditions—at sea and in the air. The Soviet/Russian model maximizes the amount of training conducted ashore and in port. This difference may be quantified in the number of days a ship spends at sea in a given year or the number of pilot flying-hours per year. The increasing availability of sophisticated shore-based trainers that accurately simulate real-time operational conditions has to some degree lessened the difference between the two general training models.

The Chinese Navy historically followed the Russian model; during the late 1950s the PLAN translated more than one hundred Soviet naval training manuals and published training guidelines. The leadership emphasized a cautious, step-by-step approach to training—not surprising for a new navy.

Today, PLAN surface ships spend more time underway each year, and pilots fly approximately 140 hours per year, both substantially more than ten years ago. These increases perhaps reflect a shift from the Soviet to the U.S. system of maximizing training at sea. The PLAN is also placing emphasis on a realistic shore-based training infrastructure.[64] Operating effectively at sea is physically demanding and requires actual training at sea. This is especially true for proficiency in complex, integrated joint operations.

China's 1985 shift in strategic focus to "high-tech wars on the periphery" called for a concomitant shift in PLAN training and exercising. Offshore defense requires at-sea training in open-ocean navigation, seamanship, logistics, and operations—especially surveillance, command and control, and multiship formation training. Coordinated training among subsurface, surface, and aviation units recognizes technological advances in maritime operations based on automation and integrated operations. Hence, the PLAN is expanding its exercise infrastructure and regimen to include more multiunit operational training, although the degree to which the above requirements are actually exercised is not clear. The PLAN shares responsibility for coastal defense with PLA coastal defense units and with personnel and weapons—principally antiair and antisurface missile batteries—manned at specific points along China's long coast.[65]

The PLA explains its training paradigm in a historical context: "Each major mass-scale military training campaign has invariably [been] accompanied . . . by the study of new knowledge [including] studying cultural knowledge in the 1950s and 1960s; studying science in the 1980s; and studying high technology at present. . . . The ongoing mass-scale campaign of military training with science and technology [makes it] . . . imperative to let [soldiers] practice using their equipment." This training program must also, in the PLA view, be integrated with developing technologies and instituted throughout the training infrastructure: "When the new equipment is still in the stage of preliminary research, military academies and schools should already introduce related courses; while the new equipment is being produced after design finalization, military academies and schools should be equipped with it first and incorporate it into the curriculum; as the new equipment arrives in units, the relevant mainstay personnel responsible for its command, operation, and maintenance should take up their positions with the arrival of the equipment, and . . . training [be] provided to the units in a timely manner."[66]

This idea was stated more simply more than two decades ago when the PLAN commander justified "long-distance training in the oceans" by stating that "the Navy belongs to the sea. . . . [I]t is necessary to undergo training [on] the oceans, [and] become adapted to a life at sea for long period of time." General Fu Quanyou illustrated possible conflict between "down to earth" exercises and budgetary concerns by noting the importance of "simulated training," "on-base training," and "training management," as opposed to training under battlefield conditions.[67]

The PLAN possesses only two dedicated training ships: the 10,000-ton *Shichang* and the midshipmen training ship *Zheng He*. The former is designed to take advantage of modular installations that enable it to serve interchangeably for surface navigation training for up to two hundred people or to embark two or three helicopters for aviation training. This last capability reportedly has included aircraft carrier training. The vessel may also have the capability to serve as a fleet command and control ship. *Shichang* can also serve as a supply ship or a hospital ship when the appropriate modules are installed.[68] Its first voyage reportedly was a training cruise for reserve PLAN personnel, and it has participated in several major exercises, including a July 2000 East China Sea Fleet operation dedicated to logistics training utilizing civilian shipping.

The Navy has joined its sister services in emphasizing training to improve logistics performance; most notable of such efforts was Stride 2009, a national exercise that moved four Army divisions across several of China's military regions. Naval exercises have continued to draw on civilian resources as part of the "socialization of logistics," perhaps representing current examples of people's war. These include civilian involvement in "advanced scientific-technological" achievements in "military research projects," civilian longshoremen supporting submarine rearming, and civilian vessels and facilities resupplying PLAN units. China's Navy in 2010 appears capable of supporting its operating forces despite the complexity of its disparate platforms and systems. The three fleets include, for example, sixteen different destroyer and frigate classes.[69]

Individual ship training is a prerequisite for multiship training exercises. Crews of all new and overhauled ships receive training and certification from their parent fleet's training center before assuming combat duties with the operating forces. A sampling of individual and small-unit training indicates a "building-block" approach, with training progressing in both complexity and scope until a unit is qualified to join fleet-level operations. Such building-block events include training in small-craft maneuvering, sea-lane interdiction, reconnaissance, submarine positioning and navigation, landing ship formation steaming, Marine Corps landing drills, weapons and sensor systems exercises, and aviation unit familiarization with new equipment. This training is conducted by shore-based teaching staff who both train and evaluate operational personnel, including commanding officers.[70]

The PLAN is striving to make its training more realistic. The Nanjing and Guangzhou MRs, for instance, are credited with conducting "in-depth studies" on joint amphibious operations, with the Navy emphasizing "naval blockade, underwater surprise-defense, and mining of harbor piers," and the Air Force including in its training "low-altitude maritime attack" against ships. Throughout, the concern is to ensure that "training is as close to real combat as possible."[71]

PLAN efforts to modernize training facilities and processes are marked by three characteristics. First, modernization efforts are experimental in nature: postexercise analysis is used to evaluate standardized exercises and derive doctrinal and tactical improvements. Second, joint and combined arms operations are emphasized, often with "blue" (i.e., enemy) and "red" forces opposing each other. Third, despite the assertions about the RMA and the importance of injecting "science and technology" into training, the PLAN continues to emphasize the importance of people over machine and technology.[72]

The PLA seems uncertain how best to mix the human element with "the application of science and technology" so that its forces can operate "under informatized conditions." The RMA is often mentioned, but its impact on military education and training is not clear. The director of the GSD's Officer Training Bureau described five features of this revolution in military affairs. It is (1) changing the components of the armed forces, especially in the campaign formation between different services; (2) introducing new combat means; (3) generating much larger combat space; (4) creating new modes of operations; and (5) inventing new methods of combat engagement.[73] An extensive series of articles in *Jiefangjun Bao* show concern with combined training and promote the use of training simulators as a means both to save money and to enhance training, although there seems to be some uncertainty regarding how to go about this.[74] One rather extreme PLA view is that "we should [understand] the change from 'two armies pitted against each other in front of [their] positions' into 'confrontation on the net.'" On a high-tech battlefield, network confrontation is more important than firepower confrontation.[75]

Various articles emphasize information warfare (IW) and what the U.S. Navy calls "network-centric warfare," but most simply repeat buzzwords without offering realistic links between concept and operational practice. For example: "The main contents of training . . . are: basic theory, including computer basics and application, communications network technology, the information highway, digitized units and theaters, electronic countermeasures, radar technology, . . . together with . . . IW rules and regulations, IW strategy and tactics, and theater IW and strategic IW; information systems . . . information weapons . . . simulated IW . . . protection of information systems, computer virus attacks and counterattacks, and jamming and counter-jamming of communications networks."[76]

On a more prosaic level, PLAN training has focused on "multidimensional attacks against targets on the ground from the air and sea," with classroom courses on amphibious landings.[77] Technical training has been modernized to include logistical and other support facets of maritime warfare.[78]

It is not clear that training is conducted with the same methodology and to the same standards in all three fleets. Although the PLAN Headquarters' Training Department should ensure Navy-wide uniformity, there are probably significant differences among the three fleets' training regimens that would complicate interfleet operations. Each fleet is commanded by a different admiral, faces different strategic and operational environments, and deploys different ships and aircraft.

EXERCISES

China's secrecy hinders efforts to identify and analyze PLAN exercises. One source claims that the Navy "successively held as many as a hundred large-scale blue-water combined training programs and exercises" between 1979 and 1999.[79] An excellent 1996 study identifies ninety-six significant (division-size or larger) PLA training exercises conducted between January 1990 and November 1995—about sixteen per year. The Navy participated in thirty-six of these, with half of that number also involving the Army, the Air Force, or both.[80] Fifteen of the thirty-six are characterized as "combined arms exercises," and fifteen involved amphibious training. The exercises were conducted fairly equally among the three different fleets, with the North Sea Fleet conducting thirteen and the East Sea and South Sea fleets ten each. Some of this training probably involved units from more than one of the fleets operating together, but that information is not available. One interesting facet is that despite appearing to be oriented primarily toward amphibious warfare, the South Sea Fleet engaged in approximately the same number of amphibious training exercises (six) as did the East Sea and North Sea fleets (five each). The PLA may also have established dedicated amphibious warfare training areas in the East Sea Fleet's AOR.

Although the PLA has seven "joint teaching and joint training bases," the Navy does not appear to have engaged in many complex interfleet exercises.[81] The most sophisticated exercise examined in the 1996 study was conducted in November 1995 on Dongshan Island and coincided with Taiwan's legislative elections. Apparently, "a ground force element of at least regimental size conducted an amphibious landing supported by perhaps a battalion of amphibious tanks and six or more transport helicopters with assault troops." The exercise included air support by Su-27 and A-5 aircraft, airborne operations, PLAN fire support, and multiple landing beaches, and demonstrated a "viable command and control system." The authors of the study perceptively noted, however, that the exercise was a public relations event that demonstrated the PLA's limitations as well as its capability for conducting joint and combined-arms warfare. Nonetheless, the Dongshan exercises were conducted on a large scale each year from 2000 to 2004.[82]

Additionally, since 1997 PLAN amphibious ships have conducted a series of significant exercises. Although China has never conducted a division-scale or larger joint amphibious exercise, its amphibious force is believed capable of landing at least one infantry division on a beach, depending on the mix of equipment and stores for immediate resupply. If China were to use its merchant fleet, its capacity to move forces would increase, although inadequate air defense, lack of experience in formation steaming, and lack of ability and training in cross-beach movement of forces would be critical shortcomings.[83]

The PLAN has maintained a steady program of exercises during the past decade, which indicates serious intent to improve its ability to conduct amphibious, combined arms, integrated, and joint operations. The roughly even spread of exercise types among the three fleets shows a desire to develop fleets with relatively balanced capabilities—and perhaps reflects Beijing's opinion that none of the three fleets operates in a more threatening theater than the other two. The one exception to this balance is the assignment of the only two Marine Corps brigades to the South Sea Fleet, accompanied by the PLAN's new large amphibious vessel. This probably indicates that the Marines' primary mission concerns the land features in the South China Sea and not the amphibious warfare focus per se of the Chinese Navy. Hence the presence in the Nanjing and Guangzhou MRs of two amphibious infantry divisions and an amphibious armored brigade with the obvious mission of preparing to operate against Taiwan.

The PLAN exercise program has grown steadily in both frequency and complexity; it apparently is carefully designed to train all three fleets from individual unit drills through complex joint exercises. Militia and reserve forces reportedly are included in some of the exercises. All warfare areas—antisurface, antisubmarine, antiair, submarine, electronic, amphibious, and mine warfare—are included, as are logistics, combined arms, navigation, and C4ISR. Also notable are the exercises focused on incorporating civilian maritime resources into PLAN missions. Other exercise areas have included base defense, emergency maintenance, and damage repair by both shore- and sea-based units. Of special note are the joint exercises with Russia, such as Peace Mission 2005. China has also employed the PLAN in multilateral exercises in both the Pacific and Indian oceans, demonstrating increasing confidence in its Navy's capabilities, as exemplified in Peace-09, the significant multinational exercise hosted by Pakistan in 2007.[84]

The PLAN is emphasizing joint exercises in a multiple-threat environment, operating at greater distances and for longer periods at sea, and operating in bad weather and at night. An annual series of humanitarian-oriented exercises has taken place in the Hong Kong area since the early 1980s, usually in January. These "sea and air rescue exercises" (SAREX) have been conducted primarily by the U.S. Coast Guard and its Hong Kong counterpart; since 1997 they have included participation by both U.S. Navy and PLAN units. In 1999 and 2000 the SAREX participants included representatives from Vietnam's nascent coast guard as well. A similar but much larger exercise was recently conducted among units from Beijing, Hong Kong, and Macao. The exercise in October 2008 was the largest to date, including units from the U.S. Navy, Air Force, and Coast Guard as well as Hong Kong and the PLA.[85] The PLAN's exercises with foreign navies have been conducted at a conservative level of activity, but according to Beijing have included since 2000 "thirty-seven joint military drills . . . in areas including non-proliferation of weapons of mass destruction, security defense of sea-land-air channels, antiterrorism and joint search and rescue."[86]

Jiang Zemin's frequent calls to apply science and technology to training exercises were underlined by a "naval-aeronautical-antisubmarine" exercise in April 1999 that demonstrated the North Sea Fleet's efforts to exercise many of the values described in the new combat regulations. The fleet's Air Force Command Center controlled forces ashore, in the air, and at sea, and the use of the satellite GPS was cited as an example of incorporating "science and technology" into the proceedings. The exercise was "live," with operational units participating in all phases of training. Doctrinal impact was achieved through postexercise analysis and a "lessons learned" process aided by collated, computerized "radar and command guidance" information. Hu Jintao has continued his predecessor's emphasis on science and technology in military exercises; Lianhe 2008 was a particularly complex PLAN operation with sea- and shore-based elements.[87]

These exercises demonstrate PLAN efforts during the past fifteen years to focus on translating the "science and technology" logo into meaningful exercises. The 2008 Navy Military Training Working Conference focused on this problem, touting the development of multifunctional training systems for surface and subsurface warfare, to include simulated missile, gun, and torpedo targets that are "increasingly more scientific and closer to the requirements for actual combat." ASW exercises have been most often reported as evidence of the progress being made in naval warfare proficiency—evidence that seems convincing in terms both of the technology employed and the personnel performance demonstrated. These attributes were noted in April 2009 when Admiral Wu Shengli summed up the PLAN's exercise program to date: "In the past decade the People's Navy has organized more than thirty combat operations group campaign exercises at sea. . . . [T]he Navy has focused on comprehensively boosting its overall combat operations capabilities," focusing on testing new tactics, operating in joint exercises in all warfare areas in "a complex electromagnetic environment." He also noted that "training far out at sea has become routine," although he did not delineate the distances involved.[88]

IDEOLOGY AND PROFESSIONALIZATION

The emphasis on training military personnel who are both ideologically "sound" and professionally competent was noted earlier. At one level, this becomes a question of allocating training hours; for instance, how many hours each week does a newly commissioned naval officer aboard a Luzhou-class destroyer spend studying Marxism-Leninism-Maoism, and how many studying the maintenance and operation requirements of the complex radar system for which he is responsible?[89]

Reorganization of military schools and the attempt to modernize their curricula and ties to the operating forces are evidence of the torch having been passed from the revolutionary generation to the one leading the Navy into the twenty-first century. The old ideological struggle in the PLA between political reliability ("red") and professional knowledge ("expert") has reached an apparently viable compromise: professionally qualified naval officers who are dedicated to China and to its Communist Party rulers.

While the question of political reliability remains an issue with China's leadership, it is almost certainly a marginal concern in everyday PLAN operations. Modernization has been explicitly embraced and has been accompanied by increasing professionalization. This in turn means that an officer will become a specialist as his or her career progresses, because the increasing complexity of modern, technologically intense sensor and weapons systems demand increasingly specialized knowledge. Such knowledge is gained only through schooling and repeated operational tours in the same warfare specialty, with the same system, or both. Warfare specialties include air/antiair, surface/antisurface, submarine/antisubmarine, mine, electronic, engineering, and command and control.

Another aspect of this question is PLA officers' view of themselves "as chief protectors of China's territorial interests and national honor."[90] The PLA may never directly govern China, but the PRC's history is one of close military-civilian rule; from 1949 until the 1990s the nation's rulers were both military and civilian figures. Jiang Zemin was the first truly civilian ruler of China since 1911; Hu Jintao is now the second.

The increasing professionalization in the PLAN does not necessarily detract from its loyalty to the CCP, of course, but that possibility appears to be a matter of concern to the leadership in Beijing. Today's officer corps is undoubtedly more technologically oriented and professionally educated than at any time since 1949. It also is the product of a distinctly military—rather than political—career. This might be expected to lead to an increasingly strong sense of cohesiveness and esprit among officers, including strong nationalistic leanings. "Paradoxically," however, in the words of Ellis Joffe, "professionalism has intensified, rather than reduced" the involvement of PLA leaders determining Beijing's policies, especially with respect to Taiwan. This conclusion may be reflected in the frequent pronouncements by civilian and military leaders of the PLA's loyalty to the party and the demand for "a strategic move for strengthening the spiritual pillar of the military forces [to] guarantee the troops' political steadfastness and ideological and moral purity."[91]

The organization for exercising political control in the military has not, on paper, changed since the founding of the PLAN, but the reality is different because military and political elites are no longer identical.[92] This may in turn be contributing to a separation of the officer corps from the CCP, a separation exacerbated by the generally much-reduced role of the party throughout Chinese life. By regulation, both the commander and the political commissar are responsible for their unit. In the early years of the PLAN the commissar had to approve the commanding officer's orders. This became a particular point of contention following the Korean War. The relief of both PLAN commanders and political commissars after the Ming 361 accident illustrated this situation.

The political commissar represents the party in PLAN operational units. The commissar's original role in a Leninist military was to serve as co-commander of the unit, with perhaps a determining voice in operational decisions. Current political commissar duties instead focus on several important but essentially nonoperational areas. The commissar's importance as military decision maker has declined as increasingly complex systems and technology have come to characterize the Navy; twenty-first-century political officers must become professionally competent if they are to affect the military decision-making process in a positive way.[93]

Political commissars are also better educated and trained now than in past years. They face professional military education requirements similar to their "professional" counterparts, including attendance at National Defense University courses. A unit's political commissar is still an important individual with significant duties. These focus on personnel management and include (1) political education and advocating various PLA reforms, such as Jiang Zemin's "five sentence" prescript; (2) personnel assignments; (3) retirements and demobilization: helping to find employment for the large number of personnel demobilized as the result of recent force reductions; (4) reserve units: serving as party educators with local reserves and militia to ensure that their training is in accordance with CCP dictates; (5) housing assignments; (6) personnel morale and welfare; and (7) enforcement of regulations. They are also responsible for conducting psychological, legal, and media warfare ("three warfares") activities in their unit.[94]

Today's PLAN political commissar is primarily an educator in CCP and Navy theory ("political work") and regulations, a personnel officer, and a counselor; his position as party representative still carries weight. A recent *Jiefangjun Bao* article sums up the commissar's responsibilities:

It is difficult to raise great enthusiasm for troop training in science and technology and more difficult to continue it persistently. . . . [But improving] the purposefulness of the political work in the training can sweep obstacles from the path. . . . When troop training reforms face frustrations, a boost of enthusiastic encouragement can often help officers and soldiers rise again with force and spirit to overcome difficulties. . . . [P]olitical officers at all levels should conscientiously study the essence of the CMC's directive, [and] arduously study and master the laws and characteristics of the troop training in science and technology. . . . We should go far into the training ground . . . regarding the political work in the process of the troop training.[95]

Political commissars are further admonished to "take the top responsibility for the military modernization construction on the precondition of adhering to the principle of 'politically qualified.'" The CCP continues to insist "on putting ideological and political work first, and pushing forward the innovative development of ideological and political work, to ensure the Party's absolute leadership over the armed forces." To this end, in April 2008 the CMC approved the Regulations of the Chinese People's Liberation Army on the Work of Servicemen's Committees. The committees are organizations through which individual military unit servicemen "exercise their democratic rights and carry out mass activities." They also

> advise on combat readiness training, education and management, logistical support, and weaponry and equipment management . . . make recommendations on issues concerning the immediate interests of officers and men, such as the selection and promotion of non-commissioned officers, selection of qualified enlisted men to enter military educational institutions . . . for technical training, and . . . for commendations and rewards; . . . supervise officers and men on the performance of their duties and observation of law and discipline; and . . . protect the collective interests of the unit, and the legitimate rights and interests of officers and men.

Each committee is supposed to be made up of five to seven members chosen nominally by secret ballot but "under the leadership of the unit Party branch . . . and the guidance of the unit commanders."[96]

The Navy's political department manages officer promotions and assignments. The former are conducted by promotion boards that gather information on the officer through written and oral reports. Officers receive annual evaluations as well as a special evaluation when eligible for promotion. They are evaluated for political character, military and specialty knowledge and achievements, and physical fitness. Based on these records, the officer's political department makes a recommendation to the local CCP committee, which will either authorize promotion (for junior officers) or make a further recommendation up the chain of command. The party remains firmly in control of

the process. Officers must meet both time-in-grade and time-in-rank requirements; except for promotion from ensign to lieutenant (junior grade), these are
usually three years in grade and four years in rank. Since the promotion clock
for academy graduates starts when they enter the academy, this means normal
promotion points as follows for total service: ensign to lieutenant (jg), 6 years;
lieutenant (jg) to lieutenant, 10 years; lieutenant to lieutenant commander, 14
years; lieutenant commander to commander, 18 years; commander to captain,
22 years; and captain to senior captain, 26 years.[97]

CONCLUSION

The PLAN serves a nation with a rapidly expanding economy and an increasingly well-educated population. The positive aspects of this situation include
a pool of better-educated and intellectually more qualified personnel from
which officers and enlisted personnel may be drawn for service in a Navy that
is increasingly dependent on sophisticated technology. The situation also has
negative aspects, however, given the reduced motivation for young men and
women to elect naval service rather than enter the booming economy.

Once in the PLAN, personnel are subject to an apparently logical, progressive structure of education and training. The education-training-exercise
paradigm is coherent on paper but is hampered by the short service term
of recruits, the decentralized administration of training, and the developing
operational objectives for the PLAN as a whole. Furthermore, the priority
assigned ideological training in the Navy is unclear but certainly continues to
affect professional development.[98]

While public assessments by the PLAN invariably praise operational
training and exercises, an undertone of dissatisfaction is apparent. The frequent
admonitions to educate, train, and exercise in accordance with the dictates of
high technology and modern methods reflect this feeling. The account by two
senior captains who served as on-scene observers of one of the U.S. Navy's
most advanced complex exercises, RIMPAC 98, are significant in this regard.
In an interview published in *Jiefangjun Bao,* these officers were unable to
restrain their enthusiasm for several aspects of the operational expertise they
witnessed, including equipment such as advanced automation, information-
processing technology, and night-vision systems. They particularly emphasized the "rigorous and regular personnel training"; the ability to operate at sea
for extended periods; "whole-staff, whole-system, whole-function, and whole-

course training"; the ability of equipment to operate continuously for long periods; personnel and equipment safety awareness and programs; frequent and continuing personnel education and training; systematic equipment maintenance procedures and practices; delegation of responsibility to lower-ranking officers and enlisted personnel; and shipboard cleanliness. Perhaps most telling was their emphasis on having witnessed consistent "specific efforts in a down-to-earth manner instead of shouting empty slogans." PLA representatives observed the U.S.-led Valiant Shield exercise, conducted in waters near Guam in June 2006, as well.[99]

These reports highlight the limits of our knowledge of PLAN operations and readiness, but open-source reports during the past fifteen years illustrate the PLAN's substantial progress in modernization. Several trends in training and exercises became apparent in 2009; these included joint training, training in MOOTW missions, emphasizing the integration of civilian support in military operations, training according to doctrine, and perhaps most important, training under "real-war" conditions.[100]

Indeed, the performance of China's naval task groups operating in the Gulf of Aden during 2009 are the clearest possible demonstration of the PLAN's significant strides in becoming an effective twenty-first-century force at sea. Significant self-awareness also marks the PLAN's progress; both in person and in press reports, naval officers grade their service and personnel relatively harshly. This may in turn impart a degree of caution on the part of Beijing in employing the military in pursuit of national security goals.[101] One "lesson learned" from the U.S. Navy is indicated in a 2009 description of junior officer ship-handling training—emphasizing decisiveness and professional knowledge—that could have been written by the commander of a U.S. destroyer.[102]

Admiral Wu Shengli implied global ambitions for the PLAN when he stated in 2009 that "transformation building" would create a Navy able to deal with "multiple security threats [while] accomplishing diversified military tasks." Significantly, he stated that these would include tasks beyond China's "territorial integrity [such as] maritime rights and development interests" and would include "the ability to go deep into the ocean." In another interview, Wu noted goals that included new, more capable "ships, aircraft and torpedoes, long-range missiles with high accuracy, submarines with superb invisibility and endurance and electronic weapons and facilities." He also said the PLAN would "incorporate the capacity for non-war military actions to the integrated construction of the Army's power, especially emergency offshore search and rescue and anti-terrorism activities."[103]

This delineates an ambitious program, especially in view of the difficulty any navy experiences attracting the educated personnel necessary to operate a twenty-first-century force. China is experiencing this shortage in particular in its submarine force, which requires highly intelligent, psychologically fit, dedicated enlisted personnel. The PLAN's continued progress toward achieving global maritime status will depend in large part on the national priorities set by Beijing and the national maritime strategy it follows.

CHAPTER 7

Doctrine and Operations
in the PLAN

As defined in the United States, doctrine is the "fundamental principles by which the military forces or elements thereof guide their actions in support of national objectives"; it "is authoritative but requires judgement in application."[1] Doctrine provides the crucial bridge between strategic intent and operational effectiveness. It is nominally driven by anticipated missions, perhaps illustrated by scenarios to which military planners respond. Devising doctrine for maritime warfare, which is by nature multidimensional and is becoming more so in the twenty-first century, poses complex challenges.

Chinese military doctrine has undergone major development since the PRC was founded in 1949. No longer is continental war China's overriding strategic concern; preparation for contingencies involving maritime territory and challenges have contributed to the increased status and resources allocated to the PLAN. The end of the Cold War and China's expanding economy brought about a basic shift in doctrinal thought. Nonetheless, doctrinal influences from the Mao era are still in effect. These include confronting a technologically and logistically superior adversary, the need to develop the ability to defeat a superior adversary, and the continued viability of "people's war."

This last remains relevant, although not as defined by Mao Zedong. The concept was justified in 2008 by General Bai Zixing, director of the Defense Ministry's Recruitment Office, because "the tremendous strength of war stems from the people, and no changes have taken place in the people's decisive role in warfare." That means, today, taking full advantage of civilian human and material resources in time of military conflict, described as "joint military-civilian action."[2]

OPERATIONAL DOCTRINE

One of the PLA's recently revised regulations—perhaps the most important in terms of war-fighting direction—is "The Chinese PLA Program for Combined Campaigns." This document connotes a strategy–doctrine–operational art–tactics progression that could describe twenty-first-century PLAN capabilities. Throughout, the Combined Campaigns program emphasizes the importance of standardization, science, and technology, which "have now become the key factor in deciding upon the outcome of a war." Because the PLA is entering "a new stage of historical development" at the strategic level, it must learn from "several recent local wars."[3]

The Combined Campaigns Regulation requires the PLA to "strive to take the initiative" in war while further refining "the people's war strategy and the people's war tactics." This modernization process may indicate a break with the Maoist doctrine of fighting a "people's war at sea." The early PLAN resorted to a form of guerrilla warfare at sea because of its operational focus on inshore waters, its lack of oceangoing warships, and the dominance of leaders with an Army background. Today, "people's war" does not mean Maoist guerrilla war; it means involving all of China's personnel and societal resources in fighting a war under modern "high-tech" conditions.

The Combined Campaigns Regulation first delineates "the principle of unity," emphasizing that the "new-generation PLA" regulations must "uphold a unified combat ideology," to include training and tactics. Second, it applies to both single-service and joint combat operations: naval units "will have clear-cut combat regulations to abide by and a unified combat ideology to follow in different types of combat operations launched at different levels." Third, at the operational level, the new regulation addresses local wars fought under high-technology conditions. This has yielded "tactics with Chinese characteristics," with "informationalization" (or "informatization") the key word in describing the environment in which PLAN strategists anticipate having to fight. The new tactics include a new command system that applies to logistic support, political work, information war, "an electronic confrontation battle," and "an anti–air raid battle." These tactical elements have high priority in PLAN training activities. The importance of science and technology is again underlined, with those factors embodied in training activities that emphasize the use of simulators, joint campaigning, the systematic application of force, and a combat environment "in light of an information war and a digitized battlefield."

This and the other new regulations promulgated by the Central Military Commission (CMC) during the past decade show a firm appreciation of the basic characteristics of modern warfare, demonstrated—or at least preshadowed—in the Persian Gulf War, the allied campaign in Kosovo, and the post-9/11 wars in Iraq and Afghanistan. The regulations also seem to reflect PLA frustration at China's laggard pace in being able to operate at the new level. The Combined Campaign Regulation, for instance, closes with a call for "optimizing" new weapon development and "developing a batch of offensive means capable of simultaneously serving as a deterrent 'trump card'" in combat operations. It further calls for the "informationalization" of "existing PLA weaponry and equipment [to heighten] PLA combat effectiveness as quickly as possible."

The Navy is tasked with PLA-wide goals, including the following:

- Developing new tactics and techniques to defeat a high-technology enemy—the mantra of PLAN training and force structure modernization.
- Relying on only limited amounts of foreign weapons and equipment. This goal is still a long way from being fulfilled, although the indigenous Chinese defense industry is significantly increasing its ability to provide modern maritime weapons systems.
- Developing joint operational capability—a training goal frequently emphasized but still in progress.
- Focusing on information warfare, including precision attack ("informatization").
- Reorganizing command, control, and communications (C3) to meet the requirements of modern warfare.

For the PLAN, this has translated into "management of the sea," including dexterous "use of the sea ... to protect the country's maritime rights and interests, to serve the maritime politics and economy, and to become a powerful support for the revitalization of the maritime undertaking in the new century and the development of new achievements in maritime productivity." Furthermore, the Navy is expected to expand its operations into extraregional waters and for power projection ashore.[4]

The *Chinese Naval Officers' Manual* lists the following operational missions for the various PLAN warfare communities:

- Surface fleet: attack enemy warships; maritime surveillance; antisubmarine warfare; merchant ship convoys; amphibious warfare; logistics; mine warfare; search and rescue; and coastal defense.

- Submarine force: attack enemy naval bases and coasts; maritime patrol and reconnaissance; strategic nuclear strikes; logistic lift; mine warfare; search and rescue.
- Air force: attack enemy naval installations; antisurface warfare; antiair warfare; defend PLAN surface and submarine forces during operations; maritime reconnaissance; early warning; communications; antisubmarine warfare; logistic lift; amphibious warfare; mine warfare; search and rescue.
- Marine Corps: forward base seizure; coastal defense; and amphibious warfare.[5]

This list contains some unusual features. The first is that strategic nuclear strikes are assigned to a submarine force that will be capable of executing such missions only when the new Jin class becomes operational, perhaps in 2010. The second is assigning logistic lift to submarines, a concept long abandoned by other navies. The third is that electronic warfare is not mentioned as a mission, although it would figure into targeting for various antiship cruise and ballistic missiles. Fourth, ASW is not assigned to the submarine force. Finally, no mention is made of special operations or joint operations for any element of the PLAN. This list of missions does illustrate, however, China's recognition that modern maritime warfare is multidimensional and becoming steadily more complex as information-age developments are adapted for naval use.

The locus of doctrinal development within the PLAN is not obvious. It is not clear, for instance, that the Navy's Beijing headquarters has a determinative position in originating doctrine, especially in view of each of the geographic fleets having its own training department. Discussions with PLAN officers indicate that significant doctrinal development occurs at the fleet or military region level, or both, which could lead to significant differences among the operational fleets. Final doctrine promulgation almost certainly does originate with PLAN Headquarters, however, given the necessity to ensure adherence to PLA objectives and strategy.

The operational capability to execute doctrine is measured by "readiness"—the ability of a particular ship, squadron, or even fleet to carry out assigned tasks effectively. A fully combat-ready navy unit would be well-trained enough to be able to carry out successfully all assigned missions. Hence, "readiness" is a measure of a navy's training, doctrine, and administration processes. We have little evidence of PLAN combat-readiness on a continuing basis, although specific exercises such as those conducted in the vicinity of the Taiwan Strait in

1995–2004, with Russia in the past decade, and those highlighted by Admiral Wu Shengli in 2009 evince a respectable level of readiness.

The Navy has been working steadily to improve its ability to operate farther offshore and to engage in integrated and joint operations under the rubric of "offshore defense," as noted in the 2006 Defense White Paper. This embodies the Maoist tenet to "take the initiative and to annihilate the enemy."[6] PLAN employment is currently highlighted by the 2009 counterpiracy deployments to the Gulf of Aden. Less obvious is the apparent doctrinal employment demonstrated by submarine employment: the eight patrols conducted in 2008 were double the number conducted in 2007. This is not an impressive number of patrols for a force of more than fifty boats, but it does indicate Beijing's increased attention to employing submarines.[7]

Innovative operational doctrine can compensate to a degree for material shortfalls. The chief lesson of Desert Storm and Kosovo, where U.S. superiority in military technology and operational power was graphically demonstrated, may well be that Chinese maritime power for at least the next fifty years will lack the capability for successful direct confrontation with American forces. Instead, the PLAN will have to rely on speed, mobility, flexibility, and initiative in a contest involving the United States. A logical step in such a conflict would be to gain the initiative through preemption. This does not necessarily require a surprise attack but could be achieved by seizing the initiative at a time of significant U.S. naval weakness.

Chinese analysts and strategists consider aircraft carriers as the center of gravity of the U.S. potential for interceding in a Taiwan scenario. U.S. intervention in the 1996 Taiwan Strait crisis reemphasized for the PLAN the importance of sophisticated weapons and the Maoist precept of seeking the initiative within the concept of informationalization to counter potential U.S. participation in a western Pacific conflict. Hence, a great deal of attention is being devoted to preventing effective carrier operations. A 2001 article identified the carriers then in the U.S. fleet and described a carrier's primary weakness as the inability "to conceal its traces," providing an avenue for attack by missiles and torpedoes. Other analysts have suggested attacking with mines, electronic warfare, submarine "ambush," and manned aircraft—everything in the PLA arsenal, in other words, although at least one writer noted that to be successful, an anticarrier operation must be an integrated, joint effort. These methods differ little from those the Soviet Union attempted to implement during the Cold War, and they continue to appear in Chinese open sources.

By the end of 2009, PLAN anti–aircraft carrier doctrine had apparently settled on two primary courses. First, China would deploy submarines to widely dispersed patrol stations in the Philippine and East China seas to slow the approach of aircraft carrier groups to the theater of action; second, antiship ballistic and long-range cruise missiles would be employed to score at least mission kills on the carriers.[8]

Doctrine, however, has often followed rather than preceded operational capability. The Chinese Navy learned from its failures and successes in the Taiwan Strait in the 1950s, and was successful against the South Vietnamese Navy in 1974 and against the Vietnamese Navy in 1988 in the South China Sea. The reorganization of the Marine Corps is evidence of the PLA's development of operational doctrine for power projection.[9] The Corps contributed six hundred troops to the 1974 takeover of the Paracels. Although remaining a small force, the Corps has continued to increase in capability, with a primary mission of amphibious operations in the South China Sea.

To be successful, operational doctrine must be linked directly to capabilities. The PLAN is aware of the increasing complexity of maritime warfare; a past director of the PLAN's Research Institute described future conflict scenarios in futuristic terms of three "theaters": space, undersea, and electromagnetic: "Land-based arms will be sharply improved [and] will be able to powerfully strike and intercept formations at sea. . . . In sea-air combat, electronic warfare and missile strikes, particularly long-distance strikes by warships, their carrier-based aircraft, and aerial combat fighters, will become the essential forms. . . . The appearance of underwater aircraft carriers and undersea mine-laying robots, and even the construction of seabed military bases, will sharpen surface-undersea combat. In sea-space combat, space-based methods and forces are going to have a very conspicuous status in future naval warfare."[10]

Clearly, the PLAN has been striving to take advantage of advances in military technology, often referred to as the revolution in military affairs (RMA). Systems acquisition, personnel education and training, and fleet exercises address capabilities that fall under the "RMA with Chinese characteristics" rubric. The military-industrial and PLAN infrastructures are not yet capable of implementing them, but given the inherent uncertainties of an RMA, China's efforts in that direction should not be discounted.

The PLAN is testing new doctrine through increasingly intense and advanced training and exercises. The most far-reaching developments in doctrine and capability should result from the Navy's 2009 operations in the Gulf of Aden. In addition to operational warfare missions, these deployments seem to demonstrate the successful implementation of the doctrinal "three warfares": legal, media, and psychological operations.[11]

PLAN research and development efforts appear focused on creating a Navy able to carry out a regional maritime strategy, supported by China's research and development process, which has mostly recovered from the fifty years of violent political changes that rent the educational and scientific fabric of the country in the last century. China currently is able to build capable, modern warships, albeit still relying significantly on foreign systems. The ships built in 2010 are a significant improvement over those of 2000, which were often constructed on a 1970 technological base and were hence obsolete when commissioned. These older ships are not without capability, but they would have to be employed imaginatively, if conservatively.

Naval purchases during the past two decades, especially those from Russia, have demonstrated China's determination to speed the pace of naval modernization as well as its still developing ability to produce naval systems indigenously.[12] The ships and systems acquired in the final decades of the twentieth century have given China "a significant main naval fighting force," but one inadequate "to have all-around (three-dimensional) control of blue water." The PLAN leadership clearly understood what was needed to fulfill its doctrinal ambitions.[13]

Chinese naval planners appear also to understand the U.S. Navy's overwhelming superiority and are seeking the capability to avoid or counter it without directly challenging its potentially dominant role in maritime Asia. Two examples of the difference in PLAN and U.S. Navy capabilities are submarine-launched ICBMs and fleet air defense (AAW).

China's seaborne nuclear deterrent has been extremely weak—a missile may have been successfully launched from its single Xia-class ballistic-missile submarine (FBM) in 1988. The United States, on the other hand, in March 1999 conducted its eighty-first consecutive successful launch and flight to target of an ICBM, in that case a Trident D-5. By 2010, however, the PLAN will deploy Jin-class FBMs armed with JL-2 ICBMs capable of targeting the continental United States.[14]

Prior to 2000 the PLAN's newest warships were the Luhai-class destroyer and Sovremenny-class ships purchased from Russia, both types equipped with very limited air-defense missile systems. The United States deploys more than forty combatants armed with Aegis, by far the most capable AAW system in the world. In 2010, however, the PLAN deploys three new classes of destroyer—Luyang I, Luyang II, Luzhou—and two of frigates—the Jiangkai and Jiangkai II—with much more advanced AAW capabilities, although probably still lagging well behind the Aegis system.

Planners use specific scenarios to devise strategies. Defense of sea lines of communication (SLOCs) is one scenario—or rather, strategic ambition—that would appeal to naval planners. Expanding or building PLAN and Naval Aviation bases in the Spratly Islands and on Burmese territory would provide a starting point for a Chinese role in controlling the Malacca and associated straits. It would place the PLAN astride the points vital to China's increasing dependence on offshore petroleum resources, and indeed, to the economic life of East Asia. These would not be easy missions to accomplish on a lasting basis, however, given both operational requirements and the political unease created among the states of South and Southeast Asia.

Operational Implications

The success of its Navy's operational doctrine will be measured by China's ability to exercise power at sea. This in turn means capability to accomplish maritime missions ranging from sea denial to controlling or significantly affecting events ashore. The objective may be a continent or a small island; the means can range from a demonstration offshore or a port visit to launching cruise missiles, landing special operations forces from a submarine, or a full-scale amphibious invasion.

Amphibious operations pose three basic problems.[15] First, forces must be transported to the objective. In a large-scale effort—one involving more than one or two divisions of troops—the PLAN apparently intends to augment its amphibious lift capacity with merchant ships. Civilian vessels have participated in amphibious exercises since at least 1994, and the Navy has a program for refitting merchant ships for possible use as amphibious lift, although history shows that using civilian troop lift is very problematic.[16]

Second, safe transport of amphibious forces requires control of the sea. Here, China must employ its surface fleet, everything from patrol boats to DDGs, to protect the ships transporting invasion forces and to ensure logistical support of the force after it lands. Mine warfare could also play a significant role in this regard by safeguarding PLAN assembly points in mainland harbors. The paucity of PLAN mine-hunting and mine-clearing capability, however, would also make Taiwan's employment of defensive minefields more effective. PLAN AAW capability would be significantly enhanced by the effective employment of the Luzhou and Luyang classes, which would be key to PLAN task force operations. Taiwan's navy, however, will still be able to challenge the PLAN's ability to establish sea control.

Third, both the safe transport of the invasion force and its defense after the initial landing require control of the air. Here, China must be able to call upon the resources of the PLANAF, the PLAAF, and shore-based ballistic and cruise missiles. Taiwan's small but capable air force could pose a serious challenge to China's attempts to gain control of the air.

China has never possessed a robust capability to transport and land troops under combat conditions. The PLAN is increasing this capability, however, highlighted by the commissioning of its first landing platform dock (LPD), the Yuzhao class.[17] China's large and growing merchant fleet gives the PLAN access to enough civilian vessels to embark several divisions of troops. Mobilization of some of these assets has been exercised, but the existence of a regularized system of merchant vessel mobilization is problematical, and arguments that civilian shipping can be used in a successful amphibious assault against Taiwan are unconvincing.[18]

If China intends to claim the South China Sea as sovereign waters, as the Law of the Territorial Sea and Contiguous Zones passed in February 1992 implies it will, the PLAN will have to be able to enforce article 10 of that law, which asserts that "foreign naval vessels . . . must obtain China's permission before proceeding through the South China Sea," and foreign submarines must surface and fly their country's flag. Foreign naval vessels that do not comply can be evicted.[19] The PLAN does not possess this capability in 2010, and its modernization program is at least ten years away from being able to "evict" U.S. or other well-managed naval forces from the South China Sea.

The PLAN does have the ability to routinely deploy and maintain ships in the South China Sea. In mid-October 1996, for instance, the PLA reportedly conducted a fifteen-day exercise "seizing islands."[20] This drill, as well as those conducted with Taiwan as the obvious objective between 1995 and 2004, are examples of the PLAN exercising in support of national strategic objectives: the linkage between training and exercising and maritime strategy is more significant than the technological complexity of the actual training.

At this writing, the PLAN is still developing the technological sophistication and personnel expertise required to fulfill its doctrinal paradigm. Admiral Shi Yunsheng listed five attributes of a modern navy: (1) strengthened "research on naval strategies"; (2) "vigorous development of high-tech equipment"; (3) personnel "with modern and scientific and technological qualities" trained to operate its "modern equipment"; (4) effective "medium- and long-term" plans; and (5) modernized main equipment.[21] All five pose a challenge to the modernizing PLAN.

Shortfalls in meeting these objectives may be at least partially compensated for by innovative operational doctrine. The dramatic advances in U.S. military technology demonstrated during the past two decades appear to offer such an opportunity to some PLA strategists. One has written, for instance, that "cruise missiles are the vanguard, aerial strength is the main power, and the ground, sea, air, space, and electromagnetism are integrated. This will become a basic mode for the recent and future high-technology regional war."[22]

The PLAN has made significant strides toward adapting state-of-the-art naval warfare methods, including taking advantage of the electromagnetic spectrum, employing space-based assets, developing a family of cruise missiles, and improving its capabilities in joint and integrated operations. Additionally, the use of reserve and maritime militia forces continues to receive attention as a means of supplementing fleet manning. A former Fujian MR commander couched this in Maoist terms: "Maritime militia guerrilla warfare under high-tech conditions includes carrying out feints to deceive and confuse the enemy, conducting harassment raids on enemy targets on the sea, and carrying out blockades, blocking, striking, and bombing to destroy the enemy's island (or coastal) facilities." He characterized guerrilla warfare at sea as requiring thorough planning and preparation, "scientific organization," unified command and close coordination, stealth, seizing the initiative, and fast-paced operations. His further emphasis on "rational use" perhaps indicates the practical limits of this concept, but it may be applied to the 2009 harassing of U.S. surveillance vessels in the East and South China seas.[23]

The PLAN also faces the complex problem of integrating the industrial, personnel, and technological means to deploy an integrated joint force at sea. Nuclear deterrence is also receiving increased priority with the building of China's first class of operational strategic missile submarines, at least two of which are operational in 2010. These Jin-class ships are capable of launching the JL-2 ICBM, which has a range of at least 3,888 nm. The Jin-class FBM enables China for the first time to put a strategic deterrent to sea that poses a credible threat to the United States.[24]

Finally, effective naval force requires air power, and no aspect of PLAN modernization attracts more interest and generates more concern than Beijing's apparent decision to acquire aircraft carriers. These will provide China with sustainable air cover for the long-range power projection needed to seize and hold disputed territory such as the Spratly Islands. A PLAN carrier force operating east of Taiwan could attack that island's air defense forces on two fronts if the PLA were able to coordinate carrier-based attacks with shore-based attacks from the mainland.[25]

The arrival of USS *Independence* and USS *Nimitz* in the Taiwan area in March 1996 demonstrated the effectiveness of aircraft carriers as political instruments. Furthermore, senior PLA officers appreciated the operational importance of two carriers versus one: the deployment of one American carrier would have constituted a diplomatic signal; the deployment of two constituted an operationally effective force able to fly air-strike missions twenty-four hours a day for several days.[26]

The 1996 crisis forcefully reminded the PLA of America's ability to command the seas in East Asia and the severe limitations on PLAN capability that U.S. opposition would pose. Indeed, it probably spurred the Chinese to increase the pace of naval modernization, just as the Soviet Union did following the 1962 Cuban Missile Crisis. The Soviet Navy's very impressive Okean exercises in 1975 demonstrated its arrival as a naval force to be reckoned with; the Chinese Navy's 2009 operational deployment of several task groups to the Gulf of Aden similarly demonstrated the advances made since 1996.

Aircraft carriers are a means, however, not an end. PLAN strategists who favor large carriers are likely pursuing the wrong objective, for at least two reasons. First, the PLAN's most crucial shortcoming is the lack of air power at sea. Shore-based air power offers a more efficacious route to control of airspace in regional waters than does building a fleet of carriers. Second, with the increasing capabilities and relatively low cost of unmanned air vehicles (UAVs), especially as demonstrated by U.S. forces in Southwest Asia, the days of the exorbitantly expensive carrier with its flock of pricey manned aircraft are numbered. A true RMA demonstration by China would have its Navy build and deploy large UAV "carriers."

Aerial refueling is crucial to the offshore employment of air power. China has developed the capacity to refuel tactical aircraft in the air but has been slow to expand the capability throughout Naval Aviation or the PLAAF. Chinese press coverage of the October 1999 parade marking the PRC's fiftieth anniversary included pictures of a close formation of an aerial tanker and two tactical aircraft, although they were not hooked up; the sixtieth anniversary parade in October 2009 did not include even this demonstration.[27]

Air control is another basic element in air power. Given the strong influence of Soviet doctrine in the PLA during the past sixty years, it is logical to assume that the PLAAF and Naval Aviation follow the relatively rigid Soviet model of very close control. That may not be a disadvantage if PLAN operational missions are tightly focused on limited offshore tasking such as coastal patrol, ship surveillance, and sector-limited air defense, but that model would be inadequate for open-ocean operations.

The employment of maritime air power becomes even more demanding in other operational scenarios such as ASW, amphibious assault operations, and area defense. Israel's refusal in the summer of 2000 to complete the sale to China of its first dedicated airborne air control platform, an Israeli-modified Il-76 Russian aircraft mounting a Phalcon radar, delayed Beijing's acquisition of this basic need until at least 2008—when the Chinese-built version crashed on a test flight, reportedly killing several of its design personnel.[28]

Another factor in deploying air power over the ocean is the relationship between Naval Aviation and the PLAAF. China's air defense system is based on geographical sectors rather than service capability or doctrine, which implies that joint maritime flight operations are not routinely exercised and joint doctrine for such operations has not been systemically developed by the two "air forces." Indeed, PLAAF operations over water likely concentrate on classic air intercept and pursuit operations, while Naval Aviation's operational doctrine focuses on fleet support missions such as surveillance and ASW. Interviews with PLA officers and exercise reports likewise indicate that interservice flight operations are not common. The effects of the lack of joint flight operations between the two air forces may have been ameliorated after the PLAAF increased its overwater flights in 1996, to the point that such maritime operations had become routine by 2000, although joint exercises have not been reported since 2001.

Additionally, while the PLA has assigned coastal air defense missions by service, and both the PLAAF and Naval Aviation conduct maritime strike exercises, the National Defense University's 2003 *Science of Campaigns* fails to address the employment of shore-based air in the five maritime categories it identifies.[29] The relationship between Naval Aviation and PLAN surface forces is also a relatively recent development, with doctrine still under development. The first such "joint exercise" was described in 2006, although these drills have since become more common among the Navy's warfare communities.[30]

China is almost certainly going to deploy at least one aircraft carrier during the coming decade. National pride, more than immediate operational requirements, is driving this decision, although longer-range strategic ambitions to possess a Navy capable of extraregional power projection on a sustained basis may well factor into Beijing's decision, especially following the Gulf of Aden deployments.

A carrier requires such a large financial and personnel investment that it embodies the state: loss of a carrier in combat would thus be not just a ship lost, but a national loss. The special ships needed to defend a carrier are just beginning to make their appearance in the PLAN. These new DDGs and FFGs provide a robust capability to defend the carrier against surface, subsurface, and aviation threats. The carrier also requires replenishment-at-sea ships to keep it (and its escorts) supplied with fuel, ordnance, and other supplies.

PLAN acquisition of a carrier will raise doubts about China's strategic intentions among other Asian nations, who will interpret it as a historically typical development of massive naval power by an economically powerful state. The construction of several aircraft carriers will occur only if the Taiwan issue, relatively quiescent since the Ma Ying-joue administration took office in May 2008, continues toward apparent peaceful resolution, enabling the PLAN to focus on other national security concerns that are more susceptible to justifying expanded maritime air power.[31]

One such mission is defending China's SLOCs, which Beijing considers a vital national interest. The first level of SLOC defense is safeguarding the sea-lanes in China's claimed territorial waters, which requires a regionally capable Navy in the Yellow Sea, the East China Sea west of the Japan-Philippines line, and the South China Sea. The PLAN already possesses most of the assets necessary to defend its coastal SLOCs; that is, those within 100 nm of its coast.[32] The next level of SLOC protection includes regional sea-lanes that extend throughout East Asia from the Sea of Japan to the Andaman Sea west of Malacca, a mission the PLAN currently is only marginally capable of executing.[33] A more ambitious goal is defense of shipping along the very long SLOCs from China's ports to the energy-rich Southwest Asian and East African littorals. The PLAN does not possess the platforms or experience to defend these SLOCs, which stretch more than 5,000 nm.

Beijing has been making increasingly effective use of the Navy as a diplomatic instrument, nominally to emphasize China's peaceful intent and to demonstrate a policy of creating "harmonious seas."[34] The many port visits and other interactions with foreign nations have concomitantly increased concerns about China's growing maritime power and ability to enforce its policies in distant waters.

Foreign port visits are not new for the PLAN. The Navy's first circumnavigation occurred in 2002, with two ships spending 132 days at sea or in foreign ports, setting the tone for a very busy first decade of the new century. The Chinese Navy operated globally for the first time in 2007 as its warships visited ports in eleven countries and conducted exercises with the French, Spanish, Russian, and British navies during a deployment to Europe. The joint exercise with the Royal Navy was perhaps the most significant of these events because it included the PLAN's first operations with an aircraft carrier. While this cruise was in progress, other Chinese warships visited Australia and New Zealand, and two ships visited Pakistan, which meant concurrent PLAN operations near three continents.

This impressive schedule was followed in 2008 by Chinese warships deploying for eighty-seven days to Asian and European waters and visiting eight countries. Most notable, however, has been the PLAN's continuous operational deployment of three-ship task groups to the Gulf of Aden, starting in December 2008 and continuing at least to mid-2010, in response to the increasing incidents of piracy and other crimes at sea in that area. Almost three hundred piracy incidents were recorded in 2008 involving some 1,500 pirates who took 889 crew members hostage. The combined ransoms yielded an estimated US$250 million.[35]

China has deployed five three-ship task groups to the Gulf of Aden, each composed of two destroyers or frigates and an underway replenishment ship, with embarked helicopters and special operations forces detachments. The first task group deployed in December 2008 and was relieved on station in April 2009; the third task group arrived in the gulf in July, and the fourth trio of ships departed China at the end of October to relieve it.[36]

One interesting facet of these deployments is that they have combined units from China's different fleets. An East Sea Fleet helicopter detachment sailed with the South Sea Fleet destroyer *Wuhan* in the second task group, and the third and fourth task groups both drew on ships from the East Sea Fleet. These joint efforts will spread the "lessons learned" from these distant operations throughout more of the PLAN.[37]

By all accounts, the ships have performed well during their deployments. A convoy system was established for merchant ships requesting protection, cooperative relations were instituted with other navies operating in the gulf, and a logistics system was quickly constructed. The first task group escorted 33 Chinese- and foreign-flag merchant ships within a month of arriving on scene and 179 ships during its three months on station; the third task group escorted 174 merchant ships during its time on station.[38]

When the first PLAN task group departed China in December 2008, it was viewed as a test of the Navy's readiness, equipment capability, and personnel performance; following that group's relief in theater and return to China, Chinese "experts" stated that "the Somalia operation showed the Chinese Navy was still a long way from being strong enough to protect China's expanding maritime rights and interests."[39] A more accurate evaluation would be that the PLAN ships in the gulf have apparently performed at the same approximate level as have those of other navies attempting to accomplish a very difficult mission.

In addition to ship deployments, China has followed a policy of interaction with foreign navies through personnel visits and educational exchanges. Approximately thirty-five Chinese naval officers attended foreign military or civilian educational institutions in 2006–7. PLAN delegations visited seventeen countries in 2008, and ninety-seven foreign officers attended Chinese naval academies or institutes. This record does not come close to that of the U.S. Navy, but it is still impressive and demonstrates China's appreciation of the employment of naval power in peacetime.

A newly emphasized mission area for the PLAN is military operations other than war (MOOTW). China's 2006 and 2008 Defense White Papers highlighted MOOTW, but doctrinal support remains undeveloped. An article in China's military newspaper lists twelve "operations other than war," including joint military exercises, military deterrence, disaster relief, and rescue; another notes the establishment of "five specialized forces" for flood and disaster relief; post-earthquake rescue; emergent rescue forces for nuclear, chemical, and biological disasters; transportation facilities; and international peacekeeping. Successful conduct of MOOTW requires full implementation of the "three warfares" as well as heightened readiness by the PLA and associated interagency forces. A key PLAN platform for these nonmilitary missions will be China's new hospital ship, *Peace Ark,* which conducted its first humanitarian mission in late 2009, albeit in Chinese territory.[40]

TACTICAL ENVIRONMENT

Planners also use specific opponents in tactical planning, represented by the "blue forces." The PLAN does not aspire to match U.S. naval power in the next half-century but is surely viewing other regional navies with a calculating eye. Russia's Pacific Fleet normally includes eight SSBNs, perhaps sixteen modern nuclear-powered attack submarines, a nuclear-powered guided-missile cruiser (reportedly inactive), no more than a dozen other guided-missile cruisers and destroyers, at least a dozen minesweepers, and six LSTs, but apparently has no underway replenishment ships. This nominally significant fleet suffers from a lack of logistical support and is of doubtful readiness.[41]

The United States has mutual defense treaties with Japan, South Korea,

Australia, and the Philippines. All but the Philippines maintain notable navies, the most formidable being the euphemistically named Japanese Maritime Self-Defense Force (JMSDF). The PLAN does not deploy forces with the technological sophistication or personnel expertise to match the JMSDF. Furthermore, the United States is working to ensure the technological modernity of the JMSDF, which already includes Aegis-equipped ships, modern (if conventionally powered) submarines, air-capable surface ships, and a modern maritime air arm trained and equipped to operate out to one thousand nautical miles from the home islands. Most significant, perhaps, is Japan's acquisition of three LSTs and two destroyers that are really small aircraft carriers. These ships extend Tokyo's maritime reach from the Bering Sea to the Luzon Strait between Taiwan and the Philippines. Japan clearly possesses both the technology and facilities to build larger aircraft carriers.

Japan's maritime power includes one of the world's leading shipbuilding industries as well as fishing and commercial fleets that are among the largest in the world. Tokyo is modernizing its combat ships and aircraft at a steady pace. Thus, it may remain the most powerful navy in Asia and, more important, maintain a position from which it can easily expand and further modernize rapidly to fill in behind any American withdrawal from the region. That situation may change, however, if the Hatoyama government elected in mid-2009 follows through on its policy of reducing defense expenditures. A halt or significant slowdown in Japan's naval developments will redound directly to China's benefit and lead quickly to a maritime imbalance in the East China Sea. Even before Hatoyama's election, the ground force dominated Japan's defense budget, receiving more than 30 percent versus the JMSDF's 23 percent.[42] Japan is continuing to build on what is already the most modern and powerful naval force in Asia other than the U.S. Seventh Fleet, however, and clearly has the financial, personnel, industrial, and technological-scientific resources to become Asia's dominant maritime force. The perception in Tokyo that the strategic situation in East Asia is changing dramatically—a significantly decreased U.S. military presence, for instance, or a dramatically more capable PLAN—might well lead Japan to seek such dominance to ensure its strategic interests in the East China Sea and the SLOCs.

The PLAN would also have difficulty opposing the Republic of Korea Navy (ROKN). South Korea is modernizing and expanding its navy, although ROKN planning scenarios probably look toward Japan rather than China as a likely opponent. It is no accident that Korea in 2009 gave the name *Dok Do* to its first helicopter carrier, since that is the name of the group of rocks whose ownership is disputed with Japan. Seoul classifies this 19,000-ton ship as a landing platform dock (LPD), but it is a much more capable ship than that. The ROKN includes almost forty surface ships armed with either Harpoon or Exocet surface-to-surface missiles (SSMs). The most significant ship acquisition program is building Aegis-equipped destroyers; seven had joined the fleet by 2009, and two more are scheduled for service by 2012. South Korea also deploys twelve modern conventionally powered submarines as well as significant mine warfare and special warfare forces. Equally important is the fact that this small country is currently as capable as China of producing state-of-the art military technology.

Australia deploys a small but extremely professional and capable force of surface combatants, submarines, and aircraft. It is one of the few Asian navies with the capability to support itself at sea over long distances. Its neighbor, New Zealand, offers equally professional naval personnel, but successive governments in Wellington have reduced the navy to a very small force with limited capability.

Despite its status as China's primary disputant in the South China Sea, the Philippines simply does not have a navy (or air force) of any significance. Manila's periodic declarations that the navy will be modernized and expanded have come to naught. Reasons for this inaction include a weak national treasury, weak national leadership, political maneuvering, an uneasy civil-military relationship dating back to Philippine independence in 1946, and a lack of clear strategic goals. These factors contribute to the legislature's refusal to finance a capable navy, while resurgent rebellions by the New People's Army in the north and Islamic groups in the south have forced the military to concentrate on internal security. The Philippines has few resources available for contesting maritime territorial claims. Manila's mutual defense treaty with the United States was reinvigorated by the visiting forces agreement passed by the Philippine Senate in 1999, especially in terms of U.S. assistance in Manila's struggle against various insurgent and terrorist groups; but that treaty probably does not apply to the South China Sea islands disputed with Beijing. Furthermore, Manila has been pursuing diplomatic and economic accommodation with Beijing rather than challenging China's campaign to solidify its presence in the South China Sea.

Taiwan is modernizing its navy, but at a slow pace because national government priorities do not highlight defense modernization.[43] Most troublesome for Taiwan's exercise of naval power is, quite simply, geography. The island's propinquity to the mainland will make it difficult for Taipei to counterbalance

Beijing's air power. In other words, the future promises a degree of Chinese air superiority that will cancel out any Taiwanese superiority at sea. Taiwan's navy includes two old submarines built in 1980 and two ancient boats built in 1944; efforts to acquire more submarines have failed in the face of Chinese protests to potential sources such as France, Germany, and the Netherlands. Taiwan has been more successful in acquiring surface ships. Four ex-U.S. *Kidd*-class DDGs, six modern *La Fayette*–class missile ships of French design, six FFG-7-type guided-missile frigates of U.S. design built in Taiwan, and eight ex-U.S. *Knox*-class frigates form the island's surface combatant force.

Other Asian nations, especially Indonesia, Singapore, Malaysia, and Thailand, are also modernizing their navies, although their efforts are still constrained by the effects of the economic disaster that struck in July 1997.[44] Indonesia is—for at least the third time—trying to expand its navy in recognition of its nature as an archipelago and the increasing need to guarantee communications between Jakarta and outlying provinces subject to secessionist movements. Beijing's territorial ambitions in the southern South China Sea also concern the Indonesians. Jakarta's effort, based on the purchase of six Harpoon-equipped corvettes from the Netherlands and sixteen ex–East German corvettes, has apparently been productive. The Indonesian Navy already included two modern conventionally powered submarines and eight capable surface ships, most armed with SSMs. The navy also includes a large patrol/coastal force, necessary for a nation of almost countless islands stretching across several thousand miles of Southeast Asia's southern rim.

Jakarta still faces a complex maritime strategic situation. The navy must defend the coastal waters and oil fields; safeguard Indonesian territorial and maritime claims against the Philippines, Malaysia, and other neighbors; and enforce Indonesian sovereignty over oil and natural gas fields in the South China Sea against possible Chinese encroachment. Finally, the navy plays an important role in maintaining national unity.

Singapore continued to modernize its armed forces throughout the recent economic slowdown. The island state has created a centralized, coherent joint defense system with a naval arm of missile-firing surface combatants, submarines, and shore-based air power.[45]

Malaysia's efforts to increase its naval strength have slowed, although new surface combatant vessels are being acquired and three submarines were deployed by 2008. The first of a new class of missile-armed corvettes joined the Malaysian Navy in March 2000.[46]

Thailand halted naval modernization because of the 1997 economic crash and has not resumed it in a meaningful fashion. The only significant additions to the Thai Navy during the past decade have been two *Gaeta*-class mine hunters and three indigenously built small patrol craft. While Thailand continues to benefit from its close military relationship with the United States, highlighted by the biannual Cobra Gold exercises and supported by defense agreements between the two nations, material improvements to Thailand's navy are on hold, due primarily to domestic political uncertainties.[47] Bangkok continues to play a wily international game and has purchased significant quantities of arms from Beijing, including six frigates now armed with Harpoons or the Chinese version of Exocets.[48] The two countries signed a Plan of Action for the Twenty-first Century in February 1999. The plan includes mutual visits by senior officials, increased trade and cooperation in science and technology, and "reviving existing arms purchase plans," which have not significantly improved Thailand's navy.[49]

The Thai Navy also includes two Harpoon-armed *Knox*-class frigates leased from the United States and two other Harpoon-armed corvettes, but its most significant warship is a small aircraft carrier. *Chakri Naruebet*, built in Spain in 1997, displaces about 12,000 tons, has a "ski jump" flight deck with two aircraft elevators, and can embark a combination of twelve helicopters and vertical-takeoff-and-landing (VTOL) aircraft. The carrier has a nominal mission of SAR and humanitarian operations and is equipped with quarters for the royal family. Thailand's was the first Asian navy since 1945 to deploy integral sea-based air power, although it has operated the carrier very infrequently.[50] This capability positions Thailand to take the lead in any confrontation between the Southeast Asian nations and an outside power—such as might develop with China over South China Sea territorial claims. Thailand has no claims in that sea, however. The Thai domestic political situation remains unsettled, and a policy of remaining friendly with China almost completely eliminates the possibility that Bangkok would assume a military leadership role in Southeast Asia, especially if it were perceived as countering Beijing's presence.

Vietnam's participation with India's navy and coast guard in "joint training and exercises" has been accompanied by modest steps to modernize its naval and air force strength.[51] Vietnam is acquiring additional Kilo-class submarines from Russia. Its modernization policy has been overshadowed, however, by a determined campaign to resolve border disputes with Beijing and to deal with China's increasing presence in Southeast Asia peacefully and multilaterally, primarily through the Association of Southeast Asian Nations (ASEAN).

India's formidable navy is composed largely of Soviet- and Russian-designed ships, submarines, and aircraft, but also includes a British-built aircraft carrier. It poses a major counterforce to any Chinese ambitions to extend a naval presence into the Indian Ocean, and makes such ambitions impractical for at least the next decade. India is also building an indigenously designed carrier, *Vikrant*, due for commissioning in 2017, while awaiting delivery of a modernized Russian Kiev-class carrier, originally named *Admiral Gorshkov*. This ship has been delayed in conversion in Russia, and reportedly has suffered from unexpected engineering difficulties and huge cost overruns.[52]

Sino-Indian relations remain uneasy, and New Delhi apparently interprets Beijing's activities in Burma as evidence of a policy to establish a presence on the western approaches to the South China Sea. Recent joint statements to "resolve to maintain peace along [their] borders" aside, India does not welcome a Chinese naval presence in "its" ocean.[53] Indian naval operations included 1999 visits to the Persian Gulf and the Mediterranean Sea, and exercises with South Korea, Vietnam, and Japan in 2000. A new naval doctrine announced in December 1999 envisions an Indian Navy in 2010 built around two aircraft carriers (the ex-British *Hermes*-class carrier is to be decommissioned), and cruise missile–firing submarines and long-range maritime patrol aircraft. This plan is well on its way to fulfillment with India's first indigenously produced nuclear-powered submarine being launched in 2009.[54]

In sum, indigenous Asian Pacific navies include the extremely formidable JMSDF and the rapidly improving ROKN. Australia's navy is also modern and capable, but very small. Singapore, Malaysia, Indonesia, and Thailand all have modern navies, but only by operating in concert could they pose a challenge to the PLAN. The political situation in Southeast Asia makes that highly unlikely.

Given Korea's and Japan's distance from the South China Sea, and the constitutional and historical factors that inhibit Tokyo, China faces no naval force south of Taiwan with which it need be seriously concerned—other than the U.S. Seventh Fleet, assisted by Australia. That is a formidable force, however, since even peacetime American naval forces in East and Southwest Asia usually include two aircraft carriers; four nuclear-powered submarines; a dozen cruisers and destroyers, most of them armed with Aegis; four to six underway replenishment ships; and an amphibious ready group. This group includes a very large (48,000 tons displacement) helicopter carrier and two other large amphibious ships operating in support of the Marine brigade based on Okinawa. Air assets include two Navy and one Marine Corps air wings, and three numbered U.S. air forces.

This situation provides parameters to PLAN officers developing operational doctrine, who can focus on two general factors: the advent of new technology at sea and the U.S. naval presence in the Asia-Pacific region. These are significant factors that may be imposing a syllogism on the development of maritime doctrine in China: (1) any mission must be couched in terms of the PLAN's ability to execute it; (2) no traditional naval mission can be completed without U.S. dispensation; and hence (3) the PLAN must devolve nontraditional means for carrying out its assigned missions. If PLAN strategists are in fact engaged in this sort of strategic "Easter egg hunt," they will fail to develop effective operational effectiveness, all their talk of RMA and Sun Zi notwithstanding.

TAIWAN

PLAN strategists in 2010 still face one overriding scenario: the potential employment of naval force against Taiwan. Chinese political and senior military leaders certainly would prefer peaceful resolution of the island's status, but the spring 2000 election of a Democratic Progressive Party government and Beijing's refusal to renounce the possible use of force both meant that for the eight years of the Chen Shui-bian administration, PLAN planners were working to develop efficient and effective plans for employing naval force against Taiwan. These plans probably covered the gamut of maritime operations from submarine and air surveillance of Taiwanese ship traffic to a full-scale amphibious invasion of the island.

While the degree of crisis over Taiwan's status has relaxed since the Kuomintang Party under President Ma Ying-jeou assumed power in 2008, PLAN operational thought about Taiwan probably remains focused on four alternative military courses of action: amphibious assault, blockade (including employment of surface ships, submarines, and mines), attacks on the island's command authorities ("decapitation"), and "deterrent strike."[55] Amphibious assault from the sea is, of course, the classic military attack to capture an island. This is a difficult, complex operation to carry out successfully, requiring the attacker not merely to match the defender's forces, but to outnumber them by a five-to-one ratio.[56] In 1944 U.S. Army planners believed that an assault on Taiwan was unsupportable because it would require seven infantry divisions—approximately 150,000 combat troops plus an additional 220,000 support personnel.[57]

PLAN planners will have to take into account the typically bad and change-able weather in the Taiwan Strait and the lack of suitable landing beaches on the island's coasts. The strait is subject to high winds and seas, often above those forecast, and is susceptible to typhoons during much of the year. The lack of beaches is compounded by the presence of broad mud flats, tidal ranges of up to fifteen meters, and complex currents.[58]

PLAN officers also have to face the usual plethora of military planning issues. These range from the manning status of ships to the troop-carrying capacity of individual landing craft; from the availability of aircraft bed-down sites on the mainland to the availability of the communications frequencies and troop rations required for extensive operations at sea. One vital factor, viewing the present platforms and capabilities of the Chinese and Taiwan militaries, is that the PLAN would have a very difficult time establishing control of the Taiwan Strait. Without air and sea control, at least for the period required for specific maritime actions against Taiwan, the PLAN surface fleet could accomplish little. Hence, planners have to assume that the PLAN may not be able to eliminate the Taiwanese Navy. No doubt they are seeking a way to neutralize their potential adversary, perhaps through surprise and deception, special operations and psychological warfare, and information warfare.

Even more important than these issues is, of course, the role of the United States. Clearly, for the foreseeable future, the PLAN will not be able to conduct significant operations on or above the sea without U.S. acquies-cence or the absence of U.S. forces due to other commitments. This does not mean, however, that the PLAN is helpless in the face of active U.S. opposi-tion. For one thing, ASW is so difficult that the United States will not be able completely to foreclose PLAN submarine operations. For another, China might launch a military action against Taiwan at a time when U.S. forces are relatively unalert and no U.S. aircraft carrier strike group is operating in the western Pacific. The potential U.S. role provides impetus for PLAN planners to devise a way to present Washington with a fait accompli—to achieve mili-tary victory before the United States is able to intervene decisively and deal the Chinese forces severe losses.[59] The PLAN would then be able to carry out specific missions against Taiwan with minimal U.S. naval interference—at least for a short period, perhaps ten days.

An effective air and sea blockade would cause severe damage to Taiwan. PLAN submarines and mines could essentially close the island's two signifi-cant commercial ports, Keelung and Kaiohsung. Furthermore, Beijing could claim that mines laid around Taiwan were within China's territorial waters and hence did not violate international law, as long as the appropriate warnings to mariners were issued. Beijing could further announce that merchant ships scheduled to call at Taiwan's ports had to first stop at a mainland port to embark a pilot who would safely navigate the ship through the minefields.

Taiwan's weak minesweeping force consists of four twenty-year-old coastal mine hunters obtained from Germany and eight ex-U.S. and ex-Belgian minesweepers that are forty to fifty years old. China's dedicated mine warfare forces are also small, but mines can be laid by almost any surface ship, as well as by aircraft. Significantly, PLAN surface combatants are required annually to exercise laying mines, not a common practice in most navies. Mines are easy to distribute and difficult to counter. Not only is minesweeping laborious, but just the announcement that mines have been laid would play havoc with commercial shipping to the island.

A U.S. decision to assist Taiwan in breaking a Chinese blockade would pose several problems to Washington. First, the U.S. Navy has a limited mine-clearing capability, and except for two small ships located in Japan, these ships and helicopters could not arrive in the Taiwan area without significant delay. Second is the legal problem of minefields laid in China's claimed territorial waters. Third, would the United States decide to attack the mainland source of the mines? That would constitute escalation on a grand scale.

U.S. analysts have addressed the problem posed by China's formidable inventory of mines and their usefulness as an adjunct to PLAN operations, particularly in a Taiwan scenario in which they could be used to blockade or at least isolate the island. These analyses do not sufficiently take into account the time required to lay an effective, controllable minefield; scattering mines across an area, as Iraq did in 1990–91, is little more than an act of terrorism and not conducive to achieving policy aims. The analyses do, however, describe a serious operational capability and a developed mine warfare doctrine against which fleet units—surface ships, aircraft, and submarines—have exercised. This doctrine reportedly includes as mission objectives "blockading enemy bases, harbors and sea lanes; destroying enemy sea transport capabilities; attacking or restricting warship mobility [aircraft carriers are specifically mentioned]; and crippling and exhausting enemy combat strength."[60]

The third Chinese military option is the one most often discussed in the media: the use of ballistic and cruise missiles, and perhaps manned aircraft, to bombard Taiwan. China's missile launches in the spring of 1996 of course contribute to the discussion of this option, but an effective missile barrage would have to overcome three significant hurdles. The first of these is topography: Taiwan is a large, mountainous island, not a "billiard table" target. Second, the mainstays of China's present ballistic missile inventory—the M-9 and M-11—have only moderate-sized warheads, 500 and 800 kg, respectively. More important, however, their accuracy—previously 300 and 600 m, respectively—has improved during the past decade to a CEP (one-half the distance around the aim point within which the missile should be expected to land) of 50 m or better. China is also increasing its inventory of land-attack cruise missiles, which are generally more accurate than ballistic missiles but typically carry smaller warheads.[61]

China's missile force could inflict great death and destruction on Taiwan and its people, but even several hundred of these missiles fired very accurately should not be able to force the Taipei government to surrender, given strong popular will on the island. Although the existence of more than one thousand missiles poised against Taiwan serves as a deterrent force, the third, and most important, hurdle is the will of Taiwan's people to resist. China is unlikely to deploy enough naval transports to carry a force across the strait sufficient for a successful amphibious assault within at least the next ten years. Taiwan is too big to be bombed into submission by manned bombers and ballistic missiles, and the island could stockpile enough energy resources, obtain sufficient supplies by air, and prevent implementation of a complete blockade to make that option work—if the will to resist is present.[62]

What course of action will Beijing select to resolve the tough strategic questions posed by Taiwan and the East and South China seas? The Navy provides the weapons and manpower, and develops the operational doctrine and well-trained tactical proficiency, but this must be framed by a coherent maritime strategy.

CONCLUSION

The dominant doctrinal concept for China's Navy is "offshore defense." But that phrase raises two crucial issues. First, the PLA's *Science of Military Strategy* states that "striking only after the enemy has struck does not mean waiting for [the] enemy's strike passively"; if any country violates China's "sovereignty and territorial integrity," China has "the right to fire the first shot." So much for the PLAN taking the first round or for Beijing's oft-proclaimed policy of "no first use" of nuclear weapons.[63] Second is how "offshore" is defined. It can be defined as "green water" or "blue water" or (by an increasing number of Chinese writers) as the area within the first island chain. Or "offshore" can be defined by the range of PLA airpower and PLAN capability, by China's territorial claims, or by China's potential maritime opponents. Most useful, however, is a definition of "offshore" that is applied to the naval operational objective at hand. In 2010 this remains Taiwan, but other scenarios—East China Sea, South China Sea, SLOC defense—have gained in prominence, especially with the 2009 deployments to the Gulf of Aden, which are truly "offshore" operations. It must be remembered, however, that virtually all decisive naval battles throughout history have been fought in littoral waters— within two hundred nautical miles of a coastline.

The Gulf of Aden deployments have also demonstrated unprecedented Chinese naval cooperation with other nations. Beijing in early November 2009 convened a conference of concerned nations seeking "the best formula of international cooperation" for countering the pirates. Meanwhile, near-daily informal cooperation with other naval forces in the gulf included attendance by the PLAN commander at a Combined Maritime Forces conference in Bahrain in May 2009.[64]

The linkage between doctrine and strategy for the PLAN is most accurately phrased in variations on a Mahanian theme. It is not "command of the sea" per se, because Beijing evinces no evidence of pursuing a global, Wilhelmine navy, but rather building a twenty-first-century Navy capable of achieving national security objectives—despite possible opposition from the United States or other maritime powers. Hence, "sea denial" is the most applicable of the classic maritime theories for China's ambitions. It is essentially a negative concept, but one attractive to a rising naval power with China's access to mines, missiles, submarines, and shore-based aircraft.

CHAPTER 8

China's Maritime Strategy

A decade ago, a prominent strategist at China's Academy of Military Science cited defense as the continuing central theme in both continental and maritime strategy in China. Lieutenant General Mi Zhenyu claimed that while imperial China fought sea battles, the "basic format in ancient times was 'land as primary, sea as secondary.'" Today, he continued, "equal consideration is given to 'land and sea,'" and Beijing considers "the ocean as its chief strategic defensive direction." Mi averred that "China's political and economic focus lies on the coastal areas [and] for the present and a fairly long period to come, [its] strategic focus will be in the direction of the sea."[1]

This thought is discussed more specifically in a paper from China's Naval Command Academy that identifies "four strategic tasks" for the Navy: protecting national "territorial sovereignty" and "safeguarding" its "water rights"; "ensuring the unification of the motherland and protecting social stability"; diplomatic activities; and providing security for national development. In practical terms these mean preventing Taiwan's independence, enforcing Beijing's claims in the East and South China seas, presence on the global scene, and defending China's economic interests.[2]

Alfred Thayer Mahan and Julian Corbett are probably the best-known maritime strategists of our time. Although they wrote at the turn of the twentieth century, they are still widely studied by navies, including the PLAN. Mahan and Corbett addressed the basic question of how maritime power can best be used to defend vital national interests, as do more recent maritime thinkers such as America's Wayne Hughes, Russia's Sergei Gorshkov, Great Britain's Colin Gray, and China's Liu Huaqing.

The classic maritime strategic concept is "command of the sea," defined most simply as the ability to use the sea while denying its use to an adversary. "Sea control," a lesser but still powerful concept, is defined as a nation's ability to "command" an area for a limited period of time sufficient to achieve limited strategic goals. Analogous to sea control is "sea denial": preventing an adversary from using a discrete maritime area for a discrete period of time without necessarily using it oneself. The PLAN combines these elements in its definition of command of the sea: "employing sea forces to gain control of a particular maritime area for a particular period of time . . . to eliminate potential threats to the friendly side in a particular area, gain freedom of action on the sea for the friendly side, and enable the friendly side to effectively utilize the ocean to undertake political, military, and economic action; and when necessary, to strip the enemy's command of the sea, and stop him from using the ocean (or) cause his maritime activities to be limited."[3] Sea denial is subsumed in this definition and is a particularly attractive option in littoral waters for even a small naval power if it has access to mines, missiles, small surface ships and submarines, and shore-based aircraft—as does the PLAN.

The *PLAN Encyclopedia* lists several factors as influencing modern naval strategy, including:

- training and education programs leading to professional specialization of the officer corps;
- naval systems and platforms costs, capabilities, and sustainability;
- national scientific and industrial infrastructure for research, development, and production of naval warfare technology and systems;
- the ability to derive doctrine and tactics;
- the ability to administer, operate, and command and control tactical units beyond individual ships;
- sources of intelligence, and its production, analysis, and dissemination;
- service-wide naval strategic planning;
- national maritime leadership; and
- the effectiveness of naval strategists in the national strategy-making structure.[4]

We will use these factors as a measure of China's development of a maritime strategy—with the addition of "geography," which should head the list but is instead a glaring omission.

Maritime strategy should reflect Colin Gray's dictum that "man lives on the land, not on the sea, and conflict at sea has strategic meaning only with reference to what its outcome enables, or implies, for the course of events on land." Gray cautioned, however, that in all the history of war, "the enemy who is confined to a land strategy is in the end defeated."[5] In other words, a maritime strategist must remember that command of the sea, sea control, and sea denial are all means, not ends; they serve only to promote a nation's ability to directly affect events on the land.

STRATEGY, POLITICS, AND GEOGRAPHY

China's current campaign to modernize its military follows the sea-change in strategic thinking that occurred in 1985, when expectations of global nuclear war or large-scale conflict with the Soviet Union gave way to a focus on small, local wars on China's periphery.[6] Planners envisioned five types of local, limited wars: small-scale conflicts in disputed border areas, conflicts over disputed islands or ocean areas, surprise air attacks, deliberate incursions into China, and counterattacks by China against an aggressor or "to uphold justice and dispel threats."[7] This was an important shift for Chinese maritime strategic thought—a shift from a general strategy of coastal defense to one of offshore defense. The Navy also moved from Army acolyte to prominent participant in possible operational scenarios, including threats from Japan, Taiwan, and India, and dealing with contentious maritime claims.

PLAN Strategy: 1949–1960

Soviet advisers brought to China the Soviet "Young School" of maritime strategy, which emphasized coastal defense by a navy of small surface craft and submarines. The Young School developed in the Soviet Union shortly after World War I based on conditions particular to postrevolutionary Russia, and was designed for

- a new regime that was under military and political attack by several capitalist countries and had not completely quelled domestic fighting;
- a regime that *expected* to be attacked by capitalist nations, with amphibious attack a current fact and future threat, especially from "the ultimate bastion of imperialism, the United States";[8]

- a navy in disarray and almost entirely manned by captured/defecting former enemy personnel;[9]
- budgetary shortages that limited the amount available to spend on expensive naval systems;
- lack of an industrial infrastructure to produce indigenously modern naval armaments; and
- a maritime frontier hemmed in by adversarial fleets and bases.

These conditions also applied to China in 1949, as did the additional problem of no recent maritime tradition. The Young School concept was attractive to early PLAN strategists because it required a defensive navy that would be relatively inexpensive to build and could be quickly manned and trained. Furthermore, the concept was analogous to guerrilla war at sea.[10]

The Soviet Union sent an initial cadre of 500 naval advisers to China in 1950; between 1,500 and 2,000 were present by 1953. These advisers paralleled the Chinese chain of command from Beijing headquarters to individual ships and squadrons, thus providing the means for inculcating Soviet naval doctrine throughout the new Chinese Navy. "Large numbers" of Chinese officers, including the new head of the PLAN, General Xiao Jingguang, received training in the Soviet Union. Xiao was twice a student in Moscow and spoke fluent Russian; he was both "an excellent administrator" and "a staunch Maoist who could be counted upon to adhere to whatever line the chairman espoused."[11]

Although China's maritime strategy in the early 1950s was primarily defensive, Beijing worked to develop the offensive capability to recover the offshore islands still occupied by the KMT, a campaign expected to culminate in the conquest of Taiwan.[12] When he inspected PLAN units in February 1953 during the Korean War, Mao Zedong justified the need for "a strong Navy for the purposes of fighting against imperialist aggression."[13] In December of that year he assigned the PLAN three priority missions: eliminate KMT naval interference and ensure safe navigation, prepare to recover Taiwan, and oppose aggression from the sea. Chinese and Taiwanese forces resumed amphibious attacks and counterattacks, which ended in Beijing's possession of all the significant offshore islands except Jinmen, Mazu, and of course Taiwan. The PLA also succeeded in stopping most of the attacks on Chinese merchant and fishing vessels, as well as the Taiwanese raids on the mainland. In less than a decade the PLAN had been organized, sent to sea, and proven effective as a Soviet-style coastal defense force, all the while adhering to the rubric of people's war.

The Korean War did not change Beijing's belief that relatively short-range defensive sea forces could counter the American invasion threat; no blue-water Chinese Navy was planned after 1954. The Navy's attempts to modernize, with an emphasis on technology and technical training, took place under a coastal defense strategy.

Attempts in the 1950s to develop a specific and perhaps independent strategic role for the PLAN fell victim to the triumph of politics over technology. Throughout the ideological turmoil of the late 1950s and the 1960s Beijing invested heavily in a determined effort to develop nuclear weapons and missiles as well as the nuclear-powered submarines from which they could be launched.[14]

A New Situation: 1960–1976

Despite the drive to produce modern strategic weapons, Mao's concept of people's war continued to guide the small Navy as well as the other branches of the PLA, as did continued adherence to the Young School—modified by some significant naval developments. By the end of the decade, relations with the Soviet Union had deteriorated to the point of armed conflict along the Amur River. The former ally was now the enemy, and the former enemy—the United States—would soon become China's strategic ally.

The Soviet threat in the 1960s and the PLA's lack of mobility drove China's national security strategy to continue fielding very large ground forces supplemented by a coastal Navy. The PLAN's coastal defense role was modified only by the development in the 1960s of nuclear-powered attack and ballistic missile submarines that later joined the fleet from 1970 to 1991.

The Navy continued to follow a strategy of coastal defense during the Great Proletarian Cultural Revolution (GPCR), which meant serving as an extension of the Army and little modernization. People's war held that technology and weaponry were insignificant compared with the effect of revolutionary soldiers imbued with Mao's ideology.

After the Great Proletarian Cultural Revolution

PLAN strategic missions still operated under the dictates of the Young School during the 1970s. Assistance to the Army; offshore patrol against criminal activities such as smuggling, piracy, and illegal immigration; lifesaving; and safety of navigation were the Navy's missions. Beijing also saw its ancient antagonist, Japan, reemerge as a strong maritime force.

Meanwhile, the Soviet Navy in the 1960s and 1970s underwent a dramatic change under the leadership of Admiral Sergei Gorshkov, partly as a result of the Cuban Missile Crisis, which demonstrated Soviet maritime weakness. Under Gorshkov's guidance the Soviets attempted to build a worldwide fleet to match that of the United States. This fleet's missions in time of war would be defense of offshore areas, countering an adversary's strategic strike systems, sea control in fleet ballistic missile (FBM) submarine operating areas, strategic nuclear strikes, disrupting an adversary's SLOCs, and protecting friendly SLOCs. Gorshkov's maritime strategy also included specific peacetime tasks: showing the flag, gaining international respect, supporting economic interests, managing crises, limiting an adversary's options, exercising local sea control, and fighting in local wars.[15]

A similar naval metamorphosis did not occur in China, but the growth and modernization of the Soviet Navy heightened Beijing's concern. People's war was no longer deemed an adequate maritime strategy. Chinese planners began thinking about projecting naval power against potential Soviet actions beyond coastal waters. Always present, but second to concern about the Soviet Union, was the determination to ensure the viability of Beijing's territorial claims throughout East Asia. Taiwan was the most important of these, but China was also concerned about its claims in the East and South China seas.

China ended the 1970s with a limited strategic view of the maritime environment. Deng Xiaoping reemphasized the Navy's role as a coastal defense force, a view retained throughout the first half of the 1980s. At that point the Navy came to be viewed as something more than an adjunct to the ground forces. China's coastal concentration of economic interests and military bases, widening maritime interests, and increased budget resources after 1979 did give rise to increased interest in a stronger Navy. China also completed developing a seaborne nuclear deterrent force, based on Mao's earlier declaration that the Navy had to be built up "to make it dreadful to the enemy."[16] Although the single FBM China deployed about 1980 was a national rather than a naval asset, the Xia gave the PLAN a nuclear deterrent mission for the first time.

Liu Huaqing's Vision

The chief architect of China's emerging maritime strategy in the 1980s was General Liu Huaqing. As early as 1982 Liu directed the PLAN's Naval Research College to elaborate a strategy of "offshore defense." By "offshore" Liu meant the ocean area from China's coast to approximately the first island chain, defined by a line through the Kurile Islands, Japan and the Ryukyu Islands, Taiwan, the Philippines, Borneo, and Natuna Besar.[17]

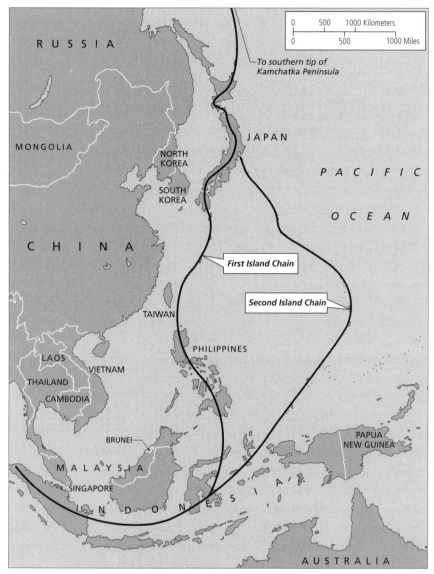

Admiral Liu Huaqing's island chains. (Bernard D. Cole)

Liu observed that "the strategic position of the Pacific is becoming more important [and] as China is gradually expanding the scale of its maritime development, the Chinese Navy will have to shoulder more and heavier tasks in both peacetime and war." He argued that "the scope of sea warfare operations has extended from the limited space of air, the surface, the water, and coasts, to all space from under the sea to outer space and from the sea inland. . . . In order to safeguard China's coast, resist possible foreign invasion, and defend our maritime rights and interests, it is only right and proper that China should attach great importance to developing its own Navy, including 'emphatic' development of its submarine force."[18]

Liu wanted to change the maritime element of China's national strategy from coastal defense to "offshore defense,"[19] a strategy that included stubborn defense near the shore, mobile warfare at sea, and surprise guerrilla-like attacks at sea. These three tenets continued to pay homage to Maoist concepts of war fighting but were significant because of Liu's emphasis on moving China's maritime defense seaward.[20]

"Offshore" in this construct has been variously defined as ranging from 150 to 600 nautical miles, but Liu delineated two strategic maritime areas the nation must be able to control. The first of these, under phase 1 of the strategy, includes the Yellow Sea facing Korea and Japan; the western East China Sea, including Taiwan; and the South China Sea.[21] These fall within China's defined area of vital national interests: territorial claims, natural resources, and coastal defense. The area is also delineated by the first island chain, with 2000 the goal for establishing Chinese control of this area. The PLAN in 2010 still has not achieved Liu's 2000 goal, but has made significant progress toward doing so.

The second strategic maritime area, under phase 2 of Liu's strategy, is delineated by the "second island chain," a north–south line from the Kuriles through Japan, the Bonins, the Marianas, and the Carolines, and would give Beijing control of all of East Asia's vast ocean areas, nominally by 2020.[22] China's ability to control this area would require very significant national resources for its Navy and Air Force as well as two unlikely conditions: the United States would have to withdraw its military presence from the region, and Japan would have to sit idly by in the face of U.S. withdrawal and not engage in an arms race with Beijing to ensure continued Japanese maritime superiority.

The third stage of Liu's maritime strategy has the PLAN becoming a global force by 2050. A step toward this goal occurred in the spring of 1997 when, within a three-month period, China deployed multiship task groups composed of warships and logistics support vessels to Southeast Asia and to North, Central, and South America. More significant were the PLAN's 2002 circumnavigation and, particularly, the 2009 operational deployments to the Gulf of Aden, the widest-ranging Chinese naval deployment since the voyages of Zheng He between 1405 and 1433.

Ironically, defining "phases" of maritime theaters by fixed geographic boundaries reveals a strong continentalist perspective, even in the mind of China's most prominent post-1949 admiral. It violates the central tenet of classic maritime strategy that while the soldier thinks of terrain and theaters, the sailor of necessity thinks in wider terms outside immediate physical limits—there is no "terrain" at sea.[23]

Liu's emphasis is understandable, however, given his Army background and early Soviet training, and the continuing influence of Soviet/Russian naval strategic thought in China during his tenure in command. By the mid-1980s the USSR's maritime strategy had settled on a division of its coastal waters into defense zones ranging outward about 2,000 nm. Liu Huaqing's maritime "phases" almost certainly owe their origin to those Soviet "zones." The inner-most of the zones was called the "area of sea control"; the second was the "area of sea denial"; and the third was a broad region for long-range reconnaissance and submarine interdiction. The first and second Soviet zones, which extended seaward 1,500 nm, closely match Liu's two island chains, the second of which lies about 1,350–1,500 nm from China's coast.

The similarity between the Chinese and Soviet maritime strategic concepts is sharply drawn in an article by Liu's successor as PLAN commander, Zhang Lianzhong, who in 1988 identified three maritime defense areas for the PLAN:

> The exterior perimeter [encompasses] the seas out to the first chain of islands. This region will be defended by conventional and nuclear submarines (some of which will be armed with anti-ship missiles), by naval medium-range aircraft and by surface warships. The submarines will play a dynamic role to ensure defense in depth, including the laying of mines in the enemy's sea lines of communication. The middle defense perimeter extends 150 miles from the coast and comes within, but in most cases does not reach, the first chain of islands. Anti-ship aircraft, destroyers and escort vessels will carry the main burden in this area. The interior defense perimeter extends to sixty miles from the coast. This will be the theater of operations for the main naval air force, fast-attack boats and land-based anti-ship missile units.[24]

Since 2000

Liu's strategy outlined the direction for the PLAN's future modernization and growth. It envisioned control of vast oceanic expanses, a very difficult task simply by virtue of the geography, not to mention that other nations would object to Chinese hegemony over such a large portion of the earth's surface. Despite missing the target year for sea control inside the first island chain, the Navy's long peacetime deployments and current operations in the Gulf of Aden demonstrate the viability of Liu Huaqing's vision. The island chain concept remains active in Chinese naval thinking, with a focus on Taiwan as a "key point" in the chain. Furthermore, Liu's timeline was essentially repeated in Beijing's 2006 Defense White Paper, indicating consistency in China's strategic long view.[25]

Liu directed study and elaboration of his strategic concepts, which emphasized naval missions well to seaward of the coastal zone that formed the basis for past PRC maritime strategy.[26] It is likely that his three-phase strategic progression was designed primarily for domestic consumption, to win resources for the PLAN. Liu was apparently following a path similar to that of naval expansionists in turn-of-the-century America and Germany as they built modern navies in conjunction with their nations' rapidly expanding economies.

PLAN modernization requires a well-articulated offshore mission supporting China as the strongest maritime power in East Asia and as a major power in the Pacific. A direct line may be drawn from Sergei Gorshkov to Liu Huaqing: the former was an instructor at the Voroshilov Naval Academy in Leningrad when the latter was a student at the school. Echoes of Alfred Thayer Mahan's theories also appear in the strategic thought of both men.

The PLAN has made significant progress adopting the Soviet maritime strategic objectives of the 1970s. FBM operating areas appear to be in the offing, with construction of a large submarine base on Hainan Island, at the head of the South China Sea, for instance. The Navy's "strategic nuclear strike" capability likewise appears to be a near-term accomplishment as the Jin-class submarines join the fleet.[27] The PLAN has also been engaging in peacetime strategic missions almost identical with those outlined by Gorshkov—who cited the American threat as his basic justification for a strong navy. Writing in 1975, the Russian admiral accused the United States of following an "oceanic strategy" of aggression against the Soviet Union.[28] Chinese strategists today use similar words; the Soviet-Russian maritime strategic influence remains strong in the PLAN.

Maritime Strategic Interests

In the Fourteenth Party Congress political report, released in 1992, General Secretary Jiang Zemin described the PLA's mission as "defending the unity, territorial integrity, and maritime rights and interests of the homeland."[29] This was the first time Jiang had addressed "maritime rights and interests." He later pledged the PLAN "to safeguard the sovereignty of China's territorial waters, uphold the country's unity and social stability and create a safe and stable environment for the nation's economic development." This emphasis has been repeated by Jiang's successor, Hu Jintao, since he took office in 2002.[30]

PLAN strategic goals begin with defense of the homeland: defending China's maritime borders. Recent diplomatic accomplishments have at least nominally resolved border disputes with all of China's continental neighbors, allowing Beijing to focus on maritime disputes. Vice Admiral Cheng Mingshang, the PLAN's vice chief in 1991, argued that the Navy was vital to China's national security as "the tool of the state's foreign policy. . . . An international Navy can project its presence far away from home. It can even appear at the sea close to the coastal lines of the target countries. . . . This has made the Navy the most active strategic force in peacetime, a pillar for the country's foreign policy and the embodiment of the country's will and power."[31] Liu Huaqing also cited the concentration of modern economic interests and growth in the special development zones clustered along China's seaboard as economic justification for a strong PLAN, stating that "the Chinese Navy must live up to the historical responsibility to grow rapidly up into a major power in the Pacific area in order to secure the smooth progress of China's economic modernization."[32]

In the fall of 1995 Jiang Zemin described China as "a continental power, and a coastal power as well." He noted the coastal region's "dense population, with its scientific, technological, and economic levels," stating that "the ocean as a natural protective screen covers this region of strategic significance. . . .We can be sure that the development and utilization of the ocean will be of increasingly greater significance to China's long-range development. This being the case, we must see the ocean from a strategic plane, and . . . set out new and higher requirements on navy building. We must . . . step up the pace of Navy modernization to meet the requirements of future wars."[33]

Anticipated war scenarios were modified over time, of course, but China's North Sea Fleet was responsible for countering any southward movement of the Soviet Pacific Fleet in the period between the 1960 split with the Soviet Union and that empire's dissolution in 1989. While this is no longer a significant mission, the North Sea Fleet still faces a difficult maritime situation: Russia, South Korea, and Japan all possess capable navies. Although Russia's fleet is only a shadow of its former self, those of South Korea and Japan are increasing in both numbers and capability.

Japan looms very large on China's horizon. Ancient disputes and rancor combined with World War II grievances and suspicion of future Japanese aggression create an edgy relationship. It is inherently a maritime relationship given the seas that lie between the two nations, forming a natural barrier to any but seaborne or airborne interaction. Beijing's evaluation of Tokyo's intentions must also take into account Japan's alliance with the United States, especially with respect to the implications of the 1997 security guidelines as they may apply to Taiwan. If Tokyo and the United States interpret those guidelines' reference to "waters surrounding Japan" as including Taiwan, then China would face a much more complicated situation in the strait.[34]

Chinese analysts have written openly that "the basic characteristic of China's diplomatic strategy is that, at present and for a long time to come, in terms of the main strategic tasks that China has to resolve and the main strategic pressures that it must bear, China's strategic focal points are all to the southeast." These include Taiwan as the essence of Beijing's strategic concerns. Despite concern about the United States, China refuses to renounce the use of military force to ensure the reunification of Taiwan. Beijing must count on the PLAN for policy options ranging from intimidation to outright invasion. The East China Sea Fleet presumably has local planning responsibility for contingency operations involving Taiwan, and also has been tasked with executing many diplomatic missions, as naval headquarters has assigned several recent significant distant deployments to that fleet.[35]

The South China Sea is second to Taiwan as a PLAN concern. This contiguous sea embodies important economic, political, and nationalistic strategic issues for Beijing; Liu Huaqing noted the PLAN's mission to secure the "vast resources" of this sea. China has maintained an unwavering position on its sovereignty over much of the area, backed by its actions against U.S. surveillance ships in 2009.[36] The National People's Congress passed the Law of the Territorial Sea and Contiguous Zones in February 1992, midway through Liu's tenure as China's senior uniformed officer. This act implies that China claims as sovereign territory almost all of the South China Sea, ocean as well as land areas.

China's strategic concern about India centers on the latter's nuclear arsenal and missiles. This capability, combined with the Sino-Indian border dispute and Beijing's concern for China's ally, Pakistan, gives India a special position in China's strategic view. Another concern must be India's desire to be involved in the South China Sea, recently evidenced in New Delhi's agreement with Hanoi to conduct mutual naval training events.[37]

China has been increasingly active in Burma, in part because of Beijing's concerns about the heavy flow of illegal drugs across the border into Yunnan Province, but also for reasons of economic gain and concern about India's intentions. China has also begun construction of an oil pipeline from the Andaman Sea through the length of Burma and into Yunnan Province, significantly increasing China's strategic stake in the troubled country.[38] The regional press has reported three Chinese approaches in Burma. First is the sale of military equipment, amounting to more than $2 billion since 1990 and accompanied by military technical support and advisers. The equipment ranges from small arms to oceangoing warships, including ten Hainan-class coastal patrol craft and six Houxin-class missile boats.[39] Second, Chinese military personnel have been reported in Burma, building and improving maritime facilities at Hainggyi, Akyab, and in the Mergui Islands off Burma's isthmian coast. Third, there have been reports of Chinese activity at what may be electronic monitoring facilities on the Cocos and Hangyi islands in the Andaman Sea. Such facilities would provide Beijing's naval commanders with intelligence on Indian and other naval forces in the Indian Ocean.[40]

China and Burma have announced a "framework of future bilateral relations and cooperation" that addresses increased trade and economic relations; forestry, tourism, culture, and judicial cooperation; joint attacks on transnational issues; and general regional cooperation.[41] Military issues are not discussed in this agreement, which is similar to those China has signed with other Southeast Asian nations. There is no hard evidence that China is establishing a naval presence in the eastern Indian Ocean, but the rationale for a PLAN presence in these waters is obvious: maritime concerns arising from China's dependence on trade and imported petroleum, and fears that an unfriendly India could control the Indian Ocean SLOCs on which China depends.

China's maritime strategy is linked inextricably to continued economic growth in the twenty-first century, which in turn depends on reliable foreign sources of energy. As discussed earlier, this imported petroleum comes primarily from the Middle East, over sea-lanes that pass through the Indian Ocean and the South and East China seas. These routes also pass through several geographic choke points, including the Luzon and Taiwan straits, the

Strait of Malacca, and the Strait of Hormuz. PLAN strategists have identified four strategic sea-lanes: east across the Pacific from the Western Hemisphere, south from Australasia, west through the Indian Ocean from Southwest Asia and Africa, and north through the Sea of Okhotsk.[42] China can project almost no naval control over these choke points, except for the Taiwan narrows, but the PLAN may want to correct this deficiency, beginning with a naval presence in the western approaches to the South China Sea. Beijing believes a strong PLAN is vital to resolving all these (and many other) issues of national security concern.[43]

AN OPEN-OCEAN NAVY?

Fulfilling Liu Huaqing's three-phase program requires task groups of missile-firing, power-projection-capable ships supported by nuclear-powered submarines and maritime air power.[44] The PLAN has made remarkable progress toward reaching this goal during the little more than twenty years since Liu delineated his strategy. The task groups operating in the Gulf of Aden throughout 2009 have in fact been composed of ships equipped with capable antisurface and antiair missiles, helicopters, and special operations detachments, supported by underway replenishment ships. They have achieved productive relations with local countries and have utilized space-based command and control. Meanwhile, China has launched new classes of conventionally and nuclear-powered submarines, while aircraft carrier acquisition has emerged over the horizon.

Liu's naval strategy is comprehensive, focusing on missions concerning Taiwan, asserting China's claims to offshore territories and natural resources, defending the homeland against invasion, and strategic deterrence. Strategy, however, is a starting point for national security, not its consummation. Senior military and civilian leaders will have to embrace Liu's concept and allocate the resources to provide the PLAN with the capability to fulfill strategic goals if China is to become a global maritime force.[45]

PLAN Capabilities to Fit the Strategy

Admiral Shi Yunsheng attributed several features to China's twenty-first-century Navy. It has an "offshore defense" strategy; it is "strong with science and technology"; it carries "more advanced weapons," including "warships, submarines, fighters, missiles, torpedoes, guns, and electronic equipment";

and it has trained personnel and "more qualified people."[46] Although logistics and sustainment at sea and information warfare are missing from this list, it delineates accurately how the PLAN has progressed during the past decade to "improve its capacity to win a war at sea."[47]

China faces five major maritime security situations in Asia: Japan and the East China Sea, Taiwan, the South China Sea, India, and vital SLOCs. The Navy is slowly achieving a greater role within the Army-dominated PLA and in the national security policy process. Casting the United States as the adversary facilitates these efforts, given U.S. naval dominance throughout Asia.

The PLAN offers China's leaders a flexible, ready instrument for applying power, and Beijing has not hesitated to use it: witness the 1974, 1988, 1995, and 1998–99 actions in the South China Sea; and the 2008–2010 operations in the Gulf of Aden. Offshore defense is a maritime strategy with clear offensive implications: Beijing is moving its strategic line seaward from the coast, demonstrating that the Navy has a key role in China's twenty-first-century strategy. For the PLAN, a strategy of offshore defense includes missions to contain and resist foreign aggression from the seas, defend China's territory and sovereignty, and safeguard the motherland's unification and marine rights.[48] These strategic objectives translate into complex and difficult specific missions:

- preparing for operations against Taiwan, including deterring further steps toward independence;
- defending Chinese claims in the East and South China seas;[49]
- maintaining a strategic deterrent force against the United States (and possibly India, Russia, and Japan);
- protecting vital SLOCs—some lying a great distance from China; and
- serving as a diplomatic force.[50]

Beijing's developing maritime strategy seeks to encompass both modern technology and neo-Maoist doctrine, as in "the use of strategy can reverse the balance of combat strength." An effective maritime strategy will have to overcome recognized shortcomings in doctrine, equipment, and training.

The PLAN is not yet the dominant naval power in East Asia, even apart from the U.S. maritime presence. The JMSDF is superior in some respects, and the Republic of Korea Navy (ROKN) would be a difficult opponent. Even the Taiwanese Navy would not be a pushover for the PLAN, although its bases—particularly its primary base at Tsoying—are vulnerable to air attack and blockade. Clearly, a wise maritime strategist in Beijing would not, in the event of conflict, pose the PLAN "one-on-one" against any of these modern naval forces.

A more thoughtful strategy would be required for the PLAN to achieve specific goals in the face of opposition by the U.S. Navy, the JMSDF, or the ROKN. Such a strategy would almost certainly employ information warfare to counter the advanced military technological superiority of these fleets—a capability often discussed and reportedly exercised by the PLAN. Another strategic step in such a conflict would be to gain the initiative through preemption. This does not necessarily require a "bolt from the blue," but could be achieved by seizing the initiative at a time of significant naval weakness on the part of the adversary.[51]

PLAN strategists have described the sea as the "new high ground of strategic competition" and urged attention to five areas of international rivalry: ocean islands, sea space jurisdiction, marine resources, maritime strategic advantage, and strategic sea-lanes. The seas are both "a protective screen" and "a marine invasion route." Naval missions are seen as, first, coastal defense; and second, control of the "sea space," which is "four dimensional," including air, surface, subsurface, and the seabed. The Asia-Pacific region is viewed as a "priority region of maritime strategic competition," with control of the seas involving "science and technology, and military. . . . Military control of the seas means achieving and defending national unification, defending national maritime territorial sovereignty and maritime rights and interests, protecting legitimate maritime economic activities and scientific research, and ensuring a peaceful and stable climate for national reform, opening, and coastal economic development, by dealing with possible maritime incidents, armed conflicts, and local wars." The PLAN "has an inescapable mission. . . . The twenty-first century is going to be a maritime one."[52]

The PLAN's strategic responsibilities are challenging. First, the distances involved in securing just the South China Sea are daunting to a Navy weak in air power, AAW, ASW, and amphibious lift, although recent exercises and the Gulf of Aden deployments show significant progress being made in command and control, and logistics sustainment. Second, the Taiwan military is formidable enough, at least on paper, to make any assault on that island a significant military and political problem. Third, in the JMSDF the PLAN would face a more experienced and professional adversary. To be effective, China's maritime strategy must compensate for the PLAN's material shortcomings and lack of operational experience. Nevertheless, the PLAN today is a formidable force within littoral East Asia and is viewed in the region as a vehicle for aggression.[53]

Given the continued presence of peaceful borders to the north and west, Beijing's national security priorities for at least the next decade will lie to the maritime east and southeast. The PLAN must be able to control East Asian seas to accomplish Beijing's strategic aims, but China is still working to overcome a previously weak technological and industrial infrastructure. Maintaining a regionally dominant Navy will be challenging.

The PLAN has other twenty-first-century naval missions. First is establishing an effective nuclear deterrent force at sea as the core of a maritime strategy for the new millennium. Second is maintenance of a naval presence throughout Asia, using port visits to the nations of the region—to include Southwest Asia, with an occasional foray to Europe and the Western Hemisphere. Within this general policy of presence the PLAN will be focused, as part of a joint force with the PLAAF, on specific objectives that in turn require a credible power-projection force, with enough amphibious and logistics capability to take and hold disputed territory in the East and South China seas. A third mission is pursuit of SLOC defense (likely avenues are expanding a presence west of Malacca, including in Southwest Asia). This mission will gain prominence only if Beijing decides that the United States is more of a maritime threat to than a guarantor of these long SLOCs on which China depends.

Finally, the question of Taiwan will continue to dominate national security strategy discussion until the island's status is resolved. PLAN leaders will have to ensure that their force remains a key player in plans to prevent Taiwan's de jure independence and coerce its reunification in a manner that will not consume all of its modernization efforts. Given present and probable future budget resources, it would not be in the PLAN's interest, for example, to build a massive amphibious force that would represent a strategic tradeoff with increased high-technology war-fighting capability at sea.

The first stage of Liu Huaqing's reported strategy—to control China's adjacent seas out to the first island chain, is attainable within the next ten years, but only if Beijing continues the present national prioritization of resource allocation to the Navy, and if Japan and the United States continue to allow it to occur. Tokyo remains consumed with a problematic economy and domestic politics; Washington remains focused on Southwest Asia. Hence, neither is actively challenging Beijing's regional ascendancy.

Comparison to Germany's late-nineteenth-century naval building program to catch up to Great Britain's navy is not a valid analogy in China's case. Imperial Germany in the late 1890s already possessed an industrial-technological-scientific infrastructure equal and perhaps superior to its competitor, Great Britain; China fails to match this status vis-à-vis the United States or Japan, but has taken huge steps forward during the past two decades and may soon displace South Korea as the world's largest shipbuilder.[54]

CONCLUSION

Earlier in this chapter I listed nine factors that affect a nation's development of a maritime strategy. How does China measure up in 2010?

First, training and education programs have been reorganized and continue to receive attention as the officer corps becomes more professional and specialized. Modern training and education systems and methodology are being adopted within a more flexible system; however, time devoted to political education may be considered detrimental.

Second, PLAN modernization is focusing on naval systems and platforms costs, capabilities, and sustainability as new systems and platforms are bought on the global market and produced in China. An additional portion of the national military budget is being allocated to the Navy; the previously weak indigenous infrastructure has been improved and continues to increase in capability, but the modernization efforts continue to struggle with its low starting point and continued dependence on foreign systems and technology.

Third, the national scientific and industrial infrastructure for research, development, and production of naval warfare technology and systems is improving, but it remains relatively weak for the design and buildup of state-of-the-art systems from drawing board to operational force; hence the continued, if reduced, reliance on foreign sources.

Fourth, the ability to derive doctrine and tactics is clearly advancing, as evidenced in publications; military education, training, and exercises, especially those focused on joint operations; and integrated systems employment.

Fifth, the ability to administer, operate, and command and control tactical formations continues to improve, as demonstrated by the administrative reorganization of the past decade and recent long-range deployments of small flotillas, but is still a question mark at the fleet and theater levels.

Sixth, intelligence—sources, production, analysis, and dissemination—probably absorbs major resources in the PLAN, but its role and influence are unclear.

Seventh, service-wide naval strategic planning appears to be ongoing, with apparent focus not on matching a potential adversary's (i.e., the United States) strengths but on avoiding those strengths.

Eighth, while another naval commander with Liu Huaqing's influence is unlikely to emerge, China's national leadership appears to have recognized the value of a strong Navy.

Finally, while the Army remains the dominant service, the Navy's status has been enhanced by the Gulf of Aden deployments and increased "presence" missions and will continue to rise in proportion with the degree of crisis in maritime situations, such as Taiwan, the East and South China seas, or in the missions other than war highlighted in recent Chinese literature.

China is pursuing a maritime strategy consciously designed to achieve near-term national security objectives and longer-term regional maritime dominance through both combatant and merchant fleets. In the near term, Beijing is building a Navy capable of decisively influencing the operational aspects of the Taiwan and the East and South China sea situations, should diplomacy and other instruments of statecraft fail. Establishing an operational PLAN and Naval Aviation presence in the Spratlys or on Burmese territory would provide the basis for a major Chinese role in controlling the Malacca and its associated straits, key to the economic life of East Asia.

Taiwan as a priority for the Chinese Navy means a continued emphasis on power projection ashore and emphasis on littoral warfare, as well as a sea denial capability. This broad mission area forms one part of the PLAN's apparent goal of deploying a force capable of extraregional operations. The term in the maritime strategic lexicography that most closely describes Beijing's maritime ambition in 2010 is "sea denial"; that is, capable of ensuring the accomplishment of regional strategic objectives despite possible interference by the United States. This does not represent a uniquely Chinese strategy, but is a classic maritime strategic option followed by continentalist powers such as Wilhelmine Germany and the Soviet Union.

A less well-known description of Beijing's naval ambitions is "flotilla defense," a term used by Sir John Fisher, Great Britain's First Sea Lord, in the early years of the last century. Fisher was concerned that Britain's large fleet of battleships would not be able to operate safely in the narrow seas surrounding Britain in the face of the torpedo threat from submarines and small surface craft. Hence, he advocated flotilla defense to safeguard the nation from invasion and attack, using submarines and torpedo-launching small craft to defeat attempts by large enemy ships to attack British ports and shore points.[55]

If the flotilla defense concept is applied to the relatively constricted Chinese coastal waters within the first island chain, then China ten years ago—like Britain circa 1907 and the Soviet Union in the 1920s—was focused on a Navy capable of little more than expanded coastal defense. Homeland security and regional waters retain pride of place in Beijing's maritime priorities, but the deployments to the western Indian Ocean demonstrate China's maturing view of naval power as guardian of global economic interests. The value to the nation of its rich offshore mineral and biological resources, and its dependence on seaborne trade and transportation are clearly understood in Beijing.

Conclusion

I mperial China for the most part ignored the sea except for brief periods and specific campaigns. Republican China was simply too preoccupied with the civil war and Japanese invasion to focus on naval development. The communist regime installed in 1949 maintained for almost fifty years a traditional Chinese view of its Navy as a secondary instrument of national power.

Mao Zedong recognized in 1950 that deploying a Navy to conquer Taiwan required development of expertise in amphibious warfare, seaborne logistics, and maritime air power, but his plan to organize a strong Navy was aborted because of the Korean War and thereafter limited by domestic political events, especially the disastrous Great Leap Forward. Later, naval development was severely impacted during the 1960s by the Sino-Soviet split and the Great Proletarian Cultural Revolution (GPCR). Only at the end of the 1970s, after the end of the GPCR and the post-Mao power struggle, was the PLAN in a position to "take off."

That did not happen, although the People's Liberation Army Navy did benefit in the 1980s from a relatively close relationship with the United States, from whom China purchased advanced naval systems, including LM2500 gas turbine engines and Mk-46 antisubmarine warfare torpedoes. The sanctions that followed the June 1989 Tiananmen Square massacre ended U.S. naval assistance, and China has since turned to Europe, Israel, and especially Russia. The following two decades have seen a dramatic increase in China's naval capabilities.

In 2007 the PLAN's commander argued, "We must build a powerful Navy . . . to maintain the safety of the oceanic transportation and the strategic passageway for energy and resources, [and] to defend the unification of our nation." This statement alludes to the fact that almost all of China's primary sovereignty concerns lie in the maritime arena: Taiwan; territorial and seabed resource disputes with Japan in the East China Sea; similar disputes with Vietnam, the Philippines, Brunei, Indonesia, and Malaysia in the South China Sea; and sea lines of communication across the Indian Ocean endangered by piracy in the Gulf of Aden. Additionally, the government's authority relies in significant part on continued economic growth, which in turn relies on maritime trade and energy flows.[1]

Chinese naval history has been marked by some notable consistencies. First, while the maritime element of China's national security has never held top priority in Beijing's strategic calculations, it has rarely been ignored. The PLAN has in fact transformed itself from a coastal defense force to one capable of offshore defense during the past quarter-century. This transformation has focused on increasing the mobility of fleet units and on their ability to engage and prevail at sea over lengthier periods and greater distances than previously. The Navy has acquired new weapon systems, but even more important have been personnel, organizational, and procedural improvements focused on training, logistics, and maintenance.

Second, Chinese naval efforts have been closely linked to the nation's economic development. China's economic boom of the past quarter-century has been concentrated in the coastal cities and provinces. The increasing concentration of industrial, technological, commercial, informational, and even agricultural wealth within a five-hundred-mile coastal belt is one spur to naval expansion and modernization. Beijing is addressing this strategic situation both by directing future development toward China's western provinces and by developing a modern Navy. President Hu Jintao emphasized in 2007 that "the overall strategic interests of national security and development [demand that] we must take both economic development and national defense into consideration and make our country prosperous and our armed forces powerful."[2]

Third, China's dependence on overseas trade for so much of its economic development presents the PLAN with a classic maritime mission. The overwhelming majority of this trade is carried by Chinese and foreign merchant ships over sea-lanes that crisscross the world; the security of such global SLOCs demands international cooperation because the PLAN does not possess the forces to defend other than coastal SLOCs. In fact, SLOC security is guaranteed so long as the United States continues serving as guardian of the world's sea-lanes. This guardianship is especially effective given the concurrent U.S. and Chinese strategic priorities, as represented in part by Washington's emphasis on defending the SLOCs most important to China's import of petroleum from the Middle East and Africa.

This in turn invites discussion of the so-called string of pearls strategy, which some observers believe signifies Chinese naval expansion throughout the Indian Ocean. The evidence simply does not support such a strategic ambition by Beijing. The "pearls" most often mentioned are "Chinese naval bases" on Burma's Andaman coast; at Chittagong, Bangladesh; at Hambantota on the southern coast of Sri Lanka; and at Gwadar, Pakistan. These places may be of use to China, especially to its merchant fleet, but they are not naval bases. This conclusion is supported by the 2009 deployments of PLAN task groups to the Gulf of Aden; these ships are relying for resupply and crew rest not on the "pearls" but on the same commercial ports and other resources that the U.S. and other navies deploying to the area use.

The Chinese security presence in Burma is apparently limited to listening and observation outposts; Chittagong is far up the Bay of Bengal, and hence distant from Indian Ocean east–west shipping routes; Hambantota is a relatively small commercial project on a fifteen-year development timeline; Gwadar is a commercial port managed by a Singaporean company. Overlying any such discussion of Chinese naval ambitions in the Indian Ocean is the presence of India, itself a significant naval power mustering nuclear submarines and aircraft carriers—and hardly friendly to China. Any PLAN efforts in the Indian Ocean would require New Delhi's acquiescence.[3]

Fourth, the PLAN is increasing its capability to prevent formal Taiwan independence, primarily by building a submarine force able to isolate the island. China is not building a Navy capable of extended, large-scale assault operations. It lacks seaborne air power, and it has no fixed-wing-capable ships, only nascent in-flight refueling capability, no airborne air control, and limited joint operational capability with the PLAAF. The advent of an operational aircraft carrier during the coming decade will mark the beginning of such capability. Ensuring the security of China's insular territorial claims in the South and East China seas is a viable mission, but the PLAN in 2010 lacks the force in both numbers and capability to dominate these limited regional theaters in the face of U.S. and possibly even Japanese opposition.

Fifth, Chinese naval developments continue to be marked by significant interaction with foreign navies, as they have from the mid-nineteenth century. A limited but enduring reliance on Soviet/Russian advisers, strategy, equipment, technology, and engineers has continued, and Russian maritime strategic and material influence remains a significant factor in the PLAN. Beijing is obviously willing to profit from Moscow's economic distress and other domestic problems. The two nations' strategic situations also retain some similarity, based on geography and history, if not ideology. Currently, the relationship revolves around two points: China's hunger for Russian energy supplies and its concern about the continuing U.S. role as the world's only superpower. Russia remains in demographic decline, with an economy dependent almost entirely on energy resources. Although its military is a shadow of its former self, it still offers an innovative and productive military research-and-development sector, to which China is attracted.

PLAN reliance on foreign sources has been reduced during the past decade, however, as China's military-industrial complex has become both more capable and more willing to research, design, develop, and produce the modern systems needed by the Navy. This has resulted from increased dedicated technological expertise, research-and-development facilities, manufacturing plant, and a more profitable public sector market, through which industry is able to earn profits not as readily available from naval customers.

Sixth, while naval doctrine development in China is not transparent, descriptions of recently conducted naval exercises have used the right labels for twenty-first-century navies: joint warfare, systems integration, coordinated subsurface-surface-aviation operations, centralized command and control. Evaluation of PLAN capabilities is clouded by unquantifiable factors, but while the PLAN has never engaged in a major campaign or combat at sea, the dedication, courage, and resourcefulness of its personnel should not be doubted.

Furthermore, Beijing's willingness to resort to force even when significantly outgunned should impart a cautionary message for strategists viewing China's possible reactions to specific issues, especially Taiwan's efforts to resist reunification.[4] In other words, China will continue to be constrained by U.S. (and perhaps Japanese) naval force but will not hesitate to employ the PLAN in situations involving sovereignty claims.

PLAN SHORTCOMINGS

The PLAN recognizes its equipment deficiencies as well as the difficulties involved in correcting them. General Cao Guangchuan, director of the General Armaments Department in the 1990s and later minister of defense, complained that poor pay made it "difficult for his department to retain top-quality scientists and researchers," and that "the task of developing the Navy's armaments is arduous."[5] The PLAN surface forces suffer in several significant warfare areas.

Antiair Warfare

Modern sea power is to a large extent defined by air power, in terms both of aircraft, manned and unmanned, and of missiles, cruise and ballistic. The PLAN is finally moving to ameliorate this weakness in launching the Luyang II–class DDGs. That ship's Aegis-like system is the Chinese Navy's first to offer an effective area AAW defense; previous combatants offered only a point-defense capability. A point-defense system is designed to defend its own launching ship; an "area-defense" system has the capability to defend a formation of ships. The key to this difference is the area-defense system's range and its ability to detect and process multiple targets simultaneously, especially targets with a crossing component in their fire-control solution, meaning the missile is not headed for the ship with the radar, in which case the missile would be approaching the ship on a steady bearing, not drifting left or right.

The Luda and Jianghu classes were designed without any surface-to-air missile (SAM) system; the four *Sovremenny*-class combatants acquired from Russia are armed with the point-defense SA-N-7 system; the Luhu, Luhai, and Jiangwei classes are equipped with the French-built Crotale or its Chinese version, the HQ-6/7—also point-defense systems. Even the Luyang I and Luzhou classes commissioned with the Luyang IIs in the middle of this decade, while armed with very potent AAW missiles, lack a true area-defense capability.

Antisubmarine Warfare

ASW is another crucial PLAN warfare weakness. Detecting submarines, especially from a surface ship, is a very difficult process, and the PLAN does not appear to be taking advantage of available ASW technology, especially in the field of passive detection—some of it forty years old. Despite promising developments using satellite-based radar to find submarine wakes and airborne lasers to detect submarines at depth, sound transmission through water (sonar) remains the most reliable way to detect a submarine.

There are two broad categories of sonar operation. Passive sonar involves listening for undersea noises generated by the submarine; active sonar uses echo ranging to find a submarine by bouncing an audible signal off the target's hull. This transmission does not occur in a straight line; the sound is "bent" by water depth, salinity, currents, and temperature. Furthermore, the ship trans-mitting an active sonar signal can be detected at about twice the distance at which it can detect a submarine. ASW helicopters and aircraft can also employ active sonar, but a better detection method is passive sonar: using hydrophones to detect the distinctive sound pattern—the "acoustic signature"—of a subma-rine. Passive sonar does not reveal the ASW ship's location, but it requires a quiet ship that generates very little noise. In both cases, sonar effectiveness is markedly decreased in most coastal waters due to decreased water depth, increased ship traffic, increased sea life, and the mixture of fresh and salt water.

Sonar is also categorized by its frequency. Lower-frequency active sonars are capable of extremely long range detection but are most useful on the open ocean, because the littoral topography induces reverberations when sonars are operated in the active mode. High-frequency sonars have a shorter opera-tional range but offer better target definition (resolution) than low-frequency systems; they are useful in coastal waters and at short range. It is possible for a ship to be equipped with both a relatively low frequency sonar for detecting submarines and a high-frequency sonar to be used in shallow water or when attacking an underwater target.

Both active and passive sonars may be mounted on the hull of a ship, towed behind it on a long cable, or towed on a shorter cable as variable-depth sonar (again, either active or passive). The two systems allow the sonar to be placed below thermal layers in the water, enhancing the range and the probability of detecting submarines. Variable-depth sonar may use both active and passive means, and is usually more effective in the open ocean than in coastal waters.

PLAN ships make almost exclusive use of hull-mounted, active, medium-frequency sonar. This probably represents a financial and operational compro-mise, because this sonar type is the least expensive and simplest to operate of the various types discussed above. Beginning with the two Luhus, which became operational in 1993 and 1996, PLAN escorts have been equipped with towed, variable-depth sonars in addition to hull-mounted medium-frequency equip-ment. Also, China's Navy lacks significant airborne ASW resources, with only a dozen old aircraft assigned to the ASW mission; there is no open-source knowledge that China has deployed sea-bottom listening arrays in its coastal waters. A serious ASW effort would encompass all these systems, properly integrated and supported by timely operational and technical intelligence.

Systems Integration

A warship is inherently a "system of systems," and the PLAN is in the early stages of integrating its operations across the complex warfare mission areas. This requires the effective integration of shipboard, airborne, and shore-based systems in pursuit of the desired operational mission objective. Prior to the advent of the Luhu and Jiangwei classes of combatants, China's surface ships had very limited systems integration, and only basic central combat direction systems. Since 2000, however, the PLAN has made significant progress in this crucial area of integrating the sensor, weapon, and command and control functions. The integration problem is complicated by China's practice of building ships that incorporate a combination of foreign and Chinese-built components within the same system—a French-designed missile system with a Chinese air-search radar, for instance.

Beyond individual ship systems integration is the need for interunit integration that maximizes the synergy among the systems and units of a task group, a task force, and a fleet. The U.S. concept of net-centric warfare presently is the epitome of this paradigm. The PLAN is certainly aware of the developments in net-centric warfare, but as discussed in Chapters 7 and 8, reported PLAN training and exercises indicate that the force remains on a very shallow learning curve toward achieving integration.[6]

Effective joint operations require interservice coordination and integrated systems as well. China's leaders understand the vital necessity of the PLA's being able to conduct joint operations effectively, but this is a difficult objective to reach, from peacetime doctrinal determination through combat operations. PLA training plans and observed exercises show a Chinese military force moving slowly to achieve cross-service and cross-warfare area capabilities.[7]

Maintenance and Supply

The maintenance of its front-line combatants is another area at which the PLAN strives to improve. Even the newest combatants—the Luzhou and Luyang classes—face supply and maintenance problems attributable to the foreign origin of many of their weapons and sensor systems and propulsion plants. France, the Netherlands, Italy, the United States, Ukraine, and Russia have all played a role in the design and/or manufacture of China's newest warships. This causes difficulties in training personnel in equipment maintenance as well as supply support, including acquisition of appropriate test equipment.[8]

These combinations reduce system efficiency and hence decrease warship lethality, and are exacerbated by China's practice of building small classes of two to four ships. PLAN officers recognize the benefits of systems integration and equipment commonality, and the slow development probably is due to budgetary limitations, the mix of indigenous construction and foreign purchases, and the small number of ships in most PLAN classes.

The loss of the crew of the Ming-class submarine (hull number 361) in 2003 apparently resulted in part from defective maintenance during a recently completed shipyard stay. Afterward, the PLAN's administrative organization for maintenance, material upkeep, and personnel training was overhauled. Another apparent result was the 2004 centralization of the Navy's spare-parts system, a move that may have improved parts availability and equipment reliability fleet-wide but has also caused resentment among shipboard officers because it reduces their control over readiness.[9] Such complaints are common among shipboard officers in most navies, however, and these changes will probably prove effective in improving PLAN equipment readiness.

Intelligence, Surveillance, and Reconnaissance

A final notable PLAN weakness is in ISR capability. This is in part the result of China's highly centralized and rigid command structure and in part because the Navy is just beginning to venture into net-centric warfare. This capability is being directly approached from various angles, including submarine detection, helicopter OTH missions, and space-based assets.

The foregoing are "weaknesses" from a U.S. perspective, however. For instance, the PLAN may rely for air defense on submarines and antiship ballistic missiles limiting the ability of U.S. aircraft carriers to engage Chinese forces rather than on the expensive development of their own maritime force of fixed-wing aircraft. There is nothing uniquely Chinese about "asymmetry" in military operations, but no opponent should doubt PLAN commanders' ability to adapt and innovate in operational situations.

PLAN RESOURCE ACQUISITION

Today, indigenously built PLAN ships evolve through a process involving the Navy, state-owned enterprises, and private industry. The first step in the construction process is the Navy's expression of the need for a specific ship with desired characteristics. The origin of such requests is not clear; the

Naval Research Institute and the Naval Research Center in Beijing probably contribute, as do the Naval Command College in Nanjing and the fleet commanders. Once a request for a new ship is approved by the PLAN and the CMC, it is passed to the China Shipbuilding Corporation (CSC), a state-owned enterprise. The CSC works with the Navy to finalize the design and then negotiates the shipbuilding program with a shipyard, which may be privately owned. PLAN construction representatives are stationed at the shipyard as liaison during the construction process.[10]

Foreign purchases, such as the acquisition from Russia of Kilo-class submarines, *Sovremenny*-class DDGs, and Su-27/30 aircraft, make headlines, but naval purchases abroad have declined during the past decade as indigenous capabilities have improved.[11] This may reflect Russia's reluctance to provide its most recent military equipment to China, but more likely it results from Beijing's knowledge that reliance on foreign arms purchases both retards the growth of its own defense industry and to a degree mortgages the military to the originating country for spare parts and maintenance assistance.

China's practice of building small classes of warships in relatively rapid succession speaks to a willingness to incorporate developments as they emerge. It also demonstrates the PLA's readiness to invest the resources necessary to pursue this expensive practice. The practice may fit well with China's diffuse military-industrial complex and PLAN budgetary limitations. The practice will likely continue, despite the difficulties in training and maintenance that result.

THE FUTURE FORCE

Admiral Yu Guoquan, director of the Department of Naval Equipment Technology and Warships division in 1995, outlined a version of twenty-first-century naval systems. The fact that his writing may mirror that of American analysts does not detract from its impact within the PLAN. New naval weaponry, he wrote, would have six features: (1) improved reconnaissance and observation, precise targeting, and better weapon-sensor integration, creating quicker reaction time; (2) increased lethality; (3) increased mobility and speed, and hence shorter engagements; (4) improved protective and survival systems; (5) increased emphasis on electronic jamming and targeting; (6) and multiple dimensions.[12]

PLAN growth depends directly on resources allocated by the government. An extraregional Navy will be built only if one of two decisions is made. First, the Navy must continue to receive an increasing percentage of available military funding, perhaps one-half or one-third of the total. This is will be difficult to achieve in the Army-dominated PLA. Second, continued double-digit increases in Beijing's annual military expenditures depend on continued economic growth, probably at least 5–7 percent of GDP.

By 2020 the PLAN will probably number approximately 70 modern surface combatants, 4–6 new ballistic-missile submarines, and 50 modern attack submarines, perhaps 10 of them nuclear-powered. The old submarines—the Han- and Xia-class nuclear-powered and Romeo-class conventionally powered boats—will have been decommissioned or placed in reserve. The Navy's attack submarine force will include approximately 15 Song-, 12 Kilo-, 10 Yuan-, and fewer than 15 Ming-class boats. Additionally, the two new Shang-class subs will likely be followed by construction of a follow-on SSN class, the Type-095.

The amphibious and logistical force will be more modern, but current building efforts make it unlikely that the PLAN will include more than approximately two dozen amphibious ships of 2,000 tons displacement or larger, featuring perhaps 4 LPDs of the Type-071 or follow-on class. At least 8 modern replenishment-at-sea ships, 2 in the North and East Sea fleets, and 4 in the South Sea Fleet, are likely to have joined the PLAN.

Naval Aviation's future is shadowed by resource and doctrinal competition with the PLAAF and within the PLAN among the different warfare communities (surface, subsurface, aviation, Marine Corps). One can easily imagine the PLAN ceding pride of place to the Air Force in the effort to garner an increasing share of PLA funding for the Navy's surface and submarine communities. The naval aviators do not appear to occupy a strong position in these bureaucratic battles. A large, U.S.-style aircraft carrier is unlikely to be deployed by 2020, but one or two *Varyag*-type air-capable ships will almost certainly have joined the PLAN, with an eventual goal of providing one "carrier" to each of the three fleets.

The Marine Corps is unlikely to expand beyond its present two brigades because the Army is training additional divisions as amphibious specialists. Hence, the Corps will retain South China Sea missions as its primary amphibious tasking while the Army retains primary responsibility for Taiwan. The Corps' role as a "rapid reaction" unit probably means, however, that its operational assignments will be determined more by the CMC General Staff Department than by the South Sea Fleet commander.[13]

Prospective PLAN numbers are large by Asian standards and reflect several specific factors. First, Beijing's number-one "national security" priority will remain keeping the Chinese Communist Party (CCP) in power. This requires a continued emphasis on fostering a strong and growing economy, which in turn means that military budgets will increase in proportion to economic growth.

Second, Beijing's primary maritime strategic goal of defending China against seaborne invasion is not urgent given the absence of any such threat. Other strategic concerns include the East and South China seas, coastal and regional SLOC defense, and the preservation of offshore resources. All require capable naval forces, and Beijing is allocating the resources to build the requisite Navy at a moderate pace. Even concern about Taiwan's status has failed to spur dramatic naval expansion at the expense of Army domination of the PLA.

Third, the Chinese polity continues to change. The revolutionary generation of military-civilian leadership is all but extinct; current and future leaders are and will be *either* civilian or military, barring the unlikely rise of a military officer to national leadership. The PLA will continue to assume a more professional character, a process that may isolate the Navy and the other services from China's civilian population. Defense Minister Chi Haotian discussed this as a concern of the national leadership in September 1998, and it is very much a concern to Beijing in 2010. The PLA's senior political officer stressed that "maintaining the Party's absolute leadership is our military's political priority" and that the PLA must "resolutely resist . . . 'nationalizing the military.'"[14]

China's growing economy and concomitant increasing global presence and influence are facts, but as one experienced PLAN flag officer noted: "China lacks the strategic power to actively influence and shape the direction and process of major international affairs. . . . China's military power lags far behind its political, diplomatic, and cultural power to better protect its national interests in the world. China gravely lacks a military deterrent and real combat capability to effectively address both traditional military threats as well as [MOOTW operations]." An official journal gives an even stronger view: "Currently, the military capacity of our Army does not fit the requirements for fulfilling the new mission. Our [Navy] cannot fully satisfy the needs involved in protecting our oceanic rights." Finally, in June 2009, after noting that "the party central leadership and the CMC take the Navy as a priority service for force building," the PLAN chief of staff complained that "there remains a substantial gap between our work and the requirement of fighting decisive battles to win decisive victories, and many bottleneck issues that restrict the enhancement of our combat capabilities have yet to be solved."[15]

These views strengthen the conclusion that China's Navy will continue to modernize at a moderate pace, with its near- and mid-term objectives a regional rather than a global force. From Beijing's perspective, the PLAN must be able to prevent another Asian navy from interfering with China's national security objectives, and to at least give pause to American maritime intervention. A globally capable PLAN would have to be able to project power around the world, from the western Pacific to the western Atlantic, an ambition apparently beyond China's goals for at least the first half of the twenty-first century.[16] Of course, even a regionally capable PLAN will have to be factored into any calculation of global strategic forces given East Asia's size, population, and economic importance.

Increased Chinese maritime presence at a few particularly sensitive political-military points, such as the Malacca Strait and the far reaches of the Indian Ocean—as represented by the current Gulf of Aden deployments— heightens this need to factor China into global strategy. The PLAN in the past twenty years has built a solid record of naval presence with visits to more than thirty countries, a program normal to a nation of China's geographic, economic, political, and cultural importance.

Further maturation of the PLAN's role in national security priorities will depend on how naval power and maritime economic interests are viewed in Beijing. The value to the nation of its rich offshore mineral and biological resources, and its dependence on seaborne trade and transportation, are clearly understood. Those interests have been categorized as the "five rivalries": over ocean islands, sea space jurisdiction, marine resources, the maritime strategic advantage, and strategic sea-lanes.[17]

China's naval modernization will continue for several reasons. First is Beijing's determination to gain the respect due to a great power, which includes deploying a great Navy. Second is the determination for regional dominance, to ensure that regional nations do not undertake unwelcome policies. Third, even following peaceful resolution of Taiwan's status, Beijing will consider a strategically capable Navy necessary to counter U.S. and possibly Japanese power. The fourth reason is momentum: the current buildup has given rise to a wide range of long-term programs and powerful interests—perhaps best described as China's military-industrial complex—that have developed a life of their own.[18] A possible fifth reason is domestic politics: no communist system has been able to establish systemic, orderly leadership succession. China may be the first, but that has yet to be proven; any leadership contest will involve the participants valuing the loyalty of a strong military, especially given the PLA's role as a "party army."

Despite the steady growth of China's Navy, the U.S. fleet remains the determinant factor in East Asian maritime crises. It will continue to fill that role for as long as the United States has the will to maintain its presence. Beijing recognizes this dominance, as well as the importance of a peaceful international environment; PLAN arguments for extraregional naval capability will receive cautious support within the Central Military Commission.

Modern Chinese military tradition does not include stationing forces outside China. The statement on military modernization by then–Defense Minister Xu Xiangqian in October 1979 is worth quoting: "The modernization of national defense cannot be divorced from the modernization of agriculture, industry, science and technology and, in the final analysis, is based on the national economy. . . . Blindly pursuing large-scale and high-speed development in building national defense will invariably and seriously hinder the development of the national economy and will harm the base of the defense industry."[19]

Economic priorities and the need to defend the world's longest land border with the most nations over every known type of terrain and climate still argue against Liu Huaqing's ambition for a global Navy. Instead, Beijing is building and deploying a Navy capable of ensuring coastal defense and the success of discrete campaigns to enforce sovereignty claims and safeguard regional SLOCs. Conflicts with Taiwan and in the East and South China seas are the scenarios that top the list of potential maritime conflicts.

China requires the ability to prevail in an area 200–1,000 nm off its coast for a period of ten to thirty days. This in turn requires a Navy able to prevail inside the first island chain, which the PLAN in 2010 is only marginally able to do against the United States or Japan, depending on timing, objectives, and the opposing force. Even Taiwan's navy would present formidable opposition if it fought well.[20] The PLAN in 2020 will remain unable to guarantee mission success if opposed by the U.S. Navy, but the other Asian maritime forces do not presently appear on a course of modernization that promises continuing ability to preclude Chinese naval success. It will remain America's responsibility to maintain its economic and military presence, as well as the historic character of American ideology, if Chinese maritime hegemony is not to prevail in Asia.

How China defines its national security interests during the next decade will determine the type of Navy it will deploy, but Beijing believes the nation's security objectives can be attained by modernizing its current naval force structure. Although not clear in 2010, it is more than possible that Beijing believes current maritime concerns are serious enough to change China's historic dependence on continental power. In that case, China might build a Navy able to challenge for command of the sea throughout the East and South China seas, the western Philippine Sea, and the eastern Indian Ocean.

Although characterized as strategically defensive, PLAN doctrine can be operationally and tactically offensive in Western terms in light of the nature of "offshore defense." Beijing sees the United States as the primary threat to its strategic interests. The United States is the world's most powerful naval power and is the dominant power inside the first island chain. Hence, the confluence in their minds of the United States as the guarantor of Taiwan's independence and that island's characterization as the key in the island chain constraining China.

China's use of its Navy for diplomatic purposes and to counter actual or perceived threats to national interests will become increasingly common as that force gains in credibility and experience. The PLAN's self-confidence is an important issue directly affecting the civilian leadership's readiness to employ the Navy to defend national interests. This self-evaluation appears to be modest, as indicated in numerous articles published since 2006. The mantra is congratulatory to a point, but then concludes that "the quality of our officers and soldiers . . . military capability . . . modernization of our military . . . weaponry and armaments . . . personnel . . . logistics . . . structure and staffing . . . cannot match the requirements of winning information-centric local wars." Even the 2009 Gulf of Aden operations have been described by Chinese "experts" as showing that the PLAN is "still a long way from being strong enough to protect China's expanding maritime rights and interests [due to] problems in helicopter maintenance, logistic supplies and telecommunications on the open sea."[21]

Despite these doubts, the current modernization path will result by 2020 in a Chinese Navy that is capable across the spectrum of warfare areas from coastal defense to nuclear deterrence. The PLAN will pose a serious obstacle to effective U.S. naval intervention in western Pacific conflicts—involving Taiwan, for instance—barring a refocusing of U.S. defense priorities to ensure that the current emphasis on counterinsurgency/counterterrorism does not result in a continued shrinking number of U.S. Navy and Air Force platforms and stagnated development of capabilities for high-end warfare.

Notes

Introduction

1. Author's interviews with foreign military attaches in Beijing and with senior U.S. Navy officers in Washington, D.C. For popular accounts of this event, see Kathrin Hille, "China Parades Its Naval Prowess," *Financial Times,* 23 April 2009, at http://www.ft.com/cms/s/0/08b321fc-3007-11de-a2f8-00144feabdc0,dwp_uuid=9c33700c-4c86-11da-89df-0000779e2340.html (accessed 17 June 2009); Dennis Blasko, "Military Parades Demonstrate China's Concept of Deterrence"; pictures of the event are at "China Holds Landmark Parade to Mark PLA Navy's 60 Anniversary," at http://news.xinhuanet.com/english/2009-04/23/content_11243632.htm (accessed 17 June 2009). Guo is quoted in "PLA Navy Urged to Beef Up Muscle for Security," *Xinhua* (Beijing unless otherwise stated), 26 April 2009, at http://www.chinadaily.com.cn/china/2009-04/26/content_7717061.htm (accessed 01 November 2009). He is one of two CMC vice chairmen and equivalent to the U.S. Chairman of the Joint Chiefs. Hu is quoted in Su Shiliang (Chief of Staff of the People's Liberation Army Navy), "Persistently Follow the Guidance of Chairman Hu's Important Thought on the Navy's Building," *Renmin Haijun* (Beijing), 06 June 2009, 3, in OSC-CPP20090716478009.

2. The event is described in "China Marks 60th Anniversary of Navy," *Xinhua,* 24 April 2009, at http://news.xinhuanet.com/english/2009-04/25/content_11252438.htm (accessed 17 June 2009).

3. This discussion relies on "CMC's Guo Boxiong Urges Improving PLA Capabilities to 'Fulfill Historic Missions," *Xinhua,* 27 September 2005, in OSC-CPP200509273 20021; and Daniel M. Hartnett, "The PLA's Domestic and Foreign Activities and Orientation," testimony before the U.S.-China Economic and Security Review Commission, hearings on "China's Military and Security Activities Abroad," Washington, D.C., 04 March 2009, at http://www.uscc.gov/hearings/2009hearings/

written_testimonies/09_03_04_wrts/09_03_04_hartnett_statement.pdf (accessed 13 August 2009). The CMC is the supreme military policy-making commission; it issues directives relating to the PLA including senior appointments, troop deployments, and arms spending. CCP senior leaders hold the CMC's most important posts. See http://english.gov.cn/links/cmc.htm (accessed 27 June 2009) for current CMC membership.

4. *China's National Defense in 2004*, ch. 3, at http://english.peopledaily.com.cn/white-paper/defense2004/defense2004.html (accessed 18 November 2009); known hereafter as Defense White Paper, with the year of issue.

5. Defense White Paper, 2008, at http://xinhuanet.com/english/2009-01/20/content_10688124.htm (accessed 17 June 2009).

6. Quoted in Cui Xiaohuo and Peng Kuang, "Navy Chief Lists Key Objective," *China Daily*, 16 April 2009, at http://www.chinadaily.com.cn/china/2009-04/16/content_7681993 (accessed 16 June 2009).

7. A useful survey by Chinese maritime strategists is Shi Chunlin, "A Commentary on Studies of the Last Ten Years Concerning China's Sea Power," *Xiandai Guoji Guanxi* (Bejing), 20 April 2008, 53–60, in OSC-CPP20080603590001.

8. *Indianapolis* was sunk by a Japanese submarine while steaming alone from Tinian to the Philippines; at that time (1945), the U.S. Navy lacked an adequate tracking system for such voyages and the ship was not missed for several days, which resulted in a delayed search and loss of hundreds of sailors (see Stanton, *In Harm's Way: The Sinking of the U.S.S. Indianapolis*). *Kursk* sank when a torpedo exploded onboard while the submarine was submerged; rescue efforts by the Russian government were slow and ineffective (author's discussion with former U.S. naval attaché in Moscow).

9. Paul H. B. Godwin was the first observer from whom I heard the caution about aspirations; for the second, see Erickson and Wilson, "China's Aircraft Carrier Dilemma," n. 93.

10. Defense White Paper, 2008; Xu Zi, "Maritime Geostrategy," 56–57.

11. This paragraph draws heavily on the excellent work by Fravel, "China's Search for Military Power."

12. Ye Zicheng, "China's Sea Power Must Be Subordinate to Its Land Power," *Guoji Xianqu Daobao* (Beijing), in OSC-CPP20070302455003, 02 March 2007.

13. "CCTV Reviews 30 Years of PLA's Development, 1978–2008," October 2008, in OSC-FEA20081215800637, 10–31 October 2008, 3.

14. See, for instance, "CPC Central Military Commission Calls for Armed Forces' Obedience, Unity," *Xinhua*, 02 February 2009, at http://paper.people.com.cn/rmrb/html/2009-02/02/content_184778.htm (accessed 17 June 2009). Another consideration is that the new more professional, better-educated, intellectually astute, and cosmopolitan officers need frequently to be reminded of the party's demand for unwavering loyalty.

15. Contrary to press reports, USS *Kitty Hawk* was not operating with its normal escort ships, but was conducting carrier qualifications for its air group accompanied by a single destroyer; hence, it was not searching for possible submarines. The author is indebted to a U.S. submarine officer for pointing out indications that demonstrate that the Chinese submarine did not intentionally surface near the carrier, but instead "broached," meaning that it accidentally broke the surface.

16. Richard Bitzinger, "Aircraft Carriers: China's Emerging Maritime Ambitions," *RSIS Commentaries,* 07 April 2009, at http://www.rsis.edu.sg/publications/Perspective/RSIS0352009.pdf (accessed 04 November 2009); Christopher Bodeen, 03 March 2009, *ABC News Online,* at http://abcnews.go.com/International/wireStory?id=6994934 (accessed 18 November 2009).

17. Author's conversations with Chinese naval officers and civilian security analysts; quotes by senior Chinese officials in Richard Fisher Jr., "Update: China's Aircraft Carriers," International Assessment and Strategy Center, 10 March 2009, at http://www.strategycenter.net/scholars/scholarID.4/scholar_detail.asp (accessed 17 June 2009).

18. Hall, *Japan: From Prehistory to Modern Time,* 302; and Spence, *The Search for Modern China,* 119, 219, address the Ryukyus' sovereignty.

19. Lambert Anthony B. Meñez, Cesar L. Villanoy, and Laura T. David, "Movement of Water across Passages Connecting Philippine Inland Sea Basins," paper presented at the Eighth National Symposium for Marine Science, Manila, November 2006, at http://journals.upd.edu.ph/index.php/sciencediliman/article/view/3/46 (accessed 28 June 2009). Unless otherwise specified, distances are given in nautical miles (nm), 1 of which equals approximately 1.15 statute miles or 1.9 kilometers; depth is given in fathoms, 1 of which equals 6 feet or 1.8 meters; speed is given in knots—nautical miles per hour—1 of which equals 1.151 statute miles per hour.

20. Korea also insists on calling the Sea of Japan the "East Sea" and the Yellow Sea the "West Sea." The disputed group of small rocks approximately 150 nm north of the Tsushima/Korea Strait is called "Takeshima" by Japan and "Dokdo" by Korea; the United Nations (and the United States) try to avoid the controversy by retaining the name "Liancourt," given to the rocks by the French whaling ship of that name, whose crew explored them in 1849.

21 Dutton, "Scouting, Signaling, and Gatekeeping," 4, points out that while declaring a 12-nm territorial sea, Japan and South Korea have modified their territorial seas to 3 nm in the Tsushima/Korea Strait to provide corridors through which ships may transit without entering their territorial seas. Japan has done the same for the Tsugaru, Osumi, and Soya (La Perouse) straits.

22. Author's interview with U.S. Navy meteorological officers, August 1999.

23. Bateman, Raymond, and Ho, "Safety and Security in the Malacca and Singapore Straits," 8.

24. Lloyds MIU, at http://www.lloydsmiu.com/lmiu/index.htm, cited in Katani, "Antipiracy Measures: Japan's Experience in the Malacca Strait."

25. Noer, with Gregory, *Chokepoints,* is still a useful source of information about these routes; a more current evaluation is Collins and Murray, "No Oil for the Lamps of China," 79–95.

26. Beijing's concern with its energy situation, and with Iran in particular, is discussed in Christina Lin, "China's Persian Gulf Strategy: Israel and a Nuclearizing Iran 2009," *China Brief* 9, no. 21, 22 October 2009, at http://www.jamestown.org/single/?no_cache=1&tx_ttnews%5Btt_news%5D=35633&tx_ttnews%5BbackPid%5D=13&cHash=f8bedd334d (accessed 08 November 2009).

27. Putin is cited in Thom Shanker, "Russia Is Striving to Modernize Its Military," *New York Times,* 19 October 2008, A11; Vysotsky, in "Russia Says Its Navy Ready to Thwart Any Threat to Security," *Ria Novstry,* 09 September 2008, at http://en.rian.ru/russia/20080909/116641317.html (accessed 02 November 2008).

28. Downing, "China's Evolving Military Strategy, Part 1," 130.

29. Chen Wanjun, "Interview with Sr. Capt. Yu Guoquan (Director of Division of Ships, Dept. of Armaments & Technology, PLAN)," *Jianchuan Zhishi* (Beijing), 07 July 1995, 2–3, in FBIS-CST-96-014.*

Chapter 1. China's Naval Heritage

1. Deng, *Chinese Maritime Activities and Socioeconomic Development, c. 2100 B.C.–900 A.D.,* is a well-written history of this topic.

2. See "China's Sea Route to West Asia Begins in Xuwen," *Xinhua,* 21 June 2000, in FBIS-CPP20000621000077 at, for archaeologists' theory that trading voyages may have departed from Guangdong Province as early as 200 BC, two hundred years before the Silk Road was established.

3. Needham's massive work, *Science and Civilization in China,* discusses these and related developments.

4. Deng, *Chinese Maritime Activities and Socioeconomic Development,* 41.

5. Forage, "The Foundations of Chinese Naval Supremacy in the Twelfth Century," 3.

6. Ibid., 70.

7. Lo Jung-pang, "The Emergence of China as a Sea Power during the Late Sung and Early Yuan Periods," 491.

*FBIS-CHI is the abbreviation for Foreign Broadcast Information Service, China. FBIS-CHI-99-0421, for example, indicates the 421st item referring to China published in 1999. FBIS was disestablished in 2005 and succeeded by the Open Source Center (OSC), as described at http://www.dni.gov/press_releases/20051108_release.htm (accessed 23 June 2009).

8. See Forage, "The Foundations of Chinese Naval Supremacy in the Twelfth Century," 6–7 and 19–21, for a fascinating account of two battles between Song and Yuan naval forces.

9. Fairbank, "Maritime and Continental in China's History," 1:15.

10. Forage, "The Foundations of Chinese Naval Supremacy in the Twelfth Century," 500–501, provides a brief but interesting description of these early weapons.

11. The Ming decision also reflected Chinese xenophobia, perhaps best expressed in the Qing emperor Ch'ien-lung's response to Britain's 1793 attempt to establish relations with Beijing. The emperor told Lord MacCartney, "We possess all things. I set no value on objects strange or ingenious, and have no use for your country's manufactures." The best work on Zheng He remains Dreyer, *Zheng He.* See Raudzens, "Military Revolution or Maritime Evolution," 56, for an interesting but Eurocentric interpretation of the role maritime mobility played in European imperialism.

12. Spence, *The Search for Modern China*, 53–54.

13. Fairbank, *China, a New History,* 220, relates the most famous case of corruption: the diversion of perhaps $50 million in naval construction funds to the building of the empress' Summer Palace in Beijing, complete with a large boat made of marble. The new Chinese navy was organized into four fleets. The Peiyang Fleet, organized by a leader of the self-strengthening movement, Li Hongzhang, was the most modern and powerful and by 1884 included two 7,500-ton German-built battleships. The Fujian Fleet was homeported in Fuzhou; the other two fleets were the Nanyang and Guangdong.

14. Wright, *The Last Stand of Chinese Conservatism,* 59–66, provides the most detailed description of the Sino-French War. The French had eight warships and two torpedo boats; the Chinese had eleven warships and several other craft, but all were made of wood. The French also destroyed the Chinese shore installations.

15. Swanson, *The Eighth Voyage of the Dragon,* 96ff., discusses these developments.

16. Japan's success was simplified by the fact that the forts' guns were designed only to defend against threats from seaward. The British made the same defensive mistake in Singapore in 1941, and Japanese forces took advantage of it.

17. Swanson, *The Eighth Voyage of the Dragon,* 223.

18. China was only one of several countries building navies at this time: Great Britain, Germany, France, Italy, Russia, Japan, the United States, and even Austria-Hungary were all modernizing their fleets. Those that failed spectacularly—China, Germany, Austria-Hungary—failed to develop meaningful strategic and operational frameworks for their new navies. Tyler, *Pulling Strings in China,* tells some colorful stories about another, more successful maritime force developed in China during the late nineteenth century. The ships of the Revenue Service, established as part of the Customs Service,

long supervised by Sir Robert Hart, were operated mostly by British officers. Tyler was onboard the Chinese flagship at Weihaiwei in 1895, and characterized the navy as "a monstrously disordered epicyclic heterogeneity."

19.   "The Chinese Navy," in *Shanghai Defense Force and Volunteers* (Shanghai: *North China Daily Herald*, 1929), 1302.

20.   This battle is described in Cole, *Gunboats and Marines*, 89–90.

21.   Swanson, *The Eighth Voyage of the Dragon*, 157. The "Chinese" naval forces were actually those of Zhang Xueliang, the Manchurian warlord (the "Young Marshall") who had recently sworn allegiance to Chang Kai-shek's Nationalist government. The Chinese account of this battle quoted by Swanson ends with a Soviet victory due to superior firepower, including air strikes. There was also an October 1929 clash with Soviet forces over disputed boundaries.

22.   The United States, for instance, used just two Navy transports and a commercial passenger liner to move a regiment of Marines from the United States to the Far East, and then between the Philippines and China, and between north and south China, as crises waxed and waned.

23.   PLAN Vice-Commander Zhou Xihan, 1957, quoted in Muller, *China's Emergence as a Maritime Power*, 47.

24.   Larry M. Wortzel, in "The Beiping-Tianjin Campaign of 1948–49: The Strategic and Operational Thinking of the People's Liberation Army" (paper prepared for the U.S. Army War College's Strategic Studies Institute, Carlisle, Pa., n.d., chart 1), points out that by July 1949 the PLA actually included seventy-seven "naval vessels." Hanrahan, "Report on Red China's New Navy," 847, describes the Nationalist contribution to this force as "twenty-five vessels ranging from LCTs to destroyers, representing an estimated one-fourth of the total Nationalist naval force."

25.   General Zhang Aiping, quoted in Hanrahan, "Red China's New Navy," 848. See Cole, *Taiwan's Security*, ch. 2, for an account of KMT activities during this period.

26.   Quoted in Zhang, *Mao's Military Romanticism*, 51.

27.   Hanrahan, 46–54, provides a useful description of the beginnings of the PLAN. Muller, *China's Emergence as a Maritime Power*, 13, states that approximately two thousand former Republic of China naval personnel who defected to the communist regime in 1949 formed the core of the nascent PLAN.

28.   One case is reported in Liu Yueshan, "Son-in-Law of Hu Yaobang Becomes the Political Commissar of PLA Navy amidst Senior Staff Changes," *Wen Wei Po Online* (Hong Kong), 18 July 2008, in OSC-CPP20080718710010. The reverse also occurs, if much less frequently. The author's long discussion with the Qingdao PLA Garrison deputy chief of staff for militia and reserve affairs in May 2000 revealed that this individual, a PLA senior colonel, had spent the previous twenty-two years as a naval officer,

reaching the rank of senior captain, before his transfer so the Army could utilize his engineering expertise.

29.   The Chinese missions to Moscow are discussed, in some cases with verbatim accounts, in "Inside China's Cold War." Probably the most complete account of PLAN Taiwan Strait operations in this period is He Di, "The Last Campaign to Unify China," 8. Its author worked at the Institute of American Studies of the Chinese Academy of Social Sciences and presumably had good access to PLA archives while researching this article.

30.   Blackman, *Jane's Fighting Ships: 1955–56*, 151ff., provides these numbers, but they should be treated only as estimates. Swanson, *The Eighth Voyage of the Dragon*, 196, describes such massive projects as a fortified "250-mile, 10-foot-wide communication trench paralleling the southern bank of the Yangtze River from Wusong to Jiujiang up river," and notes that a "similar trench was constructed along the coast south of Shanghai for about 200 miles."

31.   He, "The Last Campaign to Unify China," 2, points out that Mao postponed the date for assaulting Taiwan several times as PLA failures against various offshore islands emphasized the additional time required to prepare for a successful large-scale amphibious assault. Muller, *China's Emergence as a Maritime Power*, 16, gives August 1951 as the planned invasion month.

32.   He, "The Last Campaign to Unify China," 4. Marolda, "U.S. Navy and the Chinese Civil War," 139, states that by spring 1950 Beijing "had assembled a motley armada of 5,000 vessels . . . freighters, motorized junks, and sampans" for the invasion of Taiwan; these vessels were to be crewed by "30,000 fishermen and other sailors."

33.   See Donovan, *Tumultuous Years*, 206, for Truman's decision to reposition the Seventh Fleet, and 241ff. for a good account of administration thinking (Truman, Acheson, Bohlen, et al.) about the implementation of NSC-68, which effectively rearmed the United States for the Cold War and potential global war with Soviet-led communist forces: "On the last day of July 1950, Truman and Acheson had a talk about grand strategy. The eyes of the American people were glued to Korea. . . . The president and the secretary of state fixed their gaze on the Rhine and the Elbe." The Chinese reaction is in Mao Zedong, "Speech Delivered at the Eighth Meeting of the Government Council of the People's Republic of China," 28 June 1950, in Ch'en, *Mao*, 115.

34.   Quoted in Marolda, "U.S. Navy and the Chinese Civil War," 119–20.

35.   Israel, "Dwight D. Eisenhower: First Annual Message," 3015: in his 2 February 1953 State of the Union Address to Congress, Eisenhower commented that "since the 'Red Chinese' had intervened in the Korean War, he felt no longer any need to 'protect' them from an invasion by . . . Chiang K'ai-shek."

36.   Swanson, *The Eighth Voyage of the Dragon*, 187.

37.   *Dangdai Zhonggun Haijun* (Beijing: China Social Services Publishing House, 1987), translated as *China Today: The People's Navy* [hereafter *People's Navy*], in FBIS: JPRS-CAR-90-014, 16 July 1990, 7.

38.   Ibid., 10, also notes that the Soviet ships were designed for a northern climate and had some difficulty when operating in the warmer waters of the East and South China seas, which is still a concern with the *Sovremenny*-class DDGs purchased by China.

39.   *The Case of Peng Teh-huai*, 164–65. The quote about the Navy is in Swanson, *The Eighth Voyage of the Dragon*, 206–8.

40.   Quoted in *People's Navy*, 13.

41.   Chang and He, "The Absence of War in the U.S.-China Confrontation over Quemoy and Matsu in 1954–1955," 1514, describes this action during which "10,000 PLA troops . . . overwhelmed 1,086 Kuomingtang soldiers."

42.   Torda, "Struggle for the Taiwan Strait," describes these early battles, which included PLA successes as well as failures. Also see Huang, "Evolution of the PLA Navy," 3, for a tabular summation of the PLAN's war-fighting efforts during this period. Chang and He, "The Absence of War," 1504, 1510, documents this (nn. 7, 8).

43.   Other islands remained under Taiwan's control, including the Penghus, just off the southwestern Taiwan coast, as well as the Pratas Islands and Itu Abba in the South China Sea. Taiwan's attacks on the mainland continued into the 1960s. The Taiwan Strait naval campaigns are addressed in Li, "PLA Attacks and Amphibious Operations"; and in Huang, "PLA Navy at War, 1949–1999."

44.   *People's Navy*, 36, 37; Allen, Krumel, and Pollack, *China's Air Force*, 205, n. 11, also provide a useful description of PLA aircraft acquisition programs in app. E, 221–29. Swanson, *The Eighth Voyage of the Dragon*, 205, estimates 470 aircraft; a reasonable assumption is that the Navy's air arm has flown the older variants of the same aircraft flown by the PLAAF.

45.   The PLAN submarine bases were perhaps influenced by Soviet advisers; during discussions with the Allies in the 1940s and with Mao in 1950 Stalin had expressed interest in establishing a Soviet submarine base at Port Arthur (Lushun).

46.   See Christensen, *Useful Adversaries*, ch. 6.

47.   Swanson, *The Eighth Voyage of the Dragon*, 236.

48.   Blackman, *Jane's Fighting Ships, 1970–1971*, 610, credits the Soviet Navy with just four large (4,000 tons displacement) and eighty smaller (600–1,000 tons) amphibious ships spread out among all of the Soviet Union's four fleets, from the Pacific to the Baltic.

49.   *People's Navy* repeatedly emphasizes the deleterious effects of the GPCR; also see Lewis and Xue, *China's Strategic Seapower*, 206ff. Even Zhou Enlai was unable to protect these programs completely.

50.   O'Donnell, "An Analysis of Major Developmental Influences," 42, lists the PLAN's political commissar, chief operations officer, the East Sea Fleet commander, two deputy commanders, and two fleet political commissars among the "120 senior naval officers and thousands of lower ranking personnel [who] were purged."

51.   Lewis and Xue, *China's Strategic Seapower*, 147–48, 223.

52.   Blackman, *Jane's Fighting Ships, 1970–1971*, 61–66; the PLAN also included more than thirty other submarines, a collection of assorted foreign-built destroyers and escort vessels (Soviet, Japanese, U.S., British, Canadian, and Italian), and more than four hundred Chinese-built patrol craft, some of them hydrofoils and most armed with torpedoes.

53.   Cited in Muller, *China's Emergence as a Maritime Power*, 154.

54.   Lewis and Xue, "Beijing's Defense Establishment," 223, discusses Hua's decision; Deng is quoted on 224.

55.   Fred Hiatt, "Marine General: U.S. Troops Must Stay in Japan," *Washington Post*, 27 March 1990, A14, quoted Lieutenant General Henry Stackpole, USMC, commander of the 3rd Marine Expeditionary Force on Okinawa, describing the United States as "a cap in the [Japanese] bottle," a statement I confirmed in conversation with Lieutenant General Stackpole.

56.   Cheung, *Growth of Chinese Naval Power*, 28. China's Marine Corps had been disestablished in 1957 as "unnecessary," but was reestablished in 1979. The concentration of amphibious forces in the South Sea Fleet continues today, indicating that PLAN amphibious planning is aimed more at the South China Sea than at Taiwan.

57.   Moore, *Jane's Fighting Ships: 1976–77*, 100ff. The PLAN also included the first Chinese range-instrument ships for tracking guided-missile flights and the first Chinese-built amphibious transports. Mao is quoted in Muller, *China's Emergence as a Maritime Power*, 171.

58.   Deng Xiaoping, "Speech at an Enlarged Meeting of the Military Commission of the Party Central Committee," 14 July 1975, in Joint Publications Research Service: *China Reports*, no. 468, 31 October 1983, 14–22 (site now discontinued).

59.   Wilhelm, *China and Security in the Asian Pacific Region through 2010*, 42.

60.   Ibid., 32ff.

61.   Lewis and Xue, *China Builds the Bomb*, 50, 51; Liu had worked for Deng on at least two previous occasions.

62.   Liu's accomplishments are summed up in Wilhelm, *China and Security in the Asian Pacific Region through 2010*, 43.

63.   See Garver, "China's Push through the South China Sea," 1019, 1022.

64.   Lewis and Xue, *China's Strategic Seapower*, provides the best account of the FBM and JL-1 programs. A successful 1982 launch was made from a submerged platform; a

1988 attempt from the submarine probably succeeded. The Xia itself has been an operational failure, never operating on a regular basis; it apparently received an extensive
overhaul—probably involving recoring the propulsion plant—which at least enabled
the boat to participate in the April 2009 naval review conducted by China to celebrate
the PLAN's sixtieth anniversary.

65. Lieutenant-General Mi Zhenyu, PLA, "A Reflection on Geographic Strategy,"
     Zhongguo Junshi Kexue [China Military Science] (Beijing), no. 1 (February 1998):
     6–14, in FBIS-CHI-98-208. A brief popular view of China's maritime history was
     published as "Special Report: China marks 60 Anniversary of Navy," *Xinhua*, 24 April
     2009, at http://news.xinhuanet.com/english/2009-04/23/content_11240843.htm
     (accessed 27 June 2009).

66. Fairbank, *China: A New History*, discusses these factors at length.

67. Whitson, with Huang, *The Chinese High Command*, 473: "On balance, it is evident that
     the evolving Russian model of military ethic and style, especially on the issues of mili-
     tary role, commander authority, and strategy, has been the most important European
     influence to alter traditional Chinese perspectives."

68. Fravel, *Strong Borders, Secure Nation*, 1, observes that "since 1949, China has partici-
     pated in twenty-three unique territorial disputes with its neighbors on land and at sea.
     Yet it has pursued compromise and offered concessions in seventeen of these conflicts."

Chapter 2. China's Maritime Territorial Interests

1. Quoted in Schram, *The Political Thought of Mao Zedong*, 276.

2. See Ball, "Military Acquisitions," 88–89. Taiwan duplicates China's insular territorial
    claims. The Diaoyu/Senkaku Islands were known as the Pinnacle Islands in English.

3. United Nations, UNCLOS, art. 2. The United States has signed but not ratified this
    important international agreement.

4. Ibid., art. 33.

5. Ibid., art. 56. Several UNCLOS signatories, including China, have expressed a different
    interpretation of a host nation's rights within its EEZ, as will be discussed below.

6. Ibid., arts. 76–78. A nation's CS does not automatically extend out to 350 nm; it is
    subject to technical definition based on gradient and seabed composition: no more
    than 200 nautical miles from a line connecting the depths of the seabed at 1,367
    fathoms (2,500 meters) from the state's baseline.

7. Ibid., art. 121, makes an important distinction between an island and a "rock," which
    by definition "cannot sustain human habitation or economic life" on its own and which
    has no EEZ or CS. Although not specified, the inference of this article is that a "rock"

that can sustain human life is considered an "island." The moot point is whether a land formation with neither natural water nor food supply qualifies as a "rock" or an "island."

8. Ibid., art. 83 and sec. 15.

9. See Schofield, "Unlocking the Sea Bed Resources," 286–308.

10. "East Asia: Straits Challenge," *Asia-Pacific Daily News Summary*, U.S. Pacific Command Virtual Intelligence Center (VIC) (Honolulu, Hawaii), 10 February 2000, 2. This twice-daily collection of news articles is at http://vic.distributor@apan-info.net (accessed 18 December 2009).

11. China's "declarations" regarding UNCLOS are at http://www.un.org/Depts/los/convention_agreements/convention_declarations.htm#China (accessed 08 July 2009). Peter Dutton of the U.S. Naval War College brought to the author's attention Beijing's official view, in Ren and Cheng, "A Chinese Perspective," 139–46. The EEZ discussion is from Bateman, "Clashes at Sea," at http://www.rsis.edu.sg/publications/Perspective/RSIS0272009.pdf (accessed 06 July 2009). The United States "rejects any nation's attempt to place limits on the exercise of high seas freedoms within an EEZ," as stated by Department of State and Department of Defense officials; see "Testimony of Deputy Assistant Secretary of Defense Robert Scher" and "Testimony of Deputy Assistant Secretary of State Scot Marciel," both before the Subcommittee on East Asian and Pacific Affairs of the Senate Committee on Foreign Relations, 15 July 2009; the U.S. position on Beijing's legal claims under the UNCLOS is succinctly described by Dutton's testimony during these same hearings, at http://foreign.senate.gov/hearings/hearing/20090715_2/ (accessed 25 November 2009).

12. This discussion of China's submission regarding its CS is based on Manicom, "China's Claims to an Extended Continental Shelf." China announced its submission in MOFA spokesperson Ma Zhaoxu's "Remarks on China's Submission of Preliminary Information Indicative of the Outer Limits of the Continental Shelf beyond 200 Nautical Miles," Beijing, 13 May 2009, at http://www.fmprc.gov.cn/eng/xwfw/s2510/t562208.htm (accessed 11 July 2009).

13. Parker, "Chinese Overseas Bases," 1, 13; and "Chinese Scientists Leave for 26th Antarctica Expedition," *Xinhua*, 11 October 2009, at http://news.xinhuanet.com/english/2009-10/11/content_12210650.htm (accessed 11 October 2009). China had established three Antarctic stations by 2009; summaries of these efforts are Hsiao, "China en Route to Cap Antarctica," at http://www.jamestown.org/single/?no_cache=1&tx_ttnews%5Bswords%5D=8fd5893941d69d0be3f378576261ae3e&tx_ttnews%5Bany_of_the_words%5D=antartica&tx_ttnews%5Btt_news%5D=5228&tx_ttnews%5BbackPid%5D=7&cHash=c321acecb0 (accessed 06 July 2009); and de Pomereu, "Accompanying China to Antarctica," at http://www.sciencepoles.org/index.php?s=2&rs=home&uid=1361 (accessed 01 July 2009).

14. China had established a research station at 87° N by 2008, as reported in Spears, "China and the Arctic," at http://www.jamestown.org/programs/chinabrief/single/?tx_ttnews%5Btt_news%5D=34725&cHash=9638471049 (accessed 01 July 2009); and "Icebreaker *Xuelong* Sails into Arctic," *Xinhua*, 02 September 2008, at http://arctic-healy-baker-2008.blogspot.com/2008/09/china-in-arctic.html (accessed 01 July 2009). China's Arctic and Antarctic Administration manages these expeditions, while the Polar Research Institute operates China's single polar icebreaker.

15. "Spokesman on PRC Joining Indian Ocean Organization," *Xinhua*, 25 January 2000, in FBIS-20000125000826 (site now discontinued). Dialogue partners are states "with a special interest or capacity to contribute to" the IORARC but without an Indian Ocean coastline. Others in this category include Japan, Egypt, France, and Great Britain. The association's full members are Australia, Bangladesh, India, Indonesia, Iran, Kenya, Madagascar, Malaysia, Mauritius, Mozambique, Oman, Qatar, Singapore, South Africa, Sri Lanka, Tanzania, Yemen, and the UAE (the Seychelles withdrew in 2003). The IORARC held its ninth conference in June 2009 in Yemen; for the results of this meeting, see "IORARC Supported Anti-piracy Center in Yemen," *Saba*, 27 June 2009, at http://www.sabanews.net/en/news187099.htm (accessed 01 July 2009).

16. A sample of this occurred in 1995 when "Concrete Claims," *Far Eastern Economic Review*, 20 December 1995, 14, reported that "a Chinese reef-building expedition in the [Spratlys] in early November went badly wrong after hurricane-force winds and frigid temperatures wrought havoc with the naval personnel. . . . The ship returned from its 10-day mission with half of the 100 crew suffering from pneumonia and assorted injuries."

17. Catley and Keliat, "Spratlys," 7, offers these divisions.

18. Vietnam's claims are described in "South China Sea Territorial Issues," EIA, March 2008, at http://www.eia.doe.gov/emeu/cabs/South_China_Sea/SouthChina SeaTerritorialIssues.html (accessed 02 July 2009).

19. The Kilo purchase is reported in "Russia to Build Six Kilo-Class Submarines for Vietnam," *RIA-Novosti*, 27 April 2009, at http://en.rian.ru/russia/20090427/121320414.html; and "Russia to Build Fighter Jets for Vietnam," Agence France-Presse, 15 May 2009, at http://www.defencetalk.com/russia-to-build-fighter-aircraft-vietnam-18937/ (both accessed 02 July 2009). China's reaction—at least semiofficial—is in Hai Yan, "Vietnam's Military Expansion Threatens Malacca Strait," *Guoji Xianqu Daobao Online* (Beijing), 19 May 2009, in OSC-CPP20090527671004 (accessed 27 July 2009).

20. See "China-Malaysia Bilateral Relations," *Xinhua*, 02 December 2009, at http://news. xinhuanet.com/english/2005-12/02/content_3867959.htm (accessed 02 July 2009); Johnson, "Drawn into the Fray," 153–61, examines the Natuna disagreement in detail, including Jakarta's attempt to ignore the problem.

21.   Shi Ren, "Although Overall Situation in South China Sea Comparatively Stable, Hidden Trouble Becomes Prominent," *Zhongguo Tongxun She* (Hong Kong), in BBC report (Beijing), 25 July 2009, at http://www.viet-studies.info/kinhte/hidden_trouble. htm (accessed 08 November 2009).

22.   EIA, "South China Sea Region," at http://www.eia.doe.gov/emeu/cabs/South_China_ Sea/Background.html (accessed 02 July 2009). Noer, with Gregory, *Chokepoints*, provides a thorough breakdown of the merchant traffic through the South China Sea by cargo and by ship ownership and includes the monetary costs of using alternative routes in the event the Malacca or other straits cannot be used.

23.   Different sources give different numbers of land features occupied by various countries; these are from Fravel, *Strong Borders, Secure Nation*, which also provides a complete account of China's interests, policies, and actions in the South and East China seas.

24.   Harrison, *China, Oil, and Asia*, 101–2.

25.   Deng Xiaoping, quoted in "Nansha Islands—The Facts," *China Daily*, 08 May 2000, in FBIS-CPP20000508000027. This article describes the Spratlys as a "second Persian Gulf," which is a gross overstatement of its likely petroleum reserves. Also see Valencia, Van Dyke, and Ludwig, *Sharing the Resources*, 20–21. See, for instance, "South China Sea: Controversies and Solutions," *BeijingReview.com.cn*, no. 22, 04 June 2009, at http://www.bjreview.com.cn/world/txt/2009-05/31/content_197954.htm; and Li Hungmei, "China's Claims over Sea Sovereignty Must Be Distinctly Heard," *People's Daily*, 15 May 2009, at http://english.peopledaily.com.cn/90002/96417/6658601. html (both accessed 02 July 2009). The dangers of the situation are described in Eric A. McVadon, "The Reckless and the Resolute: Confrontation in the South China Sea," 2009, at http://www.chinasecurity.us/pdfs/mcvadon.pdf (accessed 25 November 2009).

26.   "Straight baselines" are sovereignty claim lines that are drawn directly ("straight") from one geographical point to another rather than in conformance with the coastline; using them enables a country to claim a much larger expanse of maritime area as sovereign territory. The U.S. position is in LeGrand, "Memorandum [on] 'Chinese Straight Baseline Declaration,'" 1: "all of the straight baselines within the Chinese declaration are excessive and not in accordance with international law." Beijing has not stated that straight baselines apply to the Spratlys. Valencia and Van Dyke, "Vietnam's National Interests and the Law of the Sea," 221, points out that Vietnam also uses straight baselines and thus claims much of the Tonkin Gulf as sovereign waters.

27.   Cited in Cheng-yi Lin, "Taiwan's Spratly Initiative in the South China Sea," Association for Asian Research, 19 February 2008, at http://www.asianresearch.org/ articles/3115.html (accessed 02 July 2009); and MOFA statement quoted in "Taiwan Reaffirms Sovereignty over South China Sea Islands," *Taiwan News*, 10 May 2009, 2.

Taiwan has not played a constructive role in settling the South China Sea territorial disputes, preferring to ride Beijing's rigid coattails; as a former senior naval intelligence officer in Taiwan said to me, "What do we have to lose?" The new "city," Sansha City, has its own Web site at http://www.sanshashi.com (accessed 16 August 2009).

28. Leifer, *China in Southeast Asia,* 7, 32; Kenney, *Shadow of the Dragon,* 67.

29. Fravel, *Strong Borders, Secure Nation,* is the best source on the Sino-Vietnamese conflict; see especially ch. 6.

30. Harrison, *China, Oil, and Asia: Conflict Ahead?* 204; Studeman, "Calculating China's Advances," 2; EIA, *South China Sea: Energy Data, Statistics, and Analysis,* March 2008, at http://www.eia.doe.gov/emeu/cabs/South_China_Sea/Background.html (accessed 23 December 2008). Studeman, 10, also identifies clashes in 1993 and 1994. This ironic situation—two American companies competing at the behest of China and Vietnam—would place the U.S. government in an interesting situation should American lives or property be lost. The best summing up of the Sino-Vietnamese contest in the South China Sea is Bateman and Emmers, *Security and International Politics in the South China Sea.*

31. Thayer, "The Structure of Vietnam-China Relations," notes that joint patrols were also conducted in December 2006, July and October 2007, and May 2008. The shooting incident is reported in "Chinese Ships Attack, Kill Vietnamese Fishermen," *Thanh Nien* (Hanoi), 13 January 2005, at http://www.thanhniennews.com/society/?catid=3&newsid=4460 (accessed 30 November 2008).

32. "China-Vietnam Joint Statement," *BeijingReview.com.cn,* no. 49, 04 December 2008, at http://www.bjreview.com.cn/document/txt/2008-12/04/content_168445_2.htm (accessed 03 July 2009), notes that the two sides "agreed to work more closely to resolve the remaining issues [and] to steadily advance the negotiations on demarcation"; Khalilzad et al., *The United States and a Rising China,* 29. An equidistant line would be in accord with the UNCLOS but at variance with China's own reservation to the treaty.

33. Zhou, "The Sino-Vietnamese Agreement," at http://www.southchinasea.org/docs/zou%20keyuan-sino-vietnam%20boundary%20delimitation.pdf (accessed 08 July 2009).

34. Montaperto, "Assurance and Reassurance," at http://www.csis.org/media/csis/pubs/0503qchina_seasia.pdf; and Montaperto, "Dancing with China," at http://www.csis.org/media/csis/pubs/0502qchina_seasia.pdf (both accessed 02 December 2008).

35. Penrose, Pincus, and Cheshier, "Vietnam: Beyond Fish and Ships," at http://www.viet-studies.info/kinhte/vietnam_beyond_fish_and_ships.htm (accessed 08 July 2009); Bateman and Emmers, *Security and International Politics in the South China Sea,* 213.

36. Qin Gang, *People's Daily Online,* 10 April 2007, at http://www.chinaconsulatesf.org/eng/xw/fyrth/t310433.htm (accessed 04 December 2008).

37. Roger Mitton, "Vietnam, China Clash Again over Spratlys—Chinese Navy Fires at Vietnamese Fishing Boats in Oil-Rich Region," BBC, 19 July 2007, at http://www.uofaweb.ualberta.ca/chinainstitute/nav03.cfm?nav03=62952&nav02=58211&nav01=57272 (accessed 08 July 2009); and "Vietnam Protests Chinese Military Exercise in Disputed Islands," *ChannelNewsAsia.com,* 24 November 2007, at http://www.channelnewsasia.com/stories/afp_asiapacific/view/313471/1/.html (accessed 08 July 2009).

38. Sutter and Huang, "Singapore Summits, Harmony, and Challenges," at http://www.csis.org/media/csis/pubs/0704qchina_seasia.pdf (accessed 04 December 2008). Thayer, "Recent Developments in the South China Sea," 17–18, notes that in an analogous administrative move to that of Beijing, in 1999 Taipei assigned administrative responsibility for the South China Sea islands that it occupies—Dongsha and Taiping—to the Kaohsiung city government. Furthermore, Vietnam has assigned administrative responsibility for the Paracels to Da Nang, and for the Spratlys to Vung Tau.

39. "Joint Statement between China and Vietnam," Ministry of Foreign Affairs (Beijing), 01 June 2008, at http://www.fmprc.gov.cn/eng/zxxx/t472321.htm (accessed 30 November 2008).

40. Nick Macfie, "China, Vietnam Seek Sea Border Resolution 'This Year,'" Reuters, 25 October 2008, at http://www.reuters.com/article/worldNews/idUSTRE49O0RI2008 1025?feedType=RSS&feedName=worldNews (accessed 05 December 2008).

41. Torode, "Tussle for Oil in the South China Sea," at https://archive.scmp.com/login.php?prev_url=https://archive.scmp.com/intermediate_checkout.php (accessed 04 December 2008) reports the pressure on ExxonMobile; Dong Ha, "BP, PetroVietnam Rearrange Gas Pipeline Overhauls Plan," *Thanh Nien,* 14 March 2007, cited in Thayer, "The Structure of Vietnam-China Relations," n. 33, discusses BP participation. The new patrol system is described in Liu Ke Cai, "China Enhances Protection of Its Rights in Disputed Sea Area—Establishment of a Regular Marine Patrol and Rights Protection System within Entire Sea Areas Shows China's Capability and Determination to Maintain Its Jurisdiction over Disputed Sea Areas," *Guoji Xianqu Daobao* (Beijing), 24 October 2008, in OSC-CPP20081031682001.

42. "China, Vietnam Senior Military Officers Discuss Closer Cooperation," english.chinamil.com.cn, 03 December 2008, at http://english.pladaily.com.cn/site2/news-channels/2008-12/03/content_1570184.htm (accessed 06 December 2008); but see "Chinese Patrol Seizes Vietnamese Boat in Paracel Islands," *Thanh Nien* (Hanoi), 04 August 2009, at http://www.thanhniennews.com/society/?catid=3&newsid=51418 (accessed 25 November 2009).

43. See Hans M. Kristensen, "New Chinese SSBN Deploys to Hainan Island China," 24 April 2008, at http://www.fas.org/blog/ssp/2008/04/new-chinese-ssbn-deploys-

to-hainan-island-naval-base.php (accessed 03 July 2009), Federation of American Scientists (FAS), 05 December 2008, reports in detail on a base equipped to home-port the Jin class; also see "Secret Sanya: China's New Nuclear Base Revealed," Jane's Information Group, 21 April 2008, at http://www.janes.com/news/security/jir/jir080421_1_n.shtml (accessed 23 December 2008).

44. Liefer, "China in Southeast Asia," 34; also see "Philippines May Protest to China over Disputed Islands," *Kyodo* (Manila), 07 November 2003, at http://findarticles.com/p/articles/mi_m0WDQ/is_2003_Nov_10/ai_n27672022/print?tag=artBody;col1 (accessed 23 December 2008). "Malaysia Building Up Military off Philippine Island," *Philippine Star* (Manila), 20 August 1998, 20A, in FBIS-EAS-98-232; Paolo Romero, "Philippine Army Spots 3 PRC, 2 SRV Ships off Spratlys," *Philippine Star,* 26 May 2000, in FBIS-SEP20000526000058; and Manny B. Marinay, "Philippine Planes Spot 5 PRC, 3 SRV Vessels in Spratlys," *Manila Times,* 16 May 2000, in FBIS-SEP20000516000057, are just three of an almost constant stream of reports of Manila's concerns about foreign vessels in its claimed South China Sea territories.

45. EIA, "Country Analysis Brief: Philippines," March 2008, at http://www.eia.doe.gov/emeu/cabs/Philippines/Full.html (accessed 08 July 2009).

46. Wolfgang Schippke, "Mischief Reef, Spratly Group," at http://www.southchinasea.org/docs/Schippke/mischief.html (accessed 23 December 2008), describes Mischief Reef as "a circular atoll with a diameter of 4 miles. [It] is awash, but has several rocks up to 6 ft above high tide."

47. The chief of the Philippine armed forces described this program to the author in the spring of 1997 but commented, "I don't expect to see a peso of it."

48. "Philippine Military Chief Says Armed Forces Not Strong Enough to Fully Defend Country," Associated Press report, *International Herald Tribune,* 04 June 2008, at http://www.iht.com/articles/ap/2008/06/04/asia/AS-GEN-Philippines-Problematic-Military.php (accessed 05 December 2008). Governance problems have plagued the Philippines since Ferdinand Marcos seized power in 1973; he was overthrown in 1986 and was followed by the well-meaning but inept Cory Aquino; her successor, former general Fidel Ramos, was honest and competent, but his successor (Estrada) was imprisoned for corruption; the Macapagal-Arroyo administration has also suffered frequent accusations of corruption and ineptness.

49. "Philippine-US Joint Military Exercises Open 31 Jan," *Quezon City BMA-7 Radio-Television Arts,* 31 January 2000, in FBIS-20000206000252, reports the exercise. Opel is quoted in Macon Ramos-Araneta, "Philippine Senate President: 'Ready for War' with US Ally," *Manila Times,* 06 February 2000, in FBIS-20000206000427; he was referring to the 1952 U.S.-Philippine Mutual Defense Treaty, but the United States does not agree that the Philippines' South China Sea claims are covered. Estrada is

quoted in "Military Exercises with U.S. Not Aimed at China," *Manila Business World,* 04 November 1999, in FBIS-EAS-1999-1104. Macapagal-Arroyo is quoted in "Arroyo Accuses Abu Sayyaf of Violating Woman Hostages; Defends Balikatan Drive Anew," *Manila Bulletin,* 08 March 2008, at http://www.highbeam.com/doc/1G1-83599185. html (accessed 06 December 2008). The 2009 Balikatan was defended by the Philippine government on 03 April 2009 at http://www.gmanews.tv/story/155526/dfa-defends-us-troops-in-balikatan-from-misbehavior-rap (accessed 06 December 2009). The 2010 exercise is reported in Mark Alvarez, "USS *Essex* Participates in Balikatan 2010," at http://www.navy.mil/search/print.asp?story_id=51797&VIRIN=81784&imagetyp e=1&page (accessed 11 March 2010).

50. Storey, "Impeccable Affair," at http://www.jamestown.org/programs/chinabrief/ single/?tx_ttnews%5Btt_news%5D=34922&tx_ttnews%5BbackPid%5D=414&no_ cache=1 (accessed 06 July 2009), gives a good account of these protests and notes that Manila is claiming Scarborough Shoals and other land features as "a regime of islands" rather than as lying within the Philippines' territorial baselines. China's MOFA responded with the wishful statement that "China possesses indisputable sovereignty over" the Spratlys "and adjacent waters" in: "China Reiterates Sovereignty in South China Sea, *Xinhua,* 03 February 2009, at http://english.people.com.cn/ 90001/90776/90883/6584831.html (accessed 09 July 2009).

51. "ASEAN Members Said Unhappy with Manila on Spratlys Issue," *Manila Business World,* 26 April 1999, in FBIS-EAS-99-0426, reports a Philippine diplomat's plaint that "even some of our ASEAN friends are either mute, timid or cannot go beyond espousal of general principle of peaceful settlement of disputes and polite words of understanding given in the corridors of meeting rooms."

52. Cited in Kiko Cueto, "Manila Said in 'Lose-Lose' Situation on Chinese Fisherman," *Abante* (Manila), 09 February 2000, in FBIS-20000209000074. The Philippines fared no better in its territorial disputes with the other South China Sea claimants; see, for instance, John McLean, "Philippines Plane Shooting by Vietnamese," *Kyodo,* 27 October 1999, at http://findarticles.com/p/articles/mi_m0WDQ/is_1999_Nov_1/ ai_57432163/ (accessed 08 July 2009), for an account of an incident in which Vietnamese forces allegedly fired at a Philippine Air Force plane.

53. Estrada is quoted in Tan Guoqi, "Jiang Zemin, Estrada Hold Talks on Ties, South China Sea, WTO, One-China Issues," *Xinhua,* 16 May 2000, in FBIS-CPP20000516000147. The Wen–Macapagal-Arroyo meeting is described in "Joint Development of the South China Sea Tops Bilateral Talks between RP and China," Republic of the Philippines, Office of the President news release, 21 November 2007, at http://www.op.gov.ph/ index.php?option=com_content&task=view&id=11151&Itemid=2 (accessed 03 July 2009).

54. Brunei's claim is described at EIA, "South China Sea: Background," March 2008, at http://www.eia.doe.gov/emeu/cabs/South_China_Sea/pdf.pdf; the Malaysia-Vietnam agreement is reported in Khairdzir Yunus, "Malaysia, Vietnam to Bring Understanding Reached over Sea Claims to UN," *Bernama*, 01 June 2009, at http://www.bernama. com/bernama/v5/newsindex.php?id=415187; Malaysia's relations with China are in "China-Malaysia Issue Joint Communiqué," *People's Daily*, 30 May 2004, at http:// english.peoplesdaily.cn/200405/30/eng20040530_144795.htm; and Li Xiaokun and Jiang Wanjuan, "Malaysia PM Wants Friendly Talks," *China Daily*, 04 June 2009, at http://english.peopledaily.com.cn/200405/30/eng20040530_144795.html (all accessed 04 July 2009).

55. See "Indonesia to Help Maintain Security in South China Sea," *Jakarta Post*, 07 December 1999, in FBIS-19991206001856. Johnson, "Drawn into the Fray," 153, quotes Shihab and Indonesian Foreign Ministry spokesperson Irawan Abidin saying, "We didn't want to make a big fuss out of it," thus nicely summarizing Indonesia's approach to disputed issues with China. For a good discussion of this agreement, see Whiting, "ASEAN Eyes China: The Security Dimension," 305–7, which notes that Indonesia "held its first prominent military exercises around the [Natuna] islands in five years" in September 1996. Indonesian Navy Chief of Staff Admiral Achmad Sutjipto is quoted in "Indonesian Navy to Set Up Four Maritime Region Commands," *Antara* (Jakarta), 17 February 2000, in FBIS-SEP20000217000078. This intention is expressed in "China, Indonesia Forge Strategic Partnership," *People's Daily*, 26 April 2005, at http://english.peopledaily.com.cn/200504/26/eng20050426_182767.html (accessed 06 December 2008).

56. "East and Southeast Asia," in *2008 World Factbook*, at https://www.cia.gov/library/ publications/the-world-factbook/geos/PG.html (accessed 04 July 2009). The Su-30 allows the PLA to maintain air cover over the full extent of the South China Sea, although for periods of less than thirty minutes over the extreme southern areas. There is a shorter 3,000-foot paved runway on Taiping/Itu Aba Island, built by Taiwan in 2003, and a 1,970-foot unpaved strip on Spratly Island itself. "PRC Scientific Station in Paracels Becomes Operational," *Xinhua*, 27 December 1999, in FBIS-19991227000472, reports "an observation networks station on crustal movement [for] earthquake forecast" had begun operation on Woody Island. The facility is more likely intended to conduct bottom surveys, with ASW applications. Other expanded facilities on Woody Island are described in Andrei Chang, "China Boosts Power on Offshore Islands," United Press International, 28 September 2008, at http://www. china-defense-mashup.com/?tag=spratly-island (accessed 04 July 2009). In a different vein, see "Conditions Improved for PLA Soldiers on Spratlys," *Xinhua*, 19 April 2000, in OSC-CPP20000419000003, for indications that assignment to one of the minis-

cule Spratly garrisons must be very low on the PLAN personnel-assignment priority list, despite resupply by helicopter and the provision of "dish antennas, high-efficiency refrigerators, karaoke equipment, and VCRs." Xiong Lei and Chen Wanjun, "Soldiers Make Reefs Home," *China Daily*, 08 May 2000, in OSC-CPP20000508000028, paints an even grimmer picture, although praising the PLAN garrisons for "raising pigs and chickens" and growing vegetables "on soil shipped from the mainland."

57. Whiting, "ASEAN Eyes China," 312; Chung, "The Spratlys and Other South China Sea Islands," 6.

58. Klintworth, "China's Naval Ambitions," 13; Zhang is quoted in Catley and Keliat, *Spratlys: The Dispute in the South China Sea*, 83.

59. Cited in Senior Captain Yan Youqiang, PLAN, "Naval Officers on International Chinese Maritime Strategy," *Zhongguo Junshi Kexue* (Beijing), 20 May 1997, in FBIS-CHI-97.

60. Cordner, "The Spratly Islands Dispute," quoted in Valencia, Van Dyke, and Ludwig, *Sharing the Resources of the South China Sea*, 39. In a November 1999 conversation with the author, Mark Valencia pointed out that continuous occupation, preferably for at least fifty years, is considered the legal standard to establish ownership; hence, the drive by claimants to build facilities—to "occupy"—the various bits of reef and land that form the Spratly Islands and other areas of the South China Sea. That is, they are actively pursuing a policy of "ownership is nine-tenths of the law"—no one more so than Beijing. Taiwan, the Philippines, and Malaysia have announced tourist attractions on some of the Spratlys (or Pratas Reef, in Taipei's case), and Malaysian president Mahathir bin Mohamad and Taiwan president Chen Shui-bian have actually visited "resorts" on their claimed islands. Valencia, *China and the South China Sea Disputes*, remains a useful account of the competing South China Sea claims; also see Dumbaugh et al., *China's Maritime Territorial Claims*, 12 November 2001.

61. "Beijing Eases Hard-Line Position in Dispute over Spratly Islands," *Washington Post*, 31 July 1995, 16; Leifer, *China in Southeast Asia*, 14.

62. Zhang Qiyue, quoted in "FM Spokeswoman Discusses South China Sea Issue," *Xinhua*, 18 May 2000, in OSC-CPP20000518000111; and, more recently, "China Hits RP Claim on Parts of Spratlys," *Asian Journal*, 19 February 2009, at http://www.asianjournal.com/dateline-philippines/headlines/1269-china-hits-rp-claim-on-parts-of-spratlys-.html (accessed 04 July 2009).

63. Liu Zhenyan, "ASEAN, PRC to Quicken Drafting of Spratlys Code of Conduct," *Xing Xian Ribao* (Bangkok), 29 April 2000, in OSC-SEP20000501000055. The workshops were funded by the Canadian International Development Agency, but Canada ended the funding in 2001. The code is at http://www.aseansec.org/13163.htm (accessed 06 July 2009). Although the code focuses on the South China Sea disputes, it would

also apply to existing maritime disputes between Thailand and Malaysia, Malaysia and Singapore, Malaysia and Indonesia, Malaysia and Vietnam, and the Philippines and Indonesia.

64.   See "ASEAN Chairman's Statement at the Sixth Meeting of the ARF," Singapore, 26 July 1999, 2, at www.aseansec.org/politics/pol_arf6.htm (accessed 04 July 2009). Qian is quoted in Lu Jianren (Chinese Academy of Social Sciences), "Security Cooperation among ASEAN Countries and Some Points of View," *Ta Kung Pao* (Hong Kong), 7 July 1999, C-1, in FBIS-CHI-99-0727. "ARF Holds First Meeting on Non-proliferation, Disarmament," *Xinhua,* 04 July 2009, at http://www.philstar. com/Article.aspx?articleId=483670&publicationSubCategoryId=200 (accessed 04 July 2009), reports on the 2009 meeting co-hosted by China, the United States, and Singapore. "ASEAN, China Forge Strategic Partnership," *People's Daily,* 09 October 2003, at http://english.peopledaily.com.cn/200310/09/eng20031009_125570.shtml (accessed 04 July 2009), reports the treaty being signed; the treaty is at http://www. aseansec.org/15271.htm (accessed 09 July 2009). Taiwan attends these meetings, albeit as "Chinese Taipei."

65.   Cited in Xiao Rui, "Spokesman on South China Sea Code of Conduct," *Zhongguo Xinwen She,* 26 November 1999, in FBIS-CPP19991128000072.

66.   "China, Vietnam Agree on Joint Exploitation in South China Sea," *Xinhua,* 04 July 2005, at http://news.xinhuanet.com/english/2005-07/19/content_3241736. htm (accessed 05 July 2009). Also see "RP, China, Vietnam to Cooperate in Spratlys Security," *Manila Bulletin,* 19 May 2006, at http://www.articlearchives.com/ environment-natural-resources/ecology/229621-1.html (accessed 05 July 2009). The agreement is at http://www.pcij.org/blog/wp-docs/RP_China_Agreement_on_ Joint_Marine_Seismic_Undertaking.pdf (accessed 05 July 2009). A harsh view of Macapagal-Arroyo's policy is provided in Wain, "Manila's Bungle in the South China Sea," *Far Eastern Economic Review,* January–February 2008, at http://newphilrevolu tion.blogspot.com/2008/03/that-controversial-barry-wain-article.html (accessed 04 March 2010). A more general view of potential cooperation is in Gu Xiaosong and Li Mingjing, "Beibu Gulf Emerging Sub-regional Integration between China and ASEAN," RSIS Working Paper no. 168, 02 January 2009, at http://www.rsis.edu.sg/ publications/WorkingPapers/WP168.pdf (accessed 10 November 2009).

67.   See "South China Sea Fishing Ban 'Indisputable,'" MOFA, Beijing, 09 June 2009, at http://news.xinhuanet.com/english/2009-06/09/content_11513280.htm; the Taiwan government agrees in a sense, in "MOFA Reaffirms Sovereignty over Spratlys," *China Post* (Taipei), 05 February 2009, at http://www.chinapost.com.tw/taiwan/foreign -affairs/2009/02/05/194708/MOFA-reaffirms.htm (both accessed 05 July 2009). Liu is quoted in Fravel, *Strong Borders, Secure Nation,* 267.

68. Sa-Nguan Khumrungroj, "PRC Official Warns ASEAN against Boosting U.S. Military Ties," *The Nation* (Bangkok), 15 March 2000, in FBIS-SEP20000315000021, issued this warning on the eve of the Bangkok ASEAN meeting, demonstrating a heavy Chinese diplomatic hand.

69. Remarks at the Nixon Center, Washington, D.C., 11 September 2009 (shown on C-Span television, Washington, D.C., 12 September 2009).

70. See "ROK, China Resume Fishing Talks in Beijing," *Korea Times*, 08 March 2000, in FBIS-KPP20000308000078; "Korea and China initialed a draft fisheries agreement in November 1998," which agreed on temporary EEZ boundaries and "Japan, China Plan Talks on New Fishery Pact," *Jiji Press* (Tokyo), 05 April 2000, in FBIS-JPP20000405000014, announcing the beginning of the latest in a series of discussions to activate "a new bilateral fishery accord." More recent is Rosenberg, "China, Neighbors Progress in Fishery Agreements," at http://www.atimes.com/atimes/China/GH19Ad02.html (accessed 05 July 2009).

71. A good analysis of these negotiations is Drifte, "Territorial Conflicts in the East China Sea," at http://www.japanfocus.org/-Reinhard-Drifte/3156 (accessed 05 July 2009); Dickie, "End the Go-Slow on Gas in the East China Sea," at http://www.ft.com/cms/s/0/1a88c200-6668-11de-1034-00144feabdc0.html?nclick_check=1 (accessed 05 July 2009).

72. The United States apparently considers the Senkakus to fall under the defense treaty with Japan; see U.S. Department of State, 24 March 2004, at http://usinfo.org/wf-archive/2004/040324/epf302.htm (accessed 05 July 2009), for the unclear statement by the DOS spokesman, Mr. Ereli: "The Senkaku Islands have been under the administrative control of the Government of Japan since having been returned as part of the reversion of Okinawa in 1972. Article 5 of the 1960 U.S.-Japan Treaty of Mutual Cooperation and Security states that the treaty applies to the territories under the administration of Japan; thus, Article 5 of the Mutual Security Treaty applies to the Senkaku Islands. Sovereignty of the Senkaku Islands is disputed. The U.S. does not take a position on the question of the ultimate sovereignty of the Senkaku Diaoyu Islands. This has been our longstanding view. We expect the claimants will resolve this issue through peaceful means and we urge all claimants to exercise restraint."

73. See Dutton, "Scouting, Signaling, and Gatekeeping," for a careful account of China's actions and Japan's responses. Beijing's attitude is typified in "PRC Foreign Ministry Spokesman Says China Sends Warships to Disputed East China Sea," Agence France Presse (hereafter AFP) report, 29 September 2005, in OSC-CPP20050929042020, which reports organization of a PLAN reserve squadron devoted to "eliminate obstacles at sea." A group of analysts investigated various East China Sea scenarios in 2006–7; the results generally were controlled—shooting incidents and accidents

often occurred, but Tokyo and Beijing quickly regained control of unintended, but still dangerous, events. Final report of this multisession effort is Michael McDevitt and Bradley Roberts, eds., *Sino-Japanese Rivalry* (Washington, D.C.: National Defense University Press, 2007), at http://www.ndu.edu/inss/Research/SRapr07.pdf (accessed 19 December 2009).

Chapter 3. China's Maritime Economic Interests

1. See Sun Zhihui, "Strengthening Ocean Administration and Composing Blue Brilliance," *Qiushi Online* (Beijing), no. 18, 16 September 2009, in OSC-CPP20090918710012; and Daniel Hartnett, "China's Maritime Security Strategy and Its Development Rationales," paper presented at the National Defense University Institute for National Security Studies conference on "China's Role in Asia: Access and Anti-access," Washington, D.C., 24 July 2008.

2. Sun, "Strengthening Ocean Administration and Composing Blue Brilliance," figures in 2010 U.S. dollars.

3. The following state-owned enterprises are referenced in this chapter: China National Offshore Oil Corporation (CNOOC), China National Petrochemical Corporation (SINOPEC), China National Petroleum Corporation (CNPC), China National Star Petroleum (CNSP), China Offshore Oil Bohai Corporation (COOBC), and China Petroleum Engineering Construction Enterprise Group (CPECEG).

4. Zhou Guangzhao, chair of the National Committee of China Association for Science and Technology, "Scientist Outlines Five Challenges for PRC in 21st Century," *Xinhua*, 24 May 2000, in FBIS-CPP20000524000031. The other four challenges listed are the aging population, agriculture, the environment, and "the information sector." Also see Tang, "China," 31.

5. Jeffrey Logan, "Energy Outlook for China: Focus on Oil and Gas," testimony before the U.S. Senate Committee on Energy and Natural Resources, 03 February 2005, cited in Saunders, *China's Global Activism*, 6.

6. Wu Wenyue and Song Yang, "Analysis of Coal Supply, Demand," *Zhongguo Meitan*, 01 May 1999, 21–23, in FBIS-20000120000370, reports significant problems in China's coal industry, including wildcat mining, provincial protectionism, internal competition among state-owned coal enterprises, disorganized transportation networks, and moving from a state-dominated to a free-market system. Many of these problems still plague the industry; for instance, see http://www.eia.doe.gov/emeu/cabs/China/Coal.html (accessed 23 August 2009); and "China Sharply Brakes Coal Liquefaction Projects," *Asia Info Services*, 08 September 2008, at http://www.highbeam.com/doc/1P1-

156060411.htm (accessed 07 December 2008), for Beijing's decision to suspend liquefaction experiments because of the excessive water required by the process—a case of
water proving to be a more valuable resource than coal.

7. See "Fire in Ice," *Ocean Explorer Explanations*, 12 July 2005, at http://www.
jamestown.org/single/?no_cache=1&tx_ttnews%5Bswords%5D=8fd5893941d6
9d0be3f378576261ae3e&tx_ttnews%5Bany_of_the_words%5D=malacca&tx_
ttnews%5Bpointer%5D=1&tx_ttnews%5Btt_news%5D=31575&tx_ttnews%5Bback
Pid%5D=7&cHash=ceecbf0a93 (accessed 08 December 2008). This thick, waxy form
of fossil fuel may be found in abundance in the seabed, but at extreme depths (600 m
or more). Some success is reported in "China Succeeds in Excavating Combustible
Ice," *People's Daily*, 25 June 2009, at http://english.people.com.cn/200706/05/
eng20070605_381172.html (accessed 23 August 2009). See Haiqi Zhang et al.,
"China's First Gas Hydrate Expedition Successful," *Methane Hydrate Newsletter*
(spring–summer 2007), 1, at http://www.netl.doe.gov/technologies/oil-gas/publica
tions/Hydrates/Newsletter/HMNewsSpringSummer07.pdf (accessed 23 August
2009), for a report on the South China Sea; a similar report for East China Sea and the
Tibetan Plateau is "Chinese Discover Natural Gas-Hydrate in Paracels," *Xinhua*, 12
April 2000, in FBIS-CPP20000412000014.

8. See, for instance, Renjie Zhou and Yadan Wang, "Residents of Inner Mongolia Find
New Hope in the Desert," China Central Television report, 14 August 2007, at http://
www.worldwatch.org/node/5286 (accessed 17 August 2009); "Renewable Energy
Development Project in China Wins Prestigious Ashden Award for Sustainable
Energy," World Bank, August 2008, at http://web.worldbank.org/WBSITE/
EXTERNAL/COUNTRIES/EASTASIAPACIFICEXT/CHINAEXTN/0,,c
ontentMDK:21873982~menuPK:50003484~pagePK:2865066~piPK:2865079~t
heSitePK:318950,00.html (accessed 17 August 2009). Also see "PRC, EU to Build
Tidal Energy Power Station," *Xinhua*, 7 January 1999, in FBIS-19990107000153;
"China to Build World's First Tidal Power Station," *Xinhua*, in *Alexander's Gas & Oil
Connections*, 4, 19 July 1999.

9. Unless otherwise noted, Chinese energy data in this chapter are from EIA, "Country
Brief: China," July 2009, at http://www.eia.doe.gov/emeu/cabs/China/Oil.html
(accessed 23 August 2009), referred to hereafter as EIA, "China." This has been the
most accurate and consistent source of such data during at least the past decade, but the
reader must be aware that there are few other objective sources on offshore petroleum
production. Particularly suspect are reports issued by Chinese oil companies. Since
they are state-owned enterprises, their data are subject to political influence: everything
China does must be reported as superior to any other nation's efforts. "China's Offshore
Oil Sector Profitable in 1998," *Asia Pulse*, 18 January 1999, for example, reports that

China "recorded an astonishing 80 percent success ratio for offshore wildcat drilling last year." Wang Xiaomu, deputy head of the China National Oil and Gas Group's Geophysics Office, is quoted in *Alexander's Gas & Oil Connections*, 11 June 1999, as saying that while "the world generally allows an error rate of 5 percent in exploration work, China has it down to 0.2 percent" ("China Has Very High Success Rate in Drilling"). One excessive Chinese estimate is in Mo Jie and Chen Bangyan, "Marine Geology High Tech Development Strategy," *Zhongguo Dizhi* [Chinese Geology] (Beijing), June 1997, in FBIS-CHI-98-013.

10.   "PRC Verifies Major Oil, Gas Field in East China Sea," *Xinhua*, 03 February 2000, in FBIS-FTS2000203000508, reports the discovery of major new oil fields. The current disagreement with Japan is discussed in Chapter 2.

11.   EIA; "Shenzhen LNG terminal plan clears first hurdle," *Shanghai Daily*, 09 March 2009, at http://www.china.org.cn/business/2009-03/09/content_17408175.htm (accessed 28 August 2009).

12.   Yao, ed., "World's Largest Oil Company Praises Co-op with China," *Xinhua*, 10 November 2008, at http://news.xinhuanet.com/english/2008-11/10/content_ 10337169.htm (accessed 08 December 2008).

13.   "Science Said Paying Off for China's Oil Resources," *Xinhua*, 09 January 2000, in FBIS-20000109000265, claims that the Bo Sea contains "oil deposits of nearly 8 billion tons, and an annual crude output of over 69 million tons."

14.   Collins, "China Fills First SPR Site, Faces Oil, Pipeline Issues," 26, cites a domestic pipeline growth goal of more than 60 percent. Valencia, "Energy and Insecurity in Asia," 88, includes a map depicting a web of "Trans-Asian Gas Pipelines" that would include central Asia, Russia, Mongolia, China, North and South Korea, Japan, Taiwan, Indochina, and Australia. The first phase of this Japanese proposal carries an estimated price tag of $4.8 trillion in 1996 U.S. dollars; this remains largely a dream in 2010.

15.   Shao Qin, "Experts Urge PRC Oil Strategy to Maintain Oil Supply," *China Daily*, 10 January 2000, in FBIS-20000110000012. Hu Jianyi, "a renowned expert with the Beijing-based Research Institute of Petroleum Exploration and Development," is also cited in this account.

16.   The refining goal is reported in "Saudi Arabia to Increase Oil Exports to China by at Least 9 Percent," *Alexander's Gas & Oil Connections*, 12, no. 19 (25 October 2007), at http://www.gasandoil.com/goc/news/nts74361.htm (accessed 16 August 2009).

17.   EIA, "China." A Chinese estimate—although by the company concerned (CNOOC)— is provided in Gong Zaishen, Zhu Weilin, and Jiang Wenrong, "Abstract: Prospects of Hydrocarbon Exploration in Bohai Bay," at http://www.searchanddiscovery.com/ abstracts/html/1998/annual/abstracts/720.htm (accessed 28 August 2009).

18. *The Petroleum Resources of China,* DOE/EIA-0501 (Washington, D.C.: U.S. Department of Energy, 1987), 66ff., provides a geological description of China's offshore basins.

19. According to the U.S. Department of Energy, "Proved reserves are estimated quantities that analysis of geologic and engineering data demonstrates with reasonable certainty are recoverable under existing economic and operating conditions." "Proved" is a very mutable term, however, since advancing technology, demand, and new discoveries of previously considered "uneconomical" reserves all affect the definition; see EIA, "Notes and Sources," 03 March 2009, at http://www.eia.doe.gov/emeu/international/Notes%20for%20Most%20Recent%20Estimates%20of%20Proved%20Oil%20and%20Natural%20Gas%20Reserves.html (accessed 10 July 2009).

20. As of 2009, Alcorn, Amoco, Anadarko, ARCO, British Petroleum, Chevron, Conoco, Crestone, Devon Energy, Eni, Exxon, Husky Energy of Canada, Mobil, Shell, and VAALCO were among these companies.

21. Valencia, *China and the South China Sea Disputes,* remains useful, but Fravel, *Strong Nation, Secure Borders,* is more current.

22. The author interviewed two analysts in November 1999 who used the same geological data and came to opposite conclusions about the presence or absence of significant petroleum reserves in the Spratlys. South China Sea data are from EIA, "South China Sea," March 2008, at http://www.eia.doe.gov/emeu/cabs/South_China_Sea/pdf.pdf (accessed 05 July 2009).

23. The text of the 1992 law is in "Law of the People's Republic of China on the Territorial Sea and the Contiguous Zone," at http://www.86148.com/englishlaw/shownews.asp?id=1781 (accessed 28 August 2009); also see Kim, "The 1992 Chinese Territorial Sea Law in the Light of the UN Convention."

24. Peter Huber and Mark Mills, "Oil, Oil, Everywhere," *Wall Street Journal,* 27 January 2005, at http://www.manhattan-institute.org/html/_wsj-oil_oil.htm (accessed 25 August 2009), reports that oil production costs in Saudi Arabia were $1–$2.50 in 2005, while those in China were close to the global average of $10–$15.

25. Qin Anmin, president of the China Petroleum Engineering Construction Enterprise Group, quoted in "China Is Actively Exploring International Oil Markets," *Xinhua,* in *Alexander's Gas & Oil Connections,* 19 July 1999, 4.

26. Huber and Mills, "Oil, Oil, Everywhere."

27. The 4 percent goal was announced in Wang Shibin, "Let Nuclear Energy Bring Benefit to Mankind," *Jiefangjun Bao* (Beijing unless otherwise noted), 27 March 2000, in FBIS-CPP20000328000036.

28. I am grateful to Captain Bernard Moreland, USCG (Ret.), the first U.S. Coast Guard liaison officer stationed in Beijing, for much of this information. Goldstein, "Chinese

Coast Guard Development," provides a useful view. China's ranking is in Lovshin, "World Fisheries," at http://www.google.com/search?sourceid=navclient&ie=UTF-8&rlz=1T4GWYE_enUS316US316&q=china%27s+fish+harvest+2008 (accessed 02 July 2009). Recent Chinese efforts to control fish harvests have been openly opposed by Vietnam, Indonesia, and the Philippines. See "Vietnam Criticizes Chinese Fishing Bans in South China Sea," Deutsche Presse-Agentur report in *Asia-Pacific News,* 18 May 2009, at http://www.monstersandcritics.com/news/asiapacific/news/article_1477907. php/Vietnam_criticizes_Chinese_fishing_bans_in_South_China_Sea_ (accessed 25 November 2009). Zhang Jin, "Indonesia Told to Release Chinese Fishermen," *China Daily,* 29 June 2009, at http://bbs.chinadaily.com.cn/redirect.php?gid=2&fid=9&tid= 638677&goto=nextoldset (accessed 02 July 2009), reports the seizure of eight Chinese fishing boats. The strength of China's fisheries patrol fleet is growing, as indicated by the conversion of PLAN frigates to patrol vessels reported in "Chinese Fisheries Administration Vessel Begins Patrol in South China Sea," *Xinhua,* 17 March 2009, at http://news.xinhuanet.com/english/2009-03/17/content_11027444.htm (accessed 02 July 2009). China's Ministry of Agriculture is the agency responsible for fisheries; its Academy of Fishery Science is divided into several geographical divisions, including those for the Yellow, East China, and South China seas. See the academy's Web site at http://www.lib.noaa.gov/china/archi/headquaters.htm (accessed 30 November 2008). The FLEC is described at http://www.sinodefence.com/navy/fisheries/ fisheries-law-enforcement.asp (accessed 25 November 2009). For ASEAN's policy, see "Note of the Chairman of the ASEAN-SEAFDEC Strategic Partnership and Fisheries Consultative Group," which reports on the group's eleventh meeting, held in Singapore in November 2008, at http://docs.google.com/gview?a=v&q=cache:bxkgbx-25fQJ:www.seafdec.org/cms/index.php%3Foption%3Dcom_phocadownload%26vie w%3Dcategory%26id%3D7:event-documents%26download%3D54:41cm_wp5%2 6Itemid%3D43+asean+fisheries+consultatie+group&hl=en&gl=us (accessed 07 July 2009). The group's conclusions are offered as "suggestions" to the member states. Also see Valencia and Van Dyke, "Vietnam's National Interests," 229ff., for a discussion of the complex fisheries claims in the South China Sea.

29. "South China Sea Fishing Ban 'Indisputable,'" *Xinhua,* 09 June 2009, at http://news. xinhuanet.com/English/2009-06/09content_11513280.htm (accessed 15 August 2009. The 2009 plan was announced in "Ministry of Agriculture Communiqué Regarding the Launch of Patrols by the Exclusive Economic Zone Fishery Agency," by the Secretariat/General Office of the Ministry of Agriculture (06 February 2009); see "Bureau of Fishery Administration and Fishing Port Superintendence in the South China Sea Region," 25 June 2009, at http://english.agri.gov.cn/ga/amoa/ iumoa/200906/t20090625_1163.htm (accessed 25 November 2009). Deborah Kuo,

"Taiwan Fishery Urges to Avoid PRC-Designated Area for Restocking Resources," Taipei Central News Agency, 26 May 2000, in FBIS-CPP20000526000078, reports the Kaohsiung Fishery Affairs Department calling for local fishing boats to follow the mainland's fishing guidelines. The Vietnamese government's opinion is in "Experts Discuss China's Detention of Vietnamese Fishermen," *VietNamNetBridge* (Hanoi), 05 July 2009, in OSC-SEP20090707124003.

30. David Rosenberg, "Managing the Resources of the China Seas." Also see "Clashes over Fish in Pacific Asia, 1994–1997," at http://www.middlebury.edu/SouthChinaSea/maps/dupont3 (accessed 25 August 2009).

31. Prabhadar, Ho, and Bateman, *The Evolving Maritime Balance of Power in the Asia-Pacific*, 5.

32. "Review of Maritime Transport, 2007," UN Conference on Trade and Development, Geneva, 2007, 121–26, at http://www.unctad.org/Templates/WebFlyer.asp?intItemID=4398&lang=1 (accessed 16 August 2009).

33. Erickson and Collins, "Beijing's Energy Security Strategy," 665.

34. "Review of Maritime Transport, 2007"; in mid-2007 South Korea was producing 45.2 percent, China 29.6 percent, and Japan 25.5 percent of the world's tankers.

35. Erickson and Collins, "Beijing's Energy Security Strategy," 665; Blair and Lieberthal, "Smooth Sailing," 7–13, convincingly makes this argument.

36. The Allies' experience defending SLOCs against German submarines in two world wars, especially the U.S. efforts in *U.S. coastal waters* in 1942, still stands as an example of the difficulty of this task.

37. One of the contentious points about Liu Huaqing's first two strategic stages is their southwestern delineation by the Indonesian Archipelago, since a line drawn through Sumatra extends this area of Chinese aspirations *west* of the Malacca Strait. This infers Beijing's ambition to control that strait, one of the world's most crucial, and one whose fate directly affects the national interests of Southeast Asian and Indian Ocean nations.

38. Author's conversation with Professor Zha Dajiong in Beijing in May 2009. Also see Storey, "China's 'Malacca Dilemma,'" 1. The 2008 data are from Erik Kreil, EIA, 30 June 2009. The phrase is usually—but probably erroneously—attributed to President Hu Jintao in a 2003 interview, and has achieved a life of its own. A good discussion of "the Malacca dilemma" is in Ross, "China's Naval Nationalism," 70.

39. Quoted in Pollack, "Energy Insecurity with Chinese and American Characteristics," 234.

40. See, for instance, "China to Start Burma Pipeline," http://www.upstreamonline.com (16 June 2009), at http://www.upstreamonline.com/live/article180931.ece (accessed 16 August 2009).

41. The most comprehensive and detailed discussion of China's developing military-industrial complex is Tai Ming Cheung, *Fortifying China*; especially see 215–34 for his discussion of ties between civil and military processes.

42. Quoted in Collins, Erickson, and Goldstein, "Chinese Naval Analysts Consider the Energy Question," 14.

Chapter 4. PLAN Establishment

1. This estimate is based on data in *The Military Balance, 2009*, 382, of active duty PLA strength: 1,600,000 Army; 255,000 Navy; 300,000–330,000 Air Force; and 700,000 "paramilitary." Several analysts have addressed past PLA manpower reductions: see Nan Li, "Organizational Changes in the PLA, 1985–1997," 330, who noted that all headquarters were reduced by 25 percent; Kuan Cha-chia, "Commander Jiang Speeds Up Army Reform, Structure of Three Armed Services to Be Adjusted," *Kuang Chiao Ching* (Hong Kong), no. 305, 16 February 1998, in FBIS-CHI-98-065 (06 March 1998); author's interviews with U.S. analysts and PLA officers, October 1999. Blasko, "A New PLA Force Structure," 263–64, notes that China's July 1998 Defense White Paper states that PLA ground forces will be reduced by 9 percent, naval forces by 11.6 percent, and air forces by 11 percent, a reduction of about 418,000 ground forces, 31,000 naval personnel, and 52,000 air force personnel.

2. The others are the Ground Forces (PLA), the Air Force (PLAAF), and the Second Artillery. There is no Chinese coast guard per se; coast guard missions are performed by several national and local organizations (see Chapter 6). Li, "The PLA's Evolving Campaign Doctrine and Strategies," 154ff.

3. Benjamin Disraeli is one possible originator of this phrase, but see http://www.york.ac.uk/depts/maths/histstat/lies.htm (accessed 14 June 2009).

4. Wang Shichang, "Face the Ocean, Challenge the Giant Waves," *Tiao Zhan: Yanh Fazhan yu Guofang Jianshe* (Beijing), *Guangming Daily Publisher*, 1989, 186, cited in Huang, "The Chinese Navy's Offshore Active Defense Strategy," 9. These figures do not address defense expenditures not included in the nominal PLA budget, such as foreign weapons. Other defense costs not included in the PLA budget include pensions, research and development, training conducted at civilian schools, and China's space program.

5. Liu Yueshan, "Son-in-Law of Hu Yaobang Becomes the Political Commissar of PLA Navy amidst Senior Staff Changes," *WenWeiPoOnline* (Hong Kong), 18 July 2008, in OSC-CPP20080718710010; Wu Shengli, quoted in Wu Shengli and Hu Yanlin, "Building a Powerful People's Navy That Meets the Requirements of the Historical

Mission for Our Army," ed. Wang Chuanzhi, *Qiushi* (Beijing) 14, July 2007, in OSC-CPP20070716710027; and even more recently in "Keep a Firm Grip on the Present-Day Issue of 'Three Guarantees'—on the Study and Implementation of CMC Chairman Hu's Important Speech Addressed to the PLA Deputation to the Second Session of the 11 National People's Congress," *Jiefangjun Bao*, 17 March 2009, 1, in OSC-CPP20090317702001.

6. Blasko, "A New PLA Force Structure," 258–88. This discussion owes much to Swaine, *The Role of the Chinese Military in National Security Policymaking*, 43ff., which also discusses other players in the national security policy-making process such as retired senior officers and those heading up the National Defense University and the Academy of Military Science. I will not discuss formal organizational or bureaucratic behavior theory, but note that I assume the national security policy-making process in China has many of the same characteristics as that in Western countries and Japan, where the formal structure of decision making—from the determination of national objectives to the allocation of finite amounts of resources to specific programs—operates in an environment of personal relationships and less formal discussion and decision making. Various elements in the defense bureaucracy, for instance, no doubt contain individuals who by virtue of longevity, special expertise, or both are able to influence policy to a degree out of proportion to their titular position.

7. PLAN organization and officeholders are identified through interviews with U.S. analysts and from PLA sources. I am indebted to Kenneth Allen and Dennis Blasko for the discussion of political commissars and shipboard organization.

8. "Accelerate Naval Transformation to Build a Strong Navy: Outlook of Work at Navy's Four Major Navy Departments in 2009," *Renmin Haijin* [official paper of the CCP committee of the PLAN] (Beijing), 01 January 2009, in OSC-CPP20090203478006.

9. Li Jun-ting and Yang Jin-he, *Overview of the Chinese Armed Forces*, 232; Zhang Wenxin, Chen Haochun, and Xu Feng, "Contend in New Battlefield for Military Transformation," *Jiefangjun Bao*, 04 June 2003, in FBIS-CPP20030605000071. NERA was created in 1983 as the Navy Equipment Demonstration Research Center; its name was changed in 2003. I am indebted to David Finkelstein and Dennis Blasko for explaining the different missions of the Haijun Junshi Xueshu yan jiusuo and the Haijun Zhuangbei Lunzheng Yanjiu Zhongxin.

10. Admiral Wang Huaiqing, the PLAN's senior political officer, was relieved at the same time. The enforcement of accountability in the Navy was signaled in 2006 by the forced resignation of another senior PLAN officer, apparently for financial malfeasance: Vice Admiral Wang Shouye, former deputy commander for logistics, was fired "on charges of economic crimes, after his mistress turned him in." See "Former Navy Deputy Commander Stripped of NPC Post," *Xinhua*, 29 June 2006, at http://www.chinadaily.com.cn/china/2006-06/29/content_629565.htm (accessed 12 April 2009).

11. Author's interviews with senior PLA officers: typical preparations for a significant foreign deployment would include ship selection from different fleets to pick the most operationally ready and best-looking ships, as well as those with the most proficient commanding officers (COs). An effort is also made to reward units that have performed unusually well. These ship nominations must be approved by the Defense Ministry, but that is likely automatic. Once selected, the ships' COs and crews are "frozen" to ensure continuity throughout the special deployment. Additional crew and officers are also usually assigned to increase the number of personnel benefiting from the special deployment (a procedure especially followed in the case of the 1997 PLAN deployment to North and South America). The ships are assigned a dedicated supply officer to help them prepare for the deployment, and crews receive special training and cultural familiarization lectures.

12. *Xinhua*, 17 August 1999, in FBIS-CHI-99-0817: "The Chinese Navy plans to recruit about 1,000 officers from non-military universities and colleges yearly beginning this autumn in an effort to meet its need for command and technical talent. . . . .[These officers] will account for 40 percent of all naval officers by the year 2010." Also see *Xinhua* (Hong Kong Service), 21 June 1999, in FBIS-CHI-99-0622, for the note that these civilian university programs will be linked to the military academy structure. This linkage is no doubt intended to maintain control of the ideological as well as the subject-matter content of the "civilian" program—the latter long a concern within the U.S. Naval ROTC program.

13. Rear Admiral Shao Zijung (college president), "Navy Engineering College Is Aimed at Developing New Naval Military Talent," quoted in *Xinhua*, 07 August 1999, in FBIS-CHI-99-0826.

14. "Put Military Academy Education in a Strategic Position of Priority Development," *Jiefangjun Bao*, 23 June 1999, in FBIS-CHI-99-0629. Also, *Xinhua* (Hong Kong Service), 21 June 1999, in FBIS-CHI-99-0622, for a *Jiefangjun Bao* report that the number of academies is being reduced in the interest of making individual schools larger and more efficient.

15. Author's visit to NRI and conversation with senior PLA officers; also see Xu Sen, "Building a Modern Naval Battlefield—Overview of the Naval Vessel Training Center," *Jiefangjun Bao*, 15 September 1999, 6, in FBIS-CHI-99-0923.

16. Author's conversations with senior PLAN officers, 2006, 2008.

17. Although Beijing claimed that this apparent fire was actually a training evolution, doubts remain; see "Chinese Submarine May Have Caught Fire in South China Sea," AFP report in Forbes.com, 30 May 2005, at http://www.forbes.com/feeds/afx/2005/05/30/afx2064270.html (accessed 12 April 2009).

18. Shi is quoted in Huang Caihong, Chen Wanjun, and Zhang Zhao, "China Enhances the Navy's Comprehensive Strength—Interview with Naval Commander VADM Shi Yunsheng," *Liaowang* (Beijing), no. 16, 19 April 1999, 13–15, in FBIS-CHI-99-0513.

19. "Zhang Wannian Steps Up Military Logistics Reform," *Xinhua,* 09 December 1999, in FBIS-FTS19991209000883, cites Zhang's statement that "it is imperative for the military to commercialize its logistics in this period of modernization." Author's conversations with PLAN shipboard officers (2004, 2006) revealed complaints about the unresponsiveness of the new centralized spare parts system.

20. Bi, "Managing Taiwan Operations in the Twenty-first Century," 11. Huang, Chen, and Zhang describe "naval port cities" being designated as central distribution points in the new logistics system. See, for instance, Huang, Chen, and Zhang, "The PLA Navy Has Enhanced Comprehensive Combat Effectiveness," *Xinhua,* 19 April 1999, in FBIS-CHI-99-0423.

21. See Mulvenon, *Professionalization of the Senior Chinese Officer Corps,* for analysis of the PLA's senior officer corps' professionalization.

22. Author's observation of relations between operational and political officers during visits to several PLAN combatants, 1994–2008.

23. Author's discussion with Admiral Shi's U.S. escort officer for his April 2000 visit to the United States revealed that Shi was most interested in U.S. naval aviation programs; C4ISR; officer and enlisted recruitment, retention, and training programs; and USCG roles, missions, and relationship with the U.S. Navy.

24. Swaine, *The Role of the Chinese Military in National Security Policymaking,* 45, describes Shi Yunsheng (PLAN commander 1996–2003) as one of "the most influential (and vocal) bureaucratic players in formulating and supervising critical components of policy," but this did not save him following the 2003 submarine disaster.

25. Quoted in "Interview with Shi." Also see Ren Yanjun, "Forging a Shield of Peace for the Republic—Part 1 of Roundup on 50 Years of Achievements in Army Building," *Jiefangjun Bao,* 06 September 1999, 1, 2, in FBIS-CHI-99-0911; and Xu Zuzhi, "Backgrounder on National Day Celebrations," *Zhongguo Xinwen She* (Beijing), 01 October 1999, in FBIS-CHI-99-1002. These press accounts all make a point of citing Shi's role in PLAN modern developments leading to "greatly improved combat capability." Wu is quoted in Wu Shengli and Hu Yanlin, "Building a Powerful People's Navy That Meets the Requirements of the Historical Mission for Our Army."

26. These lists are from Kondapalli, "China's Naval Structure and Dynamics," 1097–1109. Their accuracy is shadowed by the fact that submarine missions include neither anti-surface nor antisubmarine warfare missions, but do include "logistic lift."

27. Author's discussions with senior PLAN officers.

28. Wertheim, *The Naval Institute Guide to Combat Fleets of the World,* 107.

29. Such as very small patrol craft and harbor service craft.

30. Song Binyuan and Rao Yanwen, "Naval Flotilla Uplifts Capability of Fulfilling Diversified Military Tasks," *PLA Daily*, 03 January 2008, at http://english.chinamil. com.cn (accessed 01 June 2009); also see *China's Navy: 2007*, 39. Lou Douzi, "Looking at Navy and Air Force Dispositions Following Establishment Restructuring," *Jiefangjun Bao*, 14 July 2004, in FBIS-CPP20040715000074, offers a slightly different conclusion: that following the 2003 reorganization, "ship detachments with offensive combat capability will be directly subordinate to the fleet command," as will "the naval air force."

31. *The Military Balance 2009*, 383–84; and Saunders, *Jane's Fighting Ships: 2008–2009*, 120–25.

32. This and other shipyard information comes from Mikhail Barabanov, "Contemporary Military Shipbuilding in China," *Eksport Vooruzheniy*, 01 August 2005, in FBIS-CEP20050811949014, 11 August 2005, which while perhaps dated remains useful.

33. These 2006 unit assignments are somewhat tentative but reflect Ellis Melvin's unsurpassed knowledge of PLA organization.

34. Jin Xuejun, "Three-Parameter Positioning of Two Geostationary Satellites," 22–27; information provided to the author by an experienced U.S. intelligence officer who monitors the PLA unit identification matrix.

35. The area PLAAF commander also serves as an MR deputy commander, but one senior PLA officer informed the author that in time of war, the PLAN commander is senior to the PLAAF commander. As pointed out in Blasko, "A New PLA Force Structure," 284: "A true indicator of the PLA's commitment to joint operations would be for the commander of the Eastern or Southern Theaters to be a naval officer."

36. The seminal work on the 1979 Sino-Vietnamese conflict is O'Dowd, *Chinese Military Strategy in the Third Indochina War*.

37. See Cole, *Gunboats and Marines*, app. A.

38. Author's interviews with USCINCPAC personnel and with Mark Valencia, East-West Center, Honolulu, 1–5 November 1999. Woody Island may be capable of supporting eight fighter aircraft in hangars plus approximately twenty-four on hard stands in the open. The island does not offer a significant maintenance or freshwater wash-down capability, although additional freshwater tanks have been constructed. It also does not appear to have the ground control radar capability usually required by Chinese tactical aviators.

39. *Jane's Fighting Ships* for the past decade show this amphibious concentration in the South Sea Fleet. Two of the Qiongsha class have been converted to hospital ships; only one of the troop transports may be operationally active.

40.   Google Earth photos show the caves, but sea-level entrances are not readily visible; the base is described in Erickson and Chase, "An Undersea Deterrent?" 37. Also see Richard D. Fisher, "China's Naval Secrets," *Wall Street Journal Asia*, 05 May 2008, at http://online.wsj.com/article/SB120994205702565995.html (accessed 30 May 2009).

41.   Author's interview with senior PLAN officer, 2006; 10 June 2009 e-mail from Kenneth Allen referencing Cai Nianchi, Yu Chunguang, and Qian Xiaohu, "Naval Aviation," in *PLA Daily*, 18 December 2008, at http://www.chinamil.com.cn/site1/zbx1/208-12/18/content_1587442.htm. Also see Sae-Liu, "Chinese Expand Aerial Refueling Capability to Navy," which reports that "PLA Navy fighters conducted their first aerial refueling mission in late March" using a PLAAF H-6 tanker. PLAAF refueling exercises have been conducted since at least late 1998. This is just the tip of the iceberg; perhaps most indicative of PLANAF professionalism is whether it employs a system of operational standardization such as the U.S. Navy's Naval Air Training and Operations Procedures Standardization to increase safety and enhance operational effectiveness. While China appears to offer a complete flight-training syllabus, at least one report describes PLAN helicopter pilots undergoing flight training in France and Italy: see Hu Baoliang, Yu Zhenying, and Yu Haibo, "Falcon of the Ocean," *Dangdai Haijun* (Beijing), 01 November 2005, 20–21, in OSC-CPP20051107325002.

42.   Pacific Command (PACOM) sources showed Naval Aviation reporting to the Navy commander through the headquarters Staff Department. The CMC action is credited in Xu Feng and Sha Zhiliang, "Jiang Zemin on Modernizing Naval Aviation Units," *Xinhua*, 16 September 2002, in FBIS-CPP20021916000093. Also see Chen Wanjun and Sha Zhiliang, "Newsletter: Commanding the Winds and the Clouds between the Sea and the Sky—a True Picture of the Shipborne Aircraft Unit of the People's Navy," *Xinhua*, 21 April 1999, in FBIS-CHI-99-0502, which reports that a PLANAF helicopter unit began training for shipboard operations in the late 1970s, with the first successful operational flight occurring on 03 January 1980. Despite this article's purple prose, a 1980 date "fits" with the development of the PLAN's first helicopter-capable combatant, the Luda II–class DDG *Jinan*, which began construction in 1977.

43.   Office of Naval Intelligence, *China's Navy: 2007*, ch. 7, contains a description of China's "Naval Aviation" at http://militarytimes.com/static/projects/pages/20070313dnplanavy.pdf (accessed 08 June 2009); Lou Douzi, "Looking at Navy and Air Force Dispositions Following Establishment Restructuring," *Jiefangjun Bao*, 14 July 2004, in FBIS-CPP20040715000074; finally, "PLA Will Merge Its Naval Air Force into Three Fleets," *Tai Yang Pao* (Hong Kong), 07 August 2003, in FBIS-CPP20030807000042.

44.   The author is indebted to Kenneth Allen for describing this system of air defense.

45. Quoted in Liu Ke, "China Enhances Protection of Its Rights in Disputed Sea Areas—Establishment of a Regular Marine Patrol and Rights Protection System within Entire Sea Areas Shows China's Capability and Determination to Maintain Its Jurisdiction over Disputed Sea Areas," *Guoji Xianqu Daobao* (Beijing), in FBIS-CPP20081031682001, 24 October 2008.

46. The leading U.S. expert on China's complex system of maritime regulation organizations is Captain Bernard Moreland, USCG (Ret.), the first USCG officer stationed in Beijing, who was kind enough to share his knowledge with me. Moreland also pointed out that the United States underwent a similar bureaucratic struggle in the period 1915–27 when the former Revenue Cutter Service, U.S. Lifesaving Service, Lighthouse Service, and several other organizations were merged into the Coast Guard. Also see the attempt to explain China's coast guard at http://www.sinodefence. com/navy/coastguard/default.asp (accessed 07 June 2009), which lists an order of battle of twenty flotillas spread among twenty ports: Dalian, Dandong, Weihai, Qingdao, Taizhou, Ningbo, Haikou, Sanya, Beihai, Fangchenggang, Qinhuangdao, Taicang, Tianjin, Shanghai, Fuzhou, Quanzhou, Xiamen, Guangzhou, Shantou, and Zhanjiang. See Bateman, "Coast Guards: New Forces for Regional Order and Security," for discussion of developing Pacific coast guards.

47. Le Guoqiang, quoted in Liu Ke, "China Enhances Protection of Its Rights in Disputed Sea Areas," *Guoji Xianqu Daobao* (Beijing), 24 October 2008, 1, files at CMSI, Newport, R.I.

48. Swanson, *The Eighth Voyage of the Dragon*, 204, points out these forces' similarities to imperial predecessors.

49. Zhou Zhiquan and Chen Ming, "Missions that the Militia Could Perform to Support the Front and Participate in Naval War," *Beijing Guofang* (monthly journal of the Academy of Military Science), 15 June 2003, in FBIS-CPP20030627000184. Examples are reported in Dai Zhixin, Feng Weihua, and Yang Xiaogang, "Making a Comeback after 'Defeat': Account of How a Certain Water Transport Group Drills Hard on Support Capabilities Aiming at Actual Battles," *Jiefangjun Bao*, 06 February 2002, 2, in FBIS-CPP20020206000059; and "PLA Navy Stages Military-Civilian Integrated Ordnance Support Exercises in Ningbo," *Renmin Tupian Wang*, 23 October 2006.

50. Text of "Marine Environmental Protection Law of the PRC," *Xinhua*, 26 December 2000, in FBIS-FTS20000207000268.

51. Tang Min, "PRC Marine Environmental Protection Law Praised," *China Daily*, 03 April 2000, in FBIS-CPP20000403000020, reports that the amended Marine Environmental Protection Law came into effect on 01 April 2000. Municipal attempts to grapple with such maritime responsibilities are demonstrated in "State

Council Forms Marine Bureau in Shenzhen," *Xinhua*, 27 December 1999, in FBIS-FTS19991227000826, which reports that the "Shenzhen Marine Bureau was formed [to carry out] marine supervision." It combined the previous "separate port supervision departments under the Shenzhen Government and the Ministry of Communications." The new bureau is responsible for "managing overseas ships sailing and anchoring in Shenzhen water space, abiding by the related international marine treaty, maintaining order in sea navigation and transportation, supervising ships' anti-pollution facility, handling water pollution, maintaining public navigation facilities and regulating the shipping economy." Also see *Xinhua*, 18 June 1999, in FBIS-CHI-1999-0618, for a report that Shanghai had established a "Maritime Safety Administration, the first of its kind in China's coastal areas, . . . to supervise the management of navigation marks, the surveying of sea-routes, and the inspection of ships and maritime facilities."

52. The MSA is described at http://en.msa.gov.cn/msa/features/root/01/0104 (accessed 01 June 2009). Also see "PRC Establishes 12 State Maritime Safety Administrations," *Xinhua*, 28 December 1999, in FBIS-CPP19991228001478. The MSA's predecessor, the Bureau of Harbor Superintendency, was responsible for antipollution and SAR efforts, including the SAR coordination centers.

53. Also see "China to Establish Two Maritime Rescue Teams with Four Helicopters," *Xinhua Online*, 13 February 2004, at http://news.xinhuanet.com/english/2004-02/13/content_1313908.htm (accessed 08 June 2009).

54. The CMS is described at http://www.sinodefence.com/navy/marine-surveillance/default.asp (accessed 01 June 2009); and http://english.people.com.cn/9001/6518247.html (accessed 01 June 2009). Its activities defending maritime interests from a Chinese perspective against Japan, Vietnam, and the United States are described in Qi Lu, "China's Maritime Surveillance Sallies Forth in the Name of Responsibility and Honor," *Bingi Zhishi* (Beijing), 15 March 2009, 10–13, in FBIS-CPP20090511682009 (11 May 2009).

55. Zhang Xinxin, "The China Marine Surveillance Force Will Soon Be Incorporated into the Reserve Force of the Chinese Navy," *Renmin Haijun* [People's Navy] (Beijing), 27 October 2008, 1, in FBIS-CPP20081204318005, identifies the CMS as the force that has been responding to U.S. surveillance ships in China's claimed EEZ. Dennis Blasko brought this report to the author's attention; he also noted that it probably represented wishful thinking by the PLAN—although see Chen Wanjun and Wu Dengfeng, "Our Military's First Maritime Reservist Unit Formed," *Xinhua*, 13 May 2005, in FBIS-CPP20050513000104—a view represented in a statement by the force's deputy director, Sun Shuxian, quoted in "Sea Patrol Force to Get More Muscle," *China Daily*, 22 October 2008, at http://english.people.com.cn/9001/65/18247.html (accessed 01 June 2009).

56.   For a discussion of the legal aspects of the *Bowditch* and *Impeccable* incidents, see Pedrozo, "Close Encounters at Sea." The *Victorious* incident is described at http://www. voanews.com/english/2009-05-05-voa24.cfm (accessed 01 June 2009). All three of these ships are part of the U.S. Navy's fleet of TAGOS ships—ocean surveillance ships that gather underwater acoustical data. They are operated by civilian employees of the Military Sealift Command and use towed-array sensor systems to gather underwater acoustic data, which is then transmitted via satellite to shore stations for evaluation.

57.   *Xinhua*, 26 March 1999, in FBIS-CHI-99-0327, reports that "a three-dimensional border and coastal defense communications network . . . has been completed and become operational." *Xinhua*, 22 November 1999, in FBIS-CHI-99-0647, discusses the command and control structure for at least part of this coastal defense system.

58.   Wertheim, *The Naval Institute Guide to Combat Fleets of the World*, 108. Also, the PLAN commander recently announced the complete "missilization" of the coastal defense forces, in Chen Wanjun and Wu Dengfeng, "Wu Sheng Li: China's Coast Defense Force Missilized," *PLA Daily*, 16 April 2009, at http://english.chinamil.com. cn/site2/special-reports/2009-04/16/content_1732334.htm (accessed 15 June 2009).

59.   Good descriptions of China's civilian-military shipbuilding capabilities are Collins and Grubb, *A Comprehensive Survey of China's Dynamic Shipbuilding Industry*; and Madeiros, *A New Direction for China's Defense Industry*.

60.   China's 2004 Defense White Paper, ch. 2 ("National Defense Policy"), may be found at http://www.fas.org/nuke/guide/china/doctrine/natdef2004.html#5 (accessed 09 August 2009).

61.   This is evidenced in the carefully planned and directed deployment to the Gulf of Aden in 2008–9; also, all three fleets participated in China's most significant naval display, the April 2009 naval parade off Qingdao; see "All China's Three Fleets to Be Represented at Qingdao Naval Parade," *Xinhua*, 23 April 2009, at http://english.people.com. cn90001/90776/90785/6642892.html (accessed 23 April 2009).

Chapter 5. Ships and Aircraft of the PLAN

1.   These are North Atlantic Treaty Organization (NATO) and U.S. warfare terms; the PLAN at least informally uses them as well, as evidenced in the author's conversations with various senior Chinese officers.

2.   NATO "type" designations for military platforms and systems are used throughout; the Chinese names are included when available.

3.   These numbers are derived from different sources, primarily Wertheim, *The Naval Institute Guide to Combat Fleets of the World*, 107–36; and Saunders, *Jane's Fighting Ships: 2008–2009*, 119–59.

4. "Major U.S. Navy and Coast Guard Shipbuilding Programs (Table Dated 13 December 2008)," at http://shipbuildinghistory.com/today/statistics/navyprograms. htm (accessed 04 January 2009); Wertheim, *The Naval Institute Guide to Combat Fleets of the World*, 871–1010. These numbers reflect ships authorized and funded. But also see O'Rourke, "China Naval Modernization," 28, for the comparison of a U.S. fleet that numbered 547 ships in 1990, 318 in 2000, and 275 in 2009. This comparison does not overlook the fact that the U.S. Navy is tasked with global responsibilities, but the PLAN's deployments to the Gulf of Aden, now ongoing for more than a year, indicate expansion of that force's previous regional role.

5. PLAN interest is indicated in Chen Wanjun and Cao Jinping, "PLA Navy Develops Combat Software System for Surface Vessels," *Xinhua*, 14 November 2005, in OSC-CPP20051114042057.

6. In February 1997 the president of the Spanish shipbuilding company Bazan, which had just finished building Thailand's small carrier, visited China to give a "sales pitch" to senior PLA and civilian defense officials, but was unsuccessful. Jiang's decision is reported in Ross, "China's Naval Nationalism," 61.

7. This paragraph relies on quotes from "Aircraft Carrier Project," GlobalSecurity.Org, "Military," at http://www.globalsecurity.org/military/world/china/cv.htm (accessed 15 February 2009). The defense minister, General Liang Guanglie, is cited in several sources, possibly inaccurately; see, for instance, Li Xinran, "China Will Build Its Own Aircraft Carriers—One Day," *Shanghai Daily Online*, 23 March 2009, at http://www. shanghaidaily.com/sp/article/2009/200903/20090323/article_395201.htm (accessed 24 March 2009). Wang is quoted in Erickson and Wilson, "China's Aircraft Carrier Dilemma," 26; Liang is cited in Sengupta, "Full Steam Ahead for PLA Navy's Aircraft Carriers," which claims that China plans to build two 50,000-ton conventionally powered carriers and one 65,000-ton nuclear-powered carrier. Richard Bitzinger, "Aircraft Carriers: China's Emerging Maritime Ambitions," *RSIS Commentaries*, 07 April 2009, at http://www.rsis.edu.sg/publications/Perspective/RSIS0352009.pdf (accessed 04 November 2009), states that China is committed to building at least one carrier, with a fleet of "four to six" a possibility. A "high ranking Chinese military official," Major General Quan Lihua, is similarly quoted in Andrew Jacobs, "General Hints that China's Navy May Add Carrier," *New York Times*, 18 November 2008, at http://www.nytimes.com/2008/11/18/world/asia/18china.html?_r=1 (accessed 02 April 2009).

8. Moore, *Jane's Fighting Ships, 1990–91*, describes these ships. *Kiev* and *Minsk*, commissioned in 1973 and 1978, respectively, are members of the *Kiev* class of 40,000 tons displacement, capable of embarking up to twelve YAK-36 VSTOL aircraft and about twenty Ka-25/27 helicopters; *Varyag* is a member of the *Kuznetzov* class of

67,500 tons displacement; it has a ski-jump bow (instead of catapults), arresting cables, and can embark up to twenty-two Su-27/Su-25 fixed-wing aircraft and seventeen Ka-27/31 helicopters. Yelena Konnova and Mikhail Kozyrev, "Beijing's Aircraft Carrier Collection," *Nezavisimaya Gazeta* (Moscow), 12 May 2000, in FBIS-CEP20000516000183, reports that "not all armaments and control systems had been dismantled" on the ship.

9. Dunnigan, "Chinese Carrier Goes into Dry Dock." A useful pictorial history of *Varyag/ Shi Lang* is at http://www.jeffhead.com/redseadragon/varyagtransform.htm (accessed 15 February 2009). In an e-mail exchange with the author in late 2008, a senior PLAN officer stated that "no significant work has been done on *Varyag* in about a year."

10. These reports are summed up in Richard D. Fisher Jr., "Update: China's Aircraft Carriers," International Assessment and Strategy Center, 10 March 2009, at http://www.strategycenter.net/research/pubID.193/pub_detail.asp (accessed 28 November 2009).

11. Edward Wong, "China Signals More Interest in Building Aircraft Carrier," *New York Times*, 24 December 2008, at http://www.nytimes.com/2008/12/24/world/asia/24beijing.html?_r=1 (accessed 15 February 2009), quotes a Defense Ministry spokesman, Senior Colonel Huang Xueping, that China was seriously considering "relevant issues" about carrier acquisition, noting that carriers reflect "a nation's comprehensive power" and that China would one day use a carrier to defend its shores and its "sovereignty over coastal and territorial seas." A more confident—although no more substantive—prognosis is provided in Kenji Minemura, "China to Start Construct of 1 Aircraft Carriers Next Year," *Asahi Shimbun* (Tokyo), 31 December 2008, at http://www.asahi.com/english/Herald-asahi/TKY200812310046.html (accessed 15 February 2009). Finally, a report of China training pilots for aircraft carrier operations at Saki, Ukraine, is in "Russia to Construct Its Own Carrier Aviation Pilot Training Complex at Yeysk," *Voyenno-Promyshlennyy Kuryer* (Moscow), 21 January 2009, in OSC-CEP20090123548006. Similar training efforts apparently took place as long ago as the 1980s; Nayan Chanda, "The Right Stuff," *Far Eastern Economic Review*, 20 October 1994, 15, is one of several reports that the PLAN built a simulated aircraft carrier operating facility in northeastern China where "Chinese pilots have since 1984 been practicing simulated carrier-deck landings using arresting wires." Chanda also cites a report that "in 1987, an F8 aircraft was shot off a catapult at the Lushun Naval Base."

12. Erickson and Wilson, "China's Aircraft Carrier Dilemma," 13–45, gives historical background for PLAN desires for aircraft carriers. Possible characteristics of China's carrier, supposedly under design as "PLAN Project 9935," are given at http://www.fas.org/nuke/guide/china/aircraft/project9935.pdf (accessed 22 March 2009). A view

of the primary challenges to carrier construction is in Liu Jiangping, "What Are the 'Turbulent Currents and Treacherous Shoals' which a Modern Aircraft Carrier Must Navigate," *Jiefangjun Bao,* 01 March 2009, in OSC-CPP20070311702001. Also see Shih Jen, "Any Aircraft Carrier Built by China to Be Meant for Protecting Maritime Transportation Security," *Zhongguo Tongxun She* (Hong Kong), 06 January 2009, in OSC-CPP20090106172014, which predicts two 50,000–60,000-ton carriers.

13. Xu Zuzhi, "Chinese Navy Has Truly Become a Great Wall at Sea," *Zhongguo Xinwen She* (Beijing), 01 October 1999, concisely recaps PLAN equipment and significant events.

14. Hiramatsu, "China's Naval Advance," 120. The Xia may have been *covertly* going to sea on a regular basis, of course, but this is highly unlikely given the unanimity of foreign observers that it has largely remained in port; author's conversations with U.S. analysts. Also see Sharpe, *Jane's Fighting Ships, 1999–2000,* 115, as well as previous editions.

15. See Fisher, "How May Europe Strengthen China's Military?" International Assessment and Strategy Center, Washington, D.C., 15 January 2005, at http://www.strateg ycenter.net/research/pubID.61/pub_detail.asp (accessed 28 March 2009), for a list of European systems then already in use on board PLAN ships and submarines. Also see Anati, "China's PLA Navy (the Revolution)," 70–71, for a discussion of PLAN use of French and German systems.

16. Author's discussions with U.S. Navy analysts indicated problems with the first two Songs' weight and moment characteristics; later versions have a completely redesigned sail. The author made a brief pierside "tour" of a Type-039A (or Type-41, according to some sources) Yuan-class boat in May 2008.

17. PLAN interest in and appreciation for "stealth" in its warships is indicated in Sun Weizhou and Yang Changqing, "Present Situation and Prospects on Warship Stealth Technology," *Xindai Fangyu Jishu* [Modern Defense Technology] (Beijing), no. 2 (2005), in OSC-CPP20060124424002 (01 April 2005). Despite China's claim that the Jiangkai II is "designed and manufactured by a Chinese shipbuilder," in "Chinese Navy Sends Diplomatic Star, 'Stealth' Frigate to Continue Escort Mission in Somali Waters," *Xinhua,* 01 April 2009, at http://english.people.com.cn/90001/90776/90883/6628672. html (accessed 05 April 2009), the ship's diesels are French Pielstick models, the radars are Russian, and other systems are apparently reverse-engineered versions of Russian, Dutch, and U.S. systems. Pictures at http://www.jeffhead.com/rocnvsplan/Photo-PLAN-Jiangkai6.jpg (accessed 05 December 2009) show what appears to be the stern port for a towed array.

18. The *DOD Report to Congress on the PLA, 2008,* states that "the PLA Navy's total amphibious lift capacity has been estimated to be one infantry division of approximately 10,000 troops and equipment at one time."

19.   An early 1990s USN study included a comparison of the skills/technologies required for nuclear-powered and conventionally powered submarines; apart from the engineering plant, the most difficult challenge was training and employing welders.

20.   The PLAN's submarines are designated by both name and type: the Romeo is Type-033, the Ming is Type-035, the Kilo is Type-877 (two hulls) or -636 (ten hulls), the Song is Type-039, the Yuan is Type-039A/41, the Han is Type-091, the Xia is Type-092, the Shang is Type-093, and the Jin is Type-094. Saunders, *Jane's Fighting Ships: 2008–2009,* reports just eight Romeos in commission.

21.   Saunders, *Jane's Fighting Ships: 2008–2009,* 123. Also see Jeff Chen and Andrei Chang, "PLA Navy's Submarine Flotilla Undergoing Frequent Equipment Replacement," *Kanwa Asian Defense Review* (Toronto), no. 55, May 2009, 18–21, in OSC-CPP20090507702017, for a possibly overly ambitious description of changes in the submarine force.

22.   Wertheim, *The Naval Institute Guide to Combat Fleets of the World,* 113, reports the capabilities of the Klub-s. Several sources report the maintenance problems; see, for instance, Kathy Chen, "China's Inability to Keep Subs Running Shows Broader Woes Plaguing Military," *Wall Street Journal,* 01 August 1997, 1; "New PLAN to Train, Purchase Vessel Mix," *Jane's Defence Weekly,* 16 December 1998, 25. See Sharpe, *Jane's Fighting Ships, 1999–2000,* 117, for reports of battery (and other engineering) problems. Reports in "Chinese Subs Experience Battery, Training Problems," *Navy News & Undersea Technology,* 01 September 1997, 5, cited in Edmonds and Tsai, *Taiwan's Maritime Security,* 73 (n. 4), which repeats these reports as well as noting that Iran and India have experienced similar engineering problems with their Kilos. Marina Shatilova, "Zvezda Shipyards Receives Order to Repair Chinese Submarine," ITAR-TASS, 16 June 2000, in FBIS-CEP20000616000016, reports that the shipyard in Bolshoi Kamen, near Vladivostok, "will repair a Chinese submarine this year"; and "Russia to Repair Chinese Submarines," *Agentstvo Voyennykh Novostey* (Moscow), 28 June 2000, in FBIS-CEP20000628000244, reports that "medium repair" of one of the PLAN's Kilos would begin in autumn 2000. The maintenance program is reported in Hu Chuzhang and Yan Tao, "The First PLAN Naval Ship Maintenance Quality Management System Started Running," *Renmin Haijun,* 20 February 2009, 1, in OSC-CPP20090330682009. William Murray, a retired U.S. submarine officer now on the faculty of the U.S. Naval War College, discussed Kilo maintenance with the author.

23.   Author's conversation with U.S. submarine analysts and pierside views, and discussion of technical details on the Yuans' possible AIP characteristics in detail with William Murray; Dennis Blasko, foremost U.S. analyst of PLA developments, provided a wealth of pertinent Chinese articles on the topic, both in February 2009.

24. Several types of AIP engineering plants are also under development in France, Germany, Sweden, and the United States, but they are only slowly being adopted, which indicates problematic operational viability. A good, brief explanation of AIP technology is in Scott, "Boosting the Staying Power of the Non-nuclear Submarine," 41–50; also see Carl Otis Shuster and Erik R. Henderson, "Air Independent Propulsion Systems Primer," Cubic Virtual Analysis Center, Honolulu, 04 April 2005, at http://www.analysiscenter.cubic.com/. Regardless of early claims of forty-plus days' endurance, AIP-propelled submarines are subject to the same underwater speed limitations as other conventionally powered submarines: the faster they go underwater, the less time they can remain submerged.

25. Admiral Zhang Lianzhong, quoted in Tony Perry, "Hunting beyond Red October," *Los Angeles Times,* 21 October 1997, 1, 18.

26. *Jane's Defence Weekly* 30, 16 December 1998, 25, reports the Han's engineering problems. Sharpe, *Jane's Fighting Ships, 1999–2000,* 115, notes that a second Xia-class submarine was built but was so severely damaged by a fire that it was never commissioned. A retired USN master chief sonar operator who has listened to an operating Han cruising underwater compared the noise generated by the submarine to "two skeletons [making love] in a tin can."

27. Saunders, *Jane's Fighting Ships: 2008–2009,* 121, reports that the first Shang began construction in 1994 and was not commissioned until 2006.

28. The U.S. Office of Naval Intelligence estimated—apparently erroneously—in 2007 that as many as ten to twelve Shangs might eventually be constructed, while five Jin-class FBMs will be built; see http://www.fas.org/nuke/guide/china/ONI2006.pdf (accessed 21 March 2006). Wertheim reports the propulsion plant problems; while the JL-2 reportedly was test-fired in 2006 ("China Test-Fires New Submarine-Launched Missile," *Yomiuri Shimbun,* 18 June 2006, at http://www.highbeam.com/doc/1G1-133334253.html [accessed 22 March 2009]), it was not fully operational by the end of 2009.

29. Karniol, "China Buys Shkval Torpedo from Kazakhstan," 6. Submarine-launched anti–surface ship torpedoes may be "free-fired," but most modern weapons are "wire-guided," allowing the submarine to update target information after the torpedo is launched. Torpedoes may use several methods of homing on the target; most effective may be "wake-homing," with the torpedo finding the disturbed water that is inevitably created by a surface ship's propeller(s), and then simply following this wake to the ship. The nuclear-capable Shkval rocket-propelled torpedo travels at such a high rate of speed— perhaps up to 200 knots, far faster than other torpedoes' 40–50 knots—that targets have difficulty evading, but it is also difficult to control once it is fired. Supercavitation, which allows an underwater body to travel through a self-created bubble, is explained

in Ashley, "Warp Drive Underwater." A more technical explanation is in Castano and Gieseke, "Supercavitation Research Programmes," 44–53.

30. Chuan, FBIS-CHI-99-024; author's discussion with senior PLAN officer, November 2001.

31. See Nikolay Novichkov, "Russian Shipyards Builds Destroyer for China," ITAR-TASS (Moscow), 25 December 1999, in FBIS-FTS19991225000307. U.S. and Taiwanese analysts have both told the author that China paid $880 million for the first two ships, although $800 million *per ship* is quoted in "Russia Wraps Up Construction of Destroyer for PRC Navy," Interfax (Moscow), 23 December 1999, in FBIS-FTS19991223000319.

32. The full Russian designation for the version of this missile sold to China is "Moskit 3M-80E." *Sovremenny* characteristics are provided in Sharpe, *Jane's Fighting Ships: 2000–2001*, 119. Weapons' ranges and geographic distances are given in nautical miles, one of which equals approximately 1.15 statute miles. Craig S. Smith, "New Chinese Guided-Missile Ship Heightens Tension," *New York Times*, 09 February 2000, describes the Moskit as capable of carrying a nuclear warhead, but various annual issues of *Jane's Fighting Ships* and other sources are inconsistent on this matter. Wertheim, *The Naval Institute Guide to Combat Fleets of the World*, 589, reports that the Boeing Company acquired Moskits for testing against U.S. AAW systems.

33. Nikolay Novichkov, "First Lot of Russian Moskit Missiles Shipped to China," ITAR-TASS, 16 May 2000, in FBIS-CEP20000516000142. Roman Khrapachevskiy and Igor Ivanov, "Profits of War," ITAR-TASS, 16 May 2000, in FBIS-CEP200005170002000, reports the scheduled arrival in China of the "second batch of twenty-four missiles." For the Yakhont information, see Wertheim, *The Naval Institute Guide to Combat Fleets of the World*, 589; the full Russian designation is Yakhont 3K55E; the NATO designator is SS-N-27B.

34. Saunders, *Jane's Fighting Ships: 2008–2009*, 139.

35. Ibid., 127. "Modern-Class Destroyer to Patrol off China," *Wen Wei Po* (Hong Kong), 13 February 2000, A1, in FBIS-CPP20000214000053; and the author's discussion with U.S. analysts indicate that the *Sovremenny* class has in the past suffered serious problems with its main propulsion plant ("carryover"). Also, unless modified when acquired by the PLAN, this class will suffer from inadequate air-conditioning capacity for operations in warm waters.

36. This discussion of Chinese surface ships leans on Wertheim and Saunders, *Jane's Fighting Ships, 2008–2009*. Updated information on the Luda class is in Wertheim, *The Naval Institute Guide to Combat Fleets of the World*, 117–18. Two of the class have been retrofitted with the French-built Crotale point-defense system, with a range of 7.5 nm against incoming air targets; the sole Luda III is equipped with variable-depth sonar.

37. Author's conversations with PLAN officers and U.S. analysts. Also, Wertheim, *The Naval Institute Guide to Combat Fleets of the World*, 116–17. The U.S. systems were sold to China during the 1980s, before the post–Tiananmen Square massacre sanctions were imposed in 1989: the Luhu engines are the LM-2500 manufactured by General Electric and widely used in U.S. Navy ships, including the DDG-51 and Aegis cruiser classes. The SRBOC launches canisters of chaff—strips of metal foil cut to specific lengths—that burst at altitude above and away from the launching ship and create alternate targets for incoming missiles. Interestingly, much of the combat direction center equipment uses English-language displays and labels, as I observed during two visits on board Luhu-class DDGs, four visits onboard Jiangwei-class FFGs, and a visit to the PLAN combat systems training facility in Dalian. For pictures, see *Jianchuan Zhishi* [Naval and Merchant Ships] 7, no. 238 (1999); and *Jane's Defence Weekly*, 01 February 1999, 6, at http://www.taiwansecurity.org/News/Janes-990201.htm (accessed 08 March 2009).

38. The PLA during the past decade has been placing increasing emphasis on "conducting training in complex electromagnetic environments." See Defense White Paper, 2008, sec. III: "Reform and Development of the PLA," at http://news.xinhuanet.com/english/2009-01/20/content_10688124.htm, 3 (accessed 01 February 2009). Also see Yu Lei, "Correct Misconceptions about Training and Ensure Quality of Training," *Jiefangjun Bao Online*, 02 September 2008, in FBIS: CPP20080915088001 (15 September 2008), 6. I am indebted to Dennis Blasko for bringing to my attention this article as well as statements by past and current presidents Jiang Zemin and Hu Jintao in which they independently emphasized the importance of the PLA learning to operate in the electromagnetic spectrum.

39. Author's visits on board Luhu, Jiangwei III, and earlier classes of combatants (1994–2008) lead to the conclusion that these latest PLAN ships have significantly improved in command and control capabilities; however, a senior USN officer visiting a Luyang II ship characterized the pilothouse as "twenty-year-old technology."

40. These and other FFG characteristics are described in Wertheim, *The Naval Institute Guide to Combat Fleets of the World*, 118–22. Also see the discussion of Chinese frigates in Saunders, *Jane's Fighting Ships: 2008–2009*, 132–38.

41. Sharpe, *Jane's Fighting Ships, 1999–2000*, 125, suggests that this one Jianghu was converted to serve as a test ship for several features later installed in the Luhu and Luhai classes.

42. This and other information about the Houbei class is in Saunders, *Jane's Fighting Ships: 2008–2009*, 141; and Wertheim, *The Naval Institute Guide to Combat Fleets of the World*, 123.

43. Wertheim, *The Naval Institute Guide to Combat Fleets of the World*, 126, states that "a dozen are expected to enter service. Also see Saunders, *Jane's Fighting Ships: 2008–2009*, 147; the two sources differ on some of the numbers but agree on the generally ignored state of the PLAN's mine warfare forces.

44. Author's discussions with senior U.S. analysts have not removed previous uncertainty about the size of China's mine arsenal, but Erickson, Goldstein, and Murray, *Chinese Mine Warfare*, estimate China's mine inventory at 50,000–100,000. Also see the important translations by Lyle Goldstein of "PLA Mine Warfare: A Capabilities Assessment," *World Outlook*, May 2005, 16–21; and by Gabe Collins, of Fu Jinzhu, "The World's Mine Systems," *Naval and Merchant Ships*, November 2005, 52–55.

45. The Soviet safe-haven/bastion strategy is perceptively examined in Ford and Rosenberg, "The Naval Intelligence Underpinnings of Reagan's Maritime Strategy," 379–409. The JL-2 missile's range would not include the United States if launched from the South China Sea; that would require the Jin to operate farther north, perhaps from a Yellow Sea bastion.

46. Blasko, quoted in Minnick, "China's Gator Navy Makes Marginal Strides": "despite the recent construction of amphibious craft, the actual lift capability has not improved in over a decade," at http://www.defensenews.com/story.php?i=3899959 (accessed 15 February 2009).

47. Wertheim, *The Naval Institute Guide to Combat Fleets of the World*, 126–27. The Pielstick engines are licensed to the Shaanxi Diesel Engine Works, a state-owned factory located in Xingping City, Shaanxi Province, China. This represents an advance of sorts for China's military-industrial complex because the author previously observed Jiangwei-class frigate engines clearly marked "Siemens," apparently produced in a long-established German-Chinese joint venture.

48. Although two additional Fuqings were built, one was sold to Pakistan and one was converted to the civilian merchant fleet, indicating that the PLAN in the early 1980s was not concerned about further increasing its ability to conduct underway replenishment.

49. Wertheim, *The Naval Institute Guide to Combat Fleets of the World*, 132, 946. By contrast, the largest class of U.S. oilers, the *Henry J. Kaiser* class, can provide more than twice this amount of fuel (23,450 tons) as well as a significant amount of dry cargo.

50. Saunders, *Jane's Fighting Ships: 2008–2009*, 154.

51. Su Kuoshan and Su Dianlong, "Fourth Space Survey Vessel Enters Service," *Xinhua*, 18 July 1999, in FBIS-CHI-1999-0730, describes this ship as "belonging to . . . the State Oceanography Bureau." The Yuanwangs are described in "Yuanwang 5/6 Space Surveillance Ships," at http://www.sinodefence.com/navy/research_survey/yuanwang-5_6.asp (accessed 05 December 2009).

52. Saunders, *Jane's Fighting Ships: 2008–2009*, 119. Ts'ai Chih Sheng and Chang Sun Chien, "Red Underwater Giant," *Navy Studies Bimonthly* (Taipei), in OSC-CPP20090309312009, 01 October 2009, give estimated ranges for the JL-2 from 7,559 to 8,600 km nm; the latter would enable a Jin-class submarine in the Sea of Okhotsk to cover approximately two-thirds of the continental United States. The Federation of American Scientists, at http://www.fas.org/nuke/guide/china/nuke/index.html (accessed 01 November 2009), credits the JL-2 with a range of 4,320+ nm, while the U.S. Department of Defense shows the JL-2 with a range of "3,880+ nm" in its *Annual Report to Congress on the Military Power of the People's Republic of China: 2008* (Washington, D.C.: Office of the Secretary of Defense, 2009), 26, at http://www.defenselink.mil/pubs/pdfs/China_Military_Report_08.pdf (accessed 01 November 2009).

53. Saunders, *Jane's Fighting Ships: 2008–2009*, 140.

54. O'Rourke, "China Naval Modernization," 8; Wertheim, *The Naval Institute Guide to Combat Fleets of the World*, 107, credits the PLANAF with thirty Su-30s.

55. Kenneth Allen of the Center for Naval Analyses, the leading U.S. analyst of China's aviation forces, brought this to my attention.

56. Guo Yuanfa, "The Painstaking Development of an Ace Aircraft," *Liaowang*, 04 October 1999, 32–33, in FBIS-FTS19991209000604, reports that this aircraft had been in development since before 1984 and began entering the operating forces in 2000.

57. The Federation of American Scientists, at http://www.fas.org/nuke/guide/china/agency/plan-af-orbat-st.htm (accessed 16 February 2009), gives the number of Ka-28s as 34; Wertheim, *The Naval Institute Guide to Combat Fleets of the World*, says 28; Bussert, "China Builds Destroyers around Imported Technology," gives 24; and Saunders, *Jane's Fighting Ships: 2008–2009*, gives the low number at 10. In an April 2009 conversation, a senior PLAN officer shrugged in response to my question and said that "at least twelve" Ka-28s had been acquired.

58. Author's visit to Jiangwei III–class FFG in May 2006, during which the ship's commanding officer described his ship, then just six months in commission, as a "Jiangwei III," although neither *Jane's* nor Wertheim uses that term to designate a specific FFG class.

59. SAMAHE (Système d'Aide à la Manutention des Hélicoptères Embarques) is designed to allow for recovery and hangaring of helos in rough weather. Similar versions are the Canadian "Bear Trap" and the U.S. Recovery-Assist-Secure-Traverse (RAST) systems; all serve to move the helo into the hangar in seas up to state five, but this capability appears lacking on the Chinese ships (based on the author's visits to Luhu- and Jiangwei-class vessels). See picture of Jiangkai flight deck in Saunders, *Jane's Fighting Ships: 2008–2009*, 132.

60. O'Rourke, "China Naval Modernization: Implications for U.S. Navy Capabilities," 4–6, is the most comprehensive single document on PLAN capabilities; Stokes, *China's Strategic Modernization*, remains valuable for its synopsis of China's cruise missile development programs. Updated information is in Lum, "China's Cruise Missile Program"; and Chase, "Chinese Land Attack Cruise Missile Developments and Their Implications for the United States."

61. *Annual Report to Congress: The Military Power of the People's Republic of China, 2008*, 2, at http://www.defenselink.mil/pubs/pdfs/China_Military_Report_08.pdf (accessed 15 March 2009). Also see the extensive discussion by Richard Fisher Jr. in "China's New Strategic Cruise Missiles: From the Land, Sea and Air," 03 June 2005, at http:www.strategycenter.net/research/pubID.71/pub_detail.asp (accessed 31 March 2009).

62. The most complete work by an American analyst on China's ASBM program is Paul S. Giarra, "China's Maritime Reconnaissance-Strike Complex: Land Mobile, MaRV'd Anti-ship Ballistic Missiles (ASBMs)," PowerPoint presentation at the conference on "China in Asia: Access and Counter-access," Washington, D.C., National Defense University, 25 July 2008. The operational date of an effective ASBM, probably based on China's medium-range DF-21 missile, is unknown, although at least one source claims that it was operational in 2009: see "Chinese Develop Special 'Kill Weapon' to Destroy U.S. Aircraft Carriers," *U.S. Naval Institute Online* (31 March 2009), at http://www.usni.org/forthemedia/ChineseKillWeapon.asp (accessed 02 April 2009).

63. Minnie Chan, "Beijing to Build Large Destroyers," *Global Times*, at http://forum.globaltimes.cn/forum/showthread.php?t=7658 (accessed 28 November 2009).

Chapter 6. Personnel, Education, Training, and Exercises

1. Shichor, "Demobilization," 336–59, discusses earlier PLA demobilization steps (since 1950). The most authoritative figure is the 290,000 in ONI, *The People's Liberation Army Navy*, 32. The U.S. Navy, by comparison, in October 2008 numbered 332,262 uniformed and 184,396 civilian personnel, and 123,711 reserves.

2. Jiang is quoted in "Opening Up New Prospects for Ideological, Political Building of China's Military Academies," *Jiefangjun Bao*, 23 May 2000, in FBIS-CPP20000523000043; Defense White Paper, 2008, sec. III, may be found at http://news.xinhuanet.com/english/2009-01/20/content_10688124_4.htm (accessed 06 September 2009).

3. The normal Ming crew is fifty-five; hull number 361 may have embarked its squadron commander and staff, as well as some cadets from the Naval Academy at Dalian. "Mechanical malfunction" was the official Chinese explanation for the accident; the

submarine was semisubmerged when found, indicating that the accident probably involved a failure in ventilation and safety systems that resulted in a lack of internal oxygen when the diesel engine was started, killing all on board. See William Foreman, "Chinese Submarine Accident Kills 70," Associated Press report at http://www.dcfp. navy.mil/mc/articles/other/MingSub.htm (accessed 30 August 2009); author's interviews with U.S. submarine officers.

4. Two of the many accounts of this personnel upheaval are Ray Cheung, "Leaders Are Replaced in Naval Shakeup," *South China Morning Post* (Hong Kong), 13 June 2003, passed directly to author; and "CMC Appoints New PLA Navy Commander, Political Commissar," *Xinhua*, 12 June 2003, in FBIS-CPP20030612000174.

5. Author's interviews with senior (0-6 and higher) PLAN officers between 1998 and 2009. Also see Zhang Weiran, "PLA Becomes Smaller in Size but Stronger in Battle Effectiveness," *China Military Online*, 02 September 2009, at http://eng.chinamil.com. cn/news-channels/china-military-news/2009-09/02/content_4032392.htm (accessed 13 September 2009).

6. Li Peng is quoted in *The PRC's Effort to Assimilate Advanced US Military Technology*, GAO Report to Congress (Washington, D.C.: USGPO, 1999); Li Jinai's claim is quoted in Evan Medeiros, "Statement before the U.S.-China Economic and Security Commission Hearings on Chinese Military Modernization and Cross-Strait Politico-Military Relations," 06 February 2004, at http://www.uscc.gov/hearings/2004hearings/transcripts/04_02_06.pdf (accessed 31 October 2009).

7. Information provided by Blasko and Vellucci, "Recent Trends in PLA Navy Training and Education." This OMTE was promulgated in July 2008; see "New Outline of Military Training and Evaluation Promulgated," *PLA Daily*, 25 July 2008, at http://english.chinamil.com.cn/site2/news-channels/2008-07/25/content_1379311.htm (accessed 30 August 2009).

8. "GSH Arranges PLA's Military Training Work in 2009," *english.chinamil.com.cn*, 07 January 2009, at http://english.chinamil.com.cn/site2/news-channels/2009-01/07/content_1610805.htm (accessed 01 September 2009). The author is indebted to Dennis Blasko for this translation of the GSD directives. Also see Wu Dilun and Liu Feng'an, "Highlights of Military Training in First Half of 2009," *PLA Daily*, 09 July 2009, at http://eng.mod.gov.cn/DefenseNews/2009-07/09content_4002936 (accessed 02 September 2009).

9. Qin Jun, "Provisions Officers' of the Three Services Acquire Masterly Skills through Online Joint Training," *Jiefangjun Bao*, 30 March 2009, in OSC-CPP20090410088001.

10. Author's conversations with senior PLAN officers.

11. The 700,000 personnel reduction is reported in "China Plans to Cut Army, Boost Navy and Air Force," Reuters report from Beijing, in the *Taipei Times*, 01 October 2009,

11, at http://www.taipeitimes.com/News/front/archives/2009/10/01/2003454905 (accessed 01 October 2009). These data do not include small craft such as mine-sweepers and patrol boats.

12. Author's discussions with senior PLA officers between 2000 and 2008.

13. Personnel numbers are from Hackett, *The Military Balance, 2009,* and assume the following naval combatants' personnel strength: U.S. Pacific Fleet, 60,000; Thailand, 70,600; South Korea, 47,000; India, 53,000; Indonesia, 45,000; Japan, 34,300; Taiwan, 45,000; Malaysia, 13,940; Australia, 12,330.

14. Hackett, *The Military Balance, 2009,* 385, gives PLA Marine Corps strength as 10,000. Women were apparently fully integrated into Marine units at Zhanjiang according to one U.S. observer in 1999. Li Chang, "First Female Marine Corps of Chinese Navy," *Military Window,* no. 2 (reprinted in *Ta Kung Pao,* 15 June 1998, E1, in FBIS-CHI-98-198), reports on an all-female Marine unit in rather zoological prose: the women Marines are described "as agile as monkeys . . . light as birds . . . bold and forceful as race horses . . . crafty as foxes . . . clever as rabbits . . . and fierce as tigers."

15. Jiang is quoted in "Mechanization and Informatization Are Our Army's Double Historic Tasks," *Selected Works of Jiang Zemin* (Beijing, 2008), 3:162, trans. Blasko. Hu is quoted in "At the 15th Collective Study Session of the Political Bureau of the CPC Central Committee," *Xinhua,* 24 July 2009, in OSC-CPP20090724066017. Mobilizing civilian resources in support of the PLA is addressed in China's National Defense Mobilization Law, discussed in Peng Kuang and Cui Xiaohuo, "Defense Mobilization Law to Be Considered," *China Daily,* 14 April 2009, at http://www.chinadaily.com.cn/cndy/2009-04/14/content_7673631.htm; also see the discussion of national mobilization in China's 2006 Defense White Paper, at http://english.chin amil.com.cn/site2/special-reports/2007-01/15/content_706570.htm (both accessed 18 November 2009).

16. Jiang is quoted in Fu Quanyu, "Vigorously Conduct Military Training of Science and Technology to Strengthen Great Wall of Steel," *Quishi* (Beijing), 01 August 1999, 12–17, in FBIS-CHI-99-0902, 4; for Hu Jintao on this subject, see Mulvenon, "Hu Jintao and the 'Core Values of Military Personnel.'" For an operational note, see He Y and Si Yanwen, "A Navy Destroyer Flotilla Realizes Information Interconnections in Offshore Maneuver," *Jiefangjun Bao,* 17 December 2003, in FBIS-CPP20031218000081.

17. "China Reports High Employment for College Graduates," *Xinhua,* 13 April 2000, in FBIS-CPP20000413000172, states that "university graduates are in great demand" and that "postgraduates and students from well-known universities are being actively pursued by employers," according to the Ministry of Education in Beijing. More than 90 percent employment for 2006 college graduates is reported in Cao, *Private Higher Education and the Labor Market in China,* 130.

18. See "Army Seeks Mobility in Force Cuts," *Jane's Defence Weekly* 30, no. 25 (16 December 1998), 23; more recent pay increases are reported in Stephanie Ho, "China Boosts Military Spending," Voice of America (Beijing), 04 March 2009, at http:// www.globalsecurity.org/wmd/library/news/china/2009/china-090304-voa01.htm (accessed 02 October 2009); "CMC Promulgates Scheme to Deepen NCO System Reform," *PLA Daily*, 13 July 2009, at http://eng.mod.gov.cn/TopNews/2009-07/13/ content_4003727.htm (accessed 02 October 2009); and "Pay Raise of 50 Percent for Chinese Soldiers," *Asian Defense*, 31 March 2009, at http://theasiandefence.blogspot. com/2009/03/pay-raise-of-50-for-chinese-soldiers.html (accessed 02 October 2009).

19. "State Council, CMC Issue Winter Conscription Notice," *Xinhua*, 09 October 2000, in FBIS-CPP20001009000042. Eliminating corruption in the conscription process is discussed in "China's Annual Conscription Begins," *Xinhua*, 01 November 2000, in FBIS-CPP20001101000088; and in "PLA Raises Recruitment Standards for Women," *Xinhua*, 13 October 2009, at http://english.chinamil.com.cn (accessed 13 October 2009), which also describes the new standards for women recruits. The emphasis on college graduates is noted in "China's Annual Military Recruitment Favors College Graduates," *Xinhua*, 02 November 2009, at http://eng.china.com.cn/ news-channels/china-military-news/2009-11/02/content_4072066.htm (accessed 09 November 2009). Also see Sijin Chen, "The Challenge of Conscription in an Era of Social Change," 236.

20. *China's Navy, 2007*, 74–77. A senior PLAN officer told me in 2000 that this is allocated on a fleet basis.

21. Su Ruozhou, "Major Reform in Our Army's Service System," *Jiefangjun Bao*, 13 July 1999, 2, in FBIS-CHI-99-0811, discusses the two-year requirement; author's discussion with senior PLA officers about longer PLAN enlistments. Technical training schools vary in length, but a recruit may spend an additional three to six months in school after completing three months of "boot camp." By comparison, a technician in the U.S. Navy may spend as long as twenty-four months in schools before reporting to his/her first ship—after agreeing to extend his/her enlistment from four to six years. Furthermore, the USN trains sailors to both maintain and operate a system, while most other navies train their sailors to do one or the other. Based on the author's conversations with its officers, the PLAN follows the latter model. Also see Blasko, "New PLA Force Structure," 24.

22. Author's conversations with senior PLAN officers, 1998 and 2008.

23. This discussion draws directly from *China's Navy, 2007*, 31.

24. Quoted in "Opening Up New Prospects for Ideological, Political Building of China's Military Academies," *Jiefangjun Bao*, 23 May 2000, in FBIS-CPP20000523000043.

25. Quoted in editorial on PLA Training Conference, *Jiefangjun Bao*, 01 July 2006, 3, in OSC-CPP20060629702003.

26. The author first discussed with PLA officers implementing an ROTC-like program in China in 1994, and in 1998 discussed school assignments with a senior PLA officer in Beijing. Xhang Jiajun and Zhang Xuanjie, *Xinhua*, 28 May 1999, in FBIS-CHI-99-0601, reports that the "Second Artillery Corps signed an agreement with the Northwest Engineering University in Xian today to cultivate cadres for guided missile troops" and will "supply a certain number of outstanding university and graduate students for the Second Artillery Corps every year," with the corps establishing a "national defense scholarship" at the school to "encourage and fund" likely students. Liu Jianxin, *Xinhua*, 28 October 1999, in FBIS-CHI-99-1103, reports that the "Guangzhou Military Region and Wuhan University have signed an agreement on jointly training military cadres. . . . [T]his military region will . . . expand the selection of outstanding personnel from institutions of higher learning across the country. . . . All major military regions and armed services have separately designated one local university to be the designated school for training their own cadres." Also see "Navy to Recruit Officers from Non-military Colleges," *Xinhua*, 17 August 1999, in FBIS-CHI-99-0817; *China's Navy, 2007*, 69, also addresses these programs.

27. Wang Dianbin, "Open Up New [Personnel Sources]," *Jiefangjun Bao*, 09 May 1999, 2, in FBIS-CHI-99-0523, discusses the U.S. ROTC system and similar programs in Great Britain and Russia. The Chinese submarine service follows the practice of most navies in maintaining higher standards for its personnel: see Wang Yang, Wu Dengfeng, and Xu Xingtang," China's New-Generation Submarine Elites Have Excellent Qualities," *Xinhua*, 29 July 2007, in OSC-CPP20070815436001.

28. "PLA Navy Conducts First Sea Training for National Defense Scholarship Students," *PLA Daily*, 21 August 2003, at http://www.pladaily.com.cn/gb/defence/2003/03/21/2 0030821017019_zhxw.html (accessed 13 September 2009). Senior U.S. Navy officer's discussion with Chinese counterpart, 2001. "PLA to Enlist at Thirteen Beijing Private Colleges," *Xinhua*, 30 October 2009, at http://www.chinadaily.cn/china/2009-10/30/ content_8876116.htm (accessed 02 November 2009), reports that "about 2,500 college graduates and 600 undergraduate students have applied to the new program."

29. Chen Wanjun and Li Chaogui, "Navy Makes Advances in Equipment Modernization," *Xinhua*, 13 May 1998, in FBIS-CHI-98-137.

30. Author's interview with senior PLA officer, 2000. See Liu Jianxin, "Wuhan University, Military Agree on Training Officers," *Xinhua*, 28 October 1999, in FBIS-CHI-99-1103. Other civilian university participants include Nanchang University, Huazhong Science and Technology University, Harbin Engineering University, Northwestern Polytechnic University, China Ocean University, Huadong Ship Engineering University, Ningbo University, Nanhua University, the Nanchang Aviation Industry College, and Xi'an University (*China's Navy, 2007*, 70). Also see *Xinhua* (Hong Kong), 21 June 1999, in FBIS-CHI-99-0622, for the note that these civilian university programs will be linked to the military academy structure.

31. These programs are discussed in Vellucci, "Recent Trends in PLA Navy Training and Education." Sun Zhi and Lu Rongjun, "10,000 NDS to Receive Intensive Training during Summer Vacation," *PLA Daily*, 07 September 2009, at http://eng.mod.gov.cn/Database/Academies/2009-07/14/content_4003708.htm (accessed 08 November 2009), claims that 47,000 National Defense Scholarship students "are scattered in 117 regular higher learning institutions nationwide."

32. Quoted in Fu Quanyou, "Vigorously Conduct Military Training of Science and Technology to Strengthen Great Wall of Steel," *Qiushi* (Beijing), 01 August 1999, 12–17, in FBIS-CHI-99-0902.

33. "Military Academies Plan to Enroll 15,000 cadets," at http://english.chinamil.com.cnsite2/news-channels/2009-05/15/content_176450.htm (accessed 28 October 2009).

34. Author's discussions with officers at the Dalian Military Academy in September 1998, the PLAN First Surface Vessel Academy (in Dalian) in 1998 and 2002, and the Xian Air Force Engineering College in September 1998 and 2004 suggested that while candidates indicate their college preference when they take the examination, it is of secondary importance in the selection process. Besides military academies, other "special schools" include certain arts and literature institutions and the Beijing Opera School.

35. Hu Chuanmu and Xu Shuangxi, "CMC Promulgates Scheme to Deepen NCO System Reform," *PLA Daily*, 13 July 2009, at http://eng.mod.gov.cn/TopNews/2009-07/13/content_4003727.htm (accessed 09 September 2009). Also see "China Reveals Plan to Restructure PLA's Non-commissioned Ranks," *Xinhua*, 15 July 2009, at http://news.xinhuanet.com/english/2009-07/14/content_11708819.htm (accessed 09 September 2009).

36. Defense White Paper, 2008, sec. III.

37. Blasko, "A New PLA Force Structure," 13. Adding DOD civilians would increase the size of the U.S. "military" by approximately 50 percent.

38. "Regulations on Military Service of Active-Duty Soldiers of the Chinese PLA," ch. 1, art. 7, *Xinhua*, 11 July 1999, in FBIS-CHI-99-0728. Also see *China's Navy, 2007*, 80.

39. Defense White Paper, 2008, sec. III. China ratified the UNCLOS in 1996.

40. Yang, "From a Navy in Blue toward a Blue Water Navy," 4. "The People's Navy," 35–40, dates the establishment of the following Navy schools as follows: Andong Naval School, East China MR Naval School in Nanjing, and PLAN Academy in Dalian, all in 1949; Support Services School and Political Cadre School in Qingdao, 1952; Submarine School in Qingdao, 1953; Naval Command School and the Naval School of Mechanics, both in Dalian, 1954; Communications School and the Navy Advanced School, both in Qingdao, and the Naval Academy in Nanjing, 1957. But see Sheng Tong-liang, "Chinese Built Submarines Abandon Inflexible Soviet Methods and

Absorb Technology from Many Countries," *PLA Daily*, 18 December 2008, at http://www.dnxf.com/html/junshi_481_7888.html (accessed 12 October 2009).

41. Quoted in Mulvenon, *Professionalization of the Senior Chinese Officer Corps*, 11.

42. "Unify Our Ideas and Actions with Central Commission's Policy Decisions," *Jiefangjun Bao*, 21 June 1999, 1, in FBIS-CHI-99-0628.

43. Kondapalli, "China's Naval Training Program," 1336.

44. "Basic Military Project for Development in the New Century," editorial in *Jiefangjun Bao*, 15 April 2000, 1, in FBIS-CPP20000417000056.

45. Cited in Luo Yuwen, "Zhang Wannian Stresses Efforts to Train High-Quality New-Style Military Talent," *Xinhua*, 19 April 2000, in FBIS-CPP20000419000099. A 23 August 2000 editorial in *Jiefangjun Bao*, "Reaching Common Understanding" (in FBIS-CPP20000823000051), reemphasizes the responsibility of academies to stress "winning wars" and "eradicating corruption" while adhering "to the absolute leadership of the Party." Students were to be taught first to be "qualified in the political sense, and second in ... professional skills." Hu's address is discussed in Mulvenon, "Hu Jintao and the 'Core Values of Military Personnel.'"

46. Huang Huamin and Luo Yuwen, "Jiang Stresses Technology, Loyal Personnel in PLA," *Jiefangjun Bao*, 27 June 1999, in FBIS-CHI-99-0627. Su authored "Persistently Follow the Guidance of Chairman Hu's Important Thought on the Navy's Building," *Renmin Haijun* (Beijing), 06 June 2009, 3, quoted in U.S.-China Economic and Security Review Commission, *2009 Report to Congress*, 130.

47. Shen Yaojin and Wang Huamin, "Central Military Commission Issues Program for Education Reform and Development of Military Academies," *Jiefangjun Bao*, 15 April 2000, 1, in FBIS-CPP20000417000061.

48. Author's several visits to the PLA NDU and other professional military education institutions, 1994–2008. Quote is in Mulvenon, *Professionalization of the Senior Chinese Officer Corps*, 12.

49. Quoted in "An Important Measure for Strengthening the Training of High- and Medium-Ranking Cadres," *Jiefangjun Bao*, 21 June 1999, 1, in FBIS-CHI-99-0629.

50. Quoted in "Put Military Academy Education in a Strategic Position of Priority Development," *Jiefangjun Bao*, 23 June 1999, 1, in FBIS-CHI-99-0629.

51. Quan Xiaoshu, "Naval Contingents in Parade Highlight China's Growing Ocean Presence," *Xinhua*, 01 October 2009, at http://www.individual.com/story.php?story=107708968 (accessed 05 October 2009).

52. Author's discussions with commandant of the Guangzhou Naval Academy in May 1994 and commandants of the Dalian Naval Academy in April 1996 and May 1997. Andrew Yang, "From a Navy in Blue towards a Blue Water Navy," gives 1991 as the founding date of this academy, but that probably refers to a change in mission for the

school from training new cadets to conducting more advanced training for new officers who have already graduated from an academy.

53. Author's discussions with senior PLAN officers, 1994, 1998, and 2008.

54. "PRC's Navy Sets Up 'Practice Base' for Postgraduates," *Xinhua*, 13 December 1999, in FBIS-FTS19991212000948; author's discussions with senior PLA officers, 1998–99.

55. Author's discussions with senior PLA NDU officers, 1994–2008.

56. "PLA Officers Said 'Younger, Better Educated,'" *Xinhua*, 25 July 1997, in FBIS-CHI-97-206, reports that the average age of officers at the MR level has dropped to 57.3 from 59.3 in the last two years and that 78.4 percent of such officers are now college graduates, in contrast to 49.2 percent in 1992. Similar statistics for "combat commanders" were 51.4 years old and 90.2 percent college graduates. *China's Navy, 2007*, 68–69, reports that PLAN officers continue to be increasingly well educated.

57. Huang Caihong, Chen Wanjun, and Zhang Zhao, "The PLA Navy Has Enhanced Comprehensive Combat Effectiveness," *Xinhua*, 19 April 1999, in FBIS-CHI-99-0423, quotes Shi; Wu is quoted in the *Beijing Review*, 04 May 2009; *China's Navy, 2007* discusses the long trend in educational improvements for PLAN personnel.

58. Chen Wanjun, "Navy Improves Combat Capability," *Xinhua*, 26 July 1999, in FBIS-CHI-99-0729, discusses commanding officer "comprehensive examinations." Kondapalli, "China's Naval Training Program," 1338, lists these as "microelectronics, PERT [?], CPM [?], navigation, dynamics, telemetering and remote control, and aviation and astro-navigation."

59. "30 Years of PLA's Development, 1978–2008," CCTV-7, October 2008, 4, at OSC-FEA20081215800637 (accessed 10 October 2008).

60. Defense White Paper, 2008, sec. III.

61. Chen Yeong-kang, paper on the PLAN submarine force presented at the April 2000 CNA Conference on the PLAN. *China's Navy, 2007*, 63, fig. 19: "Rank and Grade Promotion Cycle." These numbers are based on the author's conversations with senior PLA and Taiwan Navy officers and with PLAN commanding officers aboard their ships from 1994 to 2008, with the PLAAF's 24th Air Division chief of staff in 1997 and 9th Air Division commander in 2000; and from Allen, Krumel, and Pollock, *China's Air Force Enters the 21st Century*. One senior PLAN officer told me that a submarine commander may serve in his billet for six years but operate under way for only about three hundred days during that period. The 2009 deployment to the Gulf of Aden attests to the PLAN's increased operational readiness.

62. *China's Navy, 2007*, 82. Also see "PRC's Yu Yongbo Reviews Military Propaganda Network," *Xinhua*, 26 December 1999, in FBIS-FTS20000120000818; and "PLA Information Network Begins Operations," *Xinhua*, 28 December 1999, in FBIS-FTS19991228000766.

63. Author's discussions with senior PLA officers between 1994 and 2006. *China's Navy, 2007*, 90, notes that each of China's three fleets has a training center. Also see Jiang Minjun and Si Yanwen, "A Certain Destroyer Flotilla Designates 'Training Ships; to Train Crew[s],'" *Jiefangjun Bao*, 14 June 2002, 2, in FBIS-CPP20020614000045. Particularly useful is Mulvenon, "True Is False, False Is True." Individual reports include Xu Sen, "Building a Modern Naval Battlefield—Overview of the Naval Vessel Training Center," *Jiefangjun Bao*, 15 September 1999, 6, in FBIS-CHI-99-0923; "China's New-Type Submarine Simulator Passes Expert Appraisal," *People's Daily Online*, 15 March 2004, at http://english.peopledaily.com.cn/200403/15/eng20040315_137548. shtml (accessed 10 October 2009); and "ESF Warship Training Center Expands Warship Training Capacity," *Jiefangjun Bao*, 21 July 2007, in OSC (link no longer available), accessed 28 July 2007.

64. Visits by the author and other U.S. observers, 1990–2008, to PLAN training facilities in Dalian, Qingdao, Shanghai, and Guangzhou; and to PLA training facilities in Beijing (NDU, Armored Engineering College, and Air Force Command College), Dalian (Shenyang MR Military Academy), Xi'an (PLAAF Engineering College), and Nanjing (PLA Staff and Command College), showed computerized training facilities that are improving but seemed still analogous to U.S. Navy facilities ca. 1990.

65. Bussert, "China Taps Many Resources for Coastal Defense," offers a general description of China's coastal defense organization; more specific information is provided in Blasko, "PLA Ground Force Modernization and Mission Diversification." "Coastal Defense/ Counter-terror Exercise by PLA, Police, Militia, and Reserves," *Xinhua*, 22 September 2002, at http://www.highbeam.com/doc/1P2-13323874.htm (accessed 30 September 2009), reports a related exercise while also reporting that the Second National Working Conference for Coastal Defense was conducted in Xiamen on 19–21 September 2002. A similar drill is reported in Zhang Shengzhong and Zhou Yawen, "The Return of the Naval Infantry," *PLA Daily*, 10 February 2009, at http://www.worldaffairsboard.com/ rise-china/49652-return-pla-naval-infantry.html (accessed 30 September 2009).

66. Tang Liehui, "Work Hard to Explore Optimal Solution to Man-Weapon Integration," *Jiefangjun Bao*, 15 June 1999, 6, in FBIS-CHI-99-0711; author's discussions with senior PLAN officers.

67. Admiral Zhang Lianzhong, quoted in "Navy Chief on Technical, Tactical Upgrading," Beijing Domestic Service, 05 May 1988, in FBIS-CHI-88-090; Fu is quoted in Mao Xiaochun and Chen Hui, "Chief of Staff Fu Quanyou on High-Tech Military Training," *Xinhua*, 16 October 1999, in FBIS-CHI-99-1016.

68. Baker, *The Naval Institute Guide to Combat Fleets of the World, 2000–2001*, 129; *Zheng He* is pictured in ibid., 130; it looks like a small passenger liner. The author inspected the ship in 1989 and noted that it is equipped with classrooms and various

navigation, electronics, and gunnery systems for instructional purposes. Chen Wanjun and Chen Guofang, "Birth of China's First Defense Mobilization Vessel," *Jianchuan Zhishi* [Naval and Merchant Ships], no. 2, 06 February 1997, 2, in FBIS-CHI-97-089, describes *Shichang* in detail, noting that the ship is assigned to the Dalian Naval Vessels Institute; "China Establishes First Aircraft Carrier Training Formation," *Takungpao News*, 06 June 2004, at http://www.takungpao.com/news/06/06/04/ZM-575010.htm (article no longer available on site).

69. The best current work on PLA logistics progress is Puska, "Taming the Hydra: Trends in China's Military Logistics since 2000." Specific advances in logistics efficiency are indicated in Wu Ruhui, Jin Zhifeng, and Chen Bingfeng, "Navy's 'Military Representatives' Hard at Work in Supervising Armament Development," *Jiefangjun Bao*, 10 April 2002, 10, in FBIS-CHI-2002-0410; Liu Xinmin and Xu Feng, "Chinese Submarine Unit Succeeds for First Time in Making Use of Civilian Port to Load Torpedoes," *Zhongguo Qingnian Bao* (Beijing), 01 June 2002, in FBIS-CPP20020603000058; "Comprehensive Support Formation of the PLA Navy Service Ship Group Successfully Conducts Non-contact Supply Operation to Submarine," *People's Daily*, 21 June 2003, at http://www.peopledaily.com.cn/GB/junshi/1079/1927053.html (accessed 12 October 2009); "PLA Fujian Military District to Conduct Maritime Logistic Replenishment Drill," *Wenweipo News* (Hong Kong), 23 July 2004, at http://www.allacademic.com/meta/p_mla_apa_research_citation/0/7/1/2/1/pages71219/p71219-45.php (accessed 17 October 2009); Zhou Yongwei, "Naval Aviation Unit Reforms Support Pattern," *Jiefangjun Bao*, 13 February 2004, in FBIS-CPP20040218000093; "Chinese Local Oil Tanker Replenishes Oil for PLA Navy South Sea Fleet Destroyer," *Military China*, 11 July 2006 (link no longer available); "PLA Navy Stages Military-Civilian Integrated Ordnance Support Exercises in Ningbo," *Renmin Tupian Wang*, 23 October 2006 (link no longer available); "PLA Navy NSF Repair Battalion Commander Pursues Submarine Repair," *Jiefangjun Bao*, 09 August 2007 (link no longer available). Copies of photographs provided to the author by Dr. Lyle Goldstein, director of the U.S. Naval War College's China Maritime Study Institute: "DDG168 Conducting Helo and UNREP," 2009, demonstrate the PLAN's state-of-the-art capabilities in replenishment at sea. The number of classes is listed at http://www.sinodefence.com/navy/surface/default.asp (accessed 12 October 2009).

70. Author's conversations with senior PLA officers. Xu Sen, "Building a Modern Naval Battlefield," *Jiefangjun Bao*, 15 September 1999, 6, in FBIS-CHI-99-0923, describes the North Sea Fleet training center and compares it to similar centers built by the United States, France, Great Britain, and others. Crews are trained in navigation and ship handling, weapons systems, and electronic warfare.

71.   Ren Yanjun, "Entire Army Bears in Mind Sacred Mission, Makes Ample Preparations for Military Struggle," *Jiefangjun Bao*, 12 April 2000, 1, in FBIS-CPP20000412000032, describes "the army as a whole . . . successively [sending] tens of divisions and brigades into training bases to conduct exercises under simulated and virtual battleground environments with real personnel, real vehicles, real bullets and real explosives to train for actual combat capabilities."

72.   This paragraph draws heavily on Blasko, Klapakis, and Corbett, "Training Tomorrow's PLA," 490–91. "Increasing Capacity of 'Winning Wars' Is Fundamental," *Jiefangjun Bao*, 30 January 1999, 1, in FBIS-FTS19990205000303, argues that "to firmly grasp the direction of military training that relies on science and technology, we must . . . standardize it." Kondapalli, "China's Naval Training Program," 1344–48, provides a useful list of PLAN exercises from 1957 to 1998.

73.   Major General Chen Youyuan, quoted in You Ji, "The Revolution in Military Affairs and the Evolution of China's Strategic Thinking," 350.

74.   See, for instance, three *Jiefangjun Bao* articles: Zhang Guoyu and Wang Boming, "Carry Out Scientific and Technological Training and Create Brilliant Historic Achievements," 19 January 1999, 6, in FBIS-FTS19990208000125; Li Jianyin, "On Welcoming the Cross-Century Military Training Revolution," 26 January 1999, 6, in FBIS-FTS19990209000171; and Gao Jianguo, "Change the Pattern of Personnel Training," 26 January 1999, 6, in FBIS-FTS19990208000103.

75.   Zhang Guoyu and Wang Boming, "Carry Out Scientific and Technological Training and Create Brilliant Historic Achievements" [one of a series], *Jiefangjun Bao*, 28 January 1999, 6, in FBIS-FTS19990205000009, 4, also observed that "simulation training has become a training form most close to 'actual combat.'"

76.   The PLAN's concerns with net-centric warfare are discussed in Erickson, "PLA Navy Modernization"; also see Zhang Zhenzhong and Chang Jianguo, "Train Talented People at Different Levels for Information Warfare," *Jiefangjun Bao*, 02 February 1999, 6, in FBIS-FTS19990210001865. Pillsbury, *Chinese Views of Future Warfare*, contains an extensive selection of PLA writings on the RMA and IW.

77.   Zheng Shuyan and Gao Aisu, "Group Army Trains Hard to Learn Multidimensional Maneuver Combat Skills," *Jiefangjun Bao*, 20 June 1997, 1, in FBIS-CHI-97-199.

78.   See, for instance, Chen Yuanming and Yan Jinjiu, "Chinese Navy Successfully Conducts First Wharf-Free Fuel Supply Operation under Combat Conditions," *Jiefangjun Bao*, 26 May 1997, 1, in FBIS-CHI-97-121; Zhang Peng and Wang Peihong, "PLA Navy Builds Modern Diving Facility in Qingdao," *Xinhua*, 12 May 1998, in FBIS-CHI-98-135.

79.   Si Liang, "Chinese Navy Holds Exercises Again and Again Recently and Stands in Combat Readiness," *Zhongguo Tongxun She*, 05 August 1999, in FBIS-CHI-99-0805.

80.   Blasko, Klapakis, and Corbett, "Training Tomorrow's PLA," 499–515.

81.   Shen Hairong and Chen Tangsheng, "Certain Group Army of Nanjing Military
      Region Makes Fresh Breakthrough in Its Capability of Fighting and Winning Battles
      at Sea," *Jiefangjun Bao,* 08 August 2000, in FBIS-CPP20000808000036, states that
      "the group army has built a simulated landing training site for each of its infantry regi-
      ments." Also see Liu Demao and Zhang Xianqiu, "Joint Teaching and Training Base of
      NDU and SAF Established," *PLA Daily,* 15 July 2009, at http://english.chinamil.com.
      cn/site2/news-channels/2009-07/15/content_1837286.htm (accessed 07 September
      2009).

82.   "Dongshan Drill to Enter New Stage," *People's Daily,* 03 August 2001, in
      FBIS-CPP20010803000050; "Preliminary Discussion Regarding Organizing
      Fishing Craft for Sea Crossing Operations," *Jianchuan Zhishi* (Beijing), 01
      February 2002, in FBIS-CPP20020304000243; "PLA's Annual Military Exercises
      Focus on Forced Landing Drills," *Wen Wei Po* (Hong Kong), 23 September 2002,
      in FBIS-CPP20020923000029; Oliver August, "China to Rehearse 'Taiwan
      Invasion,'" *The Times,* London, 08 July 2004, at http://www.timesonline.co.uk/tol/
      news/world/article454188.ece (accessed 12 October 2009); Bao Daozu, "Dongshan
      Set for Military Exercise," *China Daily,* 13 July 2004, at http://www.highbeam.com/
      doc/1P2-8821314.html (accessed 10 October 2009); David G. Brown, "China-Taiwan
      Relations: Unproductive Military Posturing," at http://csis.org/files/media/csis/
      pubs/0403qchina_taiwan.pdf (accessed 10 October 2009). "Beijing Plans Showdown
      with Taiwan by Resuming Dongshan Drills," *Ming Pao* (Hong Kong), 02 October
      2007 (link no longer available), reported that the Dongshan exercise would be resumed
      in 2007, apparently as a deterrent move against Taiwan's president, Chen Shui-bian,
      but the exercise was not conducted.

83.   See, for instance, Zeng Bin et al., "Sword Coming Out of the Scabbard and
      Shows Its Sharpness," *Zhanshi Bao* (Guangzhou) 2, 16 September 2003, in
      FBIS-CPP20031027000241; "Fujian Military District to Conduct Maritime Logistic
      Replenishment Drill," *Wenweipo News,* 23 July 2004 (link no longer available); "Navy,
      Army Units Conduct Sea-Land Joint Exercises on 28 April," *Jiefangjun Bao,* 02
      June 2008, in OSC-CPP20080502710007; Jeff Chen, "Chinese Military Reinforces
      Training in Landing Operations," *Kanwa Asian Defense Review* 50 (Toronto),
      01–31 December 2008, 18, at http://www.kanwa.com/ekir/ (accessed 12 October
      2009). More general assessments of PLAN amphibious capabilities are provided in
      Xinhui, "Amphibious Warfare Capabilities of the PLA: An Assessment on Recent
      Modernizations," *ChinaDefense.com,* 07 December 2008, at http://www.china-defense.
      com/pla/plaamphops/plaamphops07.html (accessed 12 October 2009); and Andrew,
      "PLA's Mechanization and Informationization Come of Age."

84. Li Jianguo, "Keeping the Seas Safe," *Beijing Review*, 22–28 March 2007, at OSC-CPP20070403715045, reports that two PLAN frigates joined warships from Pakistan, Bangladesh, France, Great Britain, Italy, Malaysia, Turkey, and the United States in this exercise.

85. Gerard P. Yoest, late director of international affairs for the U.S. Coast Guard, provided this information to the author. Not connected with the annual sea and air rescue exercises (SAREX) is a 1987 sea and air rescue (SAR) agreement between China's Bureau of Harbor Superintendency (now called the Maritime Safety Administration) and the U.S. Coast Guard. Vietnam's coast guard operates as an agency of the Ministry of Defense, while those of China and the United States operate under nominally civilian ministries—the Ministry of Communications and the Department of Homeland Security, respectively. The Macao exercise is reported in "PRC, Macao, Hong Kong Hold Joint Marine Rescue Exercise near Shenzhen," *Xinhua*, 05 June 2000, in FBIS-CPP20000605000152. Also see "Xiamen Conducts Major Emergency Exercise," http://www.Sina.com, 30 November 2004 (link no longer available); "Hong Kong: Rescue Exercise Boosts Cooperation," http://news.gov.hk, 12 July 2006, in IPR Strategic Business Information Database, at http://www.highbeam.com/doc/1G1-148075023.html (accessed 11 October 2009); David L. Smart and Ray Mooney, "U.S., Hong Kong Join Forces as SAREX 2008 Draws to Close," 04 November 2008, at http://www.navy.mil/search/display.asp?story_id=40650 (accessed 11 October 2009); and Feng Yuan, Zhang Ran, and Zhang Tao, "New China's Largest Search and Rescue Exercise Was Successfully Held in the East China Sea," *Xinhua*, 04 September 2009, at http://www.sourcejuice.com/1252890/2009/09/04/New-China-largest-search-rescue-exercise-successfully-held-East/(accessed 11 October 2009).

86. Wu Shengli, quoted in the *Beijing Review*, 04 May 2009, in *China Brief* 9, no. 13 (24 June 2009), at http://www.jamestown.org/uploads/media/cb_009_15.pdf (accessed 05 October 2009). A compilation of recent PLA exercises with other nations is provided in "PLA-Foreign Military Exercises since 2000," at http://english.chinamil.com.cn 2008-02-13 (accessed 11 October 2009). Specific exercises are reported in Tang Ying and Chen Hui, "Navies of China, Australia, and New Zealand Conduct Joint Sea Search and Rescue Exercise," *Xinhua*, 02 October 2007, at http://english.peopledaily.com.cn/90001/90776/90883/6296081.html; also reported in Brendan Nicholson and Jonathan Pearlman, "Military Exercises with Australia, US Still on Table," *Sydney Morning Herald*, 04 September 2009, at http://www.smh.com.au/world/military-exercises-with-australia-us-still-on-table-20090903-fa1c.html (accessed 11 October 2009); Si Yanwen and Zhou Yongjun, "Joint Military-Civilian Maritime Search and Rescue Exercise Held Near Zhuhai City," *PLA Daily*, 10 July 2009, at http://eng.mod.gov.cn/MilitaryExercises/2009-07/10/content_4003698.htm (accessed 13 December

2009); "China, France Conduct Joint Naval Exercise in Mediterranean," *Xinhua*, 26 September 2007, at http://english.people.com.cn/90001/90777/6270983.html (accessed 11 October 2009); and "Chinese Navy to Attend Joint Military Exercise in Pakistan," *Xinhua*, 19 February 2009.

87. "PLA Navy Completes Highly Difficult Drills," *Jiefangjun Bao*, 10 January 2000, cited in *Zhongguo Tongxun She*, 10 January 2000, in FBIS-FTS20000112001752; and Zhang Yuqing and Zhang Junlong, "Five-Dimensional Confrontation in Exercise 'Lianhe-2008' in Bohai Gulf," *Xinhua*, 22 September 2008, in OSC-CPP20080822074019; also see Minnick, "China's Gator Navy Makes Marginal Strides."

88. Wu is quoted in "PRC Navy Head: Military Exercises Boost Combat Power," *Xinhua*, 15 April 2009, in OSC-CPP20090415074018. Significant ASW exercises are reported in "Ocean Observation Laser-Fluorescence Radar Test-Flown Successfully," *Chin. comMilitaryNews*, 26 November 2003, in VIC report, 27 November 2003 (site no longer available); Yan Runbo, Tan Jingchun, and Yang Fengjing, "Firsthand On-site Witness Report on the Navy's Continuous Heterotypic Anti-submarine Drill," *Zhongguo Qingnian Bao* (Beijing), 25 June 2005, in OSC-CPP20050627000021; "North China Sea Fleet's Anti-submarine Unit Conducts Search and Destroy Drills in Designated Waters," CCTV-7 Report, 10 April 2005, in OSC-FEA20051123013669; "PLA Destroyer's Development of Combat Effectiveness," *Jiefangjun Bao*, 03 December 2007, in OSC-CPP20071203710011; "South Sea Fleet Logistics Support Unit Improves Torpedo Testing," *Jiefangjun Bao*, 25 April 2008, in OSC-CPP20080425710006; and Zhang Xiaoqi, Dai Zongfeng, and Zhu Lifang, "Deep Sea Shark Hunting," *Jiefangjun Bao*, 23 March 2009, 1, in OSC-CPP20090323710005.

89. "The People's Navy," 41, reports an ideological extreme in a 1958 report that the East China Sea Fleet commander "respond[ed] to a call by the CPC Central Committee and the CMC to undergo training as a sailor on Ship 311 [and] wears a sailor uniform with a private's insignia." Bullard, *China's Political-Military Evolution*, 27, estimates that at the height of the Cultural Revolution, 70 percent of a soldier's time was devoted to nonmilitary activities; by 1984, 70 percent was devoted to military duties. See Heaton, "Professional Military Education in the People's Republic of China," 125, for a description of the ideological character of the PLA as either "Maoist" or "Dengist": Mao stressed the importance of men over machines and held up the PLA as the socialist model that embodied his thought; Deng's concept was described in 1979 by Defense Minister Xu Xiangqian as stressing the importance of expertise and "expert" taking precedence over "red."

90. Joffe, "The Military and China's New Politics," 37. If a "superpatriotism" has developed among PLA officers, it might engender feelings similar to the concept of defending the *patria* typical of Latin American militaries. "Patria" connotes the military's belief that

it alone understands and is responsible for preserving the nation's soul. Carrying the concept to its logical conclusion has led many Latin American militaries to denigrate, disobey, and even displace their nominal civilian masters. I have recently heard from some experienced U.S. China-watchers that this in fact is occurring.

91. Ibid.; see for instance, the 82 Army Day editorial in *Jiefangjun Bao*, 01 August 2009, in OSC-CPP20090801705003, 1, which emphasizes the "absolute leadership of the party." The quote is from the PLA chief political officer and is found in Li Jingpo, "Li Jinai Gives Lecture to the Personnel in the General Political Department," *Jiefangjun Bao*, 11 April 2009, in OSC-CPP20090411722021.

92. As early as 1995, Paltiel (in "PLA Allegiance on Parade: Civil-Military Relations in Transition," 795) pointed out that "some 95 percent of military leaders have had careers in the military only," a percentage that has almost certainly continued to increase.

93. Quoted in Swanson, *The Eighth Voyage of the Dragon*, 208, which also notes that PLA commissars have not typically been the political hacks of the early Soviet Navy, but experienced officers who are as professionally competent as the ship-commanding officers. My visits to PLAN ships between 1994 and 2008 indicate that the relationship between the operational commander and senior political officer is strongly affected by their personal rapport.

94. Author's discussion with the dean of academic affairs of the PLA NDU, May 2000. Jiang listed being qualified politically and competent militarily, and having a fine style of work, strict discipline, and adequate logistical support. "Fully Implementing CPC Central Strategic Decisions," *Jiefangjun Bao*, 10 May 2000, in FBIS-CPP20000510000035, states that "the Party Committee[s] . . . at all levels . . . have earnestly placed the work of resettling [the more than 1.5 million] demobilized military cadres in a prominent position . . . [and that] party organizations at all military levels should devote great efforts to accelerating measures for ideological and political work to help demobilized cadres." Finally, Joffe and David Finkelstein made these points in discussions with the author. The "three warfares" are discussed in the *Annual Report to Congress on the Military Power of the PRC* (Washington, D.C.: Department of Defense, 2009), ch. 3, at http://www.defenselink.mil/pubs/china.html (accessed 28 October 2009).

95. The PLA's continued sensitivity to political matters is indicated in Lu Yunzhong, "Thoroughly Implement the Principle of Strictly Administering the Party," *Jiefangjun Bao*, 7 June 2000, 6, in FBIS-CPP20000607000071, which chastises "senior leading cadres" for giving in to "the temptation of fame, wealth, position, money, and beautiful women" and developing "blunted ideals and convictions, wavering spiritual pillars, a distorted outlook on the world, life, and values, and a faded memory of the party's nature and purpose." Quote is from "Providing Strong Moral Support for Winning War," *Jiefangjun Bao*, 07 May 2000, in FBIS-CPP20000508000051.

96. Defense White Paper, 2008, sec. III. See Shambaugh, "China's Commander-in-Chief: Jiang Zemin and the PLA," 219, citing Jiang's attack on "the view that the PLA should be 'nationalized'"—that is, put under state control and separated from the CCP.

97. *China's Navy, 2007*, 63–64.

98. An interesting critique of PLA training is offered in Zheng Qin, "Carrying Forward the Causes Pioneered by Our Predecessors and Forging ahead into the Future: Innovations and Development of Army Military Training," *Jiefangjun Bao*, 13 May 2008, 6, in OSC-CPP200805123710008.

99. Jiang Yuanliu, "China's Master-Degree Captain Watches US Naval Exercise," *Jiefangjun Bao*, 22 October 2000, 5, in FBIS-CHI-98-316, citing Mao Zhenggong and Jia Xiaoguang, both senior captains. Although similar PLA observations are not available in open-source documents, the Guam exercise is reported in Bai Ruixue, "Interpreting US Military Exercise in Guam," *Xinhua*, 21 June 2006, in OSC-CPP20060621047001, which focuses on the buildup of U.S. military forces in the western Pacific; and Lin Zhiyuan (a senior official at the PLA's Academy of Military Science), "Positive Signs from Sino-US Military Exchanges," *Renmin Ribao* (Beijing), 27 June 2006, in OSC-CPP200606287. U.S. views are in "China Sends First-Ever Delegation to Observe U.S. Pacific Wargames," AP report, Shanghai, 20 June 2006; see other stories at http://www.pacom.mil/exercises/vs2006.

100. Analysis of eighteen significant PLA exercises by Dennis Blasko, December 2009, testimony before Congress.

101. Author's conversations with senior PLAN officers between 2000 and 2009; Blasko, "China Looks and Finds Its Military Wanting," *Defense News* (Washington, D.C.), 21 July 2009, citing "Outside View: Know the Enemy and Know Yourself," *China Daily*, 25 July 2008, at http://www.chinadaily.com.cn/cndy/208-07/25/content_6875515. htm. (accessed 13 September 2009).

102. Liu Nan and Li Yanlin, "Watch Officer, Hold Your Head up High," *Jiefangjun Bao*, 27 February 2009, 5, in OSC-CPP20090227710009; Qi Hongbing, Huang Yuping, and Zhong Kuirun, "Display Skill in the Depths of the Ocean," *Jiefangjun Bao*, 24 May 2009, 1, in OSC-CPP20090526702029, reflects this problem for enlisted personnel; officer training challenges are discussed in Li Hongbin and Liang Qingsong, "Composite Captains Need 'Composite' Training," *Renmin Haijun* (Beijing), 23 February 2009, 2, in OSC-CPP20090409478014.

103. Quoted in "We Will Build Larger Ships," *Xinhua*, 16 April 2009, at http://www. china-defense-mashup.com/?p=3279 (accessed 12 October 2009); and Li Zhihui, Quan Xiaoshu, Zhu Xudong, "Chinese Navy Sees Role Further Afield," *Xinhua*, 22 April 2009, at http://news.xinhuanet.com/english/2009-04/22/content_11233491. htm (accessed 12 October 2009).

Chapter 7. Doctrine and Operations in the PLAN

1. *Joint Staff Officer's Guide* 1997, 0-16.

2. Quoted in Blasko, *People's War in the 21st Century*, 1; also see Godwin, "Patterns of Doctrinal Change in the Chinese People's Liberation Army," 8.

3. Ren Xiangdong, "PLA Ground, Naval, and Air Units Implement New-Generation Combat Regulations," *Liaowang*, 07 June 19, 32–33, in FBIS-CHI-99-0629, 12 pp., contains the statements quoted in this section (site no longer available).

4. "Management of the Sea in the 21st Century. Whither the Chinese Navy?" *Modern Navy* (Beijing), 01 June 2007, 6–9, in OSC-CPP20070628436012, trans. Blasko. A good brief discussion of PLAN attention to "informatized" war at sea is Erickson, "PLA Navy Modernization."

5. These lists are from Kondapalli, "China's Naval Structure and Dynamics," 1097–1109.

6. Lanzit and Chen, "Integrating China's Air Forces into Maritime Strike," 1; Defense White Paper, 2006, at http://english.peopledaily.com.cn/whitepaper/defense2006/defense2006.html; and Defense White Paper, 2008, at http://news.xinhuanet.com/english/2009-01/20/content_10688124.htm (both accessed 13 November 2009).

7. Hans M. Kristensen, "Chinese Submarine Patrols Doubled in 2008," Federation of American Scientists, February 2009, at http://www.fas.org/blog/ssp/2009/02/patrols.php (accessed 04 November 2009), although the author fails to define "patrol."

8. "China's Military to Build Anti-ship Ballistic Missiles," *People's Daily*, 18 November 2009, at http://english.people.com.cn/90001/90776/90786/6816677.html (accessed 07 December 2009); Wang Jiaisuo, "Aircraft Carriers: Suggest You Keep Out of the Taiwan Strait," *Junshi Wenzhai* (Beijing), 01 April 2001, 58–59, in FBIS-CPP20020326000218; Xin Benjian, "United States Concerned over China's Anticarrier Strategy," *Huanqiu Shibao* (Beijing), 07 February 2003, in FBIS-CPP20030212000035; Liu Dingping, "How to Battle Aircraft Carriers in a Taiwan Strait War," *Junshi Wenzhai* (Beijing), 01 July 2004, 19–22, in FBIS-CPP20040722000215. The employment of ASBMs and the idea of "disabling rather than sinking" are discussed in Dong Shihong, "Targets, Hostile Ships," *Binggong Keji* (Xian), 01 August 2004, 24–30, in FBIS-CPP20041122000266; and Li Jie, "Is the Ballistic Missile a 'Silver Bullet' against Aircraft Carriers?" *Modern Navy*, February 2008, 42–44, trans. Lyle Goldstein and Nan Li, Newport, R.I.: Naval War College CMSI. A good overview of possible ASBM employment is Stokes, *China's Evolving Conventional Strategic Strike Capability*.

9. The second Marine brigade, organized in 1998–99, doubled the number of Marines available to the South Sea Fleet. That fleet does not by itself, however, possess sufficient amphibious lift to carry both brigades.

10. Wang Zudian (cited in Shen Hongchang, "A Rudimentary Exploration of 21st Century Naval Warfare," *Zhongguo Renmin Kexue*, no. 1, 20 February 1995, in FBIS-CHI-95-113, supplement), wrote, for instance, that "cruise missiles are the vanguard, aerial strength is the main power, and the ground, sea, air, space, and electromagnetism are integrated. *This will become a basic mode for the recent and future high-technology regional war*," the battlefield for which "will be a digitized battlefield" [emphasis added].

11. Dennis Blasko highlighted this to the author, noting the embarkation of media detachments on the ships deploying to the Gulf of Aden. It is also supported by Beijing's repeated reference to the UN resolutions under which its ships are operating, and the extensive political indoctrination of the crews. Also see Cole, "U.S.-China's Counterpiracy Cooperation in the Gulf of Aden."

12. Most notable are the Kilo-class submarines and *Sovremenny*-class destroyers armed with the potent Moskit cruise missiles, but also important is the nonequipment assistance, including the services of Russian engineers. China's indigenous military-industrial complex is improving rapidly, however.

13. Shi Yunsheng, cited in Huang, Chen, and Zhang, "China Enhances the Navy's Comprehensive Strength—Interview with Naval Commander VADM Shi Yunsheng," *Liaowang* (Beijing), no. 16, 19 April 1999, 13–15, in FBIS-CHI-99-0513, 13–15. Also see Zhang Wei, *Jianchuan Zhishi*, January 1997, 8–9, in FBIS-CST-97-006.

14. Finkelstein, "China's New Security Concept," 3, makes this point; U.S. Navy staff, *Undersea Warfare*, 13, notes that two salvos of two missiles each were launched simultaneously in this latest test; Holzer, "Study: U.S. Navy Must Go beyond *Aegis* Radar Era," 3, 36, discusses the post-Aegis program.

15. Colonel Theodore L. Gatchel, USMC (Ret.), noted these points to the author.

16. Cheung, *Fortifying China*, 237; a survey of China's practice (with good pictures) is in "Ships Taken Up from Trade (STUFT)," at http://www.globalsecurity.org/military/world/china/stuft.htm (accessed 28 November 2009). Also see Wan Xiaoyun, "Problems and Solutions for War Zone–wide Mobilization under High-Tech Conditions," *Zhanyi Houwin*, 705–6, cited in Bi, "Managing Taiwan Operations in the Twenty-first Century," 12. Also see "Fujian Mobilizes Civilian Vessels in Drills," *Fuzhou Fujian Ribao*, 16 July 1999, 2, in FBIS-CHI-99-0802, for a report on an exercise in which "more than 100 civilian vessels" conducted "mobilization and drills." Furthermore, the past several hundred years of warfare have demonstrated the difficulties of organizing and controlling a nation's merchant fleet, as evidenced by the Napoleonic wars, the American Civil War, and this century's two world wars. Even early U.S. efforts in Vietnam, 1964–68, showed how difficult it is to organize a large, disparate merchant marine force to support an overseas wartime effort (unpublished manuscript by John Prados, Washington, D.C., 1992).

17. It appears that the defense budget allocation process is no friendlier to PLAN amphibious forces than it is in any other country's navy. Troop-carrying ships, no matter how vital to the power projection mission, simply have neither the glamour nor the profit margin of nuclear-powered submarines or guided-missile destroyers. Hence, the PLAN is only slowly strengthening its amphibious warfare capability. The new LPD is described at http://www.globalsecurity.org/military/world/china/yuzhao.htm (accessed 13 November 2009).

18. Wan Xiaoyun, "Problems and Solutions for War Mobilization under High-Tech Conditions," 705–6; "Fujian Mobilizes Civilian Vessels in Drills," *Fuzhou Fujian Ribao*, 16 July 1999, 2, in FBIS-CHI-99-0802.

19. Quoted in Ahrari, "China's Naval Forces Look to Extend Their Blue-Water Reach," 34. UNCLOS 1982 describes the rights of innocent passage. Valencia and Van Dyke, "Vietnam's National Interests and the Law of the Sea," 233, elaborates on China's interpretation of this article, which is shared by thirty-eight other nations, including the Scandinavian countries.

20. Logistics facilities have been built on some of the Spratlys. Sharpe, *Jane's Fighting Ships: 2000–2001*, 138ff., notes that the PLAN currently has five modern replenishment-at-sea ships plus a dozen or more smaller cargo (dry or liquid) carriers in the South China Sea Fleet that are not capable of underway replenishment. *Jiefangjun Bao*, 24 October 1996, 1, in FBIS-CHI-96-210, reports that this major exercise included joint operations among "the three armed services and the issues of coordination and supplies," and "involved sea-crossing, changing ships, and ship formations," with the troops fighting "an integrated war and [attacking] the enemy from the three dimensions." Also see Zhang Zenan's interview with Senior Captain Lin Shuangqiao, "Developing and Expanding Chinese Landing Ship Forces," *Jianchuan Zhishi* [Naval and Merchant Ships], 06 January 1997, 10–11, in FBIS-CHI-97-051; Lin is identified as the "army's chief of staff for naval operation" and an amphibious warfare expert. He describes the "vertical assault" aspect of amphibious landings and claims that the PLA demonstrated this capability in October 1995 and March 1996 exercises near Taiwan.

21. Huang, "Transformation and Refinement of Chinese Military Doctrine," 8–9.

22. Wang Zudian [identified as a Space Technology Information Research Institute researcher], "The Offensive and Defensive of High-Technology Arms Equipment," *Xinhua*, 24 May 1999, in FBIS- CHI-1999-0526.

23. Major General Chen Mingduan, "On Several Principles Which Should Be Followed in Maritime Militia Guerrilla Warfare," *Beijing Guofang*, no. 11 (15 November 1997), in FBIS-CHI-98-126. The 2009 incidents are discussed in "Pentagon Says Chinese Vessels Harassed U.S. Ship," *CNNPolitics.com*, at http://www.cnn.com/2009/POLITICS/03/09/us.navy.china/index.html (accessed 06 November 2009); and

"Foreign Ministry Spokesperson Ma Zhaoxu's Remarks on the US Surveillance Ship's Activities in Chinese Exclusive Economic Zone in the Yellow Sea," Chinese Foreign Ministry, 07 May 2009, at http://www.fmcoprc.gov.hk/eng/zgwjsw/t560950.htm (accessed 06 November 2009).

24. "China: Submarine Launched Weapons," Federation of American Scientists, at http://www.fas.org/nuke/guide/china/slbm/index.html (accessed 13 November 2009). Also see *Worldwide Submarine Challenges, 1996,* 27. The PLAN's employment scheme for its new FBM is not known; if homeported at the new Sanya facility on Hainan Island, it could be deployed on patrols in the Bo or Yellow Sea or in the open Pacific; the JL-2's range is not long enough for FBMs in a bastion within the South China Sea to range the continental United States.

25. Coordinated sea- and shore-based air operations were theorized by the Royal Navy immediately following World War I and were employed inefficiently by the United States during the Korean and Vietnam conflicts, but more effectively during the Persian Gulf War and the Kosovo campaign.

26. Author's conversations with two PLA lieutenant generals and other senior PLAN officers in May 1996. An aircraft carrier routinely conducts flight operations only twelve hours a day, primarily because it carries just one crew of flight deck personnel, who must rest after twelve hours of operations. Two carriers on station means that flight operations can be conducted twenty-four hours a day. The acquisition of air-capable ships by Thailand, South Korea, and Japan must also be galling to PLAN carrier advocates.

27. Author's conversation with PLAAF Air Division commander, May 2000; Liu and Sha, "Air Unit of the Navy Succeeds in Air Refueling," *Zhongguo Qingnian Bao,* 29 April 2000, in FBIS-CPP20000501000044, reports the PLANAF's first successful air-to-air refueling evolution on 26 April 2000.

28. Israel was apparently pressured by the United States to cancel the sale; the crash is reported in Joseph Kahn, "Crash of Chinese Surveillance Plane Hurts Effort on Warning System," *New York Times,* 07 June 2008, at http://www.nytimes.com/2006/06/07/world/asia/07china.html (accessed 04 November 2009).

29. Lanzit and Chen, "Integrating China's Air Forces into Maritime Strike," 9–10, 17–18; Kenneth Allen, interview with the author. Allen, Krumel, and Pollack, *China's Air Force Enters the 21st Century,* 120–33, discusses previous PLAAF training shortfalls.

30. Lanzit and Chen, "Integrating China's Air Forces into Maritime Strike," 19, 22–24, also notes that the PLA describes as "joint" exercises that the United States would certainly classify as single service.

31. Officers arguing against acquiring carriers would likely contend that maritime air power can be more efficiently provided by land-based forces.

32. The Allies' experience defending SLOCs against German submarines in two world wars, especially the American efforts *in U.S. coastal waters* in 1942, demonstrates the difficulty of this task.

33. As a PLAN mission, the following analysis from Collins and Murray, "No Oil for the Lamps of China?" n. 10, is worth repeating in full: "The distance from the PLAN's submarine base on the south coast of Hainan Island to the Straits of Malacca is approximately 1,200 nautical miles. PLAN diesel submarines can travel submerged quietly at a maximum speed of approximately four knots without rapidly depleting their batteries. Assuming, then, that they can travel nearly one hundred nautical miles a day, they will require twelve days to travel from their base to the Straits of Malacca. After arriving, PLAN submarines would have to operate in and around the very crowded and shallow waters of the straits against the combined, formidable, and concentrated antisubmarine efforts of the blockading force. Success for a PLAN submarine in such an environment is far from assured." But some strategists have used the UNCLOS, ratified by China in 1996, as rationale for including "military control of the seas [as] legitimate maritime economic activities." Li Jie and Xu Shiming, "The UN Law of the Sea Treaty and the New Naval Mission," *Hsien-Tai Chun-Shih* (Beijing), February 1997, quoted in Hugar, "The Sea Dragon Network," 73.

34. This quote and data in this section are from the excellent paper by Horta, "China Takes to the Sea." For an earlier description of China's use of naval diplomacy, see Allen and McVadon, *China's Foreign Military Relations,* available at http://www.stimson. org/china/pdf/chinmil.pdf (accessed 01 November 2009). An apparently complete list of foreign port visits by PLAN ships is "Major Overseas Visits of PLA Naval Ships," *China Military Online,* n.d., at http://english.chinamil.com.cn/site2/special-reports/2008-03/12/content_1737716.htm (accessed 10 November 2009).

35. See Storey, "Calming Waters in Maritime Southeast Asia"; and *Nimbus* (Singapore): RSIS, Q3/09, at http://www.rsis.edu.sg/research/maritime/Nimbus0903.pdf (accessed 01 November 2009). The Gulf of Aden data are in Stella Pende, "Pirates, Inc.," *Panorama* (Milan), 19 March 2009, 38, in OSC-EUP20090315467001.

36. See William Foreman, "China Targets Pirates in Groundbreaking Mission," AP report, 26 December 2008, at http://abcnews.go.com/International/wireStory?id=6529170 (accessed 01 November 2009); "Chinese Flotilla Sails to Relieve Ships in Somalia Escort Mission," *Xinhua,* 02 April 2009, at http://news.xinhuanet.com/english/2009-04/02/content_11118341.htm (accessed 01 November 2009); "4th China Fleet to Sail for Anti-piracy Mission," *China Daily,* 29 October 2009, at http://www.chinadaily. com.cn/china/2009-10/29/content_8869852.htm (accessed 01 November 2009).

37. "Navies Seek Better Ways to Fight Pirates," *China Daily*, 06 November 2009, at http://www.chinadaily.com.cn/china/2009-11/06/content_8921032.htm (accessed 08 November 2009). Also see Zhu Da and Yu Zifu, "Commander of USCTF 151 Visits *Zhoushan* Warship," Ministry of National Defense, PRC, 03 November 2009, at http://eng.mod.gov.cn/DefenseNews/2009-11/03/content_4100788.htm (accessed 09 November 2009); and Matthew A. Hepburn, "Chinese Admiral Visit Coalition Warship," Navy News Service, 25 November 2009, at http://www.navy.mil/search/display.asp?story_id=49865 (accessed 28 November 2009).

38. Author's discussions with senior U.S. naval officers in August 2009; comments by General Xu Caihou, vice chairman of China's Central Military Commission, 26 October 2009. Escort data are in Bao Daozu, "Navy Escorts Four Vessels on Day One," *Xinhua*, 07 January 2009, at http://www.chinadaily.com.cn/china/2009-01/07/content_7373037.htm; "Chinese Navy Completes Fifteen Escort Missions," *Xinhua*, at http://www.chinadaily.com.cn/china/2009-02/06/content_7453163.htm; "Chinese Naval Ships Return from Escort Mission," *Xinhua*, 28 April 2009, at http://www.chinadaily.com.cn/china/2009-04/28/content_7725100.htm (all accessed 01 November 2009); and Zhu Da and Yu Zhu, "Third Chinese Naval Escort Task Force Creates New Record in Escort Numbers in One Month," PRC Ministry of Defense report, 02 November 2009, at http://eng.china.mil.com.cn/news-channels/china-military-news/2009-11/02/content_4072984.htm (accessed 09 November 2009).

39. Unnamed "experts" quoted in Li Zhihui, Quan Xiaoshu, and Zhu Xudong, "Chinese Navy Sees Role Further Afield," *Xinhua*, 22 April 2009, at http://news.xinhuanet.com/english/2009-04/22/content_11233491.htm (accessed 13 November 2009).

40. Yang Zhongmin, "Firmly Enhance Capabilities for Carrying Out Diversified Military Tasks," *Jiefangjun Bao*, 16 September 2008, 6, in OSC-CPP20080916710007; Huang Wenfen and Liu Feng'an, "PLA Constructs MOOTW Arms Force System," *PLA Daily*, 14 May 2009, at http://eng.mod.gov.cn/Database/MOOTW/2009-05/14/content_ _3100858.htm (accessed 08 November 2009). The hospital ship mission is described in "*Peace Ark* Hospital Ship Makes Rounds of Visits to Island," *PLA Daily*, 30 October 2009, at http://eng.chinamil.com.cn/news-channels/china-military-news/2009-10/30/content_4071506.htm (accessed 09 November 2009).

41. Baker, *The Naval Institute Guide to Combat Fleets of the World, 2000–2001*, 584ff.; Sharpe, *Jane's Fighting Ships: 2000–2001*, 554ff.; and *Strategic Survey 1999–2000*, agree on the declining state of Russia's Pacific fleet.

42. Madeiros et al., *Pacific Currents*, 51.

43. The author's participation in meetings with Chen Shui-bian in January 2002 and Ma Ying-jeou in April 2008.

44. *Armaments, Disarmament and International Security,* 1998, 193, reports that while "military expenditure in the ASEAN countries increased by an aggregate of 52 percent over the nine-year period 1988–96," Malaysia has cut its military expenditures by at least 5 percent, Thailand by 30 percent, and South Korea by 4.1 percent.

45. Singapore Armed Forces DCOS, May 1999 interview with the author.

46. Sengupta, "RMN Receives First FS-2000 Frigate," 23, reports Malaysia's commissioning of two new British-built *Yarrow*-class guided-missile frigates in October and November 1999. Wertheim, *The Naval Institute Guide to Combat Fleets of the World,* 453, includes two operational and one training submarine, all acquired from France.

47. Army chief of staff General Chokedai Hongthong (quoted in "Thai-U.S. Military Exercises to Take Place More on Land," *Bangkok Post,* 10 April 1999, in FBIS-EAS-99-0412), stated that the eighteenth Cobra Gold exercise would include Thai-U.S. naval exercises in the Gulf of Thailand because "Thailand had received bigger U.S. financial assistance to organize this year's war games." Cobra Gold was still an important exercise in 2009, involving participation from Singapore, Japan, Indonesia, in addition to the United States and Thailand; China sent observers, as did Australia, Canada, France, Germany, India, Italy, Mongolia, the Philippines, the United Kingdom, and Vietnam. See Sung Jung-ki, "South Korean Marines to Join Cobra Gold Exercise," *Defense News,* 06 May 2009, at http://www.defensenews.com/story.php?i=4076825 (accessed 30 October 2009); and Kevin Baron, "Cobra Gold 2009," *Stars and Stripes,* 16 February 2009, at http://www.stripes.com/article.asp?section=104&article=60743 (accessed 30 October 2009).

48. Nolt, "The China-Taiwan Military Balance," 13, notes that these ships were so poorly constructed that Thailand had to rebuild their propulsion plants; Gardiner, *Conway's All the World's Fighting Ships, 1947–1995,* 59, reports that the Chinese frigates sold to Thailand "lack truly watertight doors and damage control equipment, and their sensors and weapons are largely obsolete."

49. "Chuan to Discuss Military Cooperation with China," *The Nation* (Bangkok), 23 April 1999, in FBIS-EAS-99-0422.

50. Wassana Nanaum, "Thai Navy Harriers Grounded Due to Spare Parts Problem," *Bangkok Post,* 01 June 1999, in FBIS-EAS-99-0601, reported that the carrier's aircraft were grounded until Thailand received twenty Harrier engines from the United States. "Country Report," November 1999, 12, reports the value of these engines as $84.5 million.

51. "Anonymous Indian Embassy official in Washington," quoted in Barber, "Indian Navy Exercises Seen Apt to Irk Beijing."

52. Information about *Vikrant* is at http://www.bharat-rakshak.com/NAVY/Vikrant.html (accessed 19 October 2009); the problems with the Russian ship are discussed

in "INS *Vikramaditya*: Waiting for Gorshkov," *Defense Industry Daily,* 17 August 2009, at http://www.defenseindustrydaily.com/ins-vikramaditya-may-hit-delay-cost-increases-03283/ (accessed 19 October 2009), which reports that the original 2008 delivery date has slipped to 2012, while the modernization cost, not including an air group of twelve MiG-29Ks, has reportedly risen from US$947 million to almost US$3 billion.

53. "India, China Reiterate Resolve to Maintain Border Peace," *Hindustan Times* (New Delhi), 05 April 2000. Indian External Affairs Minister Singh, during a November 1999 visit to Beijing, agreed with his hosts that there were no serious security problems between their two countries: see Tan Hongwei, "China Strives to Build a Fine Peripheral Environment," *Zhengguo Xinwen She* (Beijing), 05 September 1999, in FBIS-CHI-99-1023, for Singh's statement that India "does not regard China as a threat"—a statement that should be regarded with some skepticism. Sakhuja, at http://www.jamestown.org/single/?no_cache=1&tx_ttnews%5Btt_news%5D=35692 (accessed 28 November 2009), underlines New Delhi's lack of enthusiasm for Chinese participation in such organizations as the Indian Ocean Naval Symposium and the India-Brazil–South Africa trilateral grouping.

54. Simon Robinson, "Arming India: Can the U.S. Get a Piece?" *Time,* 20 February 2008, at http://www.time.com/time/world/article/0,8599,1714760,00.html (accessed 13 November 2009); and Lydia Polgreen, "India Launches Nuclear Submarine," *New York Times,* 26 July 2009, at http://www.nytimes.com/2009/07/27/world/asia/27india. html (accessed 19 October 2009). Bappa Majumdar, "India Launches First Nuclear-Powered Submarine," Reuters, New Delhi, 26 July 2009, at http://www.reuters.com/ article/worldNews/idUSTRE56P0CP20090726 (accessed 28 November 2009), reported that INS *Arihant* is the first of five boats to be built.

55. Scobell, "Show of Force," 129, presents the well-reasoned conclusion that "the seizure of Taiwan is now a central scenario for the PLA," with a missile assault the most likely mode of attack; a former U.S. naval attaché to China described PLAN strategists and planners as "completely focused on the Taiwan mission," a judgment with which the author agrees based on visits to the Academy of Military Science and the National Defense University in Beijing. Also see Hu Fan (research fellow at PLA NDU's Institute of Strategic Studies), writing in *Zhongguo Pinglun* and quoted in "Mainland Steps Up Preparations for Military Struggle against Taiwan," *Zhongguo Tongxun She,* 01 June 2000, in FBIS-CPP20000601000126.

56. The U.S. Marine Corps arrives at this ratio by assuming that a successful ground operation requires the attacker to have a three-to-one advantage over the defender; an amphibious assault requires an additional two for the five-to-one ratio so enough troops are available to hold the beachhead while the main body attacks inland. Yuan

Lin, "Probing Capability of Taiwan's ABMs," *Kuang-chiao ching,* no. 311, 16 August 1998, p. 61, cited in June Teufel Dreyer, "The PLA and the Taiwan Strait," *Taiwan Security Research,* July 1999, n. 24, at http://www.taiwansecurity.org/IS/Dreyer-The-PLA-and-the-Taiwan-Strait.htm (accessed 07 March 2010), argues unconvincingly that a two-to-one ratio will be sufficient.

57. See Coakley and Leighton, *Global Logistics and Strategy: 1943–1945,* 406–15, for a detailed discussion of the difficulties associated with an amphibious assault on and capture of the island.

58. Author's interview with U.S. Navy Meteorological Service officers, Pentagon, August 1999. See McVadon, "PRC Exercises, Doctrine and Tactics toward Taiwan," for a comprehensive discussion of this subject.

59. See, for instance, discussion of a "thirty-six-hour war" in Wen Jen, "PLA Deliberates Military Tactics against Taiwan," *Tai Yang Pao* (Hong Kong), 05 June 2000, in FBIS-CPP20000605000009.

60. "Four kinds of naval blockades" are identified in Gao Hongyan, "A Chat on Naval Blockade Warfare," *Hsien-Tai Chun-Shir* (Hong Kong), 05 January 2003, 54–55, in FBIS-CPP20030127000191; but more useful is Erickson, Goldstein, and Murray, "Chinese Mine Warfare," at http://www.navy.mil/navydata/cno/n87/usw/issue_33/china.html (accessed 02 November 2009), which presents a comprehensive view of the PLAN's mine warfare doctrine. The most comprehensive (but in the author's view unconvincing) study of China's ability to employ its missiles to render Taiwan's airfields inoperative is Shlapak et al., *A Question of Balance,* at http://www.rand.org/pubs/monographs/2009/RAND_MG888.pdf (accessed 05 December 2009).

61. See Michael Chase, "Chinese Land Attack Cruise Missile Developments," for a current description of China's missile program. Taiwan's ABM defenses might further decrease M-9 and M-11 effectiveness, but Shlapak paints a starker picture of the effectiveness of China's ballistic missiles in an anti-Taiwan scenario.

62. The will demonstrated by the people of the United Kingdom during World War II may be most instructive, but that observed in the populations of Germany, Japan, the Soviet Union, and ironically China during that war also demonstrate the ability of human will to withstand even horrific onslaughts.

63. *The Science of Military Strategy* (Beijing: Military Science Publishing House, 2005), 426, cited by Blasko in commenting on Chen Hui and Wang Jingguo, "Promoting the Vigorous Defense Miltiary Strategy," *Liaowang* (Beijing), no. 30, 28 July 2008, 22–23, in OSC-CPP20080804710013.

64. Author's conversations with senior U.S. naval officers, August 2009; "Naval Leaders Meet to Coordinate Counterpiracy Efforts," Navy News Service, 27 May 2009, at http://www.navy.mil/search/display.asp?story_id=45681 (accessed 18 November 2009).

Chapter 8. China's Maritime Strategy

1. Lieutenant General Mi Zhenyu, "A Reflection on Geographic Strategy," *Zhongguo Junshi Kexue* (Beijing), no. 1, February 1998, 6–14, in FBIS-CHI-98-208.

2. Quan Jinfu, "The Innovations and Development of the Chinese Navy's Strategy Theory in the New Century," Naval Command Academy paper published in the *Nanjing Journal of PLA Nanjing Institute of Politics*, 03 March 2004, 81–85, in OSC-CPP20071012436001, brought to the author's attention by Eric A. McVadon. See Erickson and Goldstein, "Gunboats for China's New 'Grand Canals'?" 49–50, for a discussion of PLAN interest in Mahan.

3. *PLAN Encyclopedia* (Beijing, 1999), trans. senior U.S. analyst. Mahan is the most famous writer on maritime strategy; see Sumida, *Inventing Grand Strategy and Teaching Command: The Classic Works of Alfred Thayer Mahan Reconsidered*, for a provocative analysis of his theories and impact. Corbett agrees more than he disagrees with Mahan, but the former's focus on the navy assisting the army to project national influence against foreign shores makes him more relevant to current PLAN development. Hill, *Maritime Strategy for Medium Powers*, 229, delineates five indicators of "sea dependence," all of which apply to China: seagoing trade, fish catches, size of merchant marine, ship building and repairing, and the offshore zone.

4. This list is a variation on the seventeen points delineated in Rosenberg, "Process: The Realities of Formulating Modern Naval Strategy," 150ff.

5. Gray, "Seapower and Landpower," 4, 3; also see Gray, *Explorations in Strategy*, 27.

6. Beijing's unhappiness with the present international environment is discussed in Finkelstein's interesting "China's New Security Concept."

7. Godwin, "Changing Concepts of Doctrine, Strategy, and Operations in the People's Liberation Army 1978–87"; Godwin, "From Continent to Periphery," 4.

8. Lenin, cited in Watson, "The Evolution of Soviet Naval Strategy," 115.

9. Muller, *China's Emergence as a Maritime Power*, 13; about two thousand former Republic of China naval personnel who defected to the communist regime in 1949 formed the core of the new PLAN.

10. Ibid., 16.

11. Ibid., 15; Swanson, *The Eighth Voyage of the Dragon*, 194, also notes that Xiao had attended the same school as Mao, in Changsha. Yang, "From a Navy in Blue towards a Blue Water Navy," 4, states that more than a hundred PLA officers were sent to study at the Voroshilov Naval Institute in 1951, while 275 officers studied with the Soviet submarine squadron at Lushun, on the Liaotung Peninsula.

12. Kondapalli, "China's Naval Strategy," 2038.

13. See Lewis and Xue, *China's Strategic Seapower*, 206ff.

14. Vertzberber, *China's Southwestern Strategy*, 144; Sharpe, *Jane's Fighting Ships: 1995–96*, 114: China built at least one Xia-class fleet ballistic missile submarine, patterned on the U.S. *George Washington*/Soviet Hotel class.

15. Quoted in McGruther, *The Evolving Soviet Navy*, 47–48, 66–67.

16. Huang, "The Chinese Navy's Offshore Active Defense Strategy," 13.

17. Quoted in Hahn, "PRC Policy in Maritime Asia," 20.

18. Quoted in Hahn, "China: Third Ranking Maritime Power—and Growing," 47. The "island chain" theory is actually an American concept, most famously discussed by Secretary of State Dean Acheson in a speech in January 1950, but originating in a 1948 Joint Chiefs of Staff study that defined a U.S. defensive perimeter running from the Aleutian Islands south through Japan, Taiwan, and the Philippines. Chinese analysts give the United States credit for the concept; see, for instance, the description of America's "three rings of encirclement around China" in Qing Tong, "2002: Focus on Guam," *Kuang Chiao Ching* (Hong Kong), no. 2 (16 October 2002), 48, in FBIS-CPP20021018000075.

19. See Jencks, "The PRC's Military and Security Policy in the Post–Cold War Era," 74, about a 1989 study ordered by Liu, *Balanced Development of the Navy in the Year 2000*, which called for a strategy of "offshore defense." Former PLAN commander Admiral Shi Yunsheng credited former President Jiang Zemin with originating this phrase, in "Jiang Made the Final Decision on Adopting Offshore Defense Strategy," *Tung Fang Jih Pao* (Hong Kong), 24 August 2001, in FBIS-CPP20010824000062.

20. See Huang, "Chinese Maritime Modernization and Its Security Implications," 225ff., for this discussion. Continued Maoist influence is discussed in Blasko, "A New PLA Force Structure," 260. A variation on the island chain designation is that of engagement zones, very similar to the system adopted by the Soviet Navy during the Cold War; for instance, Lou Douzi, "Looking at Navy and Air Force Dispositions Following Establishment Restructuring," *Jiefangjun Bao*, 14 July 2004, in FBIS-CPP20040715000074, discusses "three separate layers" of PLAN disposition.

21. Yuan, "China's Defense Modernization," 70; and Huang, "The Chinese Navy's Offshore Active Defense Strategy," 119, use the two estimates, respectively. Also see Downing, "China's Evolving Maritime Strategy, Part 1," 130; and Huang, "Chinese Maritime Modernization and Its Security Implications," 230.

22. Cited in Chen and Chai, "A Study of the Evolving PRC Naval Strategy," FBIS-CHI-97-329. Also see Huang, "The Chinese Navy's Offshore Active Defense Strategy," 16ff., for a good discussion of the first and second island chains.

23. Wylie, *Military Strategy*, 49; also see Winnefeld, *Joint Air Operations*, 66: "The soldier shapes and exploits his environment; the sailor must adjust to it."

24. Downing, "China's Evolving Maritime Strategy, Part 2," 186–91. Also see Kondapalli, "China's Naval Strategy," 2042. Nan Li, "The PLA's Evolving Warfighting Doctrine, Strategy and Tactics, 1985–95," disagrees with the Soviet analogy, instead crediting Liu's concept to PLA strategists' interior and exterior lines—a view I do not find convincing, but see his excellent paper "China's Evolving Naval Strategy," EIA Background Brief no. 343, 26 July 2007, at http://www.eai.nus.edu.sg/BB343.pdf (accessed 05 December 2009).

25. See Erickson and Mikolay, "Welcome China to the Fight against Pirates"; and Rear Admiral Zhang Deshun, quoted in "Chinese Navy's Anti-piracy Escorts Not a Short-Term Mission," *Xinhua*, 11 March 2009, at http://english.people.com.cn/90001/90776/90785/6611994.html (accessed 06 November 2009). Several Chinese analysts have discussed the importance of China being able to control the first island chain; see, for instance, "The Island Chains, China's Navy," *Modern Navy* (Beijing), 15 January 2008, in OSC-CPP20080103436010, which focuses on Taiwan and Guam as the "key points" in the island chain constraining China. The most comprehensive discussion of Beijing's strategic reasons for reuniting Taiwan with the mainland is Wachman, *Why Taiwan?* Dennis Blasko pointed out the 2006 Defense White Paper timeline.

26. Downing, "China's Evolving Maritime Strategy, Part 2," 191.

27. Three ships are normally required if one is to be on patrol at all times, although an SSBN armed with a missile capable of hitting its target without going very far to sea (e.g., the Russian Typhoon-class submarine) would not need this two-ship "backup."

28. Quoted in Watson, "The Evolution of Soviet Naval Strategy," 120.

29. Ping Kefu, "Development Strategy for Chinese Navy in 21st Century," *Jianchuan Zhishi*, no. 8, August 1994, 2–3, in FBIS-CST-96-014, 34-37.

30. Hu Jintao, for example, in "China's Hu Calls for Powerful, Combat-Ready Navy," *Washington Post*, 27 December 2006, at http://www.washingtonpost.com/wp-dyn/content/article/2006/12/27/AR2006122701888.html (accessed 06 November 2009); and "Navy Admiral: China to Develop Sophisticated Marine Weapon Systems," *Xinhua*, 15 April 2009, at http://news.xinhuanet.com/english/2009-04/15/content_11191749.htm (accessed 06 November 2009).

31. Quoted in You Ji, "Test Case," 379.

32. Quoted in Jun Zhan, "China Goes to the Blue Waters," 191.

33. Quoted in Huang Caihong, "Witnessing Maritime Exercise of the Chinese Navy," *Liaowang*, no. 45, 06 November 1995, in FBIS-CHI-95-235.

34. The guidelines are discussed at http://www.defense.gov/transcripts/transcript.aspx?transcriptid=1057 (accessed 06 December 2009).

35. This quote is from "PRC Scholar Views Prospects for Sino-Russian-US Cooperation in Central Asia," *Zhanlue Yu Guanli* (Beijing), no. 2, 01 March 2004, 34–107, in OSC-CPP20040420000264; also see Finkelstein, "China's National Military Strategy," 93, 115–17. East Sea Fleet responsibilities are discussed in Cao Zhi and Yang Zhiwang, "Interview with VADM Yang Yushu, East Sea Fleet Commander," *Xinhua,* 26 March 1997, in FBIS-CHI-97-085, which quotes Yang as stating that "the Navy serves as an important window of the Chinese military and is an important part of China's military diplomacy." The Gulf of Aden deployments have drawn primarily on South Sea Fleet ships, however.

36. Liu is quoted in Garver, "China's Push through the South China Sea," 1022–23. Also see the comprehensive discussion of the South China Sea situation in Fravel, *Strong Borders, Secure Nation.*

37. Barber, "Indian Navy Exercises Seen Apt to Irk Beijing," 1. "Intelligence," *Far Eastern Economic Review,* 20 April 2000, 4, reports that the Vietnamese Navy's deputy chief, Do Xuan Co, was exploring the possibility of repairing or even building ships in Indian shipyards.

38. James Griswold and Rick Parker, "Counter Narcotics: Burma, China, and Laos," 6–8, discuss the flow of illegal drugs from Burma and on p. 15 discuss China's response. China's investments and strategic interests in Burma are discussed in Sudha Ramachandran, "Yangon Still under Beijing's Thumb," 11 February 2005, *Asia Times,* at http://www.atimes.com/atimes/Southeast_Asia/GB11Ae01.html (accessed 06 November 2009); Josh Kurlantzk, "China, Burma, Sudan: Convincing Argument," *New Republic Online,* 11 May 2006, at http://www.carnegieendowment.org/publica tions/index.cfm?fa=view&id=18329 (accessed 06 November 2009); Tyler Chapman, "In Burma, China's Presence Grows," 05 May 2009, *RadioFreeAsia,* at http://www. rfa.org/english/blog/burma_diary/china-in-burma-04282009113356.html (accessed 06 November 2009); and Tim Johnson, "China Urges Burma to Bridle Ethnic Militia Uprising at Border," 29 August 2009, at http://www.washingtonpost.com/wp-dyn/ content/article/2009/08/28/AR2009082803764.html (accessed 06 November 2009).

39. Baker, *The Naval Institute Guide to Combat Fleets of the World, 2000–2001,* 475. Also see Brooke, "The Armed Forces of Myanmar," 14; "Myanmar's Armed Forces and Their Ongoing Campaigns," 11; and "Navy Relocating Donkyun Villagers for China-Burma Joint Military Exercises in July, August in Coastal Region," *Oslo Democratic Voice of Burma,* 01 July 2000, in FBIS-SEP20000703000062. "Burma, China to Hold Joint Military Exercises in July, August in Coastal Region," in FBIS-SEP20000703000034, reports the forcible removal of villagers to clear an exercise area for "joint military exercises" involving "planes, warships, naval vessels and Army officers from" the PLA.

40. See, for instance, Banerjee, "China: Worrying Approach," 71; Ray-Choudhury, "Trends in Naval Power in South Asia." Jencks, "The PRC's Military and Security Policy in the Post–Cold War Era," 89, discusses the contradictory reports that have been made about the military character of this construction. It must be noted that it is Indian authors who make the most extreme claims of Chinese intrusion into Burma. Senior PLA, Taiwan, and U.S. officers interviewed by the author and others maintain that relatively minor technical assistance and training by a small number of PLAN personnel is the most that is occurring. Also see Brooke, "Myanmar's Armed Forces and Their Ongoing Campaigns," 11; and Opall-Rome, "China Moves Roil Region," 1.

41. "China, Myanmar Issue Joint Statement," at http://www.china.org.cn/English.News/Politics/0606/22.htm (accessed 06 June 2000). Saritdet Marukatat and Bhanravee Tansugbhapol, "Mekong River Navigation Accord Signing Slated for March," *Bangkok Post,* 27 February 2000, in FBIS-SEP20000228000017, further explains one of these regional agreements, which aims to free up navigation on the Mekong River by China, Burma, Thailand, and Laos.

42. Erickson and Goldstein, "Gunboats for China's New 'Grand Canals'?" 51; and Cole, *Sea Lanes and Pipelines,* discuss China's economic and naval issues and energy requirements. The U.S. Department of Defense, in its 2008 report on the PLA (fig. 3, p. 12), simply identified as "China's Critical Sea Lanes" the Straits of Lombok, Sunda, Singapore, Malacca, Hormuz, and Bab el-Mandeb.

43. See, for instance, Si Yanwne and Chen Wanjun, "Navy to Develop More High-Tech Equipment," *Jiefangjun Bao,* 09 June 1999 in FBIS-CHI-99-0611, citing General Cao Gangchuan, director of the General Armaments Department, that "it is necessary to put [Navy] armament development in a prominent position of army building . . . increase armaments' scientific and technological contents; and improve the quality and speed of armament development"; and *Xinhua,* 10 June 1999, in FBIS-CHI-99-0609, citing Cao that "the Navy's rapid reaction capacity, emergency field repair ability and defense readiness must also be improved."

44. See Lewis and Xue, "China's Search for a Modern Air Force," 10, for Deng Xiaoping's statement that "the Army and the Navy both need air cover. . . . Without air cover, winning a naval battle is also out of the question."

45. One former U.S. defense attaché in Beijing stated that the PLAN and PLAAF have been receiving most of the recent PLA modernization funding—a common observation among observers of China's military. Lewis and Xue, "China's Search for a Modern Air Force," 11, claims that the 1985 strategic shift to nonnuclear war scenarios gave the Air Force and the Navy "pride of place" within the PLA. Also see Huang, "The Chinese Navy's Offshore Active Defense Strategy," 9 (table 1), for the estimate that 32.7 percent of the PLA's 1993 budget was allocated to the PLAN.

46. Quoted in *Xinhua*, 21 April 1999, in FBIS-CHI-99-0421.

47. Perhaps Shi was acknowledging the limits within which he had to operate: the United States was able to maintain a task force off the coast of West Africa for *seven months* in 1990–91 before finally evacuating civilians from strife-torn Liberia (pointed out in Till, "Maritime Strategy in the Twenty-first Century," 193). A PLA view of Internet warfare is provided in in Jia Xiaowei, "Pay Close Attention to Network Warfare Which Has Quietly Arrived," *Jiefangjun Bao*, 24 August 1999, 6, in FBIS-CHI-99-0925; and in Leng Binglin, Wang Yulin, and Zhao Weniang, "Bring[ing] Internet Warfare into the Military System Is of Equal Significance with Land, Sea, and Air Power," *Jiefangjun Bao*, 11 November 1999, 7, in FBIS-CHI-99-1227. See especially Pillsbury, *Chinese Views of Future Warfare*.

48. Shi is quoted in Huang, Chen, and Zhang, "China Enhances the Navy's Comprehensive Strength—Interview with Naval Commander VADM Shi Yunsheng," 3. Shi also called for a "scientifically feasible ... Navy development strategy" as part of the "defense development strategy ... subject to the national development strategy" (5).

49. See Lu Ning, *The Dynamics of Foreign-Policy Decisionmaking in China*, 126ff., for an interesting description of the 1988 naval conflict with Vietnam when—according to the author—PLAN forces drove national strategy.

50. Senior Colonel Huang Xing and Senior Colonel Zuo Quandian, "Holding the Initiative in Our Hands in Conducting Operations, Giving Full Play to Our Own Advantages to Defeat Our Enemy—a Study of the Core Idea of the Operational Doctrine of the PLA," *Zhongquo Junshi Kexue*, no. 4, 20 November 1996, 49–56 (site no longer available). The authors, who served at the Academy of Military Science, clearly identified the United States as "our enemy" (8), but displayed a very imperfect knowledge of American weapons systems.

51. "Bolt from the blue" was first used in modern maritime strategy in the early twentieth century to describe a possible surprise German naval attack on Great Britain. See Marder, *From the Dreadnought to Scapa Flow*, 144; and Roskill, *The Strategy of Seapower*, 104, for discussions of this concept.

52. Senior Captain Yan Youqiang ["Director of a Naval Headquarters Research Institute"] and Senior Captain Chen Rongxing, "On Maritime Strategy and the Marine Environment," *Zhongguo Junshi Kexue*, no. 2, 20 May 1997, 81–92, in FBIS-CHI-97-197. This was a good description of China's maritime strategic thought in the last decade.

53. This is the view from Manila and Hanoi; Singapore expresses its distrust of China by urging a continued strong U.S. naval presence in Southeast Asia (senior Singapore joint staff officer and deputy director, Singapore Armed Forces Training Institute, discussion with the author in May 1999); Indonesia and Thailand are at least more comfortable

with that presence, although Jakarta is concerned about Beijing's possible territorial claims in the South China Sea. Only Malaysia continues to maintain, at least in public, that China is not a threat (and the U.S. naval presence unnecessary) (deputy commandant and staff officers, Royal Malaysian Defense College, discussions with the author, May 1999). But also see Sokolsky, Rabasa, and Neu, *The Role of Southeast Asia in U.S. Strategy toward China,* 2001, at http://www.rand.org/pubs/monograph_reports/ MR1170/MR1170.ch4.pdf (accessed 05 December 2009).

54.   Furthermore, Germany built the wrong navy; it was unable to serve as more than a coastal defense force, and in the final analysis absorbed vast quantities of national resources while needlessly alienating Great Britain and other powers. See Marder, *From the Dreadnought to Scapa Flow,* vol. 1; Roskill, *The Strategy of Seapower;* Woodward, *Great Britain and the German Navy;* and Steinberg, *Yesterday's Deterrent.* China is building a twenty-first-century navy at a moderate, apparently carefully considered pace, and with specific strategic goals.

55.   Lambert, *Sir John Fisher's Naval Revolution,* 121–26, explains the concept of "flotilla defense." Jon Sumida brought this to the author's attention.

Conclusion

1.   This theme is developed in McDevitt, "Sino-Japanese Rivalry: Implications for U.S. Policy," 481–522. Also see the statement by Admiral Michael Mullen, chairman of the U.S. Joint Chiefs of Staff, that PLA improvements were "very focused" on U.S. capabilities, in William Lowther, "Targeting Uncle Sam," *Taipei Times,* 06 November 2009, 3, at http://www.taipeitimes.com/News/taiwan/archives/2009/11/06/2003457773 (accessed 18 November 2009). The quote is from Admiral Wu Shengli, who is listed as the author of "Building a Powerful People's Navy That Meets the Requirements of the Historical Mission for Our Army," *Qiushi,* no. 14, 07 July 2007, in OSC-CPP20070716710027.

2.   Mao Zedong's campaign in the 1960s to establish a "third wave" of industrial development well inland arose primarily from security rather than economic or social concerns. Hu's speech is in "Hu's Keynote Speech at [17th] Party Congress Attracts the World's Media," *Xinhua,* 15 October 2007, at http://english.peopledaily.com. cn/90002/92169/92187/6283161.html (accessed 22 November 2009).

3.   Author's conversation with a Sri Lankan firsthand observer of the Hambantota project. One of the authors of the "string of pearls" study told me that the provocative name was applied by the Office of the Secretary of Defense and not by the study's authors. Hambantota and Gwadar characteristics are discussed in B. Raman, "Hambantota and

Gwadar: An Update," South Asia Analysis Group, paper no. 3248, 12 June 2009, at http://www.southasiaanalysis.org/%5Cpapers33%5Cpaper3248.html (accessed 18 November 2009).

4. China employed military force internationally 118 times between 1949 and 1992, according to Johnston, "China's Militarized Interstate Dispute Behavior, 1949–1992."

5. Quoted in Si Yanwen and Chen Wanjun, "Navy to Develop More High-Tech Equipment," *Jiefangjun Bao*, 10 June 1999, in FBIS-CHI-1999-0611. Similar statements were attributed to then President Jiang Zemin in Pamela Pun, "PLA Told to Speed Weapons Research," *Hong Kong Standard*, 06 November 1999. Also see "Unswervingly Take the Road of Strengthening Armaments with Science and Technology," *Jiefangjun Bao*, 03 July 1999, 1, in FBIS-CHI-1999-0712, which also notes that "supply and maintenance can directly affect the generation and development of battle readiness," especially for high-technology weapons systems. The comparative status of PLA technology was last explored in Cole and Godwin, "Advanced Military Technology and the PLA: Priorities and Capabilities for the Twenty-first Century," 159–216.

6. For an explanation of this program, see Cebrowski, "The Implementation of Netcentric Warfare," at http://www.au.af.mil/au/awc/awcgate/transformation/oft_implementa tion_ncw.pdf (accessed 16 February 2009).

7. The U.S. directive to improve/implement "jointness" is codified in the Goldwater-Nichols Act of 1986, but it has taken decades for the U.S. military to realize the benefits of its provisions, and that process continues. The specific issue of C3 is explored in Bussert, "Chinese Warships Struggle to Meet New Command, Control and Communications Needs," at http://www.afcea.org/signal/articles/anmviewer. asp?a=1834&rint=yes (accessed 22 March 2009).

8. On the foreign origin of so many PLAN systems, see McVadon, "Systems Integration in China's People's Liberation Army," 225, which notes that the Luhu class incorporates "more than forty advanced foreign technologies." A more recent analysis is Bussert, "China Builds Destroyers around Imported Technology," 67–69.

9. Author's conversations with staff and shipboard officers of the North and East China sea fleets, 2003–8. But Chen Huihuang, "Certain Naval Base Enhances Field Armament Support," *Jiefangjun Bao*, 17 April 2002, in FBIS-CPP20021118000070 (18 November 2002), seems to be reporting pierside units of experts ready to assist ship crews. "Navy Sets Up First Technology Expert Station at Qingdao Base," *Renmin Haijun* (Beijing), 07 November 2007, 1, in OSC-CPP20080115478006, apparently reports a development of this "station" into a much more sophisticated organization with direct educational as well as assistance responsibilities and direct linkage to the Navy Engineering University. A good account of the Ming incident and other Chinese

submarine losses is in Goldstein and Murray, "International Submarine Rescue: A Constructive Role for China?" 167–83.

10. Author's discussions of this system with senior PLAN officers indicate that it is not significantly different from that in the U.S. Navy.

11. Yung, *People's War at Sea*, 37–38. Yang, "From a Navy in Blue towards a Blue Water Navy," also notes China's poor record of reverse-engineering combatant ships.

12. Shen Zhongchang, "A Rudimentary Exploration of 21st Century Naval Warfare," *Zhongguo Renmin Kexue*, no. 1, 20 February 1995, in FBIS-CHI-95-113, supplement, 28.

13. David Finkelstein discussed with the author the Marine Corps' probable relationship to the GSD resulting from regulations issued in 1999.

14. Chi noted in discussion with the author's delegation that one of the benefits of mobilizing the PLA to assist in flood control work that summer had been to get the military back in among the people, to rekindle the feeling—damaged by the Tiananmen Square incident—that the PLA is the military of the Chinese people. The PLA's senior political officer, General Li Jinai, is quoted in "China General Tells Troops Party Trumps State," Reuters, 01 April 2009, at http://www.reuters.com/article/worldNews/idUSTRE53029820090401 (accessed 28 November 2009).

15. Yang Yi, "Engagement, Caution," 33. The second quote is in "PRC Journal Examines China's Deepening National Defense, Military Reform," *Liaowang* (Beijing), no. 10, 09 March 2009, 98–99, in OSC-CPP20090318710007. The final quote is from Su Shiliang, "Persistently Follow the Guidance of Chairman Hu's Important Thought."

16. In terms, that is, of conventional naval power as currently understood. Technological developments—spaceborne sensor and weapons systems, for instance—may well allow China to achieve global power capabilities, albeit not in traditional naval forms.

17. Yan Youqiang and Chen Rongxing, "The Developing Trends of Naval Battles and Their Impact on PLA Campaigns," *Zhongguo Junshi Kexue* (Beijing), 20 May 1997, 81–92, in FBIS-CHI-97-197, 2, 3.

18. See Joffe, "China's Military after Taiwan," for a discussion of these factors.

19. See Wilhelm, *China and Security in the Asian Pacific Region through 2010*, 44, for the contention that long-range PLAN deployments would be a departure from Chinese military tradition and that PLAN arguments "have not convinced the CMC to allocate the resources" for a large blue-water navy. Cited in Shambaugh, "China's Defense Industries," 51.

20. The 200 nm figure is the author's estimate based on PLAN AAW capabilities and China's description of the first island chain; Qiu Yongzheng, "Chinese Submarines: Fighting for Absolute Sea Superiority," *Qingnian Cankao* (Beijing), 30 June 2004, in FBIS-CPP20040630000074, suggests 500 nm; a prominent Chinese scholar gave

"one thousand miles" as the range at which the PLAN wanted to hold U.S. carriers, in Erickson et al., "China Trip (1–14 December 2005) Report." See Cole, *Taiwan's Security: History and Prospects,* 171–85, for a discussion of Taiwan's resolve.

21. Dennis Blasko, in a PowerPoint presentation on 25 June 2008, offered a series of quotes to this effect, including President Hu Jintao quoted in "Beijing Military Region Commander Gives Lecture on Mission at Training Class," *Zhanyou Bao* (Beijing), 22 April 2008, in OSC-CPP20080618478003; and "Comment: A Military Strategy to Match Peaceful Rise," *China Daily,* 16 May 2008, at OSC-CPP200805169. The Gulf of Aden experience is addressed in "Chinese Navy Sees Role Further Afield," *Xinhua,* 22 April 2009, in OSC-CPP20090422968187.

Bibliography

Agnote, Dario. "China to Continue Military Buildup in Spratly Islands." *Kyodo News,* in *Washington Times,* 22 October 1999, sec. A.

Ahrari, Ehsan. "China's Naval Forces Look to Extend Their Blue-Water Reach." *Jane's Intelligence Review* 10, no. 4 (1998): 31–36.

Alexander's Gas & Oil Connections: News and Trends E and SE Asia. Vols. 3–7. http://www.gasandoil.com/goc/news/nts0835.htm.

Allen, Kenneth W., Glenn Krumel, and Jonathan D. Pollack. *China's Air Force Enters the 21st Century.* Santa Monica, Calif.: RAND, 1995.

Allen, Kenneth W., and Eric A. McVadon. *China's Foreign Military Relations.* Washington, D.C.: Henry L. Stimson Center, 1999.

Anati, Massimo. "China's PLA Navy (the Revolution)." *Naval Forces* 25, no. 6 (2004): 70–71.

Andrew, Martin. "PLA's Mechanization and Informationization Come of Age: Sharpening and Vanguard-2008." *China Brief* 8, no. 22 (24 November 2008). http://www.jamestown.org/programs/chinabrief/single/?tx_ttnews%5Btt_news%5D=34167&tx_ttnews%5BbackPid%5D=168&no_cache=1 (accessed 10 October 2009).

Armed Forces Staff College. *Joint Staff Officers' Guide.* Publication 1. Washington, D.C.: National Defense University Press, 1996.

"Army Seeks Mobility in Force Cuts." *Jane's Defence Weekly* 30, no. 25 (16 December 1998): 23.

ASEAN. "ASEAN Chairman's Statement at the Sixth Meeting of the ARF." July 1992, 2. http://www.aseansec.org/politics/pol-arf6.htm (accessed 11 December 2009).

Ashley, Steven. "Warp Drive Underwater." *Scientific American* (May 2001). http://people.exeter.ac.uk/tkirsano/Sciam.htm (accessed 15 March 2009).

Association of Southeast Asian Nations (ASEAN) information Web site. http://www.aseansec.org/politics/pol_arf6.htm (accessed 02 November 2009).

Austin, Greg. *China's Ocean Frontier: International Law, Military Force and National Development.* Canberra: Allen and Unwin, 1998.

Baker, A. D., III, ed. *The Naval Institute Guide to Combat Fleets of the World, 2000–2001.* Annapolis, Md.: U.S. Naval Institute, 2000.

Ball, Desmond. "Military Acquisitions in the Asia-Pacific Region." *International Security* 18, no. 3 (1993–94): 78–112.

Banerjee, Ruben. "China: Worrying Approach." *India Today,* 30 April 1994, 71.

Barber, Ben. "Indian Navy Exercises Seen Apt to Irk Beijing." *Washington Times,* 08 May 2000, 1.

Bateman, Sam. "Coast Guards: New Forces for Regional Order and Security." *AsiaPacific Issues* 65. Honolulu: East-West Center, January 2003.

Bateman, Sam, and Ralf Emmers, eds. *Security and International Politics in the South China Sea.* London: Routledge, 2008.

Bateman, Sam, Catherine Zara Raymond, and Joshua Ho. "Safety and Security in the Malacca and Singapore Straits." Singapore: Institute of Defense and Strategic Studies, May 2006.

Bi, Jianxiang. "Managing Taiwan Operations in the Twenty-first Century: Issues and Options." *Naval War College Review* 52, no. 4 (1999): 30–58.

Blackman, Raymond V. B., ed. *Jane's Fighting Ships: 1955–56.* London: Jane's Fighting Ships Publishing, 1956.

———. *Jane's Fighting Ships, 1960–61.* New York: McGraw-Hill, 1961.

———. *Jane's Fighting Ships, 1970–1971.* London: Jane's Yearbooks, 1971.

Blair, Dennis, and Kenneth Lieberthal. "Smooth Sailing: The World's Shipping Lanes Are Safe." *Foreign Affairs* 86, no. 3 (2007): 7–13.

Blanche, Bruce, and Jean Blanche. "Oil and Regional Stability in the South China Sea." *Jane's Intelligence Review* 7, no. 11 (1995): 511–14.

Blasko, Dennis. "Evaluating Chinese Military Procurement from Russia." *Joint Force Quarterly,* no. 17 (1997–98): 91–96.

———. "Military Parades Demonstrate China's Concept of Deterrence." *China Brief* 9, no. 8, 16 April 2009. Washington, D.C.: Jamestown Foundation. http://news.xinhuanet.com/english/2009-04/23/content_11243632.htm (accessed 17 June 2009).

———. "A New PLA Force Structure." In *The People's Liberation Army in the Information Age,* ed. James C. Mulvenon and Richard H. Yang. Santa Monica, Calif.: RAND, 1999.

———. "People's War in the 21st Century: The Militia and the Reserves." Paper prepared for the Center for Naval Analyses Conference "Swimming in a New Sea: Civil-Military Issues in Today's China," 21–23 March 2004, CNA Corp., Alexandria, Va.

———. "PLA Ground Force Modernization and Mission Diversification: Underway in All Military Regions." In *Right Sizing the People's Liberation Army: Exploring the Contours of China's Military,* ed. Roy Kamphausen and Andrew Scobell. Carlisle, Pa.: Strategic Studies Institute, 2006.

———. "Recent Trends in PLA Navy Training and Education." Testimony before the U.S.-China Economic and Security Review Commission, Washington, D.C., 11 June 2009. http://www.uscc.gov/hearings/2009hearings/written_testimonies/09_06_11_wrts/09_06_11_vellucci_statement.php (accessed 07 December 2009).

Blasko, Dennis J., Philip T. Klapakis, and John F. Corbett Jr. "Training Tomorrow's PLA: A Mixed Bag of Tricks." *China Quarterly* 146 (June 1996): 488–524.

Blouet, Brian. *Global Geostrategy: Mackinder and the Defense of the West.* London: Frank Cass, 2005.

Bodeen, Christopher. "Concrete Claims." *Far Eastern Economic Review,* 21 December 1995, 14.

———. "Taiwan Military Uses Pratas Islands." Associated Press, 20 October 1999.

Brooke, Micool. "The Armed Forces of Myanmar." *Asian Defense Journal* (January 1998): 14.

———. "Myanmar's Armed Forces and Their Ongoing Campaigns." *Asian Defense Journal* (March 1999): 11.

Bullard, Monte. *China's Political-Military Evolution: The Party and the Military in the PRC, 1960–1984.* Boulder, Colo.: Westview Press, 1998.

Bussert, James C. "China Builds Destroyers around Imported Technology." *Signal* 58, no. 12 (2004): 67–69.

———. "China Taps Many Resources for Coastal Defense." *Signal* 56, no. 11 (2002). http://www.afcea.org/signal/articles/templates/SIGNAL_Article_Template.asp? articleid=311&zoneid=30.

———. "Chinese Warships Struggle to Meet New Command, Control and Communications Needs." *Signal* 63, no. 6 (February 2009).

Caldwell, John. *China's Conventional Military Capability.* Washington, D.C.: CSIS, 1994.

Cao, Yingxia. *Private Higher Education and the Labor Market in China.* Boca Raton, Fla.: Universal Publishers, 2008.

The Case of Peng Teh-huai, 1959–1968. Hong Kong: Union Research Institute, 1968.

Castano, John, and Thomas Gieseke. "Supercavitation Research Programmes." *Naval Forces* 22, no. 3 (2001): 44–53.

Catley, Bob, and Makmur Keliat. *Spratlys: The Dispute in the South China Sea.* Sydney: Ashgate, 1997.

Cebrowski, Arthur K. "The Implementation of Netcentric Warfare." Office of the Director of Force Transformation, Department of Defense, Washington, D.C., January 2005. http://www.au.af.mil/au/awc/awcgate/transformation/oft_implementation_ncw.pdf (accessed 16 February 2009).

Chanda, Nayan. "China: Aiming High." *Far Eastern Economic Review,* 20 October 1994, 15.

———. "The Right Stuff." *Far Eastern Economic Review,* 20 October 1994, 15.

Chang, Gordon H., and He Di. "The Absence of War in the U.S.-China Confrontation over Quemoy and Matsu in 1954–1955: Contingency, Luck, or Deterrence?" *American Historical Review* 98, no. 5 (1993): 1500–1524.

Chapman, Richard. "Senkaku-Daioyutai Island Dispute." U.S. Pacific Command Virtual Information Center. http://www.vic.pacom.mil (accessed 29 February 2000).

Chase, Michael. "Chinese Land Attack Cruise Missile Developments and Their Implications for the United States." *China Brief* 8, no. 25 (19 December 2008). http://www.jamestown. org/programs/chinabrief/single/?tx_ttnews%5Btt_news%5D=34299&tx_ttnews%5Bback Pid%5D=25&cHash=a68be8ded7 (accessed 22 March 2009).

Chen, Kathy. "China's Inability to Keep Subs Running Shows Broader Woes Plaguing Military." *Wall Street Journal*, 01 August 1997.

Chen, Sijin. "The Challenge of Conscription in an Era of Social Change." In *Civil-Military Relations in Today's China*, ed. David M. Finkelstein and Kristen Gunness. Armonk, N.Y.: M. E. Sharp, 2006.

Chen Hurng-yu. "A Comparison between Taipei and Peking in Their Policies and Concepts Regarding the South China Sea." *Issues and Studies* 29, no. 9 (1993): 22–58.

Ch'en, Jerome, ed. *Mao. Great Lives Observed*. Ed. Gerald Emanuel Stearn. Englewood Cliffs, N.J.: Prentice-Hall, 1969.

Cheng Hsiao-shih. *Party-Military Relations in the PRC and Taiwan*. Boulder, Colo.: Westview Press, n.d.

Cheung, Tai Ming. *Fortifying China: The Struggle to Build a Modern Defense Economy*. Ithaca, N.Y.: Cornell University Press, 2009.

———. *Growth of Chinese Naval Power: Priorities, Goals, Missions, and Regional Implications*. Singapore: Institute of Southeast Asian Studies, 1990.

———. "Reforming the Dragon's Tail: Chinese Military Logistics in the Era of High-Technology Warfare and Market Economics." In *China's Military Faces the Future*, ed. James R. Lilley and David Shambaugh. Washington, D.C.: AEI and M. E. Sharpe, 1999.

"China and Malaysia Agree to Boost Defense Co-operation in the South China Sea." *Alexander's Gas & Oil Connections* 4 (19 July 1999).

"China Commits to Carrier Construction with Daunting Aircraft." *Navy News and Undersea Technology*, 23 August 1999, 1.

"China Gets to Grips with Luhu Technology Gap." *Jane's Navy International* 101 (November 1996): 8.

"China, Myanmar Issue Joint Statement." 2000. http://www.china.org.cn/English.News/ Politics/0606/22.htm.

"China Uses Commercial Ships to Carry Troops in Exercise." *Dow-Jones Newsletter*, 31 July 2000.

"China's Ambitions in Myanmar." *Strategic Comments* 6. London: IISS, July 2000.

"China's Offshore Oil Sector Profitable in 1998." *Asia Pulse*, 18 January 2000.

"China's Sea Change." *Far Eastern Economic Review* 163 (10 February 1999): 6.

"Chinese Naval Presence Rising off Japan." *Japan Times*, 22 March 2000.

"The Chinese Navy." In *Shanghai Defense Force and Volunteers*. Shanghai: *North China Daily Herald* [1929?].

"Chinese Subs Experience Battery, Training Problems." *Navy News and Undersea Technology,* 1 September 1997, 5.

Ching, Frank. "Manila Foiled in Spratly Row." *Far Eastern Economic Review,* 8 April 1999, 33.

Christensen, Thomas J. *Useful Adversaries: Grand Strategy, Domestic Mobilization, and Sino-American Conflict, 1947–1958.* Princeton: Princeton University Press, 1996.

"Clashes over Fish in Pacific Asia, 1994–1997." 1999. http://www.middlebury.edu/SouthChinaSea/maps/dupont3 (accessed 17 December 2009).

Coakley, Robert W., and Richard M. Leighton. *Global Logistics and Strategy: 1943–1945. The United States Army in World War II.* Ed. Stetson Conn. Washington, D.C.: Center of Military History of the U.S. Army, 1989.

Cole, Bernard D. *Gunboats and Marines: The United States Navy in China.* Newark, Del.: University of Delaware Press, 1982.

———. "The Real Sand Pebbles." *Naval History* 14, no. 1 (2000): 16–23.

———. *Sea Lanes and Pipelines: Energy Security in Asia.* Greenwich, Conn.: Praeger, 2008.

———. *Taiwan's Security: History and Prospects.* London: Routledge, 2006.

———. "U.S.-China's Counter-piracy Cooperation in the Gulf of Aden." Freeman Report. Washington, D.C.: CSIS, May 2009.

Cole, Bernard D., and Paul H. B. Godwin. "Advanced Military Technology and the PLA: Priorities and Capabilities for the Twenty-first Century." In *The Chinese Armed Forces in the 21st Century,* ed. Larry Wortzel. Carlisle, Pa.: U.S. Army War College Strategic Studies Institute, 1999.

Collins, Gabriel. "China Fills First SPR Site, Faces Oil, Pipeline Issues." *Oil & Gas Journal* 105, no. 31 (2007): 20–29.

Collins, Gabriel, and Andrew S. Erickson. "Tanking Up: The Commercial and Strategic Significance of China's Growing Tanker Fleet." *Geopolitics of Energy* 29, no. 8 (2007): 2–11.

Collins, Gabriel, Andrew S. Erickson, and Lyle Goldstein. "Chinese Naval Analysts Consider the Energy Question." Draft paper for presentation at the annual meeting of the APSA, Chicago, 31 August 2007.

Collins, Gabriel, and Michael C. Grubb. *A Comprehensive Survey of China's Dynamic Shipbuilding Industry: Commercial Development and Strategic Implications.* U.S. Naval War College, China Maritime Studies 1 (August 2008).

Collins, Gabriel B., and William S. Murray. "No Oil for the Lamps of China?" *Naval War College Review* 61, no. 2 (2008): 79–95.

Colton, Luke. "Chinese Naval Aviation: An Overview of PLAN Helicopters." Draft paper prepared for the Henry L. Stimson Center, 24 March 2000.

"Concrete Claims." *Far Eastern Economic Review,* 21 December 1995, 14.

Cordner, Lee G. "The Spratly Islands Dispute and the Law of the Sea." *Ocean Development and International Law* 25, no. 1 (1994): 62–74.

"Country Report." *Asian Defence Journal* (November 1999): 12.

Crawley, James W. "Chinese Navy Changing from Lean to Mean." *San Diego Union-Tribune*, 26 March 1997.

Daugherty, Leo G. "Commentary on 'PLAN Marines.'" Paper presented at the Center for Naval Analysis Conference on the PLAN, Washington, D.C., April 2000.

Deng, Gang. *Chinese Maritime Activities and Socioeconomic Development, c. 2100 B.C.–900 A.D.* Westport, Conn.: Greenwood Press, 1997.

Deng Xiaoping. "Speech at an Enlarged Meeting of the Military Commission of the Party Central Committee." *China Reports*, no. 468 (31 October 1983): 14–22.

de Pomereu, Jean. "Accompanying China to Antarctica." International Polar Foundation Web site, 14 November 2008. http://www.sciencepoles.org/index.php?s=2&rs=home&uid=1361.

Dickie, Mure. "End the Go-Slow on Gas in the East China Sea." *Financial Times*, 01 July 2009. http://www.ft.com/cms/s/0/1a88c200-6668-11de-1034-00144feabdc0.html?nclick_check=1.

Directory of PRC Military Personalities. Vols. 1999–2009. Honolulu: Serold Hawaii, Inc.

Donovan, Robert J. *Tumultuous Years: The Presidency of Harry S Truman, 1949–1953*. New York: W. W. Norton, 1982.

Downes, Erica Strecker, and Phillip C. Saunders. "Legitimacy and the Limits of Nationalism: China and the Diaoyu Islands." *International Security* 23, no. 3 (1989–90): 127–33.

Downing, John W. "China's Evolving Maritime Strategy. Part 1." *Jane's Intelligence Review* 8 (March 1996): 129–33.

———. "China's Evolving Maritime Strategy. Part 2." *Jane's Intelligence Review* 8 (April 1996): 186–91.

Dreyer, Edward L. "The Poyang Campaign, 1363: Inland Naval Warfare in the Founding of the Ming Dynasty." In *Chinese Ways of Warfare*, ed. Frank A. Kierman Jr. and John K. Fairbank. Cambridge: Harvard University Press, 1974.

———. *Zheng He: China and the Oceans in the Early Ming Dynasty, 1405–1433*. New York: Longman's, 2006.

Dreyer, June Teufel. *The PLA and the Kosovo Conflict*. The Letort Papers. Carlisle, Pa.: U.S. Army War College Strategic Studies Institute, May 2000.

Drifte, Reinhard. "Territorial Conflicts in the East China Sea—from Missed Opportunities to Negotiation Stalemate." *Asia-Pacific Journal: Japan Focus*, 01 June 2009. http://www.japanfocus.org/-Reinhard-Drifte/3156.

Dumbaugh, Kerry, et al. *China's Maritime Territorial Claims: Implications for U.S. Interests*. Congressional Research Service Report for Congress, RL31183. Washington, D.C.: USGPO, 12 November 2001.

Dunnigan, James. "Chinese Carrier Goes into Dry Dock." 14 May 2009. http://www.strategypage.com/dls/articles/Chinese-Carrier-Goes-Into-Dry-Dock-5-14-2009.asp (accessed 26 May 2009).

Dutton, Peter. "Scouting, Signaling, and Gatekeeping: Chinese Naval Operations in Japanese Waters and the International Law Implications." *China Maritime Studies Institute*, no 2. Newport, R.I.: Naval War College, February 2009.

"East Asia: Spratlys Initiative." *Oxford Analytica Brief*, 06 December 1999, 4. U.S. Pacific Command Virtual Information Center. http://www.vic.pacom.mil.

"East Asia: Straits Challenge." *Oxford Analytica Brief*, 10 February 2000, 2. U.S. Pacific Command Virtual Information Center. http://www.vic.pacom.mil.

Eckholm, Erik. "Despite Tensions, China and Japan Reaffirm Ties." *New York Times*, 30 August 2000.

Edmonds, Martin, and Michael M. Tsai, eds. *Taiwan's Maritime Security*. London: Routledge, 2003.

Energy Information Administration. *The Petroleum Resources of China*. DOE/EI-0501. Washington, D.C.: U.S. Department of Energy, 1987.

———. *South China Sea Region*. Washington, D.C.: U.S. Department of Energy, 1998.

Erickson, Andrew S. "PLA Navy Modernization: Preparing for 'Informatized' War at Sea." *China Brief* 8, no. 5 (29 February 2008). http://www.jamestown.org/programs/chinabrief/single/?tx_ttnews%5Btt_news%5D=4759&tx_ttnews%5BbackPid%5D=168&no_cache=1 (accessed 12 October 2009).

Erickson, Andrew S., and Michael Chase. "An Undersea Deterrent?" *U.S. Naval Institute Proceedings* 135, no. 6/1,276 (2009). http://www.usni.org/magazines/proceedings/story.asp?STORY_ID=1907 (accessed 11 December 2009).

Erickson, Andrew S., and Gabriel Collins. "Beijing's Energy Security Strategy: The Significance of a Chinese State-Owned Tanker Fleet." *Orbis* 51, no. 4 (2007): 665–84.

Erickson, Andrew, and Lyle Goldstein. "Gunboats for China's New 'Grand Canals'?" *Naval War College Review* 62, no. 2 (2009): 43–76.

Erickson, Andrew, Lyle Goldstein, and William Murray. *Chinese Mine Warfare: A PLA Navy "Assassin's Mace" Capability*. China Maritime Studies Institute, no. 3. Newport, R.I.: Naval War College, 2009. http://www.navy.mil/navydata/cno/n87/usw/issue_33/china.html (accessed 07 February 2009).

———. "Sea Mines Constitute Key Element of PLA Navy's ASW." *Undersea Warfare* (winter 2007). http://www.navy.mil/navydata/cno/n87/usw/issue_33/china.html.

Erickson, Andrew S., and Justin D. Mikolay. "Welcome China to the Fight against Pirates." *U.S. Naval Institute Proceedings* 135, no. 3 (2009): 34–41.

Erickson, Andrew, and Andrew Wilson. "China's Aircraft Carrier Dilemma." *Naval War College Review* 59, no. 4 (2006): 13–45.

Erickson, Andrew, et al. "China Trip (1–14 December 2005) Report." Newport, R.I.: Naval War College Center for Naval Warfare Studies informal paper, 2005.

"Exploration Sags off Viet Nam." *Oil & Gas Journal* 95 (3 November 1997): 32.

Fairbank, John K. *China: A New History.* Cambridge: Belknap Press of Harvard University Press, 1992.

———. "Maritime and Continental in China's History." In *The Cambridge History of China.* Vol. 12: *Republican China: 1912–1949,* part 1, ed. John K. Fairbank and Dennis Twitchett. Cambridge: Cambridge University Press, 1983.

Farrer, Mark. "China's Air Force—Kosovo Spurs a Race to Change." *Asia-Pacific Defense Reporter* 25, no. 6 (1999): 20–21.

Fesharaki, Fereidun. "Review of China's Petroleum Demand, Supply, Organizational Reforms, and Overseas Investment." Honolulu: East-West Center, January 1998.

"Fighters Trail Philippine Plane over Spratlys." Reuters report in *Yahoo! Headlines,* 01 November 1999. http://www.newsindex.com/cgi-bin/result.cgi?

Finkelstein, David M. "China's National Military Strategy: An Overview of the 'Military Strategic Guidelines.'" In *Right Sizing the People's Liberation Army: Exploring the Contours of China's Military,* ed. Roy Kamphausen and Andrew Scobell. Carlisle, Pa.: Army War College Strategic Studies Institute, 2007. http://www.strategicstudiesinstitute.army.mil/pubs/display.cfm?pubID=784 (accessed 06 December 2009).

———. "China's New Security Concept: Reading between the Lines." Center for Naval Analysis Issue Paper. Washington, D.C.: CNA, April 1999.

Fisher, Richard. "Appendix to Chapter 5: Foreign Arms Acquisition and PLA Modernization." In *China's Military Faces the Future,* ed. James R. Lilley and David Shambaugh. Washington, D.C.: AEI and M. E. Sharpe, 1999.

Forage, Paul C. "The Foundations of Chinese Naval Supremacy in the Twelfth Century." In *New Interpretations in Naval History: Selected Papers from the Tenth Naval History Symposium Held at the United States Naval Academy, 11–13 September 1991,* ed. Jack Sweetman. Annapolis, Md.: U.S. Naval Institute Press, 1992.

Ford, Christopher A., and David A. Rosenberg. "The Naval Intelligence Underpinnings of Reagan's Maritime Strategy." *Journal of Strategic Studies* 28, no. 2 (2005): 379–409.

Fravel, Taylor. "China's Search for Military Power." *Washington Quarterly* 31, no. 3 (2008), 126–27.

———. *Strong Borders, Secure Nation.* Princeton, N.J.: Princeton University Press, 2008.

Freeman, Charles W,. Jr. "China, Taiwan, and the United States." In *Asia after the "Miracle": Redefining U.S. Economic and Security Priorities,* ed. Selig S. Harrison and Clyde V. Prestowitz Jr. Washington, D.C.: Economic Strategy Institute, 1999.

Gardiner, Robert, ed. *Conway's All the World's Fighting Ships, 1947–1995.* Annapolis, Md.: U.S. Naval Institute Press, 1995.

Garver, John W. "China's Push through the South China Sea: The Interaction of Bureaucratic and National Interest." *China Quarterly* 132 (December 1992): 999–1028.

———. *Face Off: China, the United States, and Taiwan's Democratization.* Seattle: University of Washington Press, 1997.

"Gas Tussle in South China Sea." *China Weekly Fax Bulletin.* Washington, D.C.: Orbis Publications, 24 March 1997.

Glosny, Michael. "Strangulation from the Sea: A PRC Submarine Blockade of Taiwan." *International Security* 28, no. 4 (2004): 125–60.

Godwin, Paul H. B. "Changing Concepts of Doctrine, Strategy, and Operations in the People's Liberation Army 1978–87." *China Quarterly* 112 (1987): 573–90.

———, ed. *The Chinese Defense Establishment: Continuity and Change in the 1980s.* Boulder, Colo.: Westview Press, 1983.

———. "Force Projection and National Military Strategy." In *Chinese Military Modernization,* ed. C. Dennison Lane. Washington, D.C.: AEI Press, 1996.

———. "From Continent to Periphery: PLA Doctrine, Strategy and Capabilities towards 2000." *China Quarterly* 146 (June 1996): 464–87.

———. "Patterns of Doctrinal Change in the Chinese People's Liberation Army: From Threats to Contingencies to Capabilities." Paper prepared for the Eleventh Asian Security Conference on "The Changing Face of Conflict and Strategy in Asia." Institute for Defense Studies and Analysis, New Delhi, India, February 2009.

———. "Technology, Strategy, and Operations: The PLA's Continuing Dilemma." Draft article. 1998.

Goldstein, Lyle. "Chinese Coast Guard Development: Challenge and Opportunity." *China Brief* 9, no. 23 (19 November 2009). http://www.jamestown.org/programs/chinabrief/single/?tx_ttnews[tt_news]=35747&tx_ttnews[backPid]=25&cHash=11a04a70b2 (accessed 19 December 2009).

———. "Strategic Implications of Chinese Fisheries Development." *China Brief* 9, no. 16 (05 August 2009). http://www.jamestown.org/single/?no_cache=1&tx_ttnews%5Btt_news%5D=35372.

Goldstein, Lyle, and William Murray. "International Submarine Rescue: A Constructive Role for China?" *Asia Policy* no. 5, Research Note. Seattle: National Bureau of Asian Research (January 2008): 167–83. http://www.nbr.org/publications/asia_policy/AP5/AP5_Goldstein_Murray.pdf (accessed 07 March 2009).

Gray, Colin S. *Explorations in Strategy.* Westport, Conn.: Greenwood Press, 1996.

———. "Seapower and Landpower." In *Seapower and Landpower,* ed. Colin S. Gray and Roger W. Barnett. Annapolis, Md.: U.S. Naval Institute, 1989.

Grazebrook, A. W. "New Generation Naval AAW Missiles." *Asia-Pacific Defense Reporter* 23, no. 5 (1997): 18.

Griswold, James, and Rick Parker. "Counter Narcotics: Burma, China, and Laos." U.S. Pacific Command Virtual Information Center. http://www.vic.pacom.mil (accessed 22 August 2000).

Hackett, James, ed. *The Military Balance, 2009.* London: Routledge for the International Institute of Strategic Studies, 2009.

Hagt, Eric, and Matthew Durnin. "China's Antiship Ballistic Missile." *Naval War College Review* 62, no. 4 (2009): 88–115.

Hahn, Bradley. "China: Third Ranking Maritime Power—and Growing." *Pacific Defense Reporter* 15, no. 4 (1988): 46–51.

———. "PRC Policy in Maritime Asia." *Journal of Defense and Diplomacy* 4, no. 6 (1986): 19–21.

Hall, John Witney. *Japan: From Prehistory to Modern Time.* New York: Dell, 1970.

Hanrahan, Gene Z. "Report on Red China's New Navy." *U.S. Naval Institute Proceedings* 79, no. 8 (1953): 84–85.

Harrison, Selig S. *China, Oil, and Asia: Conflict Ahead?* New York: Columbia University Press, 1977.

He Di. "The Last Campaign to Unify China: The CCP's Unmaterialized Plan to Liberate Taiwan, 1949–1950." *Chinese Historians* 5 (spring 1992): 222–45.

Heaton, William R. "Professional Military Education in the People's Republic of China." In *The Chinese Defense Establishment: Continuity and Change in the 1980s,* ed. Paul H. B. Godwin. Boulder, Colo.: Westview Press, 1983.

Henley, Lonnie D. "Officer Education in the Chinese PLA." *Problems of Communism* 36, no. 3 (1987): 55–71.

Hiatt, Fred. "Marine General: U.S. Troops Must Stay in Japan." *Washington Post,* 27 March 1990, A14.

Hill, J. R. *Maritime Strategy for Medium Powers.* Annapolis, Md.: U.S. Naval Institute Press, 1986.

Hiramatsu, Shigeo. "China's Naval Advance: Objectives and Capabilities." *Japan Review of International Affairs* 8, no. 2 (1994): 120–36.

Hirschfeld, Thomas J. "China's Aircraft Carrier Program: A Virtual Dragonfly?" *Korean Journal of Defense Analysis* 10, no. 1 (1998): 141–54.

Hobkirk, Michael D. *Land, Sea, or Air? Military Priorities, Historical Choices.* New York: St. Martin's Press, 1992.

Hoffman, Fred S. "Red Chinese Reportedly Building New Naval Base." *Seattle Times,* 7 July 1971, A4.

Holzer, Robert. "Study: U.S. Navy Must Go beyond *Aegis* Radar Era." *Defense News* (June 1999): 3, 36.

Hooten, E. R., ed. "China: Surface-to-Surface Missiles." In *Jane's Naval Weapons Systems 1996.* Coulsdon, Surrey, U.K.: Jane's Information Group, 1998.

Horta, Loro. "China Takes to the Sea." *PacNet* no. 63. Honolulu: Center for Strategic and International Studies, 18 September 2009. http://csis.org/publication/pacnet-63-china-takes-sea (accessed 31 October 2009).

Hsiao, Russell. "China en Route to Cap Antarctica." *China Brief* 8, no. 20 (23 October 2008). http://www.jamestown.org/single/?no_cache=1&tx_ttnews%5Bswords%5D=8fd5893 941d69d0be3f378576261ae3e&tx_ttnews%5Bany_of_the_words%5D=antartica&tx_ ttnews%5Btt_news%5D=5228&tx_ttnews%5BbackPid%5D=7&cHash=c321acecb0.

Huang, Alexander. "Chinese Maritime Modernization and Its Security Implications: The Deng Xiaoping Era and Beyond." Ph.D. diss., George Washington University, 1994.

———. "The Chinese Navy's Offshore Active Defense Strategy: Conceptualization and Implications." *Naval War College Review* 47, no. 3 (1994): 7–32.

———. "The Evolution of the PLA Navy and Its Early Combat Experiences." Paper presented at the Center for Naval Analysis Conference on the People's Liberation Army Navy. Washington, D.C., April 2000.

———. "The PLA Navy at War, 1949–1999: From Coastal Defense to Distant Operations." Paper presented at the CNA Conference on the PLA's Operational History. Alexandria, Va., June 1999.

———. "Transformation and Refinement of Chinese Military Doctrine: Reflection and Critique on the PLA's View." Paper presented at the CAPS-RAND Conference on the PLA. Washington, D.C., July 1999.

Huber, Peter, and Mark Mills. "Oil, Oil, Everywhere." *Wall Street Journal,* 27 January 2005.

Hugar, Wayne R. "How Far Will the Dragon Swim?" *U.S. Naval Institute Proceedings* 125 (March 1999): 48–51.

———. "The Sea Dragon Network: Implications of the International Expansion of China's Maritime Shipping Industry." Master's thesis, Naval Postgraduate School, 1998.

"India, China Agree for a Forward Looking Relationship." N.d. http://www.insidechina.com/ news.php3?id=155883. Site no longer available.

"India's Military Spending: Prospects for Modernization." *Strategic Comments* (London: International Institute of Strategic Studies, July 2000): 1, 2.

"Inside China's Cold War." *Bulletin of the Cold War International History Project* 16. Washington, D.C.: Woodrow Wilson International Center for Scholars, winter 2008.

"Intelligence." *Far Eastern Economic Review* 163 (20 April 2000): 4.

International Institute of Strategic Studies. *The Military Balance, 1999–2000.* London: Oxford University Press, 2000.

———. *The Military Balance, 2009.* London: IISS, 2009.

Isnard, Jacques. "Chinese Submarine Was 'Submarining' on a Freighter in Channel." *Le Monde* (Paris), 4 February 1999, 4.

Israel, Fred L., ed. "Dwight D. Eisenhower, First Annual Message." In *The State of the Union Messages of the Presidents, 1790–1966.* Vol. 3: *1905–1966.* New York: Chelsea House, 1967.

Jane's Web site report. http://www.taiwansecurity.org/News/Janes-990201.htm (accessed 01 December 2009).

"Japan Concerned by PRC Ships' Increasing Activities." *Sankei Shimbun* (Tokyo), 18 April 2000.

Jencks, Harlan. *From Muskets to Missiles: Politics and Professionalism in the Chinese Army, 1945– 1981.* Boulder, Colo.: Westview Press, 1982.

———. "The PRC's Military and Security Policy in the Post–Cold War Era." *Issues & Studies* 30, no. 11 (1994): 65–103.

Ji, You. "The Revolution in Military Affairs and the Evolution of China's Strategic Thinking." *Contemporary Southeast Asia* 21, no. 3 (1999): 344–64.

———. "A Test Case for China's Defense and Foreign Policies." *Contemporary Southeast Asia* 16, no. 4 (1995): 375–403.

Jian, Sanqiang. "Multinational Oil Companies and the Spratly Dispute." *Journal of Contemporary China* 6, no. 16 (1997): 591–602. http://www.informaworld.com/index/777863407.pdf (accessed 17 December 2009).

Jin, Xuejun. "Three-Parameter Positioning of Two Geostationary Satellites System with Accuracy Analysis." *Chinese Space Science and Technology* 23, no. 5 (2003): 22–27.

Joffe, Ellis. "China's Military after Taiwan." *Far Eastern Economic Review* (March 2009). http://www.feer.com/international-relations/20098/march58/chinas-military-after-taiwan (accessed 29 November 2009).

———. *The Chinese Army after Mao.* Cambridge: Harvard University Press, 1987.

———. "The Military and China's New Politics: Trends and Counter-trends." In *The People's Liberation Army in the Information Age,* ed. James C. Mulvenon and Richard Yang. Santa Monica, Calif.: RAND, 1999.

———. "Taiwan and the Chinese Military." Draft article. August 2000.

Johnson, Douglas. "Drawn into the Fray: Indonesia's Natuna Islands Meet China's Long Gaze South." *Asian Affairs* 24 (fall 1997): 153–61.

Johnston, Alastair Iain. "China's Militarized Interstate Dispute Behavior, 1949–1992: A First Cut at the Data." *China Quarterly* 153 (March 1998): 1–30.

Juo, Ting-yee. "Self-Strengthening: The Pursuit of Western Technology." In *The Cambridge History of China.* Vol. 10: *Late Ch'ing, 1800–1911,* part 1, ed. John K. Fairbank. Cambridge: Cambridge University Press, 1978.

Karniol, Robert. "China Buys *Shkval* Torpedo from Kazakhstan." *Jane's Defense Weekly* 30, no. 14 (26 August 1998): 6.

Katani, Tetsuo. "Antipiracy Measures: Japan's Experience in the Malacca Strait and Its Implications for the Horn of Africa." PowerPoint presentation at Legal Experts' Workshop on Maritime Piracy in the Horn of Africa, 07 April 2009. http://www.lloydsmiu.com/lmiu/index.htm (accessed 22 June 2009).

Kearsley, Harold K. *Maritime Power and the Twenty-first Century.* Aldershot, U.K.: Dartmouth Press, 1997.

Khalizad, Zalmay M., et al. *The United States and a Rising China: Strategic and Military Implications.* Santa Monica, Calif.: RAND, 1999.

Kim, Hyun-Soo. "The 1992 Chinese Territorial Sea Law in the Light of the UN Convention." *International and Comparative Law Quarterly* 43 (1994): 894–904.

Klintworth, Gary. "China's Naval Ambitions Stir Up Fears in Region." *Singapore Straits Times,* 01 August 1992, 13.

———. "Latest Soviet Carrier for Beijing Fleet?" *Asia-Pacific Defence Reporter* 25, no. 4 (1992): 26–27.

Kondapalli, Srikanth. "China's Naval Equipment Acquisition." *Strategic Analysis* 23, no. 9 (1999): 1509–29.

———. "China's Naval Strategy." *Strategic Analysis* 23, no. 12 (2000): 2037–51.

———. "China's Naval Structure and Dynamics." *Strategic Analysis* 23, no. 7 (1999): 1095–1115.

———. "China's Naval Training Program." *Strategic Analysis* 23, no. 8 (1999): 1333–53.

———. "Military Academies in China." *Strategic Analysis* 23, no. 1 (1999): 27–43.

Krepon, Michael, ed. *Chinese Perspectives on Confidence-Building Measures.* Washington, D.C.: Henry L. Stimson Center, 1997.

Lam, Willy Wo-Lap. "PLA Weapons to Be Upgraded by 2010." *South China Morning Post,* 15 December 1999.

Lambert, Nicholas A. *Sir John Fisher's Naval Revolution.* Columbia: University of South Carolina Press, 1999.

Lampton, David M., and Gregory C. May. "Managing U.S.-China Relations in the Twenty-first Century." Washington, D.C.: Nixon Center, 1999.

Lanzit, Kevin, and David Chen. "Integrating China's Air Forces into Maritime Strike." Paper prepared for the China Maritime Studies Institute Conference at the Navy War College, Newport, R.I., October 2007.

Lardy, Nicholas R. *China's Unfinished Economic Revolution.* Washington, D.C.: Brookings Institution, 1998.

LeGrand, C. M., Rear Admiral, Judge Advocate General Corp, USN. Memorandum for Undersecretary of Defense (Policy) and Director for Strategic Plans and Policy, "Chinese Straight Baseline Declaration." Washington, D.C., Department of Defense Representative for Ocean Policy Affairs, 21 May 1996.

Leifer, Michael. *China in Southeast Asia: Interdependence and Accommodation.* CAPS Paper no. 14. Taipei: Chinese Academy of Policy Studies, 1997.

———. "Chinese Economic Reform and Defense Policy: The South China Sea Connection." Paper presented at the IISS/CAPS Conference, Hong Kong, July 1994.

———. "Chinese Economic Reform and Security Policy: The South China Sea Connection." *Survival* 37, no. 2 (1995): 44–59.

Lelyveld, Michael. "Iran: Oil Deal with China May Have Hit a Snag." Radio Free Europe/ Radio Liberty, 22 June 2000, in *Asia Times*.

Lennox, Duncan, ed. *Jane's Strategic Weapon Systems*. Coulsdon, Surrey, U.K.: Jane's Information Group, "JSWS-Issue 22." 1999.

Levathes, Louise. *When China Ruled the Seas: The Treasure Fleet of the Dragon Throne, 1405–1413*. New York: Oxford University Press, 1994.

Lewis, John W. *China Builds the Bomb*. Stanford: Stanford University Press, 1988.

Lewis, John W., Hua Di, and Xue Litai. "Beijing's Defense Establishment." *International Security* 15, no. 4 (1991): 87–109.

Lewis, John Wilson, and Xue Litai. "China's Search for a Modern Air Force." *International Security* 24, no. 1 (1999): 64–94.

———. *China's Strategic Seapower: The Politics of Force Modernization in the Nuclear Age*. Stanford: Stanford University Press, 1994.

Li, Nan. "The Evolution of China's Naval Strategy and Capabilities: From 'Near Coast' and 'Near Sea' to 'Far Seas.'" *Asian Security* 5, no. 2 (2009): 144–69.

———. "Organizational Changes in the PLA, 1985–1997." *China Quarterly* 158 (June 1999): 314–49.

———. "The PLA's Evolving Campaign Doctrine and Strategies." In *The People's Liberation Army in the Information Age*, ed. James C. Mulvenon and Richard H. Yang, 146–57. Santa Monica, Calif.: RAND, 1999.

———. "The PLA's Evolving Warfighting Doctrine, Strategy and Tactics, 1985–95: A Chinese Perspective." *China Quarterly* 146 (June 1997): 443–63.

Li, Xiaobing. "PLA Attacks and Amphibious Operations during the Taiwan Straits Crises of 1954–1958." Paper presented at the CNA Conference on the PLA's Operational History, Alexandria, Va., June 1999.

Li Jun-ting and Yang Jin-he, eds. *Overview of the Chinese Armed Forces*. Beijing: People's Publishing Agency, 1989.

Lin, Cheng-yi. "Taiwan's South China Sea Policy." *Asian Survey* 37 (April 1997): 323–39.

Lo Jung-pang. "The Emergence of China as a Sea Power during the Late Sung and Early Yuan Periods." *Far Eastern Quarterly* 14, no. 4 (August 1955): 489–503.

Lovshin, Leonard. "World Fisheries." PowerPoint presentation, July 2008. At: http://www. google.com/search?sourceid=navclient&ie=UTF-8&rlz=1T4GWYE_enUS316US316& q=china%27s+fish+harvest+2008 (accessed 15 December 2009).

Lu Ning. *The Dynamics of Foreign-Policy Decisionmaking in China*. Boulder, Colo.: Westview Press, 1997.

"Lufeng 22-1." BP Amoco announcement, 18 October 1999, 1–3. http://www.offshore-tech nology.com/projects/lufeng/ (accessed 17 December 2009).

"Luhai Pictures." *Jane's Defence Weekly* 31, no. 5 (1 February 1999): 16. http://www.globalsecurity.org/military/world/china/luhai-pics.htm (accessed 17 December 2009).

Lum, Geoffrey T. "China's Cruise Missile Program." *Military Review* 84 (January 2004): 67–73. http://findarticles.com/p/articles/mi_m0PBZ/is_1_84/ai_n6112517 (accessed 22 March 2009).

MacFarquhar, Roderick. *Origins of the Cultural Revolution.* Vol. 2. New York: Columbia University Press, 1983.

Madeiros, Evan, et al. *A New Direction for China's Defense Industry.* Santa Monica, Calif.: RAND, 2005.

———. *Pacific Currents: The Responses of U.S. Allies and Security Partners in East Asia to China's Rise.* Santa Monica, Calif.: RAND, 2008.

Manicom, James. "China's Claims to an Extended Continental Shelf in the East China Sea: Meaning and Implications." *China Brief* 9, no. 14 (09 July 2009). http://www.jamestown.org/programs/chinabrief/single/?tx_ttnews[tt_news]=35243&tx_ttnews[backPid]=25&cHash=8ecccd9b61.

Marder, Arthur M. *From the Dreadnought to Scapa Flow: The Royal Navy in the Fisher Era.* Vol. 1: *The Road to War, 1904–1914.* London: Oxford University Press, 1961.

Marolda, Edward J. "The U.S. Navy and the Chinese Civil War, 1945–1952." Ph.D. diss., George Washington University, 1990.

McDevitt, Michael A. "The PLA Navy: Past, Present, and Future Prospects." In *Comments on the Conference on the PLA Navy.* Alexandria, Va.: CNA, May 2000.

———. "The Strategic and Operational Context Driving PLA Navy Building." In *Right Sizing the People's Liberation Army: Exploring the Contours of China's Military,* ed. Roy Kampahausen and Andrew Scobell, 481–522. Carlisle. Pa.: U.S. Army War College Strategic Studies Institute, 2007.

McDevitt, Michael, et al. "Sino-Japanese Rivalry: Implications for U.S. Policy." Final Report of CNA, IDA, NDU/INSS/ and Pacific Forum/CSIS Project Report. Washington, D.C.: CNA Corporation (30 November 2006).

McGruther, Kenneth R. *The Evolving Soviet Navy.* Newport, R.I.: Naval War College Press, 1978.

McLean, John. "Philippines Protests at Vietnam Spratly 'Attack.'" *BBC Online Network,* 28 October 1999. http://news.bbc.co.uk/hi/english/world/asia-pacific/newsic_491000/491603.stm.

McVadon, Eric. "PRC Exercises, Doctrine and Tactics toward Taiwan: The Naval Dimension." In *Crisis in the Taiwan Strait,* ed. James R. Lilley and Chuck Downes. Washington, D.C.: National Defense University Press in cooperation with AEI, 1997.

———. "The Reckless and the Resolute: Confrontation in the South China Sea." *China Security* 14 (spring 2009). http://www.chinasecurity.us/pdfs/mcvadon.pdf (accessed 25 November 2009).

———. "Systems Integration in China's People's Liberation Army." In *China's Military Faces the Future*, ed. James R. Lilley and David Shambaugh. Washington, D.C.: AEI and M. E. Sharpe, 1999.

———. "Systems Integration in China's People's Liberation Army." In *The People's Liberation Army in the Information Age*, ed. James C. Mulvenon and Richard H. Yang. Santa Monica, Calif.: RAND, 1998.

Minnick, Wendell. "China's Gator Navy Makes Marginal Strides: Amphibious Exercises Tested New Capabilities." *Defense News* (Taipei), 12 January 2009. http://www.defensenews.com/story.php?i=3899959 (accessed 15 February 2009).

Montaperto, Ronald M. "Assurance and Reassurance." *Comparative Connections: An E-Journal on East Asian Bilateral Relations* 7, no. 3. Honolulu: CSIS Pacific, 2005. http://www.csis.org/media/csis/pubs/0503qchina_seasia.pdf.

———. "Dancing with China (in a Psyche of Adaptability, Adjustment, and Cooperation)." *Comparative Connections: An E-Journal on East Asian Bilateral Relations* 7, no. 2. Honolulu: CSIS Pacific, 2005. http://www.csis.org/media/csis/pubs/0502qchina_seasia.pdf.

Moore, John E., ed. *Jane's Fighting Ships: 1976–77*. New York: Franklin Watts, 1977.

———. *Jane's Fighting Ships, 1990–91*. Coulsdon, Surrey, U.K.: Jane's Information Group, 1991.

Morison, Samuel Loring. "Indian Navy Blue Water Capability Grows as Russia's Diminishes." *Navy News and Undersea Technology*, 08 May 2000, 4.

Muller, David G. Jr. *China's Emergence as a Maritime Power*. Boulder, Colo.: Westview Press, 1983.

Mulvenon, James C. "Hu Jintao and the 'Core Values of Military Personnel.'" *China Leadership Monitor*, no. 28 (spring 2009), Hoover Institution. http://www.hoover.org/publications/clm/issues/44612967.html (accessed 09 October 2009).

———. *Professionalization of the Senior Chinese Officer Corps: Trends and Implications*. Santa Monica, Calif.: RAND, 1997.

———. "True Is False, False Is True: Virtual Is Reality, Reality Is Virtual: Technology and Simulation in the Chinese Military Training Revolution." In *The "People" in the PLA: Recruitment, Training, and Education in China's Military*, ed. Roy Kamphausen, Andrew Scobell, and Travis Tanner. Carlisle, Pa.: U.S. Army War College, Strategic Studies Institute, 2008.

Needham, Joseph. *Science and Civilization in China*. Vols. 1–6. Cambridge: Cambridge University Press, 1954–86.

"New Oil Well Producing in South China Sea." *Asia Pulse*, 15 January 1999.

"New PLAN to Train, Purchase Vessel Mix." *Jane's Defence Weekly* 30, no. 25 (16 December 1998): 25–26.

Noer, John H., with David Gregory. *Chokepoints: Maritime Economic Concerns in Southeast Asia.* Washington, D.C.: National Defense University Press in cooperation with the Center for Naval Analysis, 1996.

Nolt, James H. "The China-Taiwan Military Balance." New York: Project on Defense Alternatives, 2000.

O'Donnell, John R. "An Analysis of Major Developmental Influences on the People's Liberation Army-Navy and Their Implication for the Future." Master's thesis. Fort Leavenworth, Kans.: U.S. Army Command and General Staff College, 1995.

O'Dowd, Edward. *Chinese Military Strategy in the Third Indochina War: The Last Maoist War.* New York: Routledge, 2007.

Office of Naval Intelligence. *China's Navy: 2007.* Washington, D.C.: Office of Naval Intelligence, 2007.

————. *The People's Liberation Army Navy: A Modern Navy with Chinese Characteristics.* Washington, D.C.: Office of Naval Intelligence, August 2009.

"Oil Exploration in the South China Sea: What Is the International Business Interest in the Region?" U.S. Pacific Command Virtual Information Center. http://www.vic.pacom.mil (accessed 24 June 1999).

Opall-Rome, Barbara. "China Moves Roil Region." *Defense News,* 08 February 1999, 1.

O'Rourke, Ronald. "China Naval Modernization: Implications for U.S. Navy Capabilities—Background and Issues for Congress." Washington, D.C.: Congressional Reference Service Report RL33153, 18 November 2009.

Paltiel, Jeremy T. "PLA Allegiance on Parade: Civil-Military Relations in Transition." *China Quarterly* 143 (September 1995): 784–800.

Parker, Richard. "China's Overseas Bases." U.S. Pacific Command Virtual Information Center. http://www.vic.pacom.mil (02 February 2000).

————. "Conflicting Territorial Claims in the South China Sea: The Spratly Islands Dispute." U.S. Pacific Command Virtual Information Center. http://www.vic.pacom.mil (accessed 21 January 2000).

Pedrozo, Raul. "Close Encounters at Sea: The USNS *Impeccable* Incident." *U.S. Naval War College Review* 62, no. 3 (2009). http://www.usnwc.edu/press/review/PressReviewPDF. aspx?q=385 (accessed 01 June 2009).

Penrose, Jago, Jonathan Pincus, and Scott Cheshier. "Vietnam: Beyond Fish and Ships." *Far Eastern Economic Review* (September 2007). http://www.viet-studies.info/kinhte/ vietnam_beyond_fish_and_ships.htm.

Perry, Tony. "Hunting beyond Red October." *Los Angeles Times,* 21 October 1997, 1, 18.

"Philippine Navy Fires Warning Shots." Associated Press News, 04 February 2000. http:// search.yahoo.com.sg/search/news_sg?p=Philippine+navy&n=10.

Pillsbury, Michael, ed. *Chinese Views of Future Warfare.* Washington, D.C.: National Defense University Press, 1997.

Pollack, Jonathan D. "Energy Insecurity with Chinese and American Characteristics: Implications for Sino-American Relations." *Journal of Contemporary China* 17, no. 55 (2008): 229–45.

Prabhadar, Joshua Ho, and Sam Bateman, eds. *The Evolving Maritime Balance of Power in the Asia-Pacific.* Singapore: Nanyang University, IDSS.

Puska, Susan M. "Taming the Hydra: Trends in China's Military Logistics since 2000." Paper presented at the NBR, U.S. Army War College, and Texas A&M University Conference on "The PLA at Home and Abroad" at Carlisle Barracks, Pa., 25–27 September 2009.

Raudzens, George. "Military Revolution or Maritime Evolution? Military Superiorities or Transportation Advantages as Main Causes of European Colonial Conquests to 1788." *Journal of Military History* 63, no. 3 (1999): 631–42.

Ray-Choudhury, Rahul. "Trends in Naval Power in South Asia and the Indian Ocean during the Past Year." *SAPRA India Monthly Bulletin* (January 1996). http://www.subcontinent. com/sapra/96jan/si019603.

Ren Xiaofeng and Cheng Xizhong. "A Chinese Perspective." *Marine Policy* 29 (2005): 139–46.

"Reviving Russia's Navy." *Strategic Comments* 6. London: IISS, July 2000, 1, 2.

Rosenberg, David. "China, Neighbors Progress in Fishery Agreements." *Asia Times Online,* 19 August 2005. http://www.atimes.com/atimes/China/GH19Ad02.html.

———. "Managing the Resources of the China Seas: China's Bilateral Fisheries Agreements with Japan, South Korea, and Vietnam." *Japan Focus,* 30 June 2005. http://japanfocus.org/-David-Rosenberg/1789 (accessed 25 August 2009).

Rosenberg, David Alan. "Process: The Realities of Formulating Modern Naval Strategy." In *Mahan Is Not Enough: The Proceedings of a Conference on the Works of Sir Julian Corbett and Admiral Sir Herbert Richmond,* ed. James Goldrick and John B. Hattendorf. Newport, R.I.: Naval War College Press, 1993.

Roskill, S. W. *The Strategy of Seapower: Its Development and Application.* Westport, Conn.: Greenwood Press, 1962.

Ross, Robert S. "China's Naval Nationalism: Sources, Prospects, and the U.S. Response." *International Security* 34, no. 2 (2009): 46–81.

Sae-Liu, Robert. "Chinese Expand Aerial Refueling Capability to Navy." *Jane's Defence Weekly* 33, no. 25 (21 June 2000): 14.

Sakhuja, Vijay. "Maritime Multilateralism: China's Strategy for the Indian Ocean." *China Brief* 9, no. 22 (04 November 2009). http://www.jamestown.org/single/?no_cache=1&tx_ttnews%5Btt_news%5D=35692 (accessed 28 November 2009).

Saradzhyan, Simon. "China to Double Its Order of Russian-Made Destroyers." *Defense News* 15 (27 March 2000): 17.

Saunders, Phillip C. *China's Global Activism: Strategy, Drivers, and Tools.* Washington, D.C.: National Defense University Press, Occasional Paper 4 (October 2006).

Saunders, Stephen, ed. *Jane's Fighting Ships: 2008–2009*. Coulsdon, Surrey, U.K.: Jane's Information Group, 2008.

Schmetzer, Uli. "Shadow of China Has Philippines Looking to U.S. Military." *San Diego Union-Tribune*, 11 November 1998.

Schram, Stuart. *The Political Thought of Mao Tse-tung*. Rev. ed. New York: Praeger, 1969.

Scobell, Andrew. "Show of Force: Chinese Soldiers, Statesmen, and the 1995–1996 Taiwan Strait Crisis." *Political Science Quarterly* 115, no. 2 (2000): 227–46.

Schofield, Clive H. "Unlocking the Sea Bed Resources of the Gulf of Thailand." *Contemporary Southeast Asia* 29, no. 2 (2007): 286–308.

Scott, Richard. "Boosting the Staying Power of the Non-nuclear Submarine." *Jane's International Defence Review* 32, no. 11 (1999): 41–50.

Scully, R. Tucker (Deputy Assistant Secretary of State for Oceans, Fisheries, and Space). "International Perspectives upon Fisheries Policy." Remarks at the Fifth North Pacific Rim Fisheries Conference, Anchorage, Alaska, 01 December 1999.

Sengupta, Prasun K. "Full Steam Ahead for PLA Navy's Aircraft Carriers." *Tempur*, 05 June 2009. http://officialsite.my/tempur/index/php?option=com_content&task=view&id=432 &Itemid=2 (accessed 04 November 2009).

———. "RMN Receives First FS-2000 Frigate." *Asian Defense Journal* (November 1999): 23.

Shambaugh, David. "China's Commander-in-Chief: Jiang Zemin and the PLA." In *Chinese Military Modernization*, ed. C. Dennison Lane. New York: Kegan Paul International; Washington, D.C: AEI Press, 1997.

———. "China's Defense Industries: Indigenous and Foreign Procurement." In *The Chinese Defense Establishment: Continuity and Change in the 1980s*, ed. Paul H. B. Godwin. Boulder, Colo.: Westview Press, 1983.

———. "China's Military Views the World: Ambivalent Security." *International Security* 24, no. 3 (1999): 52–79.

———. "China's Post-Deng Military Leadership." In *China's Military Faces the Future*, ed. James R. Lilley and David Shambaugh. Washington, D.C.: AEI/M. E. Sharpe, 1999.

———. "Commentary on Civil-Military Relations in China: The Search for New Paradigms." Paper presented at the Calif.PS/RAND Conference on the PLA, Washington, D.C., July 1999.

Shambaugh, David L., Eberhard Sandschneider, and Hong Zhou, eds. *China-Europe Relations: Perceptions, Policies and Prospects*. London: Routledge, 2007.

Sharpe, Richard, ed. *Jane's Warships of the World, 1976–77*. London: Jane's Publishing Group, 1977.

———. *Jane's Warships of the World, 1989–90*. London: Jane's Publishing Group, 1990.

———. *Jane's Fighting Ships: 1995–96*. London: Butler and Tanner, 1996.

———. *Jane's Fighting Ships, 1999–2000*. Coulsdon, Surrey, U.K.: Jane's Information Group, 1999.

————. *Jane's Fighting Ships: 2000–2001.* Coulsdon, Surrey, U.K.: Jane's Information Group, 2000.

Shichor, Yitzhak. "Demobilization: The Dialectics of PLA Troop Reduction." *China Quarterly* 146 (June 1996): 336–59.

Shlapak, David A., et al. *A Question of Balance: Political Context and Military Aspects of the China-Taiwan Dispute, 2009.* Santa Monica, Calif.: RAND, 2009. http://www.rand.org/pubs/monographs/2009/RAND_MG888.pdf (accessed 05 December 2009).

Simpson, B. Mitchell, III. *Essays on Maritime Strategy.* Newport, R.I.: U.S. Naval War College Press, 1972.

Singh, Swaran. "Continuity and Change in China's Maritime Strategy." Institute for Defence Strategy and Analysis, Delhi, India, n.d.

Smil, Vaclez. "China's Energy and Resource Uses: Continuity and Change." *China Quarterly* 156 (December 1998): 935–51.

Smith, Craig S. "New Chinese Guided-Missile Ship Heightens Tension." *New York Times,* 9 February 2000.

Sokolsky, Richard, Angel Rabasa, and C. Richard Neu. *The Role of Southeast Asia in U.S. Strategy toward China.* Santa Monica, Calif.: RAND, 2001.

"South China Sea Region." Energy Information Administration of the U.S. Department of Energy (March 2008). http://www.eia.doe.gov/emeu/cabs/schina.html (accessed 17 December 2009).

Spears, Joseph. "China and the Arctic: The Awakening Snow Dragon." *China Brief* 9, no. 6 (18 March 2009). http://www.jamestown.org/programs/chinabrief/single/?tx_ttnews%5Btt_news%5D=34725&cHash=9638471049 (accessed 17 December 2009).

Spence, Jonathan D. *The Search for Modern China.* New York: W. W. Norton, 1990.

Spykman, Nicolas. *America's Strategy in World Politics: The United States and the Balance of Power.* New York: Harcourt, Brace, 1942.

Stanton, Doug, Jr. *In Harm's Way: The Sinking of the U.S.S.* Indianapolis *and the Extraordinary Story of Its Survivors.* Boston: Holt, 2003.

Steinberg, Jonathan. *Yesterday's Deterrent:* Tirpitz *and the Birth of the German Battle Fleet.* London: Macmillan, 1965.

Stockholm International Peace Research Institute. *Armaments, Disarmament and International Security.* Oxford: Oxford University Press, 1998.

Stokes, Mark A. *China's Evolving Conventional Strategic Strike Capability: The Anti-ship Ballistic Missile Challenge to U.S. Maritime Operations in the Western Pacific and Beyond.* Washington, D.C.: Project 2049 Institute, 14 September 2009. http://project2049.net/documents/chinese_anti_ship_ballistic_missile_asbm.pdf (accessed 13 November 2009).

————. *China's Strategic Modernization: Implications for the United States.* Carlisle, Pa.: U.S. Army War College Strategic Studies Institute, 1999.

Storey, Ian James. "Calming Waters in Maritime Southeast Asia." *Asia Pacific Bulletin*, no. 29 (18 February 2009). Honolulu: East-West Center.

———. "China's 'Malacca Dilemma.'" *China Brief* 6, no. 8 (12 April 2006): 1. http://www.frankhaugwitz.info/doks/security/2006_04_12_China_Energy_Security_Oil_Transportation_Coal_Jamestown_Foundation.pdf (accessed 25 August 2009).

———. "Creeping Assertiveness: China, the Philippines and the South China Sea Dispute." *Contemporary Southeast Asia* 21, no. 1 (1999): 95–118.

———. "Impeccable Affair and Renewed Rivalry in the South China Sea." *China Brief* 9, no. 9 (30 April 2009). http://www.jamestown.org/programs/chinabrief/single/?tx_ttnews%5Btt_news%5D=34922&tx_ttnews%5BbackPid%5D=414&no_cache=1.

"Stratfor's Global Intelligence Update." 14 April 1999: 2. http://alert@stratfor.com (link no longer available).

Studeman, Michael. "Calculating China's Advances in the South China Sea: Identifying the Triggers of 'Expansionism.'" *Naval War College Review* 51, no. 2 (1998): 68–90. http://www.usnwc.edu/nwc/art5-sp8.htm.

Sumida, Jon Tetsuro. *Inventing Grand Strategy and Teaching Command: The Classic Works of Alfred Thayer Mahan Reconsidered.* Baltimore: Johns Hopkins University Press, 1997.

Sutter, Robert, and Chin-Hao Huang. "Singapore Summits, Harmony, and Challenges." *Comparative Connections: An E-Journal on East Asian Bilateral Relations* 9, no. 4. http://www.csis.org/media/csis/pubs/0704qchina_seasia.pdf.

Swaine, Michael D. "Chinese Military Modernization and Asia-Pacific Security." Paper presented at the Aspen Institute's Second Conference on U.S.-China Relations, Washington, D.C., March 1999.

———. *Military and Political Succession in China.* Santa Monica, Calif.: RAND, 1992.

———. *The Role of the Chinese Military in National Security Policymaking.* Rev. ed. Santa Monica, Calif.: RAND, 1998.

Swanson, Bruce. *The Eighth Voyage of the Dragon: A History of China's Quest for Seapower.* Annapolis, Md.: U.S. Naval Institute Press, 1982.

Tang, Shiping. "China." In *Energy and Security: The Geopolitics of Energy in the Asia-Pacific,* ed. Manjeet Singh Pardesi et al. Singapore: IDSS, Nanyang Technological University, 2006.

Thayer, Carlisle. "Recent Developments in the South China Sea." Paper presented to International Workshop on "The South China Sea." Hanoi, 26–28 November 2009.

———. "The Structure of Vietnam-China Relations, 1991–2008." Paper prepared for the Third International Conference on Vietnamese Studies, Hanoi, 4–7 December 2008.

Till, Geoffrey. "Maritime Strategy in the Twenty-first Century." In *Seapower: Theory and Practice,* ed. Geoffrey Till. Portland, Or.: Frank Cass, 1994.

Torda, Thomas J. "Struggle for the Taiwan Strait: A 50th-Anniversary Perspective on the First Communist-Nationalist Battles for China's Offshore Islands and Their Significance for the Taiwan Strait Crises." Unpublished manuscript. 1999.

Torode, Greg. "Tussle for Oil in the South China Sea." *South China Morning Post,* 20 July 2008. https://archive.scmp.com/login.php?prev_url=https://archive.scmp.com/interme diate_checkout.php.

Trevethan, Sidney. "Prognosis for China." Federation of American Scientists Web site, 1999. http://www.fas.org/nuke/huide/china/agency/plan-af-orbat-st.htm.

Troush, Sergei. "China's Changing Oil Strategy and Its Foreign Policy Implications." Washington, D.C.: Brookings Institution, Center for Northeast Asian Policy Studies Working Paper (fall 1999).

Twitchett, Denis, and John K. Fairbank, eds. *The Cambridge History of China.* Vol. 14: *The People's Republic.* Part K: *The Emergence of Revolutionary China, 1949–1965.* Cambridge: Cambridge University Press, 1987.

Tyler, William Ferdinand. *Pulling Strings in China.* London: Constable, 1929.

Umbach, Frank. "Financial Crisis Slows but Fails to Halt East Asian Arms Race—Part Two." *Jane's Intelligence Review* 10, no. 9 (1998): 34–37.

United Nations. United Nations Convention on the Law of the Sea [UNCLOS]. 1982. http://www.un.org/Depts/los/stat2los.txt.

U.S.-China Economic and Security Review Commission. *2009 Report to Congress.* Washington, D.C.: USGPO, November 2009.

U.S. Geodetic Survey Report. In USCINCPaC memo of 15 September 1999 (in author's possession; source no longer available).

U.S. Navy Staff. *Undersea Warfare.* Washington, D.C.: U.S. Navy, 1999.

U.S. State Department. *Public Papers of the Presidents of the United States: Harry S Truman, 1950.* Washington, D.C.: USGPO, 1965.

Valencia, Mark J. *China and the South China Sea Disputes.* Adelphi Paper 228. London: Institute for International Strategic Studies, 1995.

———. "Energy and Insecurity in Asia." *Survival* 39, no. 3 (1997): 85–106.

———. *A Maritime Regime for North-east Asia.* New York: Oxford University Press, 1996.

Valencia, Mark J., and Jon M. Van Dyke. "Vietnam's National Interests and the Law of the Sea." *Ocean Development and International Law* 25, no. 2 (1994): 217–50.

Valencia, Mark J., Jon M. Van Dyke, and Noel A. Ludwig. *Sharing the Resources of the South China Sea.* Boston: Martinus Nijhoff, 1997.

Vellucci, Frederic. "Recent Trends in PLA Navy Training and Education." Testimony before the U.S.-China Economic and Security Review Commission, Washington, D.C., 11 June 2009.

Vertzberber, Yaacov Y. I. *China's Southwestern Strategy: Encirclement and Counterencirclement.* New York: Praeger, 1987.

Wachman, Alan. *Why Taiwan? Geostrategic Rationales for China's Integrity.* Palo Alto, Calif.: Stanford University Press, 2007.

Wain, Barry. "China, ASEAN Meeting Demonstrates Deep Divisions." *Asian Wall Street Journal*, 10 March 2000.

———. "Hanoi and Beijing Take a Step Closer." *Asian Wall Street Journal*, 12 May 2000.

———. "Manila's Bungle in the South China Sea." *Far East Economic Review*, January–February 2008: 17.

"Warships' Sale to China." *Far Eastern Economic Review* 163 (30 December 1999): 6.

Watson, Bruce W. "The Evolution of Soviet Naval Strategy." In *The Future of the Soviet Navy: An Assessment to the Year 2000*, ed. Bruce W. Watson and Peter M. Dunn. Boulder, Colo.: Westview Press, 1986.

Wertheim, Eric, ed. *The Naval Institute Guide to Combat Fleets of the World*. 15th ed. Annapolis, Md.: U.S. Naval Institute, 2007.

Whiting, Allen S. "ASEAN Eyes China: The Security Dimension." *Asian Survey* 37, no. 4 (1997): 299–322.

Whitson, William H., with Huang Chen-hsia. *The Chinese High Command: A History of Communist Military Politics, 1927–71*. New York: Praeger, 1973.

Wilhelm, Alfred D., Jr. *China and Security in the Asian Pacific Region through 2010*. CRM 95–226. Alexandria, Va.: Center for Naval Analysis, 1996.

Winnifeld, James A., with Dana A. Johnson. *Joint Air Operations: Pursuit of Unity in Command and Control, 1941–1991*. Santa Monica, Calif.: RAND, 1993.

Woodward, E. L. *Great Britain and the German Navy*. Oxford: Clarendon Press, 1935.

The World Factbook, 1999. Washington, D.C.: Central Intelligence Agency (CIA). http://www.odci.gov/cia/publications/factbook/pag.html.

Worldwide Submarine Challenges, 1996. Washington, D.C.: Office of the Chief of Naval Operations.

Wortzel, Larry M. "The Beiping-Tianjin Campaign of 1948–49: The Strategic and Operational Thinking of the People's Liberation Army." Paper prepared for the U.S. Army War College Strategic Studies Institute, Carlisle, Pa., n.d.

Wright, Mary Clabaugh. *The Last Stand of Chinese Conservatism: The T'ung-chih Restoration, 1862–1874*. Stanford: Stanford University Press, 1957.

Wylie, J. C. *Military Strategy*. 1967. Reprint. Westport, Conn.: Greenwood Press, 1980.

Xu, Zi. "Maritime Geostrategy and the Development of the Chinese Navy in the Early Twenty-first Century." *China Military Science*. 2004. Trans. Andrew S. Erickson and Lyle J. Goldstein, *Naval War College Review* 59, no. 4 (2006): 47–67.

Yang, Andrew Nien-Dzu. "From a Navy in Blue towards a Blue Water Navy: Shaping PLA Navy Officer Corps (1950–1999)." Paper prepared for the Center for Naval Analysis Conference on "The PLA Navy: Past, Present and Future Prospects." Washington, D.C., April 2000.

Yergin, Daniel, Dennis Eklof, and Jefferson Edwards. "Fueling Asia's Recovery." *Foreign Affairs* 77, no. 2 (1998): 34–50.

Yi, Yang. "Engagement, Caution." *China Security* 3, no. 4 (2007): 29–39.

Yu, Hui. "Remarks on China's Ratification of the 1982 UN Convention on the Law of the Sea." In *Asian Yearbook of International Law* 5, ed. Ko Swan Sik et al., 211–30. Amsterdam: Kluwer Law International, 1997.

Yuan, Jing-dong. "China's Defense Modernization: Implications for Asia-Pacific Security." *Contemporary Southeast Asia* 17, no. 1 (1995): 67–84.

Yung, Christopher D. "People's War at Sea: Chinese Naval Power in the Twenty-first Century." CRM 95-214. Alexandria, Va.: Center for Naval Analysis, March 1996.

Zaloga, Steven J. "Russia's Moskit Anti-ship Missile." *Jane's Intelligence Review* 8, no. 4 (1996): 155–58.

Zhan, Jun. "China Goes to the Blue Waters: The Navy, Seapower Mentality and the South China Sea." *Journal of Strategic Studies* 17, no. 3 (1994): 180–208.

Zhang, Shu Guang. *Mao's Military Romanticism: China and the Korean War, 1950–1953.* Lawrence: University Press of Kansas, 1995.

Zhang Yihong. "China Enhances the Production of the Rocket Propelled Mines." *Kanwa News,* no. 520 (20 May 1999). http://www.kanwa.com.

———. "Sino-Russian Arm Sale Is Reaching the Second Stage in 2000." *Kanwa News,* no. 112 (12 January 1999). http://www.kanwa.com.

"Zhanjiang Military Sub District, Guangdong Military District, Conducts a Military-Civilian Exercise." http://www.taungpao.com.hk (02 June 2000). Link no longer available.

Zou Keyuan. "The Sino-Vietnamese Agreement on Maritime Boundary Delimitation in the Gulf of Tonkin." *Ocean Development and International Law* 36 (2005): 13–24. http://www.southchinasea.org/docs/zou%20keyuan-sino-vietnam%20boundary%20delimitation.pdf (accessed 17 December 2009).

Index

About the Author

Bernard D. Cole is a professor at the National War College in Washington. He served thirty years in the Navy, commanding USS *Rathburne* (FF1057) and Destroyer Squadron 35. His previous books include *Taiwan's Security: History and Prospects* and *Sea Lanes and Pipelines: Energy Security in Asia*. He earned a Ph.D. from Auburn University. *The Great Wall at Sea: China's Navy in the Twenty-First Century* updates his 2001 book on the Chinese Navy.